D1377043

LIBERATION MISSION

of the Soviet Armed Forces in the Second World War

Edited
and Prefaced
by Marshal
of the Soviet
Union
A. A. Grechko

 Progress
Publishers
Moscow

Translated from the Russian
by *David Fidlon*
Designed by *Victor Korolkov*

ОСВОБОДИТЕЛЬНАЯ
МИССИЯ Советских
Вооруженных
Сил
во второй
мировой
войне

На английском языке

The authors of this book are: Major-General *I. V. Parotkin*, M. Sc. (Milit.), leader of the group, Chapter X, Colonel *N. G. Andronikov*, M. Sc. (Hist.), Chapter V, *A. V. Antosyak*, M. Sc. (Hist.), Chapter III, Colonel *M. M. Malakhov*, M. Sc. (Hist.), Chapters VII and VIII, Colonel *V. P. Morozov*, M. Sc. (Milit.), Chapter IX, Lieutenant-Colonel *A. M. Noskov*, M. Sc. (Hist.), Chapter VI, Colonel *G. K. Plotnikov*, M. Sc. (Hist.), Chapter XI, Colonel *M. I. Semiryaga*, D. Sc. (Hist.), Sections 1, 2, 3, and 5 of Chapter I and Chapter XII, Colonel *F. N. Utenkov*, M. Sc. (Milit.), Chapter IV, Colonel *A. N. Shimansky*, M. Sc. (Hist.), Chapter II, and Colonel *I. I. Shinkarev*, M. Sc. (Hist.), Section 4 of Chapter I.

This group has won the Frunze Prize for 1973 for this work.

First printing 1975

© Издательство «Прогресс», 1975

© Translation into English

Progress Publishers 1975

O $\frac{11202-492}{014(01)-75}$ 101-75

Printed in the Union of Soviet Socialist Republics

CONTENTS

Already in the first years after the October 1917 Revolution, the world's first state of the dictatorship of the proletariat had to shoulder the entire burden of the world-wide struggle against imperialism. At the cost of enormous sacrifices and privation the people of the young Soviet state smashed the excellently equipped combined forces of the internal counter-revolution and international imperialism, safeguarded the gains of the Revolution and created conditions for building socialism in the USSR. Defending Soviet power in battles against numerous enemies, the Soviet Army was at the same time upholding truly international interests. Its victories had a tremendous international impact and inspired millions of toiling people in other countries to fight for social and national liberation. "By preserving Soviet power," Lenin wrote, "we are rendering the best, the most powerful support to the proletariat of all countries in their incredibly hard struggle against their own bourgeoisie."[1]

The Second World War was a rigid test of the moral and material forces of many countries and peoples. It was the most hard-fought and devastating war history had ever known. Like the First World War it was an imperialist war which had been prepared over a period of many years by the imperialists of all countries. It broke out as a result of a fresh sharpening of contradictions in the capitalist world, and the responsibility for it devolves on the entire capitalist system. It was started by nazi Germany which acted as the shock force of world imperialism.

Yet, as distinct from the First World War, it erupted when capitalism ceased to be a world-wide social system, when besides the capitalist states there was also the Soviet Union, the first state of workers and peasants in the history of mankind.

In view of these new conditions of world social development, the war mirrored two sets of contradictions and not one. In the first place, it most forcefully reflected the contradiction between the rival imperialist powers and groups of powers as did the First World War. But there was also the new and the main contradiction of the epoch—the contradiction between the capitalist world as a whole, on the one

---

[1] *Ibid.,* Vol. 27, p. 61.

CONTENTS

1*

PREFACE

Almost sixty years ago a new type of soldier appeared on the historical scene. He had the same old grey greatcoat but there was a big red star on his cap. He was a Soviet soldier who not only did not threaten the toiling masses, but, on the contrary, was prepared to endure the greatest privations and give his life for their interests. Since then the Soviet Armed Forces have been vigilantly and reliably guarding the peaceful labour of the Soviet people and the cause of world peace.

Created by the Soviet state, the Soviet Armed Forces have unbreakable bonds with the people. Built up on the basis of the Marxist-Leninist theory, they are developing and acting under the guidance of the Communist Party of the Soviet Union. Soviet soldiers are educated in the spirit of irreconcilability towards the enemies of their country and imbued with the lofty ideas of friendship of the Soviet peoples and proletarian solidarity with the working people of all countries.

Dwelling on the building of the armed forces of the young Soviet state Lenin told the 8th Congress of the Communist Party in March 1919 that "for the first time in world history, an army, an armed force, has been created, which knows what it is fighting for; and ... for the first time in world history, workers and peasants are making incredible sacrifices in the knowledge that they are defending the Soviet Socialist Republic, the rule of the working people over the capitalists; they know that they are defending the cause of the world proletarian socialist revolution."[1]

The history of the Soviet Armed Forces offers a striking example of dedicated service to the people and fidelity to the immortal ideas of proletarian internationalism.

---

[1] V. I. Lenin, *Collected Works*, Vol. 29, p. 221.

Already in the first years after the October 1917 Revolution, the world's first state of the dictatorship of the proletariat had to shoulder the entire burden of the world-wide struggle against imperialism. At the cost of enormous sacrifices and privation the people of the young Soviet state smashed the excellently equipped combined forces of the internal counter-revolution and international imperialism, safeguarded the gains of the Revolution and created conditions for building socialism in the USSR. Defending Soviet power in battles against numerous enemies, the Soviet Army was at the same time upholding truly international interests. Its victories had a tremendous international impact and inspired millions of toiling people in other countries to fight for social and national liberation. "By preserving Soviet power," Lenin wrote, "we are rendering the best, the most powerful support to the proletariat of all countries in their incredibly hard struggle against their own bourgeoisie."[1]

The Second World War was a rigid test of the moral and material forces of many countries and peoples. It was the most hard-fought and devastating war history had ever known. Like the First World War it was an imperialist war which had been prepared over a period of many years by the imperialists of all countries. It broke out as a result of a fresh sharpening of contradictions in the capitalist world, and the responsibility for it devolves on the entire capitalist system. It was started by nazi Germany which acted as the shock force of world imperialism.

Yet, as distinct from the First World War, it erupted when capitalism ceased to be a world-wide social system, when besides the capitalist states there was also the Soviet Union, the first state of workers and peasants in the history of mankind.

In view of these new conditions of world social development, the war mirrored two sets of contradictions and not one. In the first place, it most forcefully reflected the contradiction between the rival imperialist powers and groups of powers as did the First World War. But there was also the new and the main contradiction of the epoch—the contradiction between the capitalist world as a whole, on the one

---

[1] *Ibid.*, Vol. 27, p. 61.

hand, and the socialist world represented at the time by the Soviet socialist state, on the other. This circumstance had a serious impact on the entire course of the war and in many respects determined its ultimate results. Another specific feature of the Second World War was that in it the most aggressive imperialist grouping headed by nazi Germany was not bent solely on recarving the world, as was the case in the First World War, but sought to attain world domination by enslaving and even exterminating whole nations.

In view of the specific alignment of political forces in the world and the nature of aims and tasks pursued by the fascist aggressors, the Second World War, as distinct from the first, was characterised from the very beginning by a struggle between two tendencies and the existence of the objective possibilities of the peoples waging a just war of liberation against fascism.

As they prepared the Second World War, the imperialist powers and each group of imperialist powers set on remaking the map of the world and consolidating their economic and political positions. They centred their efforts on resolving their contradictions at the expense of the Soviet Union and chiefly on destroying it as a bulwark of world peace and socialism, as the socialist homeland of all the toiling peoples.

It was with this aim in view that international imperialism fostered and placed German imperialism on its feet and encouraged the establishment of nazi rule in Germany. Abetting fascist aggression, imperialists throughout the world, especially in France, Britain and the USA, left no stone unturned in their efforts to turn Hitler's war machine eastwards, against the Soviet Union. Nevertheless, the war started in an entirely different way from what those who inspired and organised it had expected.

Having erupted as a capitalist war of aggrandisement, the Second World War within a relatively short space of time developed into a just war of liberation of the countries fighting against nazi Germany and her allies.

The resolute and steadily mounting resistance put up by the peoples of Czechoslovakia, Poland, Yugoslavia, Greece, France and other countries against the nazi aggression, already in the initial period of the war, became an important

factor of its development into an anti-fascist war of liberation. But it was the entry of the Soviet Union into the war
after it had been attacked by nazi Germany that played
the decisive role in completing this transformation.

While the imperialist powers, in the course of many
years, virtually from the end of the First World War, conducted secret and overt preparations for a new imperialist war of aggrandisement, the Soviet Union, adhering as it
did to the Leninist principles of peaceful coexistence of states
with different social systems, from the outset consistently
and with great determination worked to avert the military
threat.

Due to its class nature the Soviet Union could not be
interested in war. It is a socialist state and wars of aggrandisement are therefore alien to it, for it has no classes or
groups that would have benefited from war. Its foreign
policy rests on principles of complete equality of all nations,
big or small, and self-determination of peoples, and respect
for the independence and sovereignty of all states and peoples.

The Soviet Union's consistent peace-loving foreign policy
has always been widely supported by the fraternal communist and workers' parties and by all the progressive forces in
the world in general. Together with the Soviet Union the
communist and workers' parties warned the world about the
threat of war, exposed the anti-Soviet nature of its preparations and the special role that international imperialism had
assigned to nazi Germany. The Seventh Congress of the
Communist International held in Moscow in 1935 urged all
working people to fight against the war danger and pointed
out that "German fascism is acting like the *mailed fist of the
international counter-revolution*, as the *main instigator of
the imperialist war*, as the *inspirer of the crusade against the
Soviet Union, the great homeland of the toiling people of
the whole world*".

The Soviet Union did not change its foreign policy in the
years of the Second World War. It continued to fight relentlessly against the fascist aggressors in support of the peoples
who had come under their blows. On the basis of the community of interests of the freedom-loving peoples in the
fight against the fascist aggressors a mighty anti-Hitler coali-

tion of states and peoples was established with the Soviet Union, the USA and Britain at the head and the combined efforts of its members resulted in the historic victory over the fascist and imperialist aggressors.

The Soviet people value highly the role played by the armies of the USA, Britain, France and other countries in smashing the common enemy. But for almost three years the Soviet Union bore the main burden of the war as it faced the combined forces of the fascist aggressors single-handed.

The main battles of the Second World War were fought on the Soviet-German front where 607 enemy divisions were destroyed, routed or taken prisoner—almost three and a half times as many as on all the other fronts taken together. The Anglo-US troops in Africa and Western Europe smashed or took prisoner 176 enemy divisions. The Wehrmacht sustained 80 per cent of its casualties on the Soviet-German front. There the enemy lost the bulk of the weapons of his ground and air forces and also a considerable part of his navy.

Although the peoples of the USSR and its Armed Forces were faced with incredible difficulties in the first months after the nazi attack in June 1941, they did not concentrate on national tasks alone. In a radio broadcast on July 3, 1941, Chairman of the State Defence Committee, J. V. Stalin, declared: "The purpose of this Patriotic War of all the peoples against the fascist oppressors is not only to remove the danger hanging over our country, but also to help all the other peoples of Europe languishing under the yoke of German fascism."

In this struggle the Soviet Union undeviatingly followed Lenin's principles of proletarian internationalism. It never cultivated national enmity or racial exclusiveness among its peoples with regard to other peoples, including, of course, the German people. The Soviet people said that Hitlers come and go, but the German people remains.

The Soviet Union fought against nazi Germany for almost four years. Bitter incessant fighting went on along a vast front extending more than 4,000 kilometres from the Barents Sea to the Black Sea. In extremely difficult conditions the Soviet Armed Forces withstood the blows of Hitler's armies, stopped them and then turned them to flight. The nazi invaders and their European satellites were crushed. Nazi

Germany was forced to sign the act of unconditional sur-
render. Shortly afterwards the Japanese army in the Far
East was routed and this led to the surrender of imperialist
Japan and the victorious conclusion of the Second World
War.

The Soviet Union and its Armed Forces smashed and
drove the enemy out of the USSR and liberated the peoples of
Europe and Asia at the cost of tremendous effort and the mobilisation of all its strength. Twenty million Soviet people, or
40 per cent of the total human casualties in the Second
World War, lost their lives. More than a million Soviet officers and men were killed, and another two million were
wounded or listed as missing in the fight for the liberation of
European and Asian peoples. No other country had suffered
such great sacrifices or could have endured the trials that had
fallen to the lot of the Soviet Union.

Having routed and expelled the invaders from the territories of the countries they were liberating the Soviet Armed
Forces helped many peoples in Europe and Asia overthrow
reactionary regimes, take power into their own hands and
embark on the path of democratic development. Many of
them launched socialist construction. The new social system
in these countries was not established under pressure from
the Soviet Army, as bourgeois falsifiers of history are now
asserting, but as a result of the conditions that had matured
in the liberated countries for moving towards new social
relations, in keeping with the will and desire of their
peoples.

The Soviet Union began to render enormous military and
material assistance to the liberated countries while the war
was still on; Polish, Czechoslovak, Rumanian, Yugoslav and
French national units were raised on the territory of the
Soviet Union and with its decisive assistance. The USSR
supplied them with the necessary weapons, signal means,
transport, ammunition, fuel and other items.

During the war the Soviet Union equipped and trained,
out of these countries' citizens, 19 infantry, five artillery and
five air divisions, six infantry and airborne, eight armoured
and motorised infantry, 12 artillery and mortar, and five
engineer brigades, and many other units. By the end of the
war the total strength of these units was 555,000 and the

weapons they received from the USSR included 16,500 guns and mortars, about 1,000 tanks and self-propelled guns and over 1,600 aircraft.

Thanks to measures taken during the Second World War by the Soviet Union and the liberated countries themselves, hundreds of thousands of foreign soldiers—the Polish Army, the Czechoslovak Corps and also armies of Bulgaria, Yugoslavia and Rumania and separate units of other countries—fought shoulder to shoulder with the Soviet troops. The troops of the Mongolian People's Republic participated with the Soviet forces in routing the Kwantung Army. The comradeship-in-arms of the Soviet Army and the other armies fighting on its side strengthened in the course of the war. After the war the armed forces which the people's democracies had built up with Soviet assistance have been reliably standing guard over the revolutionary gains of their peoples.

The Soviet people's uncompromising struggle against the aggressors decisively influenced the developments at the fronts and also had a profound effect on the internal political situation in countries occupied by nazi Germany and imperialist Japan. The vast organisational and educational work conducted by the fraternal communist and workers' parties among the broad masses of people enabled them to see that the freedom and independence of all the peoples of the world depended on the outcome of the battles on the Soviet-German front.

Under the influence of the Soviet victories and with the assistance of the USSR a powerful Resistance Movement gained in scope and momentum in the occupied countries. In Bulgaria, Greece, Italy, Poland, France, Czechoslovakia and Yugoslavia it embraced more than 2.2 million people. The Resistance Movement was not a historical fortuity as bourgeois ideologists are now trying to prove, but a logical outcome of the just, liberatory character of the war against fascism, and constituted an important component of the Second World War. A significant feature of the national-liberation anti-fascist Resistance Movement was its international character which found its expression both in its objectives and the national composition of its participants.

A considerable role in activating the anti-fascist struggle

was played by Soviet citizens who found themselves in foreign countries during the war. Over 40,000 of them fought courageously shoulder to shoulder with Polish, Czechoslovak, Yugoslav, French and Italian guerrillas.

The Second World War ended in a great victory of the peoples over the forces of fascism and reaction. The defeat of nazi Germany and imperialist Japan and their allies in Europe and Asia opened the way for many countries and peoples to freedom, independence and social progress.

The events of the past war have now become history and today almost thirty years separate us from the day when its last shots were fired. But as the years race by the peoples come to appreciate more fully the immortal exploit performed by the Soviet people in that war.

The Soviet Army rendered its service to history by routing the main forces of the aggressors, delivering mankind from nazism and directly liberating the peoples of many European and Asian countries from the German and Japanese invaders. And if the grim and hideous night of fascism did not engulf the world it was due above all to the magnificent victories of the Soviet Armed Forces.

To a large extent the liberation mission of the Soviet Armed Forces was responsible for the fundamental social changes which took place in quite a few countries, the swift and extensive spread and consolidation of socialism and the serious weakening of capitalism. It inspired the Soviet troops to great feats of valour, augmented the Soviet Union's international prestige to an unprecedented degree and promoted the consolidation of all anti-fascist democratic forces of the world around the USSR.

"The Soviet Union's Great Patriotic War" state the theses of the Central Committee of the Communist Party of the Soviet Union published on the occasion of the 50th Anniversary of the Great October Socialist Revolution, "have most convincingly demonstrated that there is no power on earth capable of crushing socialism, and bringing to their knees a people dedicated to the ideas of Marxism-Leninism, loyal to the socialist Motherland, and united around the Leninist Party. These results are a stern warning to the imperialist aggressors, and a harsh and unforgettable lesson of history."

Imperialism has not changed its predatory character, continues to be the most vicious enemy of the working masses. As it has been in the past imperialism's aggressive strategy is still spearheaded against the Soviet Union and other social- ist states. As socialism strengthens its international positions, imperialism seeks to weaken the unity of the world socialist system. It tries to take advantage of the divergencies in the world revolutionary movement in an effort to split its ranks, places its ideological machine, including the mass media, at the service of anti-communism, the struggle against social- ism, against all progressive forces.

In their ideological struggle against socialism and all pro- gressive movements the imperialists are most anxious to make use of any manifestation of nationalism, particularly petty- bourgeois nationalism, which enables them to speculate on the national feelings of the working people, employ more refined methods of masking their class interests, and divide the toiling people, blunt their vigilance and international sentiments, their striving for democracy, socialism and peace. And this means that the destinies of socialism and peace are intertwined, that in present-day conditions the socialist countries, each one separately and all of them together, are faced with particularly responsible tasks.

No less topical today are Lenin's words to the effect that capital is an international force which can be defeated only by a close alliance of workers, unity of the toiling people in all spheres, including the military. Referring to what the multi-national Soviet republic achieved in developing its armed forces, Lenin said on February 2, 1920: "...we, who are faced by a huge front of imperialist powers, we, who are fighting imperialism, represent an alliance that requires close military unity, and any attempt to violate this unity we regard as absolutely impermissible, as a betrayal of the struggle against international imperialism. ... We say: unity of the military forces is imperative; any deviation from this unity is impermissible."[1]

Speaking at the 24th Congress of the Communist Party of the Soviet Union, General Secretary of the CC CPSU Leonid Brezhnev noted that the world socialist system had a quarter- century history and declared: "The Communist Party of the

[1] V. I. Lenin, *Collected Works*, Vol. 30, pp. 325-26.

Soviet Union has regarded and continues to regard as its internationalist duty in every way to promote the further growth of the might of the world socialist system." All the fraternal communist and workers' parties think the same and are acting accordingly to ensure the successful outcome of the struggle against imperialism, for socialism, peace and progress.

Lenin's behests and the urgent demands of the time oblige the Soviet Union to display the utmost vigilance, to guard the interests of socialism and peace, strengthen the might and unity of the socialist camp and all the freedom-loving democratic forces of the world.

Lately, many key problems of the history of the Second World War have become the objects of an acute ideological struggle. In this field the bourgeois propaganda has focused its efforts on misrepresenting the causes and the character of the last war, masking the real inspirers and organisers, smearing the peaceable foreign policy of the Soviet Union, its fulfilment of its internationalist duty to the peoples and the liberation mission of the Soviet Armed Forces, belittling the part played by the Soviet Union in routing the aggressors and undermining the trust of the peoples of the world in the USSR.

But try as they might bourgeois propagandists will never be able to disprove the decisive role played by the Soviet Union in smashing the aggressive forces responsible for the Second World War and deny the irrefutable fact that it waged a just, liberatory and internationalist struggle.

Reared by the Communist Party, the Soviet soldier proudly carried the banner of the liberation mission through all the trials of the grimmest of all wars, displaying boundless love for his socialist homeland and unshakable devotion to proletarian internationalism.

This book is dedicated to the liberation mission of the Soviet Armed Forces in the Second World War and is the first major study of the various aspects of this problem.

A. A. Grechko,
Marshal of the Soviet Union

foreign imperialist interference into their affairs. The Soviet Union did not change its fraternal attitude to the Chinese working people even when in its determination to disrupt Soviet-Chinese friendship the Chiang Kai-shek Government, representing the right wing of the Kuomintang, provoked an incident on the Chinese Eastern Railway in 1929 that resulted in the rupture of diplomatic relations between the two countries.

On September 18, 1931, the Japanese imperialists invaded Northeast China. In this difficult period the Soviet people remained a true friend of China's toiling masses. Giving in to popular pressure the reactionary Kuomintang Government in December 1932 re-established diplomatic relations with the Soviet Union. This created wider possibilities for assisting China in her struggle against the Japanese aggressors. The Soviet Union increased its political, moral and military assistance to the Chinese people and in August 21, 1937 the two countries signed a non-aggression treaty.

Thus, already in the thirties, the mutual assistance of the working people became an important factor of the struggle against fascism and war and restrained the aggressive forces from carrying through their plans. Were it not for the political and militant experience of international proletarian solidarity the working class had acquired in those years, the popular anti-fascist struggle in the Second World War would have been unable to attain such a vast scope.

The existence of the Soviet Union, its successes in socialist construction and its dynamic and peaceable foreign policy seriously hampered the imperialists. Of especial significance for the working people of the world was the completion of the construction of socialist society in the USSR. The solution of this great problem in conditions of a constant threat of an imperialist attack was an unprecedented exploit performed by the Soviet people under the leadership of the Communist Party.

While the Soviet people were engaged in peaceful labour, the fascist powers, which were planning to destroy the Soviet Union and redivide the world among the imperialists again, were feverishly preparing new acts of aggression.

In October 1936 Germany and Italy signed a treaty spearheaded against the Soviet Union. Shortly, Germany, Italy

Chapter I   YEARS OF TRIALS
               AND VICTORIES

1. THE SOVIET UNION
IN THE STRUGGLE
AGAINST FASCIST AGGRESSION

FOR A COLLECTIVE REBUFF
TO THE AGGRESSORS

A new situation took shape in the world in the early thirties. On the one hand, it was determined by the successes of socialist construction in the USSR and its growing influence on world affairs, and, on the other, by the offensive of reaction and fascism in a number of capitalist countries, Germany in particular.

As the general crisis of capitalism aggravated sharply during the 1929-1933 world economic crisis, reactionary bourgeois circles in a number of countries intensified their efforts to set up a fascist dictatorship. Therefore, the resolute steps of the Soviet Union and all progressive forces to unmask fascism's true face and their struggle against it were of tremendous international significance.

The mounting threat of another world carnage split the forces in the world arena into two camps: the camp of war headed by German nazism, which became the shock force of world imperialist reaction, and the camp of peace headed by the Soviet Union which rallied all progressive mankind around it.

The Communist Party of the Soviet Union immediately saw the serious threat to the cause of peace which emerged with the establishment of nazi rule in Germany and proposed to set up a system of collective security. The international significance of the Soviet Union's peaceful policy increased to a still greater extent. On December 12, 1933 the Central Committee of the CPSU(B) adopted a resolution on launching a struggle for collective security and envisaged the possibility of the Soviet Union joining the League of Nations and the conclusion of a mutual security agreement with European states.

The Party underlined that the Soviet Union's peaceful foreign policy could not by itself avert the threat of war and that it was necessary to mobilise world public opinion, and first and foremost the entire international working class. It, therefore, appealed to the working people of all countries to be vigilant, strengthen fraternal solidarity and raise an insurmountable barrier to fascism and war.

International tension mounted in the mid-1930s. Nazi Germany's aggressive actions in Europe and the creation of a hotbed of war in the Far East by the Japanese militarists aroused world-wide concern.

Under the guidance of the Communist International, the communist parties made every effort to rally all the anti-fascist and anti-war forces into a single front, both on a national and international scale. In these conditions the role of proletarian internationalism as a factor of peace mounted considerably.

An important feature of the struggle of the progressive forces to prevent the outbreak of a second world war was the fusion of the anti-war movement with the anti-fascist struggle. As a result, the ranks of the peace fighters swelled enormously and the national aims of the workers of different countries became even more closely intertwined with the internatioal tasks of the struggle against fascism.

The 7th Congress of the Communist International (July-August 1935) further strengthened the international solidarity of the working people. It summed up the vast experience of revolutionary struggle accumulated by communist parties in all countries and, on the basis of an analysis of the international situation, worked out new tactics for them. It centred its attention on the struggle against fascism and the formation of a united proletarian and popular front against fascism and war.

Of exceptional importance for the education of the working people in the spirit of proletarian solidarity was the Congress proclamation that it was the primary duty of all sections of the Communist International to help with all the means at their disposal to strengthen the USSR and to fight against the enemies of the USSR. It passed a resolution which said in part: "Both under peace conditions and in the conditions of war directed against the USSR, the strengthening of the USSR, the increasing of its power, and the assuring of its victory in all spheres and in every sector of the

struggle coincide fully and inseparably with the int the toilers of the whole world in their struggle ag: exploiters, and with the interests of the colonial pressed peoples fighting against imperialism. . ."[1]

The subsequent developments fully confirmed the ness of the analysis of the international situation r the Seventh Congress of the Communist Internatio the tactics it elaborated.

The international solidarity of the world democrat strikingly manifested itself during the war in Spain 1939), the first serious armed clash between fascisn people defending its freedom and national indep The great movement of proletarian solidarity with re Spain was organised and guided by the Communis headed by the Communist International.

The proletariat and the world democratic forces the Spanish people great moral, material and milit port. In the vanguard of the international move solidarity with the Spanish working people in th for freedom were the peoples of the Soviet Uni

Even though the Spanish republic was defeate unequal struggle against fascism, the heroic figh Spanish people acquired great international sig Developments in Spain made it clear to all the pec there should be no delay in launching a struggl fascism and that it required concerted actions part.

Simultaneously with fascist intrigues in the imperialists intensified their aggression in the Far Ea the Chinese people. The working class of the worlc with great approval the revolutionary developmer place in China under the influence of the Octobe tion in Russia which awakened the Chinese people a Marxism-Leninism within their reach. The stand: of the Chinese Revolution, Sun Yat-sen, warmly the revolution in Russia. The Soviet people show standing and support for the struggle which the Ch ple waged to deepen the revolution and for their fi

---

[1] *Seventh World Congress of the Communist Internati tions and Decisions*, Moscow-Leningrad, 1935, p. 55.

and Japan concluded the so-called anti-Comintern pact thus forming an aggressive Berlin-Rome-Tokyo axis.

In March 1938 nazi Germany embarked on her aggressive plans and occupied her first victim, Austria. Only the Soviet Government resolutely condemned Germany's aggression and advanced concrete proposals in the League of Nations to organise a system of collective security. In its statement of March 17, 1938, the Soviet Government drew the attention of the Western powers to their responsibility for the future of world peace. But the latter, however, preferred a policy of appeasement of the nazis who immediately took advantage of it to continue their aggression in Europe.

Thus the ambitions of the more aggressive forces of the imperialist bourgeoisie personified by nazism led up to the pre-war political crisis whose most vivid manifestation was the Munich deal between the Western powers and Hitler which decided the fate of Czechoslovakia.

Under the agreement signed by Hitler, Mussolini, Chamberlain and Daladier in Munich on September 30, 1938, which the Czechoslovak Government accepted despite the protests of the Czechoslovak people, the Sudeten Region and other border areas with a predominantly German population were turned over to Germany. Later Czechoslovakia had to satisfy the territorial claims advanced by Hungary and Poland.

As should have been expected, Hitler did not rest content with annexing a part of Czechoslovakia. In March 1939 German troops occupied the whole of Bohemia and Moravia which were subsequently proclaimed the "Protectorate of Bohemia and Moravia". Transcarpathian Ruthenia was turned over to Horthy's Hungary.

The Munich deal affected the vital interests of many European peoples. Its real meaning, as the Central Committee's Report to the 18th Congress of the CPSU(B) held in March 1939 pointed out, was to give the nazis parts of Czechoslovakia as payment for the promise to start a war against the USSR.

In effect the Munich deal brought the peoples of Europe to the threshold of the Second World War.

The Soviet Union was at the head of the world progressive forces which rose in defence of Czechoslovakia. On March 15, 1938, two days after the nazis occupied Austria

2*

and created a direct threat to Czechoslovakia, the Soviet Government declared that the USSR was prepared to honour its allied commitments under the 1935 Soviet-Czechoslovak mutual assistance treaty. Official Czechoslovak circles admitted that the Soviet Government's stand cooled Hitler's head. Moreover, the Soviet Government said that it was prepared to defend Czechoslovakia, even if France would be unwilling to do so.

As Germany continued to threaten Czechoslovakia's independence, the Soviet Union took serious preventive measures of a military character. It alerted and concentrated on its western borders 30 infantry and 10 cavalry divisions, an armoured corps, three armoured brigades and 12 air brigades of the Byelorussian and Kiev special military districts. Then it alerted still larger forces both in the border areas and in the military districts right up to the Volga. About 330,000 reservists were called up for service.

But the ruling bourgeois circles of Czechoslovakia headed by Eduard Benes relied solely on France and Britain and regarded Soviet assistance as an extreme and even a suicidal variant.

In the face of Hitler's aggression the Soviet Government in 1939 intensified its efforts to set up a system of collective security. The political report of the Central Committee to the 18th Congress of the CPSU(B) branded German nazis as aggressor. The Party unmasked the provocative, double-dealing game carried on by British and French ruling circles aimed at channeling the nazi aggression eastwards and inciting a war between Germany and the Soviet Union, while they themselves could sit back and enjoy themselves.

The true objectives of French and British policy were fully exposed at the Anglo-French-Soviet talks which opened in March 1939 and in the course of the negotiations on the conclusion of a military convention, which ended in failure through the efforts of the Anglo-French ruling circles.

The collapse of these negotiations threatened the Soviet Union with isolation on the international arena and the prospect of fighting Germany single-handed. Taking Japan's hostile attitude into consideration, it was quite possible that the Soviet Union would be faced with a war on two fronts. The Anglo-French ruling circles created a situation in which the Soviet Union was compelled to accept Germany's proposal to conclude a non-aggression treaty with her. This was done on August 23, 1939.

Political tension in Europe reached its peak at the end of August 1939. Encouraged and abetted by reactionary circles in Britain, France and the USA, Hitler was completing his military preparations. Nothing could now be done to avert another world conflagration. The working class, which could have overturned the plans of the bellicose reaction, was weakened by the splitting activities of the Right-wing social-democratic leaders. Moreover, the communist and workers' parties in most European countries were not the mass parties they are today, and some of them were influenced by sectarian trends. Gradually the world approached the fatal day—September 1, 1939.

THE BEGINNING
OF THE SECOND WORLD WAR

The Second World War proved to be the greatest test of endurance for many peoples. It showed the whole world the enormous viability and strength of the Soviet state, its unswerving loyalty to the Leninist principles of proletarian internationalism and preparedness to assist the victims of aggression.

On September 1, 1939, nazi Germany attacked Poland, which was unprepared to give a rebuff to the aggressors and was occupied by the end of the month.

On September 3, 1939, Britain and France declared war on Germany, and British dominions and colonies also entered the war against Germany.

Taking advantage of the stand of the British and French governments which had not given up hope of channeling the Wehrmacht's aggression against the Soviet Union, and the inactivity of the Anglo-French forces in the West, Hitler energetically prepared new acts of aggression.

On April 9, 1940, Germany invaded Denmark. Simultaneously, without a declaration of war German marines and paratroops landed in Norway, and by June 10, 1940 she was fully occupied.

The seizure of Denmark and Norway considerably improved Germany's strategic position. Fighting was still going on in Norway when on May 9, 1940 German Command ordered its troops to attack Belgium, the Netherlands and Luxemburg. Its plan was to reach the frontiers of Northern France and invade French territory by-passing the Maginot Line. Under the nazi onslaught the Netherlands surrendered on May 15, and Belgium on May 28, 1940.

France lost her allies on the continent and the road to Paris was now open to the nazi panzer columns. On June 10, Italy declared war on France. The appearance of another front, in the south of the country, aggravated France's position to an even greater degree.

Hammered by the Wehrmacht the remnants of the British forces were evacuating from Dunkirk, while the French forces which had surrendered Paris on June 14 and ceased organised resistance were retreating in panic. On June 22, 1940, in Compiegne, where on November 11, 1918 Germany signed the armistice terms with the Allies in the First World War, France signed capitulation terms with nazi Germany.

So, by the summer of 1940, as a result of the self-seeking anti-communist policy of their governments the peoples of Western Europe were subjugated by nazi Germany and lost their state independence.

By overrunning six European countries with a total population of 108 million, including France and Belgium with their highly developed industries, Hitler scored a major strategic success which had very serious international repercussions. A grave danger loomed over Britain and Churchill did not preclude the possibility of evacuating his Government to Canada.

France's unprecedentedly swift defeat was largely instrumental in promoting the myth about the invincibility of the Wehrmacht.

The nazi occupation placed democratic forces in France, Belgium, the Netherlands, Denmark and other countries in an exceptionally difficult situation. And yet despite brutal terror and repressions these forces, under the leadership of the communist parties, launched an active national-liberation struggle which came to be known as the Resistance Movement.

Nazi Germany's successes inspired other aggressors in Europe and Asia to expand the sphere of military operations. In the summer of 1940 hostilities broke out between British and Italian forces in the Mediterranean Sea, and eastern and northern Africa. On October 28, 1940, following the Greek Government's rejection of the Italian ultimatum, the troops of fascist Italy invaded Greece from Albania which they had occupied earlier. Taking advantage of the rout of France the Japanese forces invaded her colony of Indochina. Having turned this territory into an important military bridgehead, the Japanese planned to continue their expansion in Southeast Asia and the Pacific Ocean. But they had to act cautiously, keeping a wary eye on the position of the Soviet Union.

After defeating France, Hitler, who regarded himself as the master of Western Europe, tried to force Britain to capitulate too. The Luftwaffe intensified its raids on the British Isles, and nazi Germany demonstratively prepared a major landing operation. The battle for the Atlantic increased in scope and scale. Beginning with the latter half of 1940, however, Hitler switched his attention to the Soviet Union, but only a very small circle of people knew about this, even at his headquarters.

Many years later it came to light that on June 2, 1940, that is at the height of the battle for France, Hitler said that since it was all over with Britain the time had come to settle scores with Bolshevism. At a meeting in Berghof on July 31, 1940, nazi Germany's top military leaders took the final decision to attack the Soviet Union. From then on all the political, economic and military measures undertaken by nazi Germany's leaders were conducted in keeping with this general line. On December 18, 1940 Hitler signed Operation Barbarossa, the plan of war against the USSR.

Although Operation Barbarossa envisaged a lightning victory over the Soviet Union, Hitler nonetheless regarded the Soviet Union as a serious adversary who could only be defeated by utilising all the resources of the whole of Western Europe and the creation of a favourable political and military situation. He even postponed the invasion of the Soviet Union for a period in order to make sure that he would not be threatened from the rear.

On April 6, 1941 Germany invaded Yugoslavia, whose
people entered into an unequal struggle against the Wehrmacht's armoured forces, and at the same time attacked
Greece.

By the summer of 1941 Hitler decided that all political and
strategic conditions for the invasion of the Soviet Union had
been created. Together with the occupied countries (Austria,
Poland, Czechoslovakia, Yugoslavia, Greece, Albania, France,
Belgium, the Netherlands, Luxemburg, Denmark and Norway) and her satellites (Rumania, Finland, Hungary and Bulgaria) Germany had a population of 290 million, and an
enormous military and economic potential. On June 1, 1941
Germany had 8,500,000 men (214 divisions) under arms, not
counting the fairly large armed forces of her satellites.

Europe was on the threshold of developments that were
destined to bring about a radical change in the entire military and political situation obtaining in the world
at the time.

THE SOVIET UNION'S MEASURES
IN THE SPHERES OF DOMESTIC
AND FOREIGN POLICY
TO STRENGTHEN ITS SECURITY

In view of the spread of the Second World War, the Communist Party and the Soviet Government took a number of
important steps in their domestic affairs between September
1939 and June 1941.

Much was done to further boost the development of the
socialist economy. The third five-year plan was being successfully fulfilled and by June 1941 gross industrial output
reached 86 per cent and railway freight turnover 90 per
cent of the level planned for the end of 1942.

In 1940 the Soviet Union produced nearly 166 million
tons of coal, 18.3 million tons of steel and nearly 15 million tons of pig iron. Engineering and machine-tool industries expanded considerably as new production capacities
were put in operation. From January 1938 to June 1941 a
total of 2,900 industrial enterprises were put into operation.
The heavy and defence industries were developing at a
particularly rapid pace. In those years the average annual

growth of industrial output as a whole was 13 per cent, while that of the defence industry was 39 per cent. In 1930 and 1931 the defence industry annually produced 1,911 guns, 860 aircraft and 740 tanks, while the figures for 1938 were 12,687 guns, 5,469 aircraft and 2,270 tanks. A number of engineering and other big factories switched to the production of military equipment, and the construction of major war plants was launched. The Army and Navy began receiving new types of aircraft, tanks, artillery and other armaments.

The Party's line of creating the country's second industrial base in her eastern regions and the expansion of the material reserves played an exceptionally important role in preparing a rebuff to aggression. From 1940 to June 1941 the total value of the country's material reserves rose from 4,000 million to 7,600 million rubles which could ensure the conversion of the economy to a war footing and the supply of the army until the time when the economy would be able to meet the army's needs out of current production. The strengthening of labour and state discipline was one of the most important measures designed to enhance the mobilisation preparedness of the USSR. On July 26, 1940 the Presidium of the USSR Supreme Soviet issued the decree on the transition to an eight-hour working day and a seven-day working week and on prohibiting workers and employees from quitting their jobs at will. Further steps were taken to improve the quality of industrial production. In October 1940 the Presidium of the USSR Supreme Soviet decreed the establishment of the system of labour reserves as a means of ensuring the uninterrupted supply of industrial enterprises, mines and railways with manpower.

The Communist Party and the Soviet Government took serious and extensive measures to strengthen the Armed Forces. In this respect an important role was played by the transition from the mixed territorial and regular army units to a regular army system of career servicemen, the adoption of the law on universal military service, the establishment in May 1940 of the ranks of general and admiral, the introduction of one-man command in the Army and Navy, the expansion of the network of military educational establishments, and the growth and improvement of the Armed

Forces. Suffice it to say that from January 1939 to June 22, 1941 the Soviet Army received more than 82,000 guns and mortars, more than 7,000 tanks and about 18,000 combat aircraft. The naval equipment was also considerably improved: from January to November 1940 a total of a hundred warships were launched and about 270 others were being built.

Between 1939 and 1941 the strength of the Soviet Armed Forces increased 2.8 times and on January 1, 1941 totalled 4,200,000 officers and men: 125 new divisions were raised in this period.

During these years further measures were taken to improve the organisational structure of the Soviet Armed Forces and their equipment. In spite of the fact that it proved impossible to carry through all the measures designed to strengthen the country's defence capacity, prior to the war the Soviet Union created a reliable base for its military and economic might. The most convincing proof of this is that enormous difficulties and losses notwithstanding the Soviet industry during the four years of the war manufactured a vast amount of arms and military equipment—nearly 536,000 guns and mortars, more than 95,000 tanks and self-propelled guns, and more than 108,000 combat aircraft.

The Communist Party believed that in order to strengthen the defence capacity of the Soviet state it was no less important to intensify the ideological education of the Soviet people than to continue strengthening the Armed Forces and developing industry, agriculture, science and culture. The Party followed Lenin's instruction that "victory in any war depends on the spirit animating the masses that spill their blood on the field of battle". Lenin underlined: "The conviction that the war is a just cause and the realisation that their lives must be laid down for the welfare of their brothers, strengthen the morale of the fighting men and enable them to endure incredible hardships."[1]

As it expanded its ideological work among the masses, including the Armed Forces, the Party took into account that in view of the existence of a socialist state the future war would inevitably acquire a class character and develop into

---

[1] V. I. Lenin, *Collected Works*, Vol. 32, p. 137.

a decisive clash between the two opposing systems, socialism and imperialism.

The Communist Party rightly pointed out that the future war would be a rigorous test not only for the socio-economic and state system of the Soviet Union, but also for the strength of character of the Soviet troops and all Soviet people, including their patriotic and internationalist ideals.

The education of the working people in the spirit of Soviet patriotism and proletarian internationalism became a matter of great importance in view of the involved international and internal situation in which the Soviet people led by the Communist Party was building socialist society.

With the completion of the construction of socialist society in the USSR the Soviet people were motivated by such powerful forces of social development as moral and political unity, socialist patriotism, friendship of the peoples of the Soviet Union, and international solidarity with the working people of all countries. As international tension mounted the Soviet people had to intensify their efforts, heighten their political vigilance and be prepared to defend their country.

In that period the Party formulated important theoretical questions of socialist construction that went a long way towards strengthening the country's defensive capacity. The 18th Party Congress devoted serious attention to the theory of the socialist state. The Party re-emphasised that in conditions of capitalist encirclement and the threat of a military attack on the USSR the Soviet state with its army and security organs would continue to exist and strengthen even after communism had been built in the country.

The Party emphatically condemned the distorted views on the character of wars in the contemporary epoch and the attitude of the Communists to just and unjust wars. It pointed out that Communists were not pacifists and did not oppose outright all the wars of the imperialist epoch, and made the point that a war in defence of the socialist homeland would be a just war.

These important decisions of the 18th Party Congress helped heighten vigilance and the combat readiness of the Soviet Armed Forces and the Soviet people as a whole.

The Party conducted extensive work to explain the essence of the international situation to the Soviet people, unmasked

the fascist aggressors and their Anglo-French accomplices
and educated the people in the spirit of solidarity with the
working people in other countries.

These measures further enhanced the Soviet Union's economic and military might, strengthened the moral and political unity and friendship of the Soviet peoples. Moreover,
they had a serious impact on the international situation: they
forced the ruling circles in the imperialist powers to reckon
with the Soviet Union, inspired the working people in other
countries to continue the struggle for national and social liberation and filled them with hope that it would end in victory. In the sphere of domestic policy the Communist Party
and the Soviet Government invariably followed Lenin's instructions to the effect that the biggest contribution which the
land of the victorious proletariat could make to the cause of
upholding the interests of the working people of the whole
world consisted above all in the successful construction of
socialism at home.

The Soviet Union's foreign policy between 1939 and 1941
also strengthened socialism in the country and furthered the
cause of proletarian internationalism. A complicated situation took shape on the country's western borders. The USSR
could not remain indifferent to the destiny of the peoples of
Western Ukraine and Western Byelorussia when, as a result
of the defeat of Poland, they were faced with the direct
threat of enslavement by nazi Germany. On September 17,
1939 Soviet troops crossed the border and took the lives and
property of 13 million inhabitants of Western Ukraine and
Western Byelorussia under their protection. Elections were
shortly held to the people's assemblies which approached the
USSR Supreme Soviet with the request that these regions be
accepted into the Soviet Union. Their request was granted
in November 1939 by the Fifth Session of the USSR Supreme
Soviet.

In view of nazi Germany's expanding aggression in Western Europe, her overt claims to the Baltic states and the
mounting anti-Soviet activity of the nazi agents there, the
Soviet Union had to take urgent measures to strengthen its
security in the northwest. In September and October Estonia, Latvia and Lithuania concluded mutual assistance treaties with the Soviet Union and in the summer of 1940 the

revolutionary events resulted in the overthrow of the reactionary bourgeois governments and the re-establishment of Soviet power in these countries. In August 1940, in response to the requests of their peoples, Estonia, Latvia and Lithuania were admitted into the USSR.

With war raging in Western Europe the Soviet Union decided to strengthen its border with Finland whose ruling circles were ready to turn her into an anti-Soviet springboard. Relations between the USSR and Finland continued to deteriorate. On November 30, 1939 an open military conflict provoked by Finnish and international reaction broke out between the two countries. The Soviet-Finnish war which lasted three and a half months ended in victory for the Soviet Armed Forces and the signing of a peace treaty in Moscow on March 12, 1940. The international significance of this treaty was that it created the necessary conditions for tranquillity and peace in the Baltic Sea area. Another important factor was that the imperialists failed to organise a military campaign against the Soviet Union and enlarge further the orbit of the Second World War. Nevertheless, Finnish reactionary circles did not draw the necessary conclusions from this lesson and a year later plunged their country once again into an anti-Soviet venture.

By the summer of 1940 the Soviet Union had created the necessary conditions ensuring its security in the west and the northwest. But there remained one more outstanding issue which in the course of two decades had caused disputes between the USSR and Rumania, the question of Bessarabia which was seized from the Soviet republic in 1918, and which became particularly involved following the outbreak of the war when Rumania's monarchial government more and more actively gravitated towards Hitler Germany. In order to secure the inviolability of the Soviet Union's southwestern frontiers, the Soviet Government in June 26, 1940 demanded that Rumania return Bessarabia to the USSR and transfer Northern Bukovina, inhabited predominantly by Ukrainians, to the Ukrainian Soviet Socialist Republic. The Rumanian rulers were forced to acquiesce: Bessarabia was reunited with Soviet Moldavia and Northern Bukovina with the Ukrainian SSR.

The peaceful solution of the Bessarabian question created favourable conditions for the development of normal economic, political and cultural relations between the USSR and Rumania, which in the final count was an important factor of peace in Southeast Europe. But the Rumanian ruling circles did not avail themselves of this opportunity and in June 1941 attacked the Soviet Union.

Among the measures taken by the Soviet Government to strengthen the country's international position and perform its internationalist duty to the working people of other countries, an important place is occupied by the five-year non-aggression pact signed by the USSR and Japan on April 13, 1941. Under its terms both countries undertook to maintain peaceful relations and respect the territorial integrity and inviolability of each other. It was a major victory of Soviet diplomacy that in a declaration appended to the pact Japan pledged to respect the sovereignty of the Mongolian People's Republic.

THE SOVIET UNION ASSISTS
THE PEOPLES FIGHTING
FOR NATIONAL INDEPENDENCE
AND FREEDOM

The Soviet Government did everything possible to strengthen the Soviet Union's internationalist ties with working people in other countries. The Bolshevik, Leninist tradition of acting in solidarity with all the contingents of the broad revolutionary movement was rooted in the Soviet people. In the thirties Soviet representatives in the Comintern, the International Red Aid, the Communist Youth International and other international organisations called upon the working people to work together to avert war, actively to help the peoples fighting for state and national independence, and exposed the aggressive nature of imperialism and its shock force—fascism. They also exposed the treachery of the Right-wing leaders of the social-democratic parties who actively impeded the formation of a united anti-fascist front.

The Soviet Union rendered great assistance to the anti-fascist democratic forces in foreign countries. With its help prominent Hungarian, Rumanian and Finnish Communists were released from prison and allowed to move to the USSR. A number of German anti-fascists were also released and many international brigade fighters interned in France were saved.

The CPSU Central Committee and the Soviet Government provided many Czechoslovak Communists with the conditions for continuing their struggle for the liberation of their country. In keeping with a decision of the Central Committee of the Communist Party of Czechoslovakia the Political Bureau of its Central Committee headed by Klement Gottwald arrived in the Soviet Union. Subsequently its members established the Party's Foreign Bureau in Moscow and together with the Central Committee which operated illegally in Prague guided the Party's activities. Thousands of Czechs, Slovaks and Transcarpathian Ukrainians who were hounded by the Hitlerite and the Hungarian invaders fled to the neighbouring countries, the Soviet Union in the first place.

A personal example in strengthening the friendship between the Soviet and Czechoslovak peoples was set by a large group of Soviet technical experts who were working at Czechoslovak factories under the Czechoslovak-Soviet agreement of June 1938. They remained in the country even after March 15, 1939, when the country was occupied by the Germans. Undaunted by the regime of terror instituted by the nazis, Soviet citizens working at the Eksplozija Works in Semtin contacted the Czech anti-fascists and helped them acquire and spread anti-fascist literature and establish links with the Foreign Bureau of the Communist Party of Czechoslovakia. The Soviet experts pursued their internationalist duty until June 22, 1941, when they were interned by the occupation authorities.

During the Polish-German war many Poles fled to territories liberated by the Soviet troops. There were 80,000 refugees in Lvov alone, and thousands of others continued to cross into the Soviet Union in the following months right up to the outbreak of the Soviet-German war. Their number included many Polish Communists and Left-wing Socialists who were able to continue the struggle for the liberation of their country, relying on the support of the CPSU and the Soviet Government. Some of them were elected deputies to the local organs of Soviet power, the Supreme Soviets of the Ukraine and Byelorussia, the People's Seim of Lithuania and the Supreme Soviet of the USSR. Polish refugees in the

USSR were given jobs, and favourable conditions for engaging in cultural activity: Polish schools and theatres were
opened and Polish-language newspapers were published. The
Soviet Government and local Soviet organisations did everything possible to make things easier for the Polish citizens
who had temporarily been deprived of their homeland.

The Soviet Union was the only great power which came to
the defence of the legitimate national interests of the Bulgarian people, especially in the Bulgarian-Rumanian dispute
over Southern Dobruja. The Soviet Union welcomed the
report that the issue was solved peacefully by the treaty of
Craiova on September 7, 1940.

In spite of the difficulties arising from the Second World
War, the Soviet Government took a number of steps designed
to prevent the spread of the war in the Balkans and ensure the security of the Bulgarian people.

For example, in December 1939 the two countries signed
a convention on the establishment of air service between them.
The three-year treaty on trade and navigation signed in January 1940 and the agreement on trade turnover and payments
for 1940 created important conditions for improving Soviet-
Bulgarian economic relations.

The Soviet Union made yet another step in support of the
fraternal Bulgarian people. On November 19, 1940 the Soviet Government proposed that the USSR and Bulgaria sign
a pact of friendship and mutual assistance. Bulgaria's acceptance of the offer would have created a serious obstacle to the
nazis in the Balkans, strengthened her security and influenced
the entire situation in that part of Europe. The Bulgarian
leaders, however, rejected the Soviet proposal and decided
to hitch themselves still closer to nazi Germany.

In the next few months the Soviet Government continued
to uphold the interests of the Bulgarian people and expose
Germany's intrigues. For example, on January 13, 1941 the
Soviet press agency, TASS, issued a statement concerning
her preparations to occupy Bulgaria. And when the nazi forces
extended their aggression to the Balkans and moved into
Bulgaria, the Soviet Government in a statement on March 3,
1941 condemned the Bulgarian leaders for allowing the Germans to enter Bulgaria and said that their stand led to the
expansion of the war and Bulgaria's involvement in it.

Maintaining a consistently internationalist position, the Soviet Government worked hard to improve relations with Yugoslavia. In May 1940 the two countries successfully concluded economic negotiations and signed a treaty on trade and navigation. In June 1940, giving in to the demands of the popular masses, the Cvetkovic-Macek government decided to establish diplomatic relations with the USSR. The Yugoslav peoples welcomed this step with satisfaction.

Regarding the entry of German troops into Bulgaria as a threat not only to the Bulgarian but also to the Yugoslav peoples, the Soviet Union early in March 1941 offered Yugoslavia to conclude a friendship and non-aggression treaty. But to the detriment of the national interests of the Yugoslav peoples Simovitch's government took some time to make up its mind and the treaty was only signed on April 5, 1941. In this way the Soviet Union extended political and material suport to the Yugoslav people on the eve of the nazi invasion of Yugoslavia.

The Soviet Government also came out in support of the Albanian people. It officially qualified the occupation of Albania by the Italian troops as an act of aggression and a fresh attempt by the fascist states to disturb peace in Europe.

In the early period of the Second World War the Soviet Union took serious steps to prevent the extension of the sphere of military operations of the Scandinavian countries. It warned Sweden and Norway about the danger of becoming involved in the conflict and thus helped the peoples of the Scandinavian Peninsula to maintain neutrality and strengthen their co-operation with the USSR.

In this respect the conclusion of peace between the USSR and Finland in March 1940 created fresh favourable conditions. The Soviet Government met the requests of the Swedish Government to mount a search for Swedish volunteers who had fought on the Finnish side, compensate for the losses, return the detained goods and so forth.

At all stages of the Second World War the Soviet Union vigorously upheld Sweden's national sovereignty. The real threat of occupation loomed over Sweden in April 1940 when the German forces invaded Norway and Denmark. Several days later the Soviet Government informed the German Ambassador in Moscow about its concern for Sweden's neutrality and Hitler was forced to take this into account.

Though military operations in Western Europe disrupted Sweden's traditional trade ties, Soviet-Swedish relations continued to improve in 1940. True to its policy of friendship with Sweden, the Soviet Government favourably responded to a number of property claims in the Baltic republics which she put forward in connection with the entry of Lithuania, Latvia and Estonia into the USSR.

The Soviet Union was on the side of the Norwegian people during the most difficult period of its history when in April 1940 Norway was occupied by German troops. The Soviet Government maintained diplomatic relations with the legitimate government of Norway until May 1941.

The Soviet Government continued to support Denmark in the grim days of April 1940 when she was invaded by the German troops. The Soviet Union welcomed Denmark's proposal to improve trade relations. These normal trade relations were maintained in 1941, too. In May of that year Denmark conducted favourable trade talks with the Soviet Union.

In the period from 1939 to 1941 the Soviet Union considerably increased its economic and military assistance to the Chinese people. Under the Soviet-Chinese trade treaty of June 16, 1939, Soviet goods, including large consignments of military equipment and fuel poured into China. Ill and wounded officers and men of the Chinese 8th Army, led by the Communist Party of China, were brought to the Soviet Union for treatment. An additional 200 Soviet bomber and fighter aircraft were shipped to China at the beginning of 1941 when she desperately needed military aircraft to deprive the Japanese Air Force of its superiority. Right to the beginning of the Soviet-German war Soviet pilots were fighting in China.

Civil and military experts from the USSR effectively assisted the Chinese people in organising the armed struggle against the Japanese invaders.

Soviet assistance enabled the Chinese people to intensify its fight against the Japanese and strengthened its hope in the final victory.

The Soviet Union also rendered moral and political support to other peoples of Asia in their unequal struggle against the Japanese invaders.

The measures carried out by the Soviet Union in the initial period of the Second World War were of tremendous international significance.

2. HITLER GERMANY'S TREACHEROUS ATTACK ON THE SOVIET UNION AND THE CHANGE IN THE BALANCE OF FORCES ON THE WORLD SCENE

WORLD REACTION TO THE OUTBREAK OF THE GREAT PATRIOTIC WAR

On June 22, 1941, nazi Germany attacked the Soviet Union. Without a declaration of war German troops invaded the USSR in the hope of achieving a lightning victory and completely isolating the USSR. Shortly afterwards Italy, Rumania, Hungary and Finland entered the war on Germany's side.

The situation was extremely grave for the Soviet people and its Armed Forces at the beginning of the war (which is known as the Great Patriotic War).

The Soviet Union had to enter into a single-handed combat with a colossal military machine. The difficult situation was due largely to the miscalculations in assessing the possible time of Hitler's attack on the USSR and the shortcomings in the preparations to repel the first blows. At the time the Soviet troops' lack of experience in waging large-scale operations in a modern war likewise made itself felt. But even at the initial period of the war it became clear that the military venture of the nazis was doomed to failure.

In the summer of 1941, the Soviet troops waged fierce defensive battles all along the Soviet-German front and their ferocity mounted with the advent of autumn. Rallied around the Communist Party, the Soviet people rose to the defence of their country.

The involvement of the USSR in the war altered the military and political situation and the balance of forces in the world in favour of the forces fighting a just and liberatory struggle against nazi Germany.

With its enormous economic and military potential the Soviet Union became the bulwark of the united anti-fascist front of the peoples. All the freedom-loving peoples of the world realised that the future of world civilisation, the sovereignty of many states and freedom and even the physical existence of entire nations depended on the outcome of the battles on the Soviet-German front. They regarded solidarity with the Soviet Union as a matter of vital concern, as one of the most essential elements of proletarian internationalism. The Soviet people's heroic struggle evoked the admiration and won the support and sympathy of the broadest masses of working people.

The Communist Parties of the United States, Great Britain, Canada and other countries issued fervent appeals to their peoples and governments to ensure unity of action with the Soviet Union. The Communist Parties of Yugoslavia, Bulgaria and Rumania summoned the working people of their countries to intensify the anti-fascist struggle and increase assistance to the Soviet people. Operating in the grim conditions of nazi terror the Communist Party of Germany on June 24, 1941 appealed to the German people and the armed forces to overthrow Hitler. In October it again declared that Hitler "by perfidiously and treacherously attacking the Soviet Union committed a grave crime against the German people which will plunge Germany into a dreadful national catastrophe".[1] In its directive to Party organisations of June 23, 1941 the Central Committee of the Communist Party of China pointed out that in the war which the Soviet Union was waging to rebuff the fascist aggression the Soviet people were defending not only their own country, but also all the peoples struggling for liberation from fascist bondage.

The Resistance Movement mounted in all the occupied countries and in some even developed into partisan struggle. In July and August 1941 armed uprisings broke out in some parts of Yugoslavia; in the latter half of 1941 French patriots carried out hundreds of armed attacks on the German oc-

[1] *Geschichte der deutschen Arbeiterbewegung*, Vol. 5, Berlin, 1966, pp. 547, 550-52.

cupation forces. Patriots in Poland, Czechoslovakia and other countries intensified their struggle against the invader.

Hitler Germany's striving for world domination seriously threatened US and British interests. Therefore, already on June 22, 1941 British Prime Minister Winston Churchill declared that Britain would take the Soviet Union's side and render it every assistance.[1] A day later US President Franklin Roosevelt made a similar statement. Their statements had a positive impact on the consolidation of anti-Hitler forces in the world and coincided with the vital interests of the peoples of the United States and Britain and their sympathies for the world's first socialist state and the Soviet people.

Thus, the position of the main opposing forces was defined in the first days of the Soviet-German war. As regards the Japanese ruling circles, they for a time remained neutral in the Soviet-German war, while the military circles vigorously prepared to resolve Japan's contradictions with the United States in the Pacific basin by armed force. Japanese-US relations continued to deteriorate and on December 7, 1941 the Japanese attacked the US naval base at Pearl Harbour. Within a few days the Japanese troops landed in Malaya and the Philippines.

On December 11, 1941 Germany declared war on the United States and then Italy, Bulgaria, Hungary and Rumania followed suit. The Government of Manchoukuo also declared war on Britain and the United States.

The Second World War was fought in Europe, Asia and Africa on the territory of 40 states. By the end of the war the 61 countries involved had an aggregate population of 1,700 million, i.e., more than 75 per cent of the world's total, of whom 110 million had been mobilised for military service.

THE EFFORTS OF THE USSR
TO ESTABLISH
AN ANTI-HITLER COALITION

The Soviet Union's principal foreign policy objective in the years of the Great Patriotic War was to create a powerful anti-Hitler coalition. The USSR regarded this as its in-

---

[1] W. Churchill, *The Second World War*, Vol. II, pp. 331-33.

ternationalist duty before the freedom-loving peoples and its fulfilment coincided not only with the interests of the USSR, but also with the vital interests of the whole world.

As it rallied different countries regardless of their social system into the anti-Hitler coalition, the Soviet Government took into account the objective factor—the existence of acute and irreconcilable contradictions in the capitalist world, especially between Britain, the USA and France, on the one hand, and Germany, Japan and Italy, on the other. Another objective factor which made the establishment of the anti-Hitler coalition inevitable was the community of vital interests of the peoples of the capitalist states that had already been attacked by Hitler Germany or which were threatened with attack. It was natural, therefore, that they resolutely supported the USSR in the war against fascism.

The first official document which marked the beginning of the formation of the anti-Hitler coalition was the agreement for joint action by the Governments of the USSR and Great Britain in the war against Germany signed in Moscow on July 12, 1941.

In its efforts to expand the membership of the anti-Hitler coalition, the Soviet Government signed agreements with the governments in exile of Czechoslovakia (July 18, 1941) and Poland (July 30, 1941) on the restoration of diplomatic relations and mutual assistance and support in the war against Hitler Germany. On September 27, 1941 the Soviet Government was the first to extend official recognition to the Free France Committee and said that it was prepared to offer every assistance to the fighting French people.

From the outset of the Great Patriotic War, the Soviet Union tried to improve relations with the United States. But it had to surmount certain difficulties which were occasioned not only by the fact that the US was not at war, but mainly by the intrigues of US reactionary circles. Their plans were disclosed by Senator Harry Truman who said on June 24, 1941: "If we see that Germany is winning we ought to help Russia and if Russia is winning we ought to help Germany and that way let them kill as many as possible."[1]

Nevertheless, the more far-sighted US statesmen, President

---

[1] *The New York Times*, June 24, 1941, p. 7.

Roosevelt in the first place, maintained that their country's destiny depended on the Soviet Union's ability to stand up to the aggressors. They decided to give military aid to the USSR and as of November 1941 extend to it the provisions of the Lend-Lease Act under which the United States rendered military assistance to countries fighting against Hitler Germany.

An important document signed by the Allies at the first stage of the anti-Hitler coalition was the declaration issued on August 14, 1941 by Churchill and Roosevelt and which came to be known as the Atlantic Charter.

Taking into account that the declaration proclaimed a number of democratic principles conducive to the strengthening of the anti-Hitler coalition and the mobilisation of the peoples for the struggle against fascism, the Soviet Union acceded to the Charter. In a special statement of September 24, 1941 the Soviet Union once again unequivocally expounded its strategic line in international affairs. It recognised the right of each people to state independence and territorial inviolability and formulated the key objectives of the anti-Hitler coalition: abolition of racial exclusiveness; equality of nations and inviolability of state territory; liberation of the enslaved nations and the restoration of their sovereignty; economic assistance to the victims of aggression; re-establishment of democratic freedoms; destruction of the fascist regime. This document also raised the question of the post-war reorganisation of the world on the basis of collective security.

The Soviet declaration substantially supplemented and specified the programme of the anti-Hitler coalition, making it more democratic and anti-fascist in character.

The Moscow Conference of representatives of the USSR, Britain and the USA (September-October 1941), at which the Allies considered the question of reciprocal military and economic assistance in the war against Germany, was another important step towards the establishment of the anti-Hitler coalition and an indication of the Soviet Union's growing international prestige.

America's entry into the war in December 1941 following Japan's attack on Pearl Harbour created fresh conditions for the Soviet Union to continue its efforts to strengthen the anti-Hitler coalition. On January 1, 1942, in Washington representatives of 26 nations, including Soviet Ambassador to the United States, Maxim Litvinov, signed the United Nations Declaration.

The first half of 1942 witnessed fresh successes of the USSR in its political activity aimed at bringing states and peoples still closer together for the purpose of routing the aggressors and liberating the occupied countries. On May 26, 1942 the Soviet Union and the United Kingdom signed a treaty of alliance which replaced the agreement of July 12, 1941, and on June 11, 1942 in Washington the Soviet Union and the United States signed an agreement on the principles applying to mutual aid in the war against aggression.

These documents were of considerable significance because, first and foremost, they constituted the legal foundation of the anti-Hitler coalition of the peoples of the USSR, the USA and Britain; secondly, they not only frustrated the plans of the nazis to isolate the USSR, but also raised the international prestige of the USSR to a still higher level, and thirdly, they were a blow at the reactionary circles in the United States and Britain which sought to foster distrust of the Soviet Union's aims, weaken the anti-Hitler coalition and thus help nazi Germany.

The Soviet people's heroic struggle and the just, liberatory aims pursued by the USSR in the Great Patriotic War made the Soviet Union the leading and decisive force of the anti-Hitler coalition.

SOVIET ASSISTANCE TO PEOPLES
OF OCCUPIED COUNTRIES

Despite the exceptionally difficult situation in which the USSR found itself in the first months of the Great Patriotic War, it did all it could in the circumstances to help peoples in countries under German occupation. This assistance acquired the most diverse forms.

Some communist parties had their foreign bureaus in Moscow headed by such eminent representatives of the communist and working-class movement as Georgi Dimitrov, Maurice Thorez, Palmiro Togliatti, Wilhelm Pieck, Walter Ulbricht and Klement Gottwald. Assisted by the Central Committee of the CPSU and the Soviet Government these men devoted their entire political experience to the cause of liberating their peoples, taking part in the organisation of underground Party activity and the guerrilla struggle in their countries. In August and September 1941, for example, seven groups of Bulgarian Communists returned to Bulgaria from the Soviet Union. After undergoing training in the USSR, several special groups of Party workers were secretly infiltrated to Czechoslovakia to re-activate underground Party organisations.

With the assistance of the CPSU Central Committee activists of the Communist Party of Poland, which the Executive Committee of the Comintern unjustly dissolved in 1938, set up an operational group to re-establish the Communist Party in Poland. In December 1941 this group which among others included Marceli Nowotko and Pawel Finder, successfully landed near Warsaw. In the next few months other groups arrived in the country. Many German Communists who had emigrated to the Soviet Union in their time returned to Germany to organise the anti-fascist struggle there. Filled with admiration for the heroic struggle of the Yugoslav peoples the Soviet people did all they could to help them in their fight against the common enemy.

The Soviet Government rendered extensive assistance to foreign anti-fascists in their propaganda activity among the population of their countries and, in particular, provided them with broadcasting facilities. In July 1941, for example, the Hristo Botew radio station began broadcasting to Bulgaria and in the autumn of the same year the Naroden Glas radio station started transmissions to Bulgaria, too. In the latter half of 1941 the Lajos Kossuth radio station went on the air beaming of its programmes to Hungary.

Programmes from Moscow were also broadcast in Czech, Slovak, Polish, German, Finnish, French and other languages. These transmissions, in which leaders of Communist Parties and people prominent in science and culture participated, proved to be of great practical and moral help to the patriots waging an underground struggle against fascism in many European countries.

A positive role in consolidating the world anti-fascist forces, explaining the liberatory objectives of the war waged by the Soviet people and unmasking fascism's man-hating ideology was played by anti-fascist committees which were established in the Soviet Union during the war: the Anti-Fascist Committee of Soviet Youth, the Anti-Fascist Committee of Soviet Women, the Jewish Anti-Fascist Committee. An especially great part in rallying the Slav peoples in the fight against the common enemy was played by the All-Slav Anti-Fascist Committee under the chairmanship of General A. S. Gundorov of the Soviet Union. It was established at an all-Slav meeting of representatives of the peoples of the USSR, Poland, Czechoslovakia, Yugoslavia, Bulgaria and other countries which took place in Moscow on August 10 and 11, 1941. During the war it published the *Slavyane* (Slavs) magazine, organised several anti-fascist rallies, published leaflets, helped emigrants from Slav countries and carried on other activity.

Soviet trade unions maintained close contact with foreign workers' organisations. On October 15, 1941 an Anglo-Soviet Trade Union Committee was established which held several joint sessions.

The Soviet Government effectively assisted Polish citizens living in the USSR. On March 1, 1943 they began to publish the *Wolna Polska* weekly newspaper which had a circulation of about 40,000. A congress held in Moscow at the beginning of June 1943 on the initiative of Polish Communists organisationally established the Union of Polish Patriots in the USSR which subsequently embraced 100,000 persons. The Union, whose elected chairman was the Polish authoress and public figure Wanda Wasilievska, regarded the formation of Polish military units on Soviet territory which would fight together with Soviet troops for Poland's liberation as one of its most urgent tasks.

The Soviet Union provided many German POWs with an opportunity to work for Germany's liberation from the nazis. A conference of German soldiers taken prisoner by the Soviet troops was held at the end of 1941 on the initiative of German Communists. It adopted and published an Address to the German People which exposed the nazis' anti-popular aims and summoned all anti-fascists to put up a resolute fight for their country's liberation. Several anti-fascist conferences were held in 1942. Following the rout of the German forces at Stalingrad, German officers and men in the Krasnogorsk

POW camp near Moscow organised a conference on July 12 and 13, 1943 at which they established the Free Germany National Committee, and in September of the same year a group of anti-fascist generals and officers formed the Union of German Officers which joined the Free Germany National Committee which became the political and organisational centre of all German patriots. The Soviet Government placed Radio Free Germany at its disposal, and a weekly newspaper of the same name was published.

Rumanian, Hungarian and other prisoners of war harbouring anti-fascist feelings were also given an opportunity to unite and fight for the liberation of their countries together with the Soviet troops.

SOVIET TROOPS ENTER IRAN
AND THWART A FASCIST THREAT
TO THAT COUNTRY.
ASSISTANCE TO AFGHANISTAN

By the summer of 1941, nazi Germany had thousands of her secret agents in Iran and established close contact with Iranian ruling circles. There were German "advisers" in many government institutions, and the nazis used Iranian territory for raising and training groups for subversive activity in the Soviet Union. Within a few months the nazis delivered 11,000 tons of arms and ammunition to Iran and in August 1941 hundreds of German officers arrived in the country under the guise of tourists.

The expanding activity of Hitler's agents created a serious threat of a fascist coup in the country. Developments in Iran were viewed with anxiety in the Soviet Union and Britain and clashed with the vital interests of the Iranian people whose country the nazis wanted to turn into yet another theatre of the Second World War.

In these circumstances the USSR and Britain in a note of August 25, 1941 informed Iran that in the interests of self-defence they were compelled to bring their troops into the country. The USSR undertook this move in keeping with the Soviet-Iranian Treaty of 1921. On the following day a Soviet force consisting of an infantry corps of the Central Asian Military District and a cavalry corps of the Transcaucasian

Military District entered Northern Iran. Simultaneously British troops entered Southern Iran. The British ruling circles took advantage of this act to further their selfish imperialist aims.

Within several days Soviet troops were stationed in Iranian (East) Azerbaijan, Gilan, Mazandaran and Khorosan where they were warmly welcomed by the local population.

On September 8, Soviet, British and Iranian representatives signed an agreement in Teheran which inaugurated their close war-time co-operation. It was also agreed that Soviet and British troops would enter the Iranian capital. On September 16, Shah Reza Pahlavi who actively pursued a pro-Hitler policy abdicated in favour of his son Mohammed Reza Pahlavi and fled the country.

On January 24, 1942 the new Iranian Government signed a treaty of alliance with the USSR and Great Britain. The treaty developed and concretised the principal provisions of the September 8 Agreement and took into account both the interests of the countries of the anti-Hitler coalition and of the Iranian people. A special article of the treaty pointed out that the "allied states jointly pledge to make the maximum effort to support the economic life of the Iranian people against poverty and difficulties arising as a result of the present war".

As the Iranian historian Rezvani notes, "the people of Iran saw for themselves that the stationing of the Soviet Army in Iran pursues no aims other than to thwart the threat of a nazi attack on the USSR from the territory of Iran and to ensure the security of Iran herself. The Soviet troops did not interfere in Iran's internal affairs. The population was on good terms with the Soviet Army."[1]

The entry of Soviet and British troops into Iran had important international repercussions. First, it put an end to the fascist espionage and subversive network and wrecked Hitler's plans to create a new hotbed of war in the Middle East. Second, it ensured the necessary communications between the countries of the anti-Hitler coalition, thus strengthening their military co-operation in achieving victory over

---

[1] Rezvani, *Madjara-iye Azerbaijan...* Arak, 19, pp. 46-69 (in Persian).

the common enemy. Third, Iran became a member of the anti-Hitler coalition and retained her sovereignty and national independence which was in the vital interests of the entire Iranian people.

In Iran the Soviet Armed Forces directly fulfilled their mission of liberation with regard to a people of a neighbouring country faced with the threat of falling into fascist bondage.

The Soviet Union's relations with friendly Afghanistan were likewise based on its peaceful foreign policy and internationalist duty. In the first months of the Soviet-German war Afghanistan, just as Iran, was infested by German and Italian agents who worked as "advisers" in various ministries.

On October 11, 1941, the Soviet Government, with the agreement of Britain and in conformity with the Soviet-Afghan treaty of Friendship of 1921, addressed a note to Afghanistan advising that members of the German and Italian communities be evicted from the country. The Afghan Government took the advice and at the end of October 1941 the fascist agents were ordered to leave the country, and the people of Afghanistan were thus able to avoid the danger of becoming inveigled in Hitler's adventuristic plans and all the grave consequences they entailed.

3. THE ECHO
OF THE GREAT VICTORIES
OF THE SOVIET PEOPLE

THE SOVIET-GERMAN FRONT—
THE MAIN FRONT
OF THE SECOND WORLD WAR

From June 1941 to May 1945 the Soviet-German Front was the main front of the Second World War, where the destiny of the military and political objectives of the warring coalitions was decided. Preparing for war Hitler referred to the Soviet Union as the most formidable obstacle on nazi Germany's road to world domination. He refrained from invading Britain immediately for the sole reason that, as he himself admitted, Russia would have continued to fight even if

Britain had been routed, whereas with Russia down on her knees, Britain would have immediately begged for peace.[1]

In her effort to defeat the Soviet Union Germany moved the bulk of her manpower and weapons to the East. Out of the 214 divisions totalling 8.5 million men she had in June 1941, 153 divisions and 37 divisions of her satellites numbering 5.5 million men were designated for military operations against the Soviet Army.

The strength of German and satellite forces on the Soviet-German front increased in the course of the war. From December 1941 to April 1942 the German Command was forced to transfer another 39 divisions, six brigades and a large number of replacements to the East.

In May 1942 there were 226 and in November of the same year 266 enemy divisions, or about 6.2 million men, on the Soviet-German front. This was the maximum number of troops the enemy had ever concentrated against the USSR in the course of the war.

Between November 19, 1942 and March 30, 1943, in view of the enormous losses sustained in the winter campaign of 1942-1943, particularly at Stalingrad, the enemy was compelled to transfer 33 divisions and three brigades from Western Europe to the Soviet-German front. During the preparations for the 1943 summer offensive the German Command managed to concentrate only 4.8 million men, that is, 71 per cent of its army in the field, against the Soviet forces. At the time Germany's satellites had 525,000 men on the Soviet-German front. Altogether the enemy had 232 divisions, totalling 5.2 million men, facing the Soviet troops. Although another 14 divisions were transferred from the West to the Soviet-German front between July and September 1943, Germany was unable to substantially replenish her losses.

In early 1944 the Wehrmacht had 4.9 million men—198 divisions and 6 brigades, and 38 divisions and 18 brigades of her allies.

When the Soviet troops gained the state border of the USSR in the beginning of the summer of 1944, having liberated almost the whole of Soviet territory, the most battle-

---

[1] Gert Buchheit, *Hitler der Feldherr. Die Zerstörung einer Legende*, Rastatt-Baden, 1958, p. 178.

worthy enemy forces were concentrated on the Soviet-German front as before. Germany's land forces alone consisted of 179 divisions and 5 brigades and there were also 49 divisions and 18 brigades of her satellites.

From June 1941 to the middle of 1944, therefore, the number of enemy divisions on the Soviet-German front varied between 190 and 270, or up to 70 per cent of the land forces, whereas the number of the enemy divisions fighting against the US and British troops was between 9 and 20 in North Africa and between 7 and 26 divisions in Italy. The bulk of the enemy air force was also in action on the Soviet-German front.

The presence of the greater part of the enemy troops in the East indicated, in the first place, that Hitler linked the realisation of his plans for world domination with operations on the Soviet-German front. Having started the gamble in the East, he was no longer in a position to open a new front anywhere else. This meant that the United States, Britain and other countries of the anti-Hitler coalition had more or less favourable conditions in which to prepare and carry out major operations in North Africa and Italy and later in France. In the second place, the patriots in the occupied countries were able to intensify the Resistance Movement and deal more effective blows at the enemy.

The Soviet-German front was the scene of incessant and exceptionally furious fighting. Battles went on almost without respite for 1,418 days and nights, in the summer heat and the bitterly cold winters with temperatures as low as -40°C, in the spring slush and autumn rains. The Soviet troops fought in the marshes of the northwest, in the forests of Byelorussia and the Moscow area, in the steppes of the Ukraine and Kuban and in the mountains of the Caucasus.

In the course of the Wehrmacht's first campaign (summer-autumn 1941) which proved to be the most difficult test for the Soviet Army lasting five and a half months, the Soviet forces wore down and inflicted heavy losses on the enemy troops, forcing them to assume the defensive. They frustrated Hitler's plan for a lightning war and paved the way for a Soviet counter-offensive. Nazi Germany's casualties in the first two months of the war against the Soviet Union were twice as high as in all her campaigns in Europe during the preceding two years. The Germans lost a total of 402,865 men and officers, of whom 85,896 were killed, 296,670 wounded and 20,299 listed as missing.

The winter campaign of 1941-1942, and especially its main event—the rout of the enemy at Moscow—occupy an important place in the Great Patriotic War. In the course of their winter offensive the Soviet troops smashed up to 50 Wehrmacht divisions which lost more than 400,000 officers and men.

In the course of heavy fighting which took place in the southern sector in the summer and autumn of 1942, the enemy temporarily occupied an enormous area and reached the Volga and the passes of the Main Caucasian Range. But the German troops paid a high price for their successes and by November 1942 were forced to take on the defensive along the entire Soviet-German front. They managed to occupy more than 1,920,000 square kilometres of Soviet territory which prior to the war had a population of 85 million and accounted for a third of the country's industrial output. And yet, having lost two million officers and men in killed, wounded and missing in the fighting between June 1941 and the middle of November 1942 the enemy failed to achieve his ultimate objective.

The decisive development of the 1942-43 winter campaign was the Soviet victory at Stalingrad. At various stages of this battle, which lasted 200 days and nights, more than two million officers and men, 26,000 guns and mortars, over 2,000 tanks, a large number of aircraft and other equipment were in action on both sides simultaneously.

In the Stalingrad Battle, in the battle for the Caucasus and other operations carried out by the Soviet Army in the winter of 1942-43, the Wehrmacht suffered an unprecedented defeat. Between November 1942 and March 1943 the Soviet troops routed more than 100 enemy divisions whose losses amounted to about 1,700,000 men, 24,000 guns, more than 3,500 panzers and 4,300 aircraft.

The Stalingrad Battle marked a turning point in the Great Patriotic War, and in the Second World War for that matter, and inaugurated the mass expulsion of the enemy from the Soviet territory.

One of the decisive events of the Great Patriotic War was the historic battle at Kursk where the Soviet troops smashed

30 enemy divisions. The enemy lost half a million officers and men in the fighting. The shattering defeat at Kursk meant an end to the Wehrmacht's offensive strategy. Nazi Germany was on the brink of an imminent catastrophe. The Soviet Army was fully in command of the strategic initiative that had been wrested from the enemy at Stalingrad. The battle at Kursk and other developments which took place in 1943 meant that the tide of the war had irreversibly turned against the nazis.

The Soviet troops continued their offensive after the victory at Kursk. In the autumn of 1943 they reached the Dnieper and crossed it in their stride. During the battles of the 1944 winter campaign they reached the state borders of the USSR, liberating a vast territory of 329,000 square kilometres which had a population of almost 19 million before the war. Within a few months the enemy lost over a million officers and men, 20,000 guns and mortars, 8,400 panzers and assault guns, and almost 5,000 aircraft.

By the middle of 1944 the Soviet Armed Forces seriously undermined the strength of the Wehrmacht whose losses since the first day of the war reached 5.5 million men in killed, wounded and taken prisoner. The enemy was never able to recoup these enormous losses.

THE FURTHER STRENGTHENING
OF THE ANTI-HITLER COALITION

The Soviet Union's efforts to foster still closer co-operation of all the enemies of nazism and thus speed up the victorious conclusion of the war evoked the sympathy and understanding of all freedom-loving peoples. Pressing for the immediate opening of a second front in Europe, the Soviet Government was not only concerned with upholding the interests of the USSR, but also with hastening the end of the nazi occupation of the European countries, alleviating their sufferings and sacrifices, and speeding up the restoration of their state independence. The problem of the second front was more than just a problem of relations between the USSR, Britain and the USA. Its solution was vital for all the peace-loving peoples of the world. Consequently, they persistently demanded that the US and British leaders should open the second

front in Europe and were absolutely justified in doing so
since the military and political situation which took shape
at the beginning of the summer of 1942, when 75 per cent
of Germany's armed forces were firmly held down on the
Soviet-German front, favoured an Allied invasion of France.

Nevertheless, British Prime Minister Winston Churchill
informed the Soviet Government during his visit to Moscow
in the middle of August 1942 that Britain and the USA had
decided to put off the opening of the second front in Europe
from 1942 to 1943.[1] The reactionary circles in these countries
wanted to prolong the war in the course of which according
to their calculations both Germany and the Soviet Union
would be worn out.

Soviet victories in the winter of 1942-43 and the summer
of 1943 brought the final defeat of the enemy considerably
closer and placed the post-war organisation of the world
on the agenda. The Soviet programme on this matter was
expounded most fully on November 6, 1943 in a report delivered by Chairman of the USSR State Defence Committee,
J. V. Stalin, on the 26th anniversary of the Great October
Socialist Revolution. It provided for the liberation of the
peoples of Europe from the fascist invaders and assistance
to them in the restoration of their national states; the granting to the liberated peoples of Europe of the full right and
liberty to decide the question of their state system themselves; the severe punishment of the fascist war criminals responsible for the war and the suffering of the nations; the
creation of conditions in Europe completely precluding the
possibility of new aggression by Germany, and, finally, the
ensurance of long-term economic, political and cultural co-
operation between the European peoples on the basis of
mutual trust and mutual assistance.

The significant differences between the Soviet Union, on
the one hand, and its Anglo-American Allies, on the other,
in appraising the principles of post-war order of the world
came to light at the Moscow Conference of the foreign ministers of the three Great Powers in October 1943.

The Soviet side firmly upheld Poland's independence and
resolutely opposed the partitioning of Europe into spheres

---

[1] W. Churchill, *The Second World War*, Vol. 4, p. 430.

of influence, considering that this would be detrimental to the fundamental interests of the peoples. It also came forward with a democratic programme for the re-establishment of Italy's independence. Through the efforts of the Soviet representatives the conference rejected the plan which gave the Anglo-US organs the right of unlimited authority in the event of an Allied invasion of France. At the proposal of the Soviet Government the Conference adopted the Declaration on Austria expressing the desire of the three Governments to see this country, the first victim of the nazi aggression, free and independent.

The anti-Hitler coalition was further consolidated at the Tehran Conference of the Heads of Government of the USSR, USA and Britain which took place at the end of November and beginning of December 1943. The Conference decided that the second front in Europe would be opened in 1944. Meeting the wishes of the United States and Britain, the Soviet Union undertook to enter the war with Japan after the rout of nazi Germany. The conference also discussed a number of problems bearing on Poland, Iran, the future of Germany and the Italian Navy.

The significance of the Tehran Conference lay in the fact that it affirmed the ability of states with different political and socio-economic systems to agree on cardinal problems of war against a common enemy. The democratic and just nature of the conference decisions was largely due to the actual correlation of forces which took shape in the anti-Hitler coalition towards the end of 1943, when, as Winston Churchill put it, the Soviet Union became one of the strongest military powers in the world, if not the strongest, at least in Europe and Asia.

Though the Soviet Union was chiefly occupied with developments in Europe where the outcome of the entire world war was being decided, it also keenly followed developments in the Far East and in June 1943 demanded that the Japanese fold up their oil and coal concessions on Northern Sakhalin.

In September 1943 Japan offered her services to the Soviet Union as a mediator in what she calculated could be peaceful negotiations between the USSR and Germany. This was obviously a provocative venture on the part of Japanese ruling circles who wanted to save Germany from utter defeat and drive a wedge between the countries of the anti-Hitler coalition. The Soviet Union flatly rejected this proposal.

THE IMPACT OF SOVIET VICTORIES
ON PEOPLE'S RESISTANCE MOVEMENT
IN EUROPE AND ASIA

The national-liberation struggle in Europe and Asia took place in dissimilar conditions, and its character, scope and aims were influenced by a multitude of internal and external factors, of which the most decisive one was the Great Patriotic War of the Soviet people.

Soviet military victories, the courage and staunchness of the Soviet partisans, the dedicated labour of the Soviet workers, collective farmers and intellectuals inspired the peoples of Europe and Asia to fight heroically for their freedom and national independence.

A new stage in the Resistance Movement of the peoples in nazi-occupied countries was ushered in by the Soviet Army's historical victories at Stalingrad and Kursk. The partisan struggle acquired a mass character. By the end of 1943 the regular People's Liberation Army of Yugoslavia had 300,000 officers and men and controlled a considerable portion of the country. The People's National Liberation Army (ELAS) in Greece liberated almost two-thirds of the country and had 12,500 officers and men by the summer of 1943. "The numerical composition of ELAS," said General Seraphis, "began to grow rapidly after the Stalingrad battle." By the autumn of 1943 the 20-thousand strong National Liberation Army of Albania had freed many areas of the country. Gwardia Ludowa in Poland had an excellent organisational structure; its 60 brigades and detachments were in action in practically all the provinces where they tied down large enemy forces. An important development in the people's struggle against the occupation forces were the armed uprisings in the Warsaw (April-July) and Bialystok (August 1943) ghettoes which were supported by Gwardia Ludowa detachments. Dozens of guerrilla detachments in Czechoslovakia extended the scope of their operations. Two hundred thousand maquis controlled Savoie, Haute-Savoie, Correze and other departments in France. Without assistance from the Allies they liberated Corsica. The Resistance Movement gained momentum in Belgium, Norway, Denmark and other occupied countries.

Inspired by the Soviet Army's victories the peoples of China and Southeast Asia struck heavy blows at the Japanese invaders. In China the 8th and the new 4th armies, and other forces of the people's anti-Japanese Resistance Movement tied down considerable forces of the Japanese regular army. With growing determination the Korean patriots hindered the plunder of their country by the Japanese. The Vietnamese guerrillas liberated a number of regions in the North of Vietnam and gave fraternal assistance to the peoples of Laos and Cambodia.

The radical turn of the tide in the war stimulated the further consolidation of all the genuinely patriotic forces of the Resistance Movement, the extension of the social base of the enemies of fascism and the establishment of national fronts resting on the alliance of the working class and the peasantry in which the proletariat played the leading role.

Some bourgeois organisations of the Resistance Movement were forced to establish contact with the communist parties. In France a National Resistance Council was set up. Greek patriots united in the National Liberation Front (EAM). The fight of the Slovak patriots for unity of action resulted in the establishment of the Slovak National Council. A Freedom Council was set up in Denmark. Similar organisations uniting the Resistance fighters appeared in 1943 in several other countries.   The assurance of the peoples of occupied Europe in the ultimate victory over the enemy inspired by the nazi Germany's defeats on the Eastern front found its expression in the appearance of underground organs of people's rule. Thus, the Anti-Fascist People's Liberation Assembly established in November 1942 became the first parliament of new Yugoslavia. At its second session, which was held in November 1943, the Assembly elected the National Committee of Liberation of Yugoslavia, the country's Provisional Government. In Albania there were national liberation councils which functioned as organs of people's rule. In the night of December 31, 1943, 19 delegates representing various anti-fascist political parties and organisations of Poland elected the

Krajowa Rada Narodowa which became the supreme organ of the people's democratic national representation.

In 1943 there was an upsurge in the national liberation movement of the peoples of the Arab countries, particularly in the former French mandated territories of Syria and Lebanon. France's new national government headed by de Gaulle could not ignore this fact and granted independence to Syria and Lebanon where elections were shortly held, bringing representatives of the national bourgeoisie to power.

The influence and authority of the communist parties which were in the front ranks of the Resistance fighters from the first day of occupation rose considerably. They rallied the patriots, exposed traitors, fostered hatred for the invaders and formulated the tasks of national and social liberation. People were becoming more and more convinced that the Communists had every reason to maintain that the liberation of their countries depended first and foremost on the Soviet Army's victories.

In spite of the heavy losses sustained by the communist and workers' parties as a result of repressions, the world Communist movement rose to a new and higher stage in its development.

On May 15, 1943 the Presidium of the Comintern Executive Committee decided to dissolve the Communist International. The Comintern had played a great historical role in guiding the Communist movement in the pre-war period. During the Second World War the imperialist propaganda spread the lie that the Communists in different countries were acting on "orders from Moscow" and not in the interests of their peoples. The dissolution of the Comintern repudiated this calumny and stimulated the activity of the communist parties which in view of the extremely diverse local conditions had to display flexibility and be capable of making swift decisions.

The important thing about the Resistance Movement was its international character as could be seen from its tasks and its multinational composition. People of dozens of nationalities took part in the anti-fascist struggle in Poland, Czechoslovakia, France, Italy, Yugoslavia and other countries. Likewise international in character was the struggle of the inmates of many nationalities in the nazi death camps.

Soviet citizens, whom the fortunes of war had brought to Europe, played a serious role in determining the nature and scope of the Resistance Movement there. According to incomplete data more than 40,000 Soviet patriots were members of partisan detachments in Europe, including 18,000 in Poland, 5,000 in Italy, 3,000 in Czechoslovakia, 3,000 in France and over 6,000 in Yugoslavia. Soviet people were with the partisan detachments in these and other countries, but there were also detachments and brigades consisting wholly of Soviet partisans.

The title of Hero of the Soviet Union was conferred on N. A. Prokopyuk, V. A. Karasev, M. I. Petrov, N. P. Fyodorov, D. M. Karbyshev, Musa Djalil, Mehti Ganifu ogly Gusein-Zade, M. P. Devyatayev, F. A. Poletayev, and V. V. Porik, the bravest of the Soviet partisans and underground workers who fought in foreign countries.

Educated by the Communist Party in the spirit of proletarian internationalism and fraternal solidarity with the enslaved nations, the Soviet people did not spare their lives in the struggle against the German invaders.

By the spring of 1944, when the Soviet troops had reached the state border and began directly to fulfil their mission of liberation, the Resistance Movement considerably increased its influence on the character and the outcome of the war and also on the post-war order of the world.

THE VICTORIES
OF THE SOVIET ARMY
AND THE FURTHER AGGRAVATION
OF THE CRISIS OF THE FASCIST BLOC

The fighting on the Soviet-German front had a decisive impact on the situation in the nazi bloc countries. The strength of any coalition of states depends on their people's unity and cohesion which are only possible when the coalition pursues just aims and its members have equal rights. There was nothing of the sort in the nazi bloc. In the initial period of the war it was held together by Germany's military might, by propaganda which had created the myth about its invincibility and by the terroristic regimes established in its member states. These were unreliable bonds, however, and the nazi bloc could only hold together as long as Germany continued to win her battles. And so when the German troops began to suffer defeats this immediately had a negative effect on the internal political situation in each member state and on their relations.

The enormous human and material losses sustained by the Wehrmacht at Moscow forced Hitler to resort to the mobilisation of people subject to military service. Since no earlier provisions had been made for this measure, it had an adverse effect on the war economy. Germany hastily reorganised her war industry which was not geared to a protracted war. The first defeat sustained by the Wehrmacht also had an impelling effect on the morale of the country's population. That part of it which trusted Hitler's promises that the USSR would be smashed within a few weeks was afraid of a drawn-out war. At the same time the Soviet victory at Moscow inspired another part of the population, the anti-fascist workers in the first place, to continue the struggle against nazism. In 1942 anti-fascist groups under Harro Schulze-Boysen, Herbert Baum, George Schumann, Theodor Neubauer and others stepped up their operations. The Communists were the most active fighters against the fascists. In his determination to crush any Resistance movement Hitler increased the reign of terror in the country.

Some of the generals were also disenchanted with Hitler and so he retaliated by removing a number of army group commanders from their posts and appointed himself commander-in-chief of the land forces.

Italy, Rumania, Hungary and other satellites of nazi Germany were beset by increasing economic difficulties. The heavy casualties sustained by their troops on the Eastern front led to differences between them.

The communist parties intensified their efforts to overthrow the fascist regimes and pull their countries out of the anti-Soviet war. Strikes and sabotage increased at the Fiat factories in Italy, at the oilfields in Rumania and at industrial enterprises in Hungary and Bulgaria.

The Soviet victory at Moscow decisively influenced Japan's position whose ruling circles resolved to refrain from attacking the USSR and wait for the outcome of the fighting on the Soviet-German front.

Seventeen months after Hitler started the war in the East, 16 countries declared war on Germany and another 10 severed diplomatic relations with her. All this manifested the increasing isolation of the nazi bloc in the sphere of foreign policy.

Although the Soviet victory at Moscow revealed signs of instability of the nazi bloc and Germany's European rear, Germany's military and economic potential and her armed forces were still powerful enough for her to try and restore the situation on the Soviet-German front.

The Soviet Armed Forces dealt fresh blows at the nazi war machine and Hitler's "new order" in Europe at the end of 1942 and in the course of 1943. Under the influence of their historical victories at Stalingrad and Kursk, the signs of a crisis in Germany herself and in her relations with her satellites began to develop into a real crisis, expediting the disintegration of the nazi bloc and its complete isolation on the world scene.

Early in 1943 the nazis proclaimed "total mobilisation" in Germany in order to rectify the catastrophic situation with reserves and replenish the equipment lost at Stalingrad. After the defeat at Kursk another "total mobilisation" was proclaimed in the country. Although the Wehrmacht managed to make good its material losses to some extent, it became less battleworthy and its morale declined.

The defeats on all fronts made some generals and representatives of the nazi elite more and more disenchanted with Hitler, and in order to save the regime and prevent Germany from surrendering they conspired to remove Hitler from power by force.

An important feature of the internal political crisis that developed in Germany in 1943 was the further increase in the activity of the anti-fascist patriotic groups headed by the Communist Party. Seriously weakened by arrests, groups and organisations of the Communist Party continued to operate in Leipzig, Berlin and Thüringia. The Communists made an attempt to unite all the anti-fascist forces on the basis of the platform of the Free Germany National Committee.

On instructions from the Central Committee of the Communist Party of Germany, the leading organisers of the anti-fascist Resistance in the country Anton Saefkow, Franz Ja-

cob, Martin Schwantes, Theodor Neubauer and George
Schumann in the summer of 1943 set up an operational centre to guide the struggle of the Communists throughout the
country.[1]

The military defeats sustained by Hitler Germany and
her satellites aggravated the military and political crisis in
the nazi bloc, and seriously affected the situation in Italy.
By the summer of 1943 Mussolini's regime had fully discredited itself and was overthrown. In September 1943 Italy
withdrew from the bloc, thus paving the way for its disintegration. A decisive role in overthrowing fascism and promoting the liberation struggle of the Italian patriots against the
Germans who had invaded the country was played by Italian Communists. They formed Garibaldi brigades and detachments which played an important part in Italy's liberation.

Especially heavy defeats were sustained by the Rumanian
troops at Stalingrad, the Kuban area and in the Crimea. Seeing no way out of the situation, the opposition in the Rumanian bourgeoisie tried to conclude a separate peace with
Britain and the USA. There was growing discontent among the
Rumanian people with the nazis who had turned their country
into Germany's appendage deprived of all rights. It was the
Rumanian Communists who drew up a genuinely democratic
programme for saving their country. On the initiative of the
Communist Party an anti-Hitler Patriotic Front was established in the summer of 1943 and the Rumanian Communists
with the support of other patriots stepped up preparations
for an armed uprising and the disposal of the Antonescu regime.[2]

Anti-Hitler opposition also stiffened in other countries,
satellites of Germany. Its activists established contacts with
US and British representatives in the hope of negotiating a
separate peace and the entry of the troops of the Western
Allies into their countries.

But genuine democrats and patriots headed by the Communists realised that the national independence of their countries

---

[1] Wolfgang Bleyer, Karl Drechslar, Gerhard Förster, Gerhart Hass,
*Deutschland von 1939 bis 1945 (Deutschland während des zweiten Welt-
krieges)*, Berlin, 1969, p. 312.
[2] See *Romania in razboiul antihitlerist*, Bucharest, 1966, p. 33.

depended only on the victories of the Soviet Army and summoned their peoples to welcome the Soviet troops as liberators.

THE INFLUENCE
OF SOVIET VICTORIES
ON NEUTRAL COUNTRIES

The Soviet Union made every effort to rally the freedom-loving peoples for the struggle against nazi Germany and to isolate the nazi bloc. But it invariably displayed respect and understanding for those countries which for various reasons proclaimed and maintained neutrality in the war.

The policy of neutrality was officially proclaimed by Turkey, Portugal, Sweden, Switzerland and other countries, and Spain proclaimed non-belligerency. In fact, however, some of these countries did not observe the generally recognised principles of neutrality, openly supported the nazi bloc and were hostile to the Soviet Union.

In the difficult period for the USSR, when many foreign politicians predicted its destruction, Spain sent her Blue Division to the Soviet-German front, Turkey concentrated 17 divisions on the Soviet-Turkish border and other countries supplied Germany with valuable strategic raw materials. The ruling circles in some neutral countries openly called for an alliance with Germany, patronised various fascist organisations and turned their countries into nazi spy grounds against the Soviet Union and its allies.

But as the situation on the Soviet-German front changed in favour of the Soviet Union, the neutral countries changed their policy. At the end of 1942, for example, Turkish-German relations began to cool. Although Turkey did not break off economic relations with Germany, the Turkish press began to publish more and more articles criticising Germany and to call for an improvement in Soviet-Turkish relations.

Having lost his confidence in Germany's ultimate victory, Spanish dictator Franko took steps to save her and proposed to act as mediator in the conclusion of a separate peace between Germany and the Western Powers. In October 1943 Spain announced a switch from non-belligerency to neutrality.

Swedish ruling circles pursued a more independent domestic and foreign policy course. In the middle of 1943 they imposed a ban on the transit of German military personnel and materials through the country. The Swedish Government made no secret of its sympathy for occupied Denmark and helped Danish and Norwegian anti-fascists who had fled to Sweden.

Japan was in a peculiar position. Being in a state of war with the USA, Britain and other members of the anti-Hitler coalition, she was formally obliged to proclaim neutrality towards the USSR which in fact she did not observe. The Japanese troops continuously carried out acts of provocation against the Soviet Union, but did not venture to declare war. After the rout of the Germans at Stalingrad, the Japanese Government made it clear to Berlin that it was not in a position to open an anti-Soviet front in the Far East.

In this way the victories of the Soviet Armed Forces played a decisive role in helping some countries to preserve their neutrality. The international significance of this fact was that, first, it saved the peoples of Sweden, Turkey, Switzerland and other countries from nazi occupation and, second, that it restricted the sphere of war, which was a matter of considerable importance for the anti-Hitler coalition, especially in the initial period of the war.

4. THE ASSISTANCE OF THE SOVIET UNION IN THE FORMATION OF FOREIGN ARMED UNITS AND THEIR PARTICIPATION IN THE BATTLES ON THE SOVIET-GERMAN FRONT

An important way in which the Soviet Union fulfilled its internationalist duty was by rendering all-round assistance to foreign patriots in raising, arming and training their military units on Soviet territory.

Foreign military units were raised and trained under agreements between governments or at the request of the patriotic organisations of other countries. It was a difficult task, for the Soviet Union's material and technical possibilities had been sharply decreased as a result of the unfavourable developments at the front in the first months of the war. It had lost a large amount of its material reserves that had been built up for the needs of the army in peace-time, and at the same time in order to pursue the war it had to deploy a large number of land, air and naval units. The newly raised Soviet and foreign units felt an acute shortage of arms, equipment and transport facilities. Things were just as difficult with the personnel of the foreign units. There were several thousand political emigrants in the Soviet Union. Most of them were Communists and sturdy patriots, but they had practically no military training, and the problem of commanders for them was never fully solved. The shortage of officers held up the formation and training of the foreign military units.

The ruling circles and various political parties of the countries whose military units were raised in the Soviet Union had different views concerning their military tasks. The Polish and Czechoslovak governments in London, which entered into agreement with the USSR on the formation of military units in effect tried to prevent their participation in the battles against the German forces on the Soviet-German front, undermined the confidence of the soldiers in victory, sowed national discord and assigned anti-Soviet officers to command posts. In contrast to this stand, Polish and Czechoslovak Communists insisted that the units raised in the USSR should actively participate in the fighting on the Soviet-German front together with the Soviet Army and be able to uphold the interests of the working people in their countries following their liberation from the nazi yoke.

THE FORMATION
AND MILITARY OPERATIONS
OF THE POLISH TROOPS

Polish units were the first foreign troops to be raised in the USSR. The legal basis for their formation was the Agreement between the Soviet and Polish governments signed on July 30, 1941 in London. On August 14 the USSR and Poland signed an agreement in Moscow, fixing the strength of the Polish army which was being raised in the USSR at 30,000. In December the Soviet Union agreed to raise its strength to 96,000. The agreement stipulated that "the Polish army units will be moved to the front upon being brought to combat readiness. They will, as a rule, operate in units not less than divisions and will be used in conformity with the operational plans of the USSR Supreme Command".

The formation of the Polish troops was started in September 1941, and in February 1942 a field army HQ, six infantry divisions, a tank brigade and a school for junior officers were deployed in the republics of Uzbekistan, Tajikistan and Kazakhstan. The Polish Army had 73,000 officers and men. But the Polish emigre government in London, acting through General W. Anders who was placed in command of the army, did its best to prevent these divisions from being dispatched to the Soviet-German front. In response to his insistent demands the Polish Army was evacuated to Iran by August 1942.[1]

By authorising the departure of the Polish Army at such a difficult period in the Soviet Union's struggle against the armies of the fascist coalition, the Polish emigre government let down the interests of the Polish people. The Polish patriots qualified this act as betrayal of a soldier's duty unprecedented in Poland's history and non-fulfilment of the allied commitments to the USSR.

In May 1943 the formation of truly popular Polish troops in the USSR entered a new stage. Expressing the interests of the Polish people and its desire to fight arms in hand against fascism, the Union of Polish Patriots sought the Soviet Government's assistance in raising a Polish division. In the opinion of the Union of Polish Patriots the Polish Division would be the embryo of a new Polish Army which would embrace progressive ideology and the freedom-loving traditions of the Polish people and rely on the alliance and friendship with the USSR. The Soviet Government met the request and on May 6, 1943 the State Defence Committee authorised the formation of the Tadeusz Kosciuszko[2] 1st Polish

---

[1] This army was subsequently reorganised into the 2nd Army Corps. In January 1944 the Corps was transferred to the Italian Front, and in May 1944 took part in the battle at Monte Cassino.

[2] Tadeusz Kosciuszko (1746-1817), a Polish national hero who took part in the Polish national liberation movement and headed the 1794 insurrection.

Infantry Division. Colonel Zygmunt Berling[1] was appointed its commander.

It took three weeks to bring the division up to authorised strength. The principal difficulty was that of preparing the necessary number of officers, and the 920 Poles who were enrolled in Soviet military schools were put through a shortened training course. A hundred and fifty Soviet Army officers, most of whom were from western regions of the Byelorussian and Ukrainian republics and knew Polish, were assigned to medium-level command posts.

The divisional command was faced with the formidable task of turning the division into a battleworthy force in a mere three months. It was trained in line with the Soviet Army regulations, but Polish military traditions were not in the least infringed. The Polish flag, Polish anthem, Polish uniforms and Polish songs became a part of the life of its officers and men.

After six weeks of training the division received its colours and took the oath of allegiance. On July 15, the anniversary of the historic battle at Grünwald, the Union of Polish Patriots presented the Polish Ist Division with a banner bearing the inscription "For our freedom and yours".

By the time the division completed its combat training programme, several thousand Polish volunteers of conscription age had arrived in its camp, making it possible to begin the formation of other large units. On August 10, 1943 the State Defence Committee in response to the request of the Union of Polish Patriots agreed to form the Polish Ist Army Corps and to establish a school for Polish officers. Moreover, Polish sections of fifty men each were set up at the 3rd Saratov Armour and the Orjonikidze Automobile schools.

The corps consisted of three infantry divisions, including the Kosciuszko Division, an armour and an artillery brigade, air fighter regiment, and service units. Zygmunt Berling was made corps commander with Karol Swierczewski, a prominent member of the Polish revolutionary movement, second in command. Alexander Zawadski of the Communist Party of Poland was put in charge of political and educational work.

---

[1] Colonel Z. Berling was chief of staff of the 5th Infantry Division in Anders' army. He opposed the decision of the Polish emigre government to withdraw the army from the USSR and refused to go to Iran.

On September 1, 1943, the fourth anniversary of nazi Germany's invasion of Poland, the Kosciuszko Polish Ist Division was dispatched to front, while the other two divisions were still being brought up to full combat strength. It passed its ordeal by fire under the operational control of the 33rd Army of the Western Front. Acting in close co-operation with the Soviet 42nd and 290th Infantry divisions, it was ordered to breach enemy defences at Lenino and then push towards the Dnieper. The Soviet Command gave the division powerful artillery support from the army artillery group and reinforced it with a howitzer brigade, a mortar regiment and two artillery regiments.

In the course of the two-day offensive which began on October 12, the Soviet and Polish divisions seized two strongly fortified resistance centres of Tregubovo and Polzukhi and inflicted heavy losses in manpower and weapons on the enemy.

Although the success of the offensive proved to be of tactical importance only and was not exploited, the battle at Lenino was immensely significant from the political standpoint. The appearance at the front of the Polish troops symbolised the historical community of the destinies of the two Slav peoples, the revival and further development of the glorious traditions of the joint struggle of the peoples of Russia and Poland against the Teutonic knights and against tsarist autocracy and the traditions of the proletarian co-operation of the Polish internationalists with the working people of Soviet Russia in the Civil War.

For meritorious action at Lenino, the Soviet Government awarded orders and medals to 247 Polish officers and men, three of whom were conferred the title of Hero of the Soviet Union. October 12 became the birthday of the People's Polish Army.

The first success of the Kosciuszko Division showed the Polish soldier that he had chosen the shortest and the most dependable road of liberating his country. It also became obvious that the Polish troops had to receive serious training for action against the Wehrmacht. Consequently the training period of the Ist Army Corps was extended until the spring of 1944. The Soviet Union supplied the Polish units with 309 guns and mortars, 105 tanks and armoured cars, 1,425 machine guns, 6,967 submachine guns, 19,759 rifles, and also communication and transport facilities, various military equipment and uniforms.

In view of the fact that in the course of the 1944 winter campaign the Soviet troops had moved close to the Soviet-Polish border, the Union of Polish Patriots requested the Soviet Government to continue the formation of Polish troops. This request was met and on March 16, 1944 the Ist Army Corps was transformed into the Polish Ist Army. Prior to the entry of the Soviet forces into Poland, the Soviet Government authorised formation of the Polish 4th, 5th and 6th infantry divisions, a tank corps, an engineer brigade, an officers' higher school and combined Military School, the Headquarters of the Partisan Movement and the Main Headquarters of Polish Military Units.

THE ACTIVATION
AND MILITARY OPERATIONS
OF THE CZECHOSLOVAK TROOPS

The Czechoslovak military units in the USSR were raised under a treaty signed on July 18, 1941 by the governments of the USSR and the Czechoslovak Republic on mutual assistance and support in the war against nazi Germany. On September 27, in line with this treaty, the Soviet Supreme Command and the Supreme Command of Czechoslovakia signed a military agreement which defined the purpose of the formation of the Czechoslovak troops, their numerical strength and their logistic support. The agreement said that the Czechoslovak troops raised on the territory of the USSR would "participate jointly with the troops of the USSR and other Allied Powers in the struggle against Germany".

The first Czechoslovak unit activated in the USSR was a battalion commanded by the reputed anti-fascist resistance fighter Colonel Ludvik Svoboda.[1] The battalion command assumed its functions on December 12, 1941 upon receiving barrack accommodations from the Buzuluk City Soviet. The first to be enlisted were the 93 men who had remained in the USSR

---

[1] On March 30, 1968, the National Assembly elected Ludvik Svoboda President of the Czechoslovak Socialist Republic.

from the Polish Legion of the Czechoslovak forces.[1] The Communist Party of Czechoslovakia Foreign Bureau[2] headed by Klement Gottwald sent several dozen Czech and Slovak political emigrants to Buzuluk. But that was not enough to raise a full-strength battalion. In response to a request of the Czechoslovak Communists the Soviet Government allowed Soviet citizens of Czech and Slovak descent to volunteer for service in the Czechoslovak units which were being raised on the territory of the USSR.

Representatives of the Czechoslovak emigre National Defence Ministry on the selection board strove to enlist the smallest possible number of Communists and Czechoslovak patriots who had friendly feelings for the USSR.

Soviet instructors were attached to the battalion, its companies and platoons to help the command organise and carry on military training. These Soviet officers were subordinated to the representative of the Soviet General Staff assigned to the battalion.[3]

The Czechoslovak Communists put in a great deal of work to prepare the battalion morally and politically. Their discipline and progress in studies were an example for the other men; they explained to their colleagues that the way to their native land lay through joint struggle with the Soviet Army and not through Iran and the Middle East, as the emigre Czechoslovak Government proposed. Klement Gottwald and other members of the Foreign Bureau of the Communist Party of Czechoslovakia often visited the battalion. They informed the soldiers about the situation in Czechoslovakia and on the various fronts and outlined the tasks and the possible military operations which they were to carry jointly with the Soviet Army.

On January 30, 1943 the battalion left for the front where

---

[1] The Polish Legion was a detachment of Czechoslovak emigrants-volunteers who fought in September 1939 jointly with Polish troops on the territory of Poland against the nazi forces. Retreating to the east the legion numbering 900 crossed into the USSR.

[2] The Foreign Bureau consisted of Klement Gottwald, Jan Sverma, Viliam Siroky, Vaclav Kopecky and V. Boreck.

[3] The General Staff representative with the Czechoslovak 1st Battalion and later with the Czechoslovak Brigade was Lieutenant-Colonel K. T. Zagoskin with Major P. I. Kambulov as his liaison officer.

as a component part of the 3rd Tank Army of the Voronezh Front it saw action for the first time. The battalion was ordered to defend the northern bank of the Mzha River south of Kharkov and prevent the enemy from crossing the river.

Failing to overrun the defences of the 25th Guards Infantry Division at Taranovka, the German forces on March 8, 1943 struck their main blow at the positions of the Czechoslovak battalion. An exceptionally furious engagement took place for the village of Sokolovo, the main strong-point of the defence, manned by a company under Senior-Lieutenant Otakar Jarosz.

The Czechoslovak troops and the Soviet units attached to them stemmed the offensive and inflicted heavy losses on the enemy. For courage and heroism in this battle Otakar Jarosz was made Hero of the Soviet Union. He was the first foreigner to receive this title. Battalion Commander Colonel Ludvik Svoboda was awarded the Order of Lenin.

The battle at Sokolovo had great political repercussions. It proclaimed to the world that Czechoslovak troops capable of fighting arms in hand for their country's freedom and independence had been raised in the Soviet Union, and gave fresh impulse to the national liberation struggle of the Czechoslovak people. The Soviet-Czechoslovak comradeship-in-arms passed its first test.

In the course of the fighting, however, it became clear that a unit such as the Czechoslovak Ist Battalion could remain in action for a few days only and could not fulfil involved military assignments. It was, therefore, necessary to form a bigger force, namely an all-arms unit, and the question of activating a separate infantry brigade was raised.

The response of the Soviet Government to the request of the Czechoslovak comrades was expressed in the decision of the State Defence Committee of April 29, 1943 which stated: "1. Grant the request of the Czechoslovak Command concerning the formation on the territory of the USSR of the Czechoslovak 1st Infantry Brigade."

Preparations for activating elements and the brigade as a whole were launched in July under the command of Colonel Ludvik Svoboda. The brigade exercises that were held between August 27 and 31 were attended by Klement Gottwald and Jan Sverma who spoke highly of them. The inspec-

5*

tion that followed showed that the brigade was materially
well outfitted, tactically trained and capable of fulfilling
combat assignments.

On September 20, 1943 the brigade was organically assigned to the Ist Ukrainian Front and actively participated
in the battles for the liberation of Kiev and Belaya Tserkov.
The battles for these Ukrainian towns became vivid pages
in the history of the Soviet-Czechoslovak comradeship-in-
arms. The Soviet Government and the Supreme Command
commended the Czechoslovak troops for their courage and
combat efficiency, and the Presidium of the USSR Supreme
Soviet decorated the brigade with the Orders of Suvorov,
2nd Class, and Bogdan Khmelnitsky, Ist Class; 183 officers
and men were awarded orders and medals, and two, Lieutenant Sohor and Senior-Lieutenant Tesarzyk, were made
Heroes of the Soviet Union. Brigade commander Colonel
Svoboda was decorated with the Order of Suvorov, 2nd Class.

At the same time other Czechoslovak units were being
raised in the Soviet Union, including a tank battalion, an
air squadron and a paratroop brigade, whose formation was
started at the end of 1943. The paratroop brigade was the
first and only unit of its kind in the foreign troops activated
in the USSR. It was raised in the view of the need to have
mobile units within the Czechoslovak forces in the USSR
which could be transferred at short notice to Czechoslovakia
where the guerrilla struggle was acquiring increasing proportions.

The paratroop brigade consisted of approximately 3,000
officers and men. All of them were from the Slovak Division
which the fascist government of Slovakia had dispatched to
the Soviet-German front and who voluntarily surrendered
to the Soviet Army at Melitopol on October 30, 1943.

In early April 1944 the Soviet Army had almost reached
the Soviet-Czechoslovak border, a moment that had long been
waited for. In this connection the Foreign Bureau of the Communist Party of Czechoslovakia expressed the desire to raise
larger Czechoslovak units. This was fully in keeping with the
wish of the Czechoslovak people to take an active part in
liberating their country.

The Soviet Government met this request. On April 10
instructions were issued to speed up the formation of the Cze-

choslovak 1st Army Corps consisting of three brigades and an artillery, an anti-tank artillery, an anti-aircraft and an air fighter regiments.

Czechoslovak officers were trained at short-term courses in the brigades and at Czechoslovak departments in Soviet military schools.

The corps, which was under the operational control of the commander of the 1st Ukrainian Front, was ready for action by June 1944.

THE FORMATION
OF RUMANIAN TROOPS

Rumanian volunteer units in the USSR were raised at the request of political emigrants and patriotically minded prisoners of war. On October 4, 1943 after the Soviet Government had considered repeated requests from Rumanian Communists living in exile in the USSR and groups of Rumanian prisoners of war for permission to form a military unit which would fight against the nazis together with the Soviet Army, the State Defence Committee decreed the formation in the USSR of the Rumanian 1st Volunteer Division, which was later named after Tudor Vladimirescu[1], under the command of Colonel Nicolae Cambrea. The division began regular combat training in November when it had in the main been brought to full strength. Soviet instructors were attached to the division to help its officers.[2]

A great deal of work in getting the division ready for action on the Soviet-German front was carried out by the cultural and educational section. Aided by 30 Rumanian Communists who had fought in the international brigades in Spain, it educated the soldiers in the spirit of Rumanian revolutionary traditions.

---

[1] Tudor Vladimirescu (1780-1821), a Rumanian national hero. In the Russian-Turkish war of 1806-1812 he commanded a Rumanian volunteer detachment which fought on the side of the Russian troops. In 1812 he led a popular uprising against the wealthy landowners and the Turkish yoke and was killed in action.

[2] Colonel A. S. Novikov was appointed senior adviser of the group and Colonel G. M. Yeremin was the representative of the Soviet Army General Staff.

The division had completed its training period at the end of March 1944; its soldiers gave the oath of allegiance and were dispatched to the front. The Rumanian soldiers pledged to avenge the nazis for the occupation of their country and for the suffering they had brought on their people. They also pledged themselves to strengthen friendship with the Soviet people and their Armed Forces. The division was attached to the 2nd Ukrainian Front which had already entered Rumania. It had 158 guns and mortars, 212 anti-tank rifles, 605 machine guns, 2,287 submachine guns and 5,529 rifles.

THE FORMATION
OF YUGOSLAV TROOPS

The activation of Yugoslav military units on Soviet territory began in the autumn of 1943. The first to be raised was a separate infantry battalion. This was in keeping with a Soviet Government decision of November 17. Colonel M. Mesich was appointed its commander with Captain D. Georgievich as deputy commander for cultural and educational affairs and Captain M. Prishlin as chief of staff.

The formation of Yugoslav military units in the USSR was approved by the National Committee of Liberation of Yugoslavia. On February 16, 1944 Marshal Josip Broz Tito and Ivan Ribar, Chairman of the anti-fascist People's Liberation Assembly, addressed a message of greetings to the officers and men of the Yugoslav unit in the USSR. It said in part: "The Yugoslav People's Liberation Army and partisan detachments welcome you and express firm conviction that you will honourably represent our People's Liberation Army of Yugoslavia on the field of the battle, fighting shoulder to shoulder with the glorious Red Army against common enemy."

On May 8, 1944 the State Defence Committee authorised the formation in the USSR of Yugoslav 2nd Separate Infantry Battalion, a tank company, signal company and the establishment of a supply base in Kalinovka, Vinnitsa Region, for the People's Liberation Army of Yugoslavia.

In compliance with a request of Yugoslav nationals in the USSR, the formation of the Yugoslav 1st Infantry Brigade began on May 24. By the end of July it was ready for action and on August 1, 1944 it was organically attached to the 2nd Ukrainian Front. The brigade had 1,946 officers and men, 46 guns and mortars, 32 anti-tank rifles, 96 machine guns, 344 submachine guns and 1,250 rifles.

THE FORMATION
AND MILITARY OPERATIONS
OF FRENCH AIR UNITS

On the initiative of the French National Committee talks were opened in London in February 1942 on the activation of a French air unit in the USSR. These talks were continued in Moscow by General Ernest Petit who visited the USSR as head of a military mission of the French National Committee, and ended on November 25, 1942 when an agreement on the participation of French air units in the operations on the Soviet-German front was signed. It was decided to begin with the formation of a fighter squadron, the Soviet Government assuming all the expenses connected with its maintenance.

On March 25, 1943 the French Normandie 1st Fighter Squadron numbering 12 YAK-1 fighter aircraft was dispatched to the front. After its men became acquainted with the area, the squadron was incorporated into 303rd Fighter Division of the 1st Air Army and on April 1 flew its first combat mission as part of this force.

Twice, in the middle of April and in May 1943, General Petit approached the commander of the Soviet Air Force with the request to enlarge the Normandie Squadron into a fighter regiment of four or five squadrons. At the same time the question was raised of replacing the French ground personnel with Soviet mechanics.

On July 5, 1943 the Soviet Command ordered the reorganisation of the Normandie Squadron into a fighter regiment of the same name consisting of a training and three fighter squadrons. The regiment was placed under the command of Major Pierre Pouyade, with Soviet Captain I. V. Shtraukov as chief of staff and Soviet Major S. D. Agavelyan as chief engineer.

The regiment was activated at one of the 1st Air Army's frontline airfields and was fully equipped and ready for action by the end of August. For their active participation in the Smolensk offensive operation many French pilots were decorated with Soviet orders and medals.

From November 6, 1943 to May 25, 1944 the Normandie Regiment was stationed at a rear airfield near Tula where it was re-equipped with the new Soviet YAK-9 aircraft. On May 28 it joined the fighting units where it participated in military operations in Byelorussia as a part of the 303rd Fighter Division.

In August 1944 the regiment received new YAK-3 aircraft on which the French pilots flew their missions over Eastern Prussia in the following months. Between October 16 and 26 alone they shot down 105 enemy planes. For successful actions the name Nieman was attached to the name of the regiment.

In the course of its operations on the Soviet-German front the pilots of the Normandie-Nieman Regiment destroyed 268 enemy aircraft. Soviet orders were conferred on 117 French pilots, four of whom were awarded the title of Hero of the Soviet Union.

After the war at the request of General de Gaulle the Soviet Government handed over to France all the aircraft on which the French pilots fought on the Soviet-German front.

The foreign troops raised in the Soviet Union were not incorporated into the Soviet Army, and remained under Soviet operational control for the period of military operations. In all matters of internal life, foreign units were fully independent. Neither were their national traditions violated. They had their colours, uniforms, rank insignia and decorations and were trained in their own language.

All foreign units activated in the USSR were fully equipped by the Soviet Union which supplied them with the latest weapons. The local Soviets and Party organisations showed care and concern for the troops of the friendly armies. The industrial enterprises of Buzuluk, Novokhopersk, Ryazan, Kolomna and other towns took Polish, Czechoslovak, Yugo-slav and Rumanian units under their wing.

The educational departments for the most part consisting of Communists of the countries whose units were being formed played a major role in the morale-building activities in their respective units. They morally prepared the men for the struggle against fascism and for the establishment of popular rule in their countries.

5. ON THE EVE
OF FRESH BATTLES

THE SITUATION
ON THE SOVIET-GERMAN FRONT
IN THE FIRST HALF OF 1944

The third year of fighting on the Soviet-German front, 1944, became a year of decisive victories for the Soviet Armed Forces. The continuing Soviet-German clash was of critical importance for the outcome of the fighting against Hitler Germany. The Soviet side committed to action there 6.1 million men and approximately 89,000 guns and mortars, 2,167 rocket launchers, about 4,900 tanks and self-propelled guns and 8,500 combat aircraft. Besides, GHQ had large reserves at its disposal.

Although the Soviet troops had superior numbers, the enemy was still powerful and well armed. He had put up against the Soviet Army 4.9 million German and satellite troops, with more than 54,000 guns and mortars, 5,400 panzers and assault guns and 3,000 aircraft.

Seriously outweighing the enemy in men and equipment (with exception of tanks) and possessing high moral and fighting qualities, the Soviet Armed Forces which held an advantageous operational and strategic position, initiated their 1944 winter campaign with an offensive in the Ukraine on the western bank of the river Dnieper.

Here the Germans assembled their most powerful group of forces consisting of 92 divisions and 2 brigades of Army Groups South and A, which had 1,760,000 officers and men, 16,800 guns and mortars, 2,200 panzers and assault guns, and 1,460 aircraft. The Soviet Forces numbered 2,365,000 officers and men, 28,800 guns and mortars, more than 2,000 tanks and self-propelled guns, and 2,370 aircraft. These figures explain the reason why the most important battles of the entire 1944 winter campaign took place in the Ukraine.

At the end of December 1943, the 1st, 2nd, 3rd and 4th Ukrainian fronts, co-operating with ships of the Black Sea

Fleet, assumed the offensive along a huge front extending from the marshlands of the northern Ukraine to the Black Sea. The regular Soviet Army units were supported by Soviet partisans in the Ukraine, the Crimea and Moldavia. In January and February 1944 the enemy suffered smashing defeats in the area of Zhitomir and Berdichev, at Kirovograd, Rovno and Lutsk and also at Krivoi Rog and Nikopol. The results of the Korsun-Shevchenkovsky operation carried out by the 1st and 2nd Ukrainian fronts were the greatest of all. In the course of the fighting the Soviet troops surrounded ten enemy divisions and one brigade, killing or wounding 55,000 German officers and men, and taking more than 18,000 prisoners.

Having received reinforcements and regrouped its forces in early March, the 1st, 2nd and 3rd Ukrainian fronts operating between Lutsk and the mouth of the Dnieper resumed active military operations, especially in the Uman sector, while the 4th Ukrainian Front launched preparations for the Crimean Operation.

In this great battle the German 1st Panzer Army sustained a major defeat north of Kamenets-Podolsk. Rapidly crossing the Dniester, the 2nd Ukrainian Front reached the Prut, the state border of the USSR, and entered Rumania. The 3rd Ukrainian Front smashed the German 6th Army, liberated Nikolayev, Odessa and many other towns and villages in the south of the Ukraine, forced the Dniester and secured bridgeheads on its western bank.

These victories were of major political, economic and strategic significance. Having liberated the western regions of the Ukraine, the Soviet troops returned to the USSR its richest southern industrial and agricultural regions. This circumstance considerably strengthened the military and economic position of the Soviet Union and contributed to the successful continuation of the war and its victorious conclusion. The Soviet troops reached Rumania whose leaders were feverishly searching for a way out of the blind alley in which they had found themselves. The position of the enemy forces sharply deteriorated when the Soviet Army pushed into the Carpathians and split their strategic front in two.

In January 1944 the Leningrad, Volkhov and 2nd Baltic fronts went over to the offensive. After several days of furious fighting, the German 18th Army at Leningrad was forced to retreat to the west to escape encirclement. The 16th Army of Army Group North was also in serious trouble. As a result of six weeks of incessant fighting, the Soviet troops liberated Leningrad Region, a part of Kalinin Region and entered the Estonian Republic at Narva. The heroic battle for Leningrad which lasted for more than two and a half years was won. This victory was of tremendous significance for further struggle of the Soviet people against the German invader.

In January 1944, simultaneously with the offensive of the Soviet troops at Leningrad and Novgorod and in the western Ukraine, the 1st Baltic, Western and Byelorussian fronts went into action in the central sector where the enemy put up stubborn resistance and the fighting acquired a protracted character. Soviet offensive operations in the central sector from January to March 1944 tied down Army Group North with the result that being heavily battered at Leningrad and in the western Ukraine, it was unable to come to the assistance of the German forces.

The rout of the German troops west of the Dnieper put the enemy's 17th Army in a hopeless situation, it found itself sealed up in the Crimea. It consisted of seven Rumanian and five German divisions totalling over 195,000 officers and men, about 3,600 guns and mortars, 215 panzers and assault guns, and 150 aircraft.

The Crimean Operation was carried out in April and May by the 4th Ukrainian Front and the separate Maritime Army in conjunction with the Black Sea Fleet and the Azov Naval Flotilla. Overcoming bitter resistance, the Soviet forces freed Sevastopol on May 9 and three days later mopped up the remnants of the 17th Army at Cape Khersones. The Soviet troops were assisted by the Crimean partisans who harassed the enemy's logistical units.

The Crimean Operation ended in brilliant victory for Soviet arms. A hundred thousand enemy officers and men were killed or taken prisoner. Many enemy ships with troops and equipment were sent to the bottom. Whereas in 1941 and 1942 the German forces captured Sevastopol after 250 days of fighting, in 1944 the Soviet Army completely routed 200,000-strong enemy force in 35 days.

Thus ended the Soviet Army's campaign in the winter and spring of 1944. In hard-fought battles the Soviet troops destroyed 30 enemy divisions and one brigade and shattered another 142 divisions and five brigades. The enemy forces sustained tremendous losses in manpower and weapons. In order somehow to remedy the situation the German Command transferred 40 divisions and four brigades from Germany and other West European countries to the Soviet-German front.

The Soviet forces drove the enemy out of dozens of regions in the Russian Federation and the Ukraine and re-established the Soviet state border with Rumania on a 400-kilometre long sector. The Soviet Armed Forces stood now ready to liberate people of Poland, Czechoslovakia and Rumania from nazi bondage.

The victories of the Soviet troops had far-reaching international consequences, which, in particular, influenced the further strategic plans of the United States and Britain. The Allies stepped up preparations for a second front in Europe in the fear that the swift succession of events might create a situation when there would be no need for it at all.

On May 13, 1944 the Soviet, American and British Governments issued a joint Declaration regarding the four Axis satellites—Hungary, Rumania, Bulgaria and Finland—demanding that they should withdraw from the war, terminate their collaboration with Germany and declare war on her, thus shortening the war, diminishing their own sacrifices and lightening their own responsibility for the war. Nevertheless, the leaders of these countries who had closely bound up their destiny with Germany, had no intention of breaking off with her.

There was a marked growth of the Soviet Union's international prestige; it came to play a greater part in solving world problems and broadened its ties with other countries. By 1944 it had diplomatic relations with 32 countries as compared with 17 at the beginning of the war.

The emergence of the Soviet troops at the Soviet state border created a number of acute international problems, on whose solution depended the future of the countries about to be liberated by the Soviet Army and the fate of the anti-

Hitler coalition as a whole. One of the most crucial was the Polish question. During the war the Soviet Union repeated time and again that it favoured the re-establishment of a powerful, independent and democratic Poland. This view was confirmed in a statement of the Soviet Government of January 11, 1944. Nevertheless, the Polish emigre government in a note of January 15, 1944 once again made it clear that it did not want to have goodneighbourly relations with the Soviet Union. On top of that it hoped to aggravate contradictions by proposing that the Western Allies should act as mediators.

Thus, it was the Polish reactionary circles which were responsible for the fact that the relations between the two countries were still not re-established when the Soviet troops reached the Polish border. It was apparent that only democratic forces of the Polish people could restore and improve Soviet-Polish relations at that crucial period.

The Soviet Army's historic victories in the 1944 winter and spring campaign struck a fresh crushing blow at the Hitler bloc and stimulated the activity of the forces in Rumania, Hungary and Finland favouring a separate peace with the Soviet Union.

THE IMPACT OF SOVIET VICTORIES
ON THE SITUATION
ON OTHER THEATRES

The radical turn in the war achieved by the Soviet Army in 1942 and 1943, and its fresh victories in the 1944 winter and spring campaign created favourable conditions for the Anglo-US forces to step up their operations on other theatres of the war. And yet, the Allies for a long time refrained from undertaking a decisive offensive against the enemy, not because they lacked strength to do so but chiefly out of political considerations. The most important of these were the calculations of reactionary circles in the USA and Britain that Germany and the Soviet Union would bleed each other white in a single-handed combat.

Judging by their actions in Italy, the Allies displayed very little concern for hastening victory over nazi Germany. Having occupied the south of Italy, following her surrender in

September 1943, the Allied forces in the winter of 1944 advanced very slowly northward. In March 1944, after heavy fighting for Cassino, their advance stopped completely and was resumed only in the middle of May. Still another month passed before the US 5th Army captured Rome on June 4 and then slowly pursued the retreating German divisions, giving them ample time to take up deliberate defence.

But the growth of the Soviet Union's international prestige and the victories of its Armed Forces compelled the American and British governments to open the long-promised second front. On June 6, 1944 Allied troops landed in France. They managed to establish a large beach-head from where they mounted a large-scale offensive. The Allies owed their successes largely to the Soviet Army's strategic operations in the east.

The Allied landing in France seriously impaired the position of Hitler Germany which now had to fight on two fronts. The Anglo-American forces in France and Italy immobilised a part of the German army and sucked off a considerable proportion of the Wehrmacht's strategic reserves.

The military and political situation in Europe was bound to have an impact on the military operations in the Pacific Ocean, where the Allies had seized the strategic initiative in 1943. This led to an upsurge of the national liberation struggle in China and the countries of Southeast Asia occupied by the Japanese.

In February 1944 numerically superior American forces captured the Marshall Islands and intensified their operations in other parts of the Pacific Ocean. The successes of the Allied troops in the Pacific were largely due to the fact that the Japanese Command was forced to keep 27 picked divisions ready for action against the Soviet Union in Manchuria and Korea and another 26 divisions in China which were fighting against the Chinese patriots.

In this way the military, political and strategic situation which had taken shape at the fronts of the Second World War by the summer of 1944 was favourable for the countries of the anti-Hitler coalition. The Soviet Army and Allied troops held the strategic initiative firmly in their hands.

THE BALANCE OF FORCES
AND THE PLANS OF THE COMBATANTS
ON THE SOVIET-GERMAN FRONT
IN THE MIDDLE OF 1944

However important the successes of the Anglo-American forces in the Mediterranean and the Pacific, the main events of the war as before developed on the Soviet-German front. Therefore Germany and her allies continued to keep the bulk of their forces there.

By June 1944 the enemy had 4,000,000 men, about 49,000 guns and mortars, 5,250 panzers and assault guns, and nearly 2,800 military aircraft facing the Soviet Army. Germany's industry attained the highest wartime level in July 1944. In the first six months of the year her factories turned out more than 17,000 aircraft and nearly 9,000 tanks, and her steel output was more than that of the USSR.

Although Germany's position continued to deteriorate, the nazi command still hoped to escape defeat. Its plan for the summer of 1944 expounded by Field-Marshal Keitel at a conference in Sonthofen on May 5, 1944 was of a defensive nature and envisaged a war for time in expectation of events. In drawing up its plans the German Command pinned its hopes on possible contradictions erupting within the anti-Hitler coalition with the result that Germany's Anglo-American enemies would become her allies in the struggle against the USSR. That these calculations did exist was borne out by Keitel during his interrogation by a group of Soviet officers in June 1945.

Hitler no longer entertained any hopes of turning the war in his favour and in March 1944 the General Staff of the Land Forces was compelled to recognise the Soviet Army's superiority.

As regards the strategic plans of the Soviet Supreme Command, they retained their offensive nature and relied on the Soviet Union's increasing economic and military might, on the high morale, offensive spirit and mass heroism of the Soviet troops. The political and military concept of the Soviet Command's plan for the 1944 summer and autumn campaign was formulated in the Order of the Day issued by Supreme Commander-in-Chief J. V. Stalin on May 1. It set the task of routing the enemy's main strategic groupings, liberating all the occupied areas of the Soviet Union, extending a hand of fraternal assistance to the peoples of other countries, forcing the Axis satellites to withdraw from the war and helping their peoples to cast off the fascist yoke.

Accordingly, the Soviet Command concentrated enormous forces on the 4,450-kilometre front extending from the Barents Sea to the Black Sea. In June 1944, the Soviet Army in the field had about 6,500,000 officers and men, 83,200 guns and mortars, about 8,000 tanks and self-propelled guns, and 11,800 aircraft. Besides, there were Polish, Czechoslovak, Rumanian, Yugoslav and French units on Soviet territory. GHQ reserves consisted of two field, one armoured and one air armies, and a number of separate formations.

The strategic initiative firmly in its hands, the Soviet Command decided to deliver a series of strong blows in the summer of 1944 in the key sectors of the front, for which purpose it built up powerful forces.

Marshal G. K. Zhukov recalls that on April 12, 1944 GHQ adopted a decision in which the rout of the German forces in Byelorussia was designated as one of the basic tasks in the summer of 1944. In preparation for this operation it was necessary to strike a number of heavy blows in other directions with the view to diverting the maximum German reserves from Byelorussia.

The strategic map of the General Staff of May 30, 1944 showed that the Soviet troops were to go into action in the Karelian Isthmus. After that the main attack was to be launched in Byelorussia with the view to smashing Army Group Centre, free Byelorussia and start the liberation of Poland. At the same time the Ist Ukrainian Front was to go over to the offensive, wipe out Army Group North Ukraine, complete the liberation of the western regions of the Ukraine and start liberating southern Poland. In the course of their strategic offensive in the southern sector the 2nd and 3rd Ukrainian fronts were to smash Army Group South Ukraine and thus change the entire political and strategic situation in the Balkans.

A characteristic feature of the Soviet Command's plan for the 1944 summer and autumn campaign was that it specified the important political aim of the Soviet Armed Forces, that of directly assisting the peoples of other countries to cast off the fascist yoke. In setting this task the Communist Party and the Soviet Government proceeded from Lenin's well-known premise about the internationalist obligations of the socialist state and the liberatory mission of its Armed Forces.

It was a task of tremendous historical significance, and it could be set thanks to the unparalleled heroism of the Soviet troops which for three years were locked in a grim struggle with a powerful and experienced adversary and sustained heavy losses in it, and also thanks to the dedicated labour of the Soviet working class, the collective-farm peasantry and the intelligentsia who under the guidance of the Communist Party kept the troops supplied with all they needed for victory.

All Soviet troops regarded it as their international duty to help the peoples of other countries get rid of fascist bondage.

The great liberation mission of the Soviet Armed Forces which began in the middle of 1944 was prepared by the entire Soviet people, by its combat and labour exploits, its fidelity to the principles of proletarian internationalism and by the organisational and ideological activity of the Communist Party of the Soviet Union.

1. THE POLISH PEOPLE FIGHTS ON

THE CONSEQUENCES
OF GERMAN OCCUPATION

The catastrophe which overtook Poland in September 1939 was the most dreadful in the history of the Polish people. Having seized the country, the nazis deprived her of national and state independence and divided her into two parts. Poznan, Upper Silesia, Pomorie, Lodz and other economically developed regions were incorporated into Germany and their inhabitants were expelled to the other part of Poland which the Germans had turned into Governor-Generalship ruled by the hangman Hans Frank. On the future of the Polish people Frank said that "henceforth the political role of the Polish people has ended. It is proclaimed a labour force and nothing more ... we shall see to it that the very concept of Poland is erased." During the occupation period 600,000 people were evicted from the annexed regions. The eviction was accompanied by brutalities, plunder, violence and killings. The Poles were deprived of all rights. The strongest and the fittest were driven to forced labour in Germany. Three million people suffered this lot in the period from 1940 to 1943.

Having occupied Poland, the nazis immediately established a reign of unbridled terror, plunder and violence. Under the General Plan Ost they embarked on the man-hating policy of mass extermination of the Polish people. They covered the country with a network of death camps, including two giant ones, Oświęcim and Maidanek. In these two camps alone the nazis exterminated six million people, including women, old folk and children, from various European countries during the war. During the occupation period they killed about 6,028,000 Poles, or 22.2 per cent of the country's population; 5,384,000 either perished in death camps, or were executed or died in prisons from hunger or hard labour. Of the total number of Poles put to death by the nazis, 2,250,000 were children under 18 years of age; another 500,000 children were injured and a million died from illnesses.

The country's economy, her towns and villages sustained enormous damage. Tens of thousands of industrial enterprises and hundreds of thousands of peasant farms were wrecked. The nazi "new order" brought destruction, death and tears to the country.

THE PEOPLE RISE
AGAINST THE NAZIS

Neither the occupation nor the terrible conditions of the nazi regime could force the Polish people to their knees. The struggle against the invader, which began in September 1939, flared up with renewed force after nazi Germany's attack on the Soviet Union. The working class led by Communists played the leading and guiding role in this struggle.

On the initiative of the Communists the Polish Workers' Party (PWP) was formed in January 1942 in Warsaw as a result of the merger of underground revolutionary groups and organisations. It was headed by Marceli Nowotko, Pawel Finder and Boleslaw Bierut. Wladislaw Homulka was elected General Secretary of the Party Central Committee in November 1943 after the death of Nowotko and the arrest of Finder.

The PWP summoned the working class and all democratic and patriotic forces to fight relentlessly against the invader and established Gwardia Ludowa, Poland's armed underground organisation, whose first detachments went into action against the Germans in May 1942.

While the PWP advanced and carried through the idea of active armed struggle against the invader, the Polish emigre government in London and its representatives in occupied Poland resorted to the tactic of passive temporising—"standing with arms grounded". Armia Krajowa, a conspiratorial military organisation in Poland subordinated to the emigre government, also received strict orders to adhere to this tactic. Devised in the hope that Poland would be liberated by the Western Allies, this tactic was intended to preserve Armia Krajowa so that it would have the strength to play an important role in bringing the reactionary bourgeois government back to power in the country. But the Polish patriotic forces had no intention of passively standing by while the Soviet

6*

Army fought against the nazi invader, and Armia Krajowa detachments and the Polish guerrillas ever more frequently co-operated with Gwardia Ludowa. Many Soviet officers and men who had fled from POW camps also actively participated in the armed struggle of the Polish patriots. A detachment under Senior Lieutenant F. N. Kovalev was one of the first to join Gwardia Ludowa.

The desire of the broad masses in Poland to wage an armed struggle for national and social liberation, and the Soviet Army's decisive victories over the Germans forced the emigre Polish government to relinquish its temporising policy. On its instruction the main headquarters of Armia Krajowa drew up a plan code-named "Storm" providing for a series of blows at the retreating German forces, thus enabling representatives of the Polish Government in London to establish control over certain regions of the country shortly before the arrival of Soviet troops, that is, to seize power.

In the summer and autumn of 1943 the national liberation struggle in Poland assumed still greater proportions. In order to rally the forces of the people and guide its struggle and also to have an organ which could take power into its hands as soon as the Soviet Army begins liberating Poland, the Krajowa Rada Narodowa (KRN), the highest organ of the National Democratic Front, was formed on the eve of 1944 on the initiative of the PWP. The KRN consisted of representatives of the PWP, underground trade unions, Left socialist, peasants' and other organisations favouring the establishment of a strong, independent and democratic Poland. Boleslaw Bierut was elected Chairman of the KRN Presidium.

At its first sitting the KRN adopted the important decision to unite all the guerrilla groups, armed detachments and military units fighting against the German invaders into a single people's army—Armia Ludowa. It was formed out of Gwardia Ludowa detachments, which became its nucleus, militia units, guerrilla detachments and even included a number of Armia Krajowa detachments, primarily those operating in Silesia.

The KRN programme set the Polish people the task of fighting for a strong, independent and democratic Poland. It recognised that the return of Western Byelorussia and Western Ukraine to the Soviet Union was justified and underlined the need to establish durable friendly relations with the USSR.

On January 11, 1944 the Soviet Government issued a statement confirming the possibility of Poland becoming a strong and independent state, and friendly relations being established between the two countries.

THE IMPACT OF SOVIET VICTORIES
ON THE DEVELOPMENT
OF THE LIBERATION
MOVEMENT IN POLAND

During its 1944 winter and spring offensive the Soviet Army smashed the Wehrmacht's southern wing, reached the areas of Kovel and Verba south of the Pripyat and point west of Berestechko. Now only 20-60 kilometres separated it from the Polish border.

In the summer of 1944 Armia Ludowa under General Michal Rola-Zymerski had about 40,000 men in its ranks. Guerrilla detachments merged into brigades. The first was activated in February 1944. All told, 11 brigades were raised in the first half of the year. Soviet citizens made up 85 per cent of the strength of two of the five brigades which were raised in the Kielce Province in 1944. The names of Fyodor Kovalev, Vasily Volodin, Vasily Voichenko, Yakov Salnikov, Terenty Novak and many other former Soviet Army servicemen who became commanders of the guerrilla detachments of Gwardia Ludowa and Armia Ludowa are well known to the Polish people. From eight to ten thousand Soviet citizens were members of these detachments.

The entry of Soviet partisan formations into Poland tremendously stimulated the partisan movement in the country. Between February and April 1944 P. P. Vershigora's Ukrainian 1st Partisan Division and partisan formations and detachments under I. N. Banov, V. A. Karasev, G. V. Kovalev, M. Y. Nadelin, V. P. Pelikh, N. A. Prokopyuk, S. A. Sankov, V. P. Chepiga, B. G. Shangin and I. P. Yakovlev entered the southeastern areas of the country along a broad front extending from Brest to Lvov and went into action in the rear of the enemy forces. The Soviet partisans acted in co-operation with Armia Ludowa detachments and supplied them with weapons and ammunition. A total of seven large formations

and 26 separate detachments of Soviet partisans crossed into
Poland and operated in her eastern areas in 1944. Soviet and
Polish partisans strengthened their fraternal comradeship-in-
arms in joint raids and military operations.

In the spring of 1944 a KRN delegation arrived in Moscow
with the view to establishing the broadest possible co-operation with the Soviet Union. The Soviet Government recognised the KRN as the sole representative of the Polish people
and turned over the Polish Ist Army to it. The two sides agreed in principle on questions concerning their relations and
the Soviet-Polish border. The Soviet side decided to meet
the Polish delegation's request for arms, whose shortage slowed down the growth of Armia Ludowa. The Soviet Government's recognition of the KRN enhanced its prestige both in
Poland and abroad.

After inspecting Polish national military units, the KRN
delegation issued a statement which said in part: "The Polish
people will never forget the earnest attention on the part of
the Soviet people.... We regard this as a guarantee of the
great friendship of our Polish people and the fraternal Russian and Ukrainian peoples."

By the summer of 1944 the political situation in Poland
was characterised by a further intensification of the national
liberation struggle and a deepening rift between her political
forces. The democratic forces rallied around the Polish Workers' Party and the KRN, and the national liberation movement began to acquire the character of the people's democratic revolution, a development which seriously alarmed the
Polish reactionaries who were striving to prevent the victory
of the democratic forces in the country.

The Polish emigre government in London based its policy
on anti-Sovietism and in its activity against the progressive
Polish forces and the Soviet Union relied on the support of
US and British ruling circles which wanted to establish the
old reactionary bourgeois order in Poland and thus keep the
country under their influence. They tried hard to prevail
on the Soviet Union to recognise the Polish emigre government and upheld the latter's claims to the western areas of
Byelorussia and the Ukraine. The Soviet Government, however, considered that only Poland's democratic development
would solve the Polish question. This would "create the pro-

per conditions for normal Soviet-Polish relations, for solving the problem of the Soviet-Polish frontier and, in general, for the rebirth of Poland as a strong, free and independent state".[1]

The political and military situation in Poland at the time when the Soviet Army arrived at her frontiers was very complicated. Taking into account the reactionary policy of the emigre government in London and the presence of powerful German forces on Polish territory, it was clear that Poland could only be liberated with the help of the Soviet Army.

From the summer of 1944 to the spring of the following year the Soviet Army carried out several major offensive operations in Poland, involving a vast number of troops on both sides. Five Soviet fronts—27 field, five armoured and six air armies, 13 separate armoured and mechanised corps, and six cavalry corps—fought for the freedom and independence of the Polish people.

The Soviet Army's campaign on Polish territory includes two stages, as it were. In the first stage (July-September 1944) it carried out the Byelorussian and the Lvov-Sandomierz operations. In the second stage (January-May 1945) the Soviet troops conducted the East Prussian, Vistula-Oder, East Pomeranian, Upper and Lower Silesian, Berlin and Prague operations, in the course of which they routed German Army Groups A, North Ukraine, North, Vistula and Centre. Obviously Poland could not be liberated unless these strategic groupings, each consisting of from 30 to 50 divisions, had been smashed.

2. LIBERATION OF POLAND'S EASTERN REGIONS

TOWARDS THE VISTULA AND NAREW

In the summer of 1944 four fronts—18 field and four armoured armies consisting of more than 1,700,000 officers and

---

[1] *Correspondence between the Chairman of the Council of Ministers of the U.S.S.R. and the Presidents of the U.S.A. and the Prime Ministers of Great Britain During the Great Patriotic War of 1941-1945*, Moscow, 1957, Vol. I, p. 197.

men,[1] more than 38,000 guns and mortars, and about 5,000 tanks and self-propelled guns—were ready to cross the border into Poland. The land forces were supported by six air armies of the front aviation and formations of the long-range air army.

Having routed Army Group Centre in Byelorussia, the 3rd and 2nd Byelorussian fronts and the right wing of the 1st Byelorussian Front in mid July reached the line running on the Nieman river south of Kaunas, Grodno, Volkovyssk, Pruzhany and came up to Poland's state borders.

The success of this operation created favourable conditions for the 1st Ukrainian Front under Marshal I. S. Konev to begin its offensive. The Front consisted of seven field and three armoured armies, a total of 74 infantry and six cavalry divisions, 10 armoured and mechanised corps, three of them separate. Air support was provided by two air armies. All in all the front had 14,000 guns and mortars of all models and calibres, more than 1,600 tanks and self-propelled guns, 2,800 aircraft, and 843,000 officers and men, not counting the logistical units. The enemy force facing the 1st Ukrainian Front consisted of 40 divisions, including six panzer and motorised, and two brigades, numbering 600,000 men, 6,300 guns and mortars, 900 panzers and assault guns, and 700 aircraft. The purpose of the operation was to smash Army Group North Ukraine in the Lvov and Sandomierz sector.

Assuming the offensive on July 13, the 1st Ukrainian Front on July 18 breached the enemy defences at Rawa Russka and Lvov along a 200-kilometre front, advanced to a depth of 50-80 kilometres and encircled eight enemy divisions at Brody. On July 17, the 1st Guards Tank Army under Colonel-General M. Y. Katukov was moved into the breach in the Rawa Russka sector. On the same day its 44th Guards Tank Brigade commanded by Colonel I. I. Gusakovsky crossed the Western Bug and secured a bridgehead at Dobrocin. With the capture of this bridgehead the advance units crossed the Soviet border into Poland, commencing the liberation of the Polish people. On July 18, Colonel-General V. N. Gordov's 3rd Guards Army forced the Western Bug at Sokal and also crossed into Poland.

---

[1] Not counting army and front logistics and support units.

At the same time the Soviet Command increased pressure in other sectors of the Soviet-German front. On July 18 the left wing of the 1st Byelorussian Front under Marshal K. K. Rokossovsky struck a powerful blow towards Lublin. The Soviet force involved in this attack consisted of five field, one armoured and one air armies, numbering 36 infantry and six cavalry divisions, four armoured corps, 416,000 men, 1,750 tanks and self-propelled guns, more than 7,600 guns and mortars, and approximately 1,500 aircraft. The Polish 1st Army under Lieutenant-General Zygmunt Berling was a part of this force. Well-trained and fully equipped by the Soviet Union, the army consisted of four infantry divisions, a tank and a cavalry brigades and two air regiments, totalling 78,000 men, 851 guns and mortars, 130 tanks and self-propelled guns, and 44 combat aircraft.

Facing this force were nine German infantry divisions, three assault artillery brigades, more than 200 panzers, and 1,550 guns and mortars.

In the course of the operation the Soviet troops were to smash the enemy in this area, push the offensive towards Warsaw and reach the Vistula.

The left wing of the 1st Byelorussian Front attacked in the morning of July 18 and within a few hours it was clear that the offensive was developing successfully. Towards the end of July 20 a breach 130 kilometres wide and 70 kilometres deep yawned in the enemy's defences. The advancing forces gained the Western Bug along a broad front. Despite the enemy's efforts to halt the drive, the 47th, 8th Guards and 69th armies crossed the river in a number of sectors and entered Poland. Among the first were the 328th Infantry Division under Colonel I. G. Pavlovsky, the 132nd Infantry Division under Colonel Y. G. Tsvintarny, the 165th Infantry Division under Colonel N. I. Kaladze and Lieutenant-Colonel V. M. Shtrigol's 39th Guards Infantry Division.

The main forces pushed ahead at such a pace that the enemy was unable to put up a determined resistance at any of the intermediate lines. On July 22, Lieutenant-General V. Y. Kolpakchi's 69th Army and Lieutenant-General M. P. Konstantinov's 7th Guards Cavalry Corps liberated the Polish town of Chelm. The 2nd Tank Army which was moved into the breach in the attack zone of the 8th Guards

Army on July 22 executed a lightning 75-kilometre thrust
and by the evening of the same day engaged the enemy at
Lublin. On July 24 armoured units in conjunction with the
8th Guards Army drove the enemy out of the city. The commander of the 2nd Tank Army, Lieutenant-General S. I. Bogdanov who was heavily wounded in the fighting for Lublin
was replaced by Major-General A. I. Radzievsky. Pressing
home the offensive, the army's main forces on July 25 reached the Vistula and captured important enemy strong points
of Demblin and Pulawy, but failed to cross the river in their
stride without waiting for the arrival of the crossing means.
Two days later the 8th Guards and 69th armies arrived in
the area to replace the 2nd Tank Army which on July 27th
launched a swift offensive in the northerly direction along
the Vistula's eastern bank. The closer the Soviet troops drew
to Warsaw the more desperate became the resistance of the
Germans.

Determined to hold on to the bridgehead on the right bank
of the Vistula in the area of Warsaw at all costs, the German
Command decided to smash the 2nd Tank Army and avert
the threat to Praga, the suburb of Warsaw on the eastern
bank of the river. With this aim in view it assembled one infantry and four panzer divisions at Praga.

The Germans attacked on August 1 in the wake of a powerful air and artillery strike. Heavy fighting with superior
enemy forces broke out along the army's entire front. By
nightfall on August 5, after five days of bitter battles, the
enemy pushed the 2nd Tank Army away from Praga. The
Army lost about 1,900 officers and men, including more than
300 killed, about 130 tanks and self-propelled guns. At the
critical moment units of the 47th Army arrived and the enemy, having sustained heavy losses, was forced to stop his
counterattacks.

While the 2nd Tank Army was figthing at Praga, the 8th
Guards and 69th armies, using improvised means, crossed
the Vistula in the face of heavy resistance, and gained important bridgeheads at Magnoszew and Pulawy.

Polish troops fought side by side with the Soviet forces
for the bridgeheads on the left bank of the Vistula. The
Polish 1st Army reached the Vistula in the afternoon of July
28 and in the night of August 31 began to cross the river in

the zone between the 8th Guards and the 69th armies. Only an insignificant part of its forces managed to reach the opposite bank where they secured a number of small and isolated bridgeheads which had to be abandoned several days later in the face of enemy's powerful counterattacks. Even though the operations of the Polish troops failed to produce the desired results, they played a positive role in the fighting as a whole. The bridgeheads held by the Polish troops diverted considerable enemy forces, thus making it somewhat easier for the Soviet troops to gain bridgeheads on the river's western bank. Heavy fighting, especially in the Magnoszew area, broke as soon as the Soviet troops launched their attacks. The offensive of the 8th Guards Army under Colonel-General V. I. Chuikov came up against stubborn enemy resistance. The Germans tried to restore the situation at whatever the cost. During August the German Command steadily built up the forces in the area, bringing five infantry and two panzer divisions and two infantry brigades in addition to the 17th Infantry Division already operating there. Supported by a large number of aircraft, the enemy mounted several counterattacks a day in desperate attempts to dislodge the Soviet forces.

In view of the strategic significance of the captured bridgehead, the commander of the 1st Byelorussian Front, Marshal K. K. Rokossovsky, took steps to strengthen the advancing forces. The 3rd and 2nd Infantry Divisions under General S. Galitsky and Colonel A. Sivitsky, a tank brigade and other units of the Polish 1st Army were among the troops that were moved to the bridgehead. For almost the whole of August Soviet and Polish troops retained their hold on the bridgehead against the enemy's heavy pressure. Small in area —35 kilometres wide and 15 kilometres deep—the Magnoszew Bridgehead was the springboard, from which the main forces of the 1st Byelorussian Front launched the liberation of Western Poland in January 1945. On August 29, 1944, in fulfilment of GHQ orders, the armies of the 1st Byelorussian Front fighting south of Warsaw, having exhausted all their offensive capabilities, reverted to the defensive. The Soviet troops paid a heavy price to retain the bridgehead.

In the meanwhile the 1st Ukrainian Front was locked in heavy battles in the south of Poland. On July 23, after smashing the eight enemy divisions encircled at Brody, its

right-wing armies reached the line Woislawice-Grodislawi-
ce-the San river and forced the river north and south of
Jaroslav. The Front's central forces reduced the enemy at
Lvov and on July 27 liberated the city. On the same day the
3rd and 1st Guards Tank armies under Colonel-Generals
P. S. Rybalko and Y. M. Katukov liberated Przemysl, and on
July 29 the Ist Ukrainian Front's advance units reached the
Vistula between Annopol and Baranow, and shortly captur-
ed a bridgehead on the opposite bank south of Sandomierz.

The German Command made several attempts to wipe out
the bridgehead and restore its defences along the Vistula.
With this aim in view Colonel-General Harpe, Commander
of Army Group North Ukraine, threw large forces against
the Soviet troops holding the bridgehead. Heavy fighting
went on throughout August. The enemy struck powerful counterblows in a number of sectors, using up to three panzer
and infantry divisions, or two or three panzer divisions
only, in the hope of splitting the Soviet troops and sweeping them into the river. All these strikes, however, were repulsed, and the Soviet forces in the course of the fighting
captured Sandomierz, extending the bridgehead up to 75 kilometres in width and up to 50 kilometres in depth. In August
alone the 1st Ukrainian Front lost more than 122,000 officers
and men in killed and wounded. Because of the increased
resistance of the enemy, the exhaustion of the troops, the long
supply routes and the need to bring in replenishments, GHQ
on August 29 ordered the Front to assume the defensive.

At the height of the fighting on the Magnoszew and Sandomierz bridgeheads, Soviet and Polish partisans operating beyond the Vistula attacked enemy supply routes. The partisan
detachment of the Kielce province blew up 129 trains carrying troops and equipment, and demolished 48 railway and
highway bridges. The frontal attacks of the Soviet troops were
timed with the blows delivered by the partisans at the enemy's rearward positions.

While fighting was in progress at the approaches to Warsaw and for the bridgeheads on the Vistula, the 3rd and 2nd
Byelorussian fronts and the right-wing armies of the 1st Byelorussian Front were waging battles to liberate Poland's
northeastern regions where the enemy was putting up a stubborn resistance.

Repelling a series of powerful counterattacks by the enemy reserve Das Gross Deutschland Panzer Division and the 56th and 547th Infantry divisions in the first half of August, the 3rd Byelorussian Front under General I. D. Chernyakhovsky crushed the resistance of the German forces, advancing 30-50 kilometres. By the end of the month it reached the Rossieny-Augustow line and entered Polish territory north of Augustow.

The 2nd Byelorussian Front under Colonel-General G. F. Zakharov shattered the enemy's fresh reserves, and in the period from July 17 to 25 entered Poland. Among the first Soviet units to cross into Poland at Volokush, 25 kilometres northwest of Grodno, were the 153rd Infantry Division under Colonel A. A. Shchennikov and the 3rd Guards Cavalry Corps commanded by Lieutenant-General N. S. Oslikovsky. Pushing the enemy further west, the front drove the enemy out of the large industrial centre of Bialystock on July 27 and at the end of August its right-wing armies reached the Bobr and Narew rivers between Augustow and Lomza where on GHQ orders it went over to the defensive.

The 2nd Byelorussian Front attacked in close co-operation with the right wing of the 1st Byelorussian Front, whose 48th and 65th armies under Lieutenant-Generals P. L. Romanenko and P. I. Batov on July 17 entered Poland on a wide frontage between Jaluwk and Bialowieza.

In the first two weeks of September 1944 only small forces of the 2nd and 1st Byelorussian fronts were conducting local offensive operations in Poland, in the course of which they gained a bridgehead on the Narew at Rozan and Serock and also captured Praga, a suburb of Warsaw on the eastern bank of the Vistula. The German Command tenaciously defended Praga, regarding it as a jumping off ground for an attack in the southerly direction at the left flank and rear of the 1st Byelorussian Front. This enemy bridgehead constituted a constant threat to the Front and impeded the deployment of troops for an attack against Warsaw that could prove helpful to its population which on August 1 rose in arms against the Germans.

On September 10 Lieutenant-General N. I. Gusev's 47th Army, which included the reinforced Tadeusz Kosciuszko Polish 1st Infantry Division and the 1st Tank Brigade named

after the heroes of Westerplatte, went over to the offensive.
The resistance of the enemy was crushed in the course of
five days of heavy fighting, and on September 14 Praga was
liberated. During street fighting the local population courageously helped the Soviet and Polish troops. The fall of Praga
deprived the Germans of their last bridgehead on the eastern
bank of the Vistula and considerably improved the situation
of the Soviet troops in the Warsaw sector. On November 20,
1944 the Presidium of the USSR Supreme Soviet awarded
the Order of the Red Banner to the Polish 1st Infantry Division and attached the name "Praga" to its 1st Regiment,
which acted with especial distinction.

The participation of the Polish 1st Army in battles on the
territory of Poland emphasised the fact that in the liberation
of Poland as a sovereign state a definite role was played by her
own forces acting in close co-operation with the Soviet Army.

During the offensive in Poland the Soviet Army's political
organs, and Party and Komsomol organisations put in a great
deal of work to establish correct relations between Soviet
armymen and Polish soldiers and the local inhabitants. Se-
minars were held in the units to brief agitators and propagandists on the situation in Poland, Soviet-Polish relations
and the policy of the CPSU and the Soviet Government in
the Polish question. Meetings of Soviet and Polish servicemen
were also held. The reason why the Soviet Army entered
Poland was extensively explained to the local population.
Evenings of Soviet-Polish friendship were organised, and
front and army newspapers regularly published articles explaining the tasks of the Soviet troops who were fighting in
foreign countries.

The entry of the Soviet Army and the Polish 1st Army
into Poland and their advance towards the Vistula evoked
great enthusiasm among the Polish people. The population
of the liberated areas warmly welcomed the Soviet Army and
the Polish troops and expressed their profound gratitude.

Polish patriots actively helped the Soviet troops. During
the crossing of the Vistula at Baranow the peasants built rafts,
marshalled boats and established crossings together with the
Soviet forces. The Polish population also helped the troops
to repair railways and bridges.

The Soviet Union on its part rendered extensive aid to

liberated Poland. In September 1944 the Soviet Government turned over 10,000 tons of flour, medicines and other essential goods free of charge to the people of liberated Praga. Kerosene, salt, tea, soap and other vital goods were delivered to the countryside.

An important measure which further strengthened the relations between the Soviet Government and the Polish Committee of National Liberation (PCNL) was the GHQ directive of August 10, 1944 on the protection and the transfer to the Polish authorities of property plundered by the Germans from the Polish population and Polish enterprises and organisations. The directive also said that when the owners of landed estates, industrial enterprises and trading establishments were absent (including those who had fled with the retreating German troops), the commanders of the Soviet fronts operating in Poland were authorised to protect their property and officially turn it over to the Polish authorities. In fulfilment of the terms of the first Soviet-Polish trade agreement concluded in October 1944, the Soviet Union undertook to supply Polish industrial enterprises with raw materials and fuel. The same month the Soviet Government granted the Polish Committee of National Liberation an interest-free credit of 10 million rubles. The Soviet Command opened eight hospitals for the population of Praga.

Having reached the Narew and the Vistula the Soviet Army liberated Polish Lands lying east of the Vistula, or 25 per cent of Polish territory, and 5.5 million Polish citizens. In the course of the fighting the Soviet troops inflicted a series of smashing defeats on the enemy. They destroyed 14 divisions and one brigade which lost from 50 to 75 per cent of their effective strength.

Soviet casualties were also considerable. In the summer of 1944 over 97,000 Soviet officers and men were killed and about 340,000 were wounded in the fighting in Poland.

POLAND EMBARKS ON THE ROAD
OF DEMOCRATIC DEVELOPMENT

The Soviet Army's entry into Poland was a most important event in the life of the Polish people opening before them broad prospects for free democratic development. By the will of the people and under the guidance of the Polish Workers' Party a new people's democratic rule was being established in the country.

At a meeting on July 21 in Chelm the Krajowa Rada Narodowa formed the Polish Committee of National Liberation, the organ of the new, democratic rule. The decree adopted by the Rada said in part: "On the eve of decisive battles to expel the German invaders from Poland, the Krajowa Rada Narodowa is establishing the Polish Committee of National Liberation as a provisional executive authority to guide the people's liberation struggle, ensure its independence and the restoration of the Polish state."

The creation of the PCNL signified that all patriotic anti-fascist, democratic forces of the Polish people had united into a militant alliance in the struggle against the nazi oppressors, for the rebirth of a strong and independent Poland.

In its manifesto entitled "To the Polish People" on July 22 the Committee set forth the programme for the complete liberation from the German yoke and the establishment of the people's democratic rule. It proclaimed friendship and alliance with the Soviet Union as the basic principle of its foreign policy and noted that the establishment of the Soviet-Polish border should take place in line with the principle: "Polish lands to Poland, Ukrainian, Byelorussian and Lithuanian lands to Soviet Ukraine, Byelorussia and Lithuania." The western regions of Poland which had been annexed by the invader had to be returned to Poland.

July 22, 1944, the day the PCNL issued its manifesto, became the day of the founding of people's democratic Poland.

The formation of national armed forces greatly stimulated the struggle for the establishment of a free, democratic Poland. On July 21, the Krajowa Rada Narodowa issued a decree on the merger of Armia Ludowa and Polish 1st Army into a single Wojsko Polskie and the formation of the High Command of Wojsko Polskie. For the first time in Poland's history her armed forces would be the bulwark of the working people. Former commander of Armia Ludowa, Colonel-General M. Rola-Zymierski, was appointed Commander-in-Chief of Wojsko Polskie.

On July 26, 1944 the Soviet Government issued a statement which enormously contributed to the further consolidation of Poland's democratic forces under the leadership of the Polish Workers' Party and the strengthening of friendship between the Soviet and Polish peoples. The statement said that the Soviet Army together with the Polish Army had entered Poland, inaugurating the liberation of the long-suffering fraternal people from German occupation. It underlined that the Soviet troops were fully determined to smash the German armies and help the Polish people in their efforts to liberate themselves from the yoke of the German invader and establish an independent, strong and democratic Poland.

The Soviet Government declared that since the Soviet Army's military operations in Poland were conducted on the territory of a free and sovereign allied state, it did not intend to establish its administrative organs in Poland considering this to be the concern of the Polish people. It noted that the USSR did not intend to annex any part of Poland and that the Soviet Army's military operations on Polish territory were dictated solely by military necessity and the desire to help the friendly Polish people liberate themselves from German occupation.

Respecting the independence of the Polish state, the Soviet Government on July 26 signed an agreement with the PCNL on the relations between the Soviet Command and the Polish authorities after the entry of the Soviet forces into Poland. The agreement stated that as soon as one or another region of Poland was liberated the PCNL would assume full control over civil administration and continue the formation of Wojsko Polskie. It was also pointed out that the Polish units which were being activated on Soviet territory would operate in Poland.

In order to establish still closer contacts with the PCNL the Soviet Government appointed Colonel-General N. A. Bulganin as its representative with the Committee. He was directed by GHQ to act, in his relations with the PCNL, in the spirit of friendship and close co-operation and to make sure that the Soviet military organs precisely and undeviatingly observe the agreement of July 26, 1944 between the Government of the USSR and the PCNL on the relations

between the Soviet Command and the Polish administration.

The Soviet Government's statement defining the Soviet
Union's attitude to Poland and the agreement governing the
relations between the Soviet Command and the Polish administration were in effect recognition of the Polish Committee
of National Liberation as the sovereign government of Poland. They buttressed the Polish people's confidence in victory
over the German invader and were instrumental in broaden-
ing the national liberation movement and strengthening people's rule in the country.

The Soviet military authorities, which were set in Poland
by the Soviet Command when the Soviet troops entered the
country, did not control the activity of local organs of power, but only coordinated their functions with them.

Broad sections of the Polish population rallied around the
PCNL. And although reactionary elements guided by the
Polish emigre government in London intensified their campaign against the Polish Workers' Party and all progressive
forces in the country, the people vigorously supported the
PCNL in all its undertakings. This support was vividly manifested at congresses and conferences held in September 1944
by political parties representing the principal political trends
in the country.

In the resolutions at their congresses and conferences the
Stronnictwo Ludowe Party, the Polish Socialist and the Polish Democratic Parties and the Union of Advanced Peasant
Youth unanimously expressed solidarity with the political
and practical activity of the PCNL and called on all the
forces of the people to unite in the struggle against the invader and wage a merciless fight against the agents of the
Polish reaction in the country.

The US and British governments approached the Polish
question from a totally different position. They increased their
support for the Polish emigre government despite the fact
that being torn away from Poland it did not express the interests and aspirations of the Polish people and was incapable
of uniting with the democratic forces which supported the
domestic and foreign policies of the PCNL.

THE TRAGEDY OF WARSAW

The entry of the Soviet Army and Wojsko Polskie into Poland, the establishment of the Polish Committee of National Liberation and the growth of the national liberation movement in the occupied parts of the country alarmed the Polish reactionary circles. Acting on orders from the emigre government, Armia Krajowa on August 1, 1944 provoked an uprising in Warsaw paying no heed to the situation at the front and without informing the Soviet Command, thus dooming it to failure. The first 38,000 insurgents who went into action had only 1,000 rifles, 300 submachine guns, 67 machine guns, 1,700 pistols and only a two or three days' supply of ammunition. For six weeks the leaders of the uprising did not want to contact the Soviet Command and did so only in the middle of September, after the liberation of Praga.

The reactionary elements planned to gain control of Warsaw prior to the arrival of the Soviet troops and establish the emigre government in power in the capital. As regards the plans of its organisers and its political substance, the uprising was anti-Soviet in character and designed to prevent the victory of people's rule in Poland.

The Soviet Government, which learned about the uprising after it had already started, declared that the Warsaw action was a reckless and fearful gamble, taking a heavy toll of the population. This, it said, would not have been the case had Soviet headquarters been informed beforehand about the Warsaw action and had the Poles maintained contact with them. Things being what they were, Soviet Command had declared that it had to dissociate itself from the Warsaw adventure.[1]

Blinded by class hatred the reactionaries did not reckon with the military situation and summoned the almost unarmed people to fight against German panzer divisions, artillery and air force. And yet the uprising was a spark that fired the hearts of the Warsaw population. Detachments of Armia Ludowa and many volunteers joined the insurgents. The uprising was supported by the people who believed that its leadership had concerted its actions with the Soviet

---

[1] See *Correspondence...*, Vol. I, p. 254.

Army. Despite unfavourable conditions the fighting lasted 63 days.

The uprising began when the 1st Byelorussian Front was completing the Byelorussian Operation and repelling vicious German counterattacks and counterblows at the bridgeheads south of Warsaw and in the Praga area. At the time the front's right-flank armies were fighting almost 150 kilometres east of Warsaw and its central group was in action at Siedlce. The Soviet troops had to fight for every inch of the ground. By the beginning of August the German Command had brought up large forces into action against the 1st Byelorussian Front, restored the strategic front and organised serious resistance. The position of the Soviet forces was further aggravated by the fact that in the course of almost six weeks of continuous fighting they had suffered heavy losses and their supplies and artillery were lagging far behind.

In most of the infantry divisions there were two companies to a battalion and companies numbered not more than 25 or 30 men each. The battle-worthiness of tank troops decreased drastically.

The redeployment of the air force to new bases lowered its activity. From July 18 to 20 the aircraft of the 1st Byelorussian Front made 9,000 sorties, or 3,000 a day, whereas between August 1 and 13 it flew only 3,170 sorties, or 240 a day.

By the beginning of August the Soviet troops were 500 kilometres away from their supply bases. There were days when lack of fuel prevented armoured corps from taking part in the fighting. A considerable part of the artillery was lagging hundreds of kilometres behind. As a result, the pace of the offensive declined sharply.

The Polish Ist Army began to cross the Vistula to help the insurgents in Warsaw on the night of September 15, as soon as Warsaw's eastern suburb Praga had been liberated. The Polish troops were reinforced by five Soviet artillery brigades and a mortar regiment, and supported by a powerful artillery group from the GHQ reserves and the 16th Air Army. The Polish troops encountered outright treachery. They were to land at points held by the insurgents. But at the last minute the leaders of the uprising withdrew their men into the city and these footholds were taken over by the Germans.

Within four days up to six battalions of the 2nd and 3rd infantry divisions crossed the river into Warsaw. In an attempt to wipe out the bridgeheads the Germans attacked with large infantry and panzer forces supported from the air.

As soon as contact was established with the insurgents, the Soviet Command began to render them every possible assistance. From September 14 to October 1, 1944 Soviet planes parachuted 156 mortars, 505 antitank rifles, 2,667 submachine guns and rifles, 41,780 grenades, 3,000,000 rounds of ammunition, 113 tons of rations and 500 kilogrammes of medicines to the insurgents.

By September 21 the situation on the bridgeheads worsened to such an extent that the Front Command had to evacuate the units of the Polish 1st Army that had crossed the Vistula at Warsaw. Groups of insurgents and the civilians were also evacuated. The Command of Armia Krajowa refused to link up with the Polish troops and Soviet Army and surrendered on October 2, leaving the fate of the surviving insurgents in the hands of the nazis.

The Polish people paid a heavy price for the adventurism of the Polish reactionaries. The insurgents' losses totalled 22,000, the Polish 1st Army lost 5,600 officers and men and losses among civilian population of the capital amounted to 180,000. On Hitler's orders the Polish capital was levelled with the ground.

3. FROM THE VISTULA TO THE ODER

THE PLANS OF THE COMBATANTS

The Soviet Army's victories in the summer and autumn of 1944 were largely instrumental in swinging the military and political situation on the battlefields of the Second World War in favour of the anti-Hitler coalition and hastened the final rout of fascism in Europe. At the same time they created favourable conditions for the complete liberation of Poland and sharply worsened Germany's military and political situation.

Having sustained heavy losses in 1944, the Wehrmacht began to experience an acute shortage of manpower and military equipment. Compared with July 1944 the output of Germany's armaments industries declined 27 per cent by the beginning of the following year. As a result of the considerable shrinkage of her material base Germany was unable fully to replenish the steadily rising losses at the front. The strength of her armed forces declined by almost 2,700,000 men as compared with the beginning of 1944. By 1945 she had lost almost all her allies. Her armed forces had been driven out of most of the occupied countries, and, with the entry of the Soviet troops into East Prussia in the autumn of 1944, the war had come to Germany's territory. Nevertheless, the Wehrmacht was still a force to be reckoned with. At the beginning of 1945 it had 299 divisions and 31 brigades, numbering 7,500,000 officers and men, 43,000 guns and mortars, 7,000 panzers and assault guns, and 6,800 combat aircraft.

The biggest and the most battleworthy part of the German forces was still concentrated on the Soviet-German front, where the Soviet Army faced 169 divisions and 20 brigades of the Wehrmacht, and 16 divisions and one brigade of the Hungarians. These forces consisted of 3,100,000 officers and men, 28,500 guns and mortars, about 4,000 panzers and assault guns, and approximately 2,000 aircraft. The Anglo-US troops faced 107 German divisions.

The German Command wanted to drag out the war in the hope of causing a split among the participants of the anti-Hitler coalition, and based its strategic plan for 1945 on these calculations. By putting up a tenacious defence on deliberate defence lines, it hoped to wear down and maul the Soviet troops and, in the long run, force them to revert to the defensive. At the same time it planned to carry out an offensive operation in the Ardennes at the end of 1944, smash the Anglo-US forces there and seize the strategic initiative on the Western front. By effecting this strategy on the Eastern and Western fronts, the nazi leadership thought that it would be able to create favourable conditions for concluding a separate peace with the USA and Britain.

Having chased the German invader out of occupied regions of the USSR and also out of a number of countries in East and Southeast Europe, the Soviet Armed Forces by the beginning of 1945 had taken up positions for striking the final blows at nazi Germany.

Guided by the Communist Party, the Soviet people considerably expanded the socialist economy and by their dedicated labour supplied the Army with increasing quantities of military equipment.

The Soviet Armed Forces had about 6,500,000 officers and men, 108,000 guns and mortars, about 3,000 rocket launchers, nearly 13,000 tanks and self-propelled guns, and 15,500 combat aircraft pitted against the Germans. Co-operating with the various fronts were 29 Polish, Czechoslovak, Rumanian and Bulgarian divisions (326,000 men) with 5,200 guns and mortars, 203 tanks and self-propelled guns.

The enhanced might of the Soviet Armed Forces and their high combat efficiency enabled the Communist Party and the Soviet Government to set the exceptionally important military and political task of completing the rout of nazi Germany and fulfilling their great mission of liberation by helping those European peoples which were still languishing under the fascist yoke to overturn the bloody regime and win freedom and independence. The Soviet Command planned to achieve these objectives by undertaking a strategic offensive along the entire Soviet-German front, striking the main blow in the direction of Warsaw and Berlin.

Regarding the liberation of the whole of Poland as a matter of great importance, the Soviet Supreme Command assembled a powerful force which included 3,500,000 men, about 9,500 tanks and self-propelled guns, 57,000 guns and mortars, or more than a half of the effective strength committed at the Soviet-German front, for the purpose of routing the German forces there. The ground actions were supported by 7,500 aircraft.

THE SITUATION IN POLAND
IN EARLY 1945

The second phase of the fight to liberate the whole of Poland conducted by the Soviet Army and Wojsko Polskie began in January 1945. By then important socio-economic changes had taken place in the country's liberated areas. With the vigorous support of the working class, people's authorities nationalised large-scale industry, transport and banks, abolished landed estates and turned them over to the peasants and agricultural workers, and created conditions for the free and dignified life of the mass of the people.

The people's democratic reforms were carried out in the course of a bitter class struggle. In this involved situation the Polish Workers' Party further strengthened the National Front by consolidating the working class and rallying more and more people to its support. In the course of its extensive political, organisational and economic activity the Polish Workers' Party, the leading force of the National Front, developed into a mass party as the foremost representative of the working people. Between July 1944 and April 1945 its membership increased from 20,000 to 300,000, and the domestic and foreign policy of the PCNL enjoyed the support of the broad masses.

The progressive measures effected by the people's government were most displeasing to the ruling circles in the United States and Britain. The Polish reactionaries, who were particularly incensed by the fruitful co-operation and friendly relations between the Soviet Union and Poland, tried to undermine the young democratic state from within by resorting to terror against the leaders and activists of the Polish Workers' Party and other parties of the democratic bloc. The Polish emigre government and its agents in Poland centred their activity on provoking a civil war in the liberated parts of the country. But the presence of the Soviet Army which helped the new democratic rule in Poland in every possible way foiled these plans.

A key task facing the PCNL at the time was that of activating the Polish Armed Forces. It was an exceptionally difficult matter since the economy in the liberated areas was at a low level and the young people's government was unable to supply them with weapons and military equipment. The Soviet Government supplied, therefore, Wojsko Polskie with weapons, equipment, transport facilities, ammunition, fuel and partly with officers without any compensation.

As a result of the mobilisation proclaimed in the liberated areas 100,000 men were enrolled in Wojsko Polskie in the course of several months in 1944 and several tens of thousands of Poles were mobilised on Soviet territory.

In their efforts to obstruct the formation of the Polish Armed Forces, reactionary elements boycotted the measures of the Polish Workers' Party and the PCNL, prevented the patriots from joining the army, called upon them not to turn up at drafting centres and to desert. In view of the hostile attitude of the Polish reactionaries to the establishment of the people's army, the Soviet GHQ, with the agreement of the Polish Committee of National Liberation, on July 31, 1944, ordered the Military Councils of the fronts operating in Poland to inform the Polish population that:

1. The right to mobilise people subject to military service on the territory of Poland rested solely with the Polish Committee of National Liberation as the government of the Polish sovereign state. At the request of the PCNL, mobilisation could be carried out by the Soviet Command.

2. Any mobilisation arrangements carried out on Polish territory by Polish organisations not connected with the PCNL were illegal. Persons engaging in such activity were to be immediately arrested as German agents sowing discord among the Polish population. At the same time the GHQ ordered that all detachments of Armia Krajowa which did not want to fight against the German invaders side by side with the troops of Wojsko Polskie were to be disarmed.

Despite the intrigues of the reactionaries, by the end of 1944 the people's government had raised the 2nd Army of Wojsko Polskie under the command of General K. Swierczewski and raised several divisions as reserves of the High Command. The High Command, the Main Headquarters, the Air Force Command, and administrative and mobilisation organs were also established. By that time Wojsko Polskie had 10 infantry divisions, a cavalry brigade, a tank corps, two separate tank brigades, 12 artillery brigades, a mortar brigade, three anti-aircraft artillery divisions, five engineer brigades and four air divisions. The new units were fully armed with weapons and equipment. In 1944, the Soviet Union supplied Wojsko Polskie with about 200,000 rifles and carabines, about 100,000 submachine guns, 17,000 light and 10,000 heavy machine guns, more than 4,600 guns and mortars, and 249 tanks and self-propelled guns. In the last quarter of 1944 the Soviet Union manufactured 150,000 uniforms and outfits and as many pairs of boots, and sets of underwear, for the Wojsko Polskie.

The Soviet Government assigned a fairly large number of highly experienced officers and specialists for service with Wojsko Polskie. But in view of the fact that it was still very short of officers, the Polish High Command sought the Soviet Supreme Command's assistance in training Polish officers, especially for the specialist arms of the service, and also in raising more air, artillery, armoured, engineer and signal units. Meeting this request, GHQ transferred to the Polish Command an air force and an engineer school, and also a tank brigade and a reserve signal battalion to be used as a base for the establishment of a tank and a signal school. On top of that the Soviet Command reinforced the Polish Ist and 2nd armies with several of its own units. As a result, each Polish army had as much artillery as a Soviet field army.

By early 1945 Wojsko Polskie was a powerful, well-armed and equipped army with more than 3,500 guns, nearly 1,500 mortars, about 400 tanks and self-propelled guns, and 300,000 officers and men. The Soviet Union continued to assist in the formation and equipment of Polish units; by the end of the Great Patriotic War Wojsko Polskie numbered approximately 446,000 officers and men. It consisted of two field armies, a tank and an air corps, 15 infantry divisions, including a training division, five artillery, four air, one cavalry, one motorised infantry, four tank, one mortar and 12 artillery brigades and four engineer brigades and other all-arms and specialist units and elements. It had 3,740 guns and mortars, 432 tanks and self-propelled guns, and 584 aircraft. In the course of the Great Patriotic War, up to May 1, 1945, the Soviet Union supplied Wojsko Polskie with more than 300,000 rifles and carbines, 106,000 submachine guns, nearly 19,000 machine guns of all calibres, 4,800 mortars, 3,540 guns of all calibres, 670 tanks and self-propelled guns, 630 aircraft and a large number of transport vehicles, communication facilities and other equipment. About 20,000 Soviet officers, including generals, were posted with the Polish troops in these years.

On December 31, 1944 the Krajowa Rada Narodowa transformed the Polish Committee of National Liberation into the
Provisional National Government of the Polish Republic.
This was an important step towards the revival of a free,
independent and democratic Poland. Headed by Prime Minister Edward Osobka-Morawski the Provisional Government
included representatives of the main political parties, namely
the Polish Workers' Party and the Socialist, Peasant and
Democratic parties. The establishment of such a government
accelerated the unification of the Polish people for the struggle against the invaders. In keeping with its policy of maintaining and strengthening friendly relations with the democratic Poland, the Soviet Union was the first foreign state
which on January 4, 1945 recognised the Polish Provisional
Government and established diplomatic relations with it.

"This recognition," wrote the *Glos Ludu*, "offered further
proof of the heart-felt feelings of the peoples of the Soviet
Union for Poland."

The American and British governments adopted a totally
different stand. They declined the offer of the Provisional
Government to establish diplomatic relations and, in effect,
worked for its isolation.

THE VISTULA-ODER OPERATION

Preparing to repulse the offensive of the Soviet and Polish
forces in Poland, the German Command established seven
defensive lines extending to a depth of 500 kilometres between the Vistula and the Oder. The main and the most
powerful line passed along the western bank of the Vistula.

The defensive lines organised in depth passed through
many industrial centres and towns, including Modlin, Thorn
(Torun), Bromberg (Bydgoszcz), Schneidemuhl (Pila), Poznan,
Küstrin (Kostrzyn), Glogau (Glogow), Breslau (Wroclaw) and
numerous inhabited localities with stone houses.

The lines between the Western Bug and the foothills of
the Carpathians were defended by the 9th Field Army, 4th
Panzer Army and the main forces of the 17th Army of Army
Group A under the command of Colonel-General Harpe who
was replaced on January 17 by Colonel-General Schörner.

These armies consisted of 30 divisions, including four panzer and two motorised divisions, and two brigades. Moreover, 50 separate battalions subsequently committed against the Soviet troops were stationed as garrisons in Polish towns. All told, the Germans had up to 400,000 men, more than 4,000 guns and mortars, more than 1,100 panzers and assault guns, and about 300 aircraft of the 6th Air Fleet which provided the air cover.

The 1st Byelorussian and the 1st Ukrainian fronts were deployed in the central sector of the front, between the mouth of the Western Bug to Jaslo; the 2nd Byelorussian Front was in action north and the Ist Ukrainian Front south of the Western Bug, and the 4th Ukrainian Front was fighting in the south of Poland and in the Carpathians.

Deployed in a 500-kilometre zone, the 1st Byelorussian and the 1st Ukrainian fronts had 2,200,000 men, more than 34,000 guns and mortars, about 6,500 tanks and self-propelled guns, and about 4,800 combat aircraft. It was the biggest strategic group of forces ever assembled by the Soviet Union in the Great Patriotic War for a single offensive operation. With these forces GHQ planned to strike a very powerful initial blow, execute a swift offensive and thus deprive the enemy of the chance of wrecking towns, villages, factories and railways during his retreat. The Polish 1st Army which was organically assigned to the Ist Byelorussian Front was all set to begin the liberation of Warsaw. It has approximately 68,000 men, 1,260 guns and mortars, 172 tanks and self-propelled guns.

In general the situation in the Warsaw-Berlin sector of the Soviet-German front favoured the large-scale offensive which has gone down in the history of the Great Patriotic War as the Vistula-Oder Operation. It was undertaken to smash Army Group A, liberate the whole of Poland and create the necessary conditions for striking the decisive and final blow at Berlin, capital of nazi Germany.

To achieve this aim the 1st Byelorussian and the 1st Ukrainian Fronts were to deal powerful frontal blows in the direction of Poznan and Breslau, develop a swift offensive to break up the enemy's defences along their entire depth, break up the defender's forces and destroy them piecemeal.

The 1st Byelorussian Front under Marshal G. K. Zhukov

was to smash the Warsaw-Radom group, gain the line Petr-kuwek (Petruwek)-Zychlin-Lods not later than on the 12th day of the offensive and then push towards Poznan.

The main attack was to be delivered from the Magnoszew bridgehead in the general direction of Kutno. Acting in con-junction with a part of the Front's strike group, the Soviet 47th and the Polish 1st armies were to rout the German grouping at Warsaw and capture the city. The second blow was to be delivered from the Pulawy bridgehead at Lodz.

In keeping with GHQ orders Marshal I. S. Konev's 1st Ukrainian Front was to cooperate with the 1st Byelorussian Front in smashing the Kielce-Radom enemy grouping. It was to mount the main attack from the Sandomierz bridgehead at Radomsko and gain the Piotrkow-Radomsko-Czestochowa-Mechow-Bochnia line not later than on the 11th day of the offensive, and then open an offensive in the general direction of Breslau.

From the north the offensive of the main strike group to-wards Warsaw and Berlin was to be covered by Marshal Ro-kossovsky's 2nd Byelorussian Front, a part of whose forces was to advance along the eastern bank of the Vistula towards Modlin. From the south the strike group was to be supported by the 4th Ukrainian Front under General I. Y. Petrov, whose right-wing forces were to attack from the area of Jaslo.

Originally planned for the end of January 1945, the offen-sive was started on January 12 in view of the defeat of the Anglo-American forces in the Ardennes and in response to Prime Minister Churchill's request to Marshal Stalin. The Soviet Union once again fulfilled its commitments to the Allies in the struggle against the common enemy.

On January 12, 1945 the Soviet Army began its strategic offensive along a 1,200-kilometre front. A key element of this offensive was the Vistula-Oder Operation.

The operation got under way in non-flying weather, and since the air force was unable effectively to assist the land forces, the task of providing fire support for the infantry and armour on the first day of the offensive was shouldered by the artillery. It brilliantly coped with the task. The enemy sustained heavy casualties in manpower and materials, his fire system was upset and the men were morally depressed. Some enemy units were wiped out of existence and control and communications were disrupted.

By nightfall the Soviet troops had pierced the enemy fortifications through their tactical depth, wedging from 15 to 20 kilometres into the enemy's defences. From January 14 to 16 the strike forces advanced 25-50 kilometres into the German defences. The routed German 9th Army, the 4th Panzer Army and the 17th Army began to retreat, and by nightfall on January 17 the main forces of Army Group A were smashed. Piercing the enemy defences to a depth of 100-150 kilometres along a 500-kilometre frontage, the Soviet troops liberated Radom, Kielce, Radomsko, Czestochowa and other large industrial centres which the Germans had turned into strong-points.

The fighting in that period was crowned by the liberation of Warsaw by Soviet and Polish forces on January 17. Colonel-General P. A. Belov's 61st Army, advancing from the Magnoszew bridgehead, enveloped Warsaw from the south and the 2nd Tank Army under General S. I. Bogdanov, which entered into the breach by nightfall on January 16, reached the Sochaczew area west of Warsaw, outflanked the left wing of the enemy Warsaw group. At the same time the 47th Army turned Warsaw from the north. The long pincers completely disorganised the defences of the enemy forces in Warsaw and the German Command ordered its troops to withdraw from the city. As a result, the Polish 1st Army was able to strike a direct blow at the Polish capital.

The Polish 1st, 3rd and 4th infantry divisions under Brigadier-General V. Bewziuk, Colonel S. Czaijkowski and Brigadier-General B. Kiniewicz, respectively, crossed the Vistula on the night of January 16 and landed on its western bank south of Warsaw. Colonel J. Rotkiewicz's 2nd Infantry Division, taking advantage of the successful operations of Major-General F. I. Perkhorovich's 47th Army, enveloped the city from the north, and the 6th Infantry Division under Brigadier-General G. Szejpak attacked the city from the east. On January 17 Polish forces broke into the city. Simultaneously, the 61st Army entered the city from the southwest, the 47th Army from the northwest. The Polish capital was liberated by the evening of January 17.

Barbarously demolished by the nazis, liberated Warsaw was a horrifying sight. The city was blazing, and clouds of smoke shrouded the charred remains of buildings.

At spontaneous meetings in the streets the people of Warsaw with tears in their eyes thanked their liberators.

In recognition of the heroism and courage displayed by Soviet and Polish troops in the fighting for the Polish capital Soviet GHQ bestowed the name "Warsaw" on 70 corps, divisions, brigades, regiments and battalions of the Soviet Army, and on 12 divisions, brigades, regiments and battalions of the Polish 1st Army.

To commemorate the liberation of Warsaw the Presidium of the USSR Supreme Soviet struck the medal "For the Liberation of Warsaw", which was awarded to more than 682,000 officers and men who took part in the operation.

The Soviet Government extended fraternal assistance to the Polish people in rehabilitating Warsaw. It sent experts to the city who drew up a plan to rebuild Warsaw and also decided to furnish material and technical aid to cover 50 per cent of the expenditure envisaged by the plan. Moreover, as a token of friendship with the Polish people and in order to help the inhabitants of Warsaw, the Soviet Union provided them with 60,000 tons of flour and considerable quantities of medicines and dressings.

After liberating the city, the Soviet and Polish troops, helped by the local population, began mine-clearing. Within a short period of time Soviet sappers removed approximately two million mines and unexploded shells and cleared the main streets of rubble. Soviet engineers helped to build a pontoon bridge between Warsaw and Praga, and repaired the power station and the water supply.

On January 20 the Krajowa Rada Narodowa sent a message to the Soviet Government which said: "The Polish people will always remember that it owes its freedom and the possibility to restore its independent state to the brilliant victories of the Soviet arms and to the abundantly spilt blood of the heroic Soviet servicemen."

Honouring the memory of the Soviet and Polish soldiers who fell in the battles for Warsaw and other Polish cities, grateful inhabitants of Warsaw erected a monument in one of the city's many squares.

The splendid results of the Soviet offensive in the period from January 12 to 17, 1945 paved the way for an exceptionally bold and determined offensive on Poznan and Breslau. On January 19, the 1st Byelorussian Front liberated Lodz, a large industrial centre and Poland's second biggest city with fine revolutionary traditions. Beating a hasty retreat, the Germans had no time to demolish the city. They also abandoned the plundered machine-tools and equipment packed for shipment to Germany.

In order to hold up the Soviet drive towards Berlin the German Command hastily transferred additional forces from the reserves, the Western front and from other sectors of the Soviet-German front. But all its attempts to stem the offensive of the 1st Byelorussian and the 1st Ukrainian fronts at intermediate lines, including the defences along major water barriers (Bzura, Warta, Narew and Oder) fell through. The rapid pace of the offensive, in the course of which the infantry advanced from 30 to 40 and the armoured troops from 40 to 70 kilometres a day, deprived the German Command of any possibility to organise stable defences.

On January 25 the 1st Byelorussian Front broke through the Poznan line, surrounded the 62,000-strong enemy garrison in the city and on the following day reached the old German-Polish border. In five days of heavy fighting they penetrated the German border defences, reached the Oder and by February 3 gained a bridgehead on its western bank near Küstrin, within 60 kilometres of Berlin.

In the meantime the 1st Ukrainian Front pushed towards the Oder and the Upper Silesian industrial region. On January 19 its units crossed the old German-Polish border at Breslau and entered the old Polish lands which Prussia had seized in the middle of the 18th century. On the same day the 59th and 60th armies under Lieutenant-General I. T. Korovnikov and Colonel-General P. A. Kurochkin liberated Cracow, an important military, industrial, political and administrative centre.

Though the battle for Cracow was fought in difficult conditions, the Soviet Command took steps that minimum damage was caused to the city. As a result, its magnificent architectural monuments were saved from destruction, including the world-famous Wawel Castle, the unique 14th century building of the fullers' corporation (Sukiennice), the Maria Chapel with sculptures by Stwosz and Cracow University founded in 1364.

As a measure to speed up the liberation of the Upper Silesian industrian region, the Front Commander on GHQ instructions committed Colonel-General D. N. Gusev's 21st Army to action. The blow which it delivered from an area northeast of Katowice in the southerly direction, coupled with the strike to the west by the Front's left-wing armies after the liberation of Cracow, confronted the enemy group in Silesia with the threat of encirclement. To make its position even more difficult and thus force it to withdraw from Upper Silesia with the utmost speed, the Front Commander carried out a bold manoeuvre. He ordered General P. S. Rybalko's 3rd Guards Tank Army, which was approaching the Oder in the area of Namslaw, to turn and strike at the flank and rear of the enemy forces in the Upper Silesian industrial region. Since it was clear that fighting in Upper Silesia could have become drawn out and cause considerable damage to its industry, the Front Commander on GHQ orders made no attempt to prevent the enemy troops from withdrawing with the view to smashing them in an area west of the industrial region.

This was a brilliant decision. The offensive of the Front's forces from the east and the northeast and the blow delivered by General Rybalko's tanks from the northwest forced the enemy hastily to abandon Silesian towns and retreat from the region through the remaining gap in the southwesterly direction. On January 28, following a resolute attack, the 59th and 21st armies liberated Katowice, the centre of the Dombrowski coal region, and on January 29 the Upper Silesian industrial region was cleared of all German forces. This enabled the Polish Government quickly to restore and re-open Silesian industrial enterprises and mines.

By the beginning of February the 1st Ukrainian Front reached the Oder in its operational zone and gained important bridgeheads at Breslau, Ratibor (Raciborz), Olau (Olawa) and northwest of Oppeln (Opole). With the 1st Byelorussian and the 1st Ukrainian Front entrenched on the Oder and the liberation of the Upper Silesian industrial region, the Vistula-Oder Operation was brought to a close.

As in the summer of 1944, the Polish people meritoriously contributed to the cause of liberating their country. Together with the Soviet Army Polish troops battered the enemy in heavy engagements; partisans who operated behind enemy lines attacked his communications and depots; and the urban and rural inhabitants made every effort to help the Soviet Army.

In the course of the Vistula-Oder Operation the Soviet troops routed Army Group Centre, formerly Army Group A, liberated a large part of Poland with her capital Warsaw, commenced military operations in Germany and gained the immediate approaches to Berlin.

During their 20-day offensive the Soviet troops smashed the 30 divisions the enemy had at his disposal at the outset and also a large number of the 40 divisions which the German Command committed in the course of the fighting. Thirty-five enemy divisions were destroyed and 25 lost from 60 to 75 per cent of their manpower. The Soviet troops took prisoner 147,000 officers and men and seized approximately 1,400 panzers and assault guns, nearly 14,000 guns and mortars, 1,360 aircraft and large quantities of other military equipment.

The Vistula-Oder Operation was closely coordinated with the general plan of the Soviet offensive in East Prussia and the Western Carpathians.

The offensive in East Prussia began on January 13. Striking powerful blows, the 2nd and 3rd Byelorussian fronts swiftly broke through the entire depth of the enemy defences. On January 26 the strike group of the 2nd Byelorussian Front reached the Baltic Sea at Elbing (Elblag) and cut off Army Group North (until January 26 called Army Group Centre) from the main forces of the Wehrmacht. At the end of January the 3rd Byelorussian Front reached Frisches Haff (Kaliningrad Bay) north and south of Königsberg (Kaliningrad). Coordinating their operations the two fronts by the end of January had enveloped the East Prussian group of enemy forces and split it into three parts which were later wiped out by the 3rd Byelorussian Front. On February 8, the 2nd Byelorussian Front, whose left-flank armies in fulfilment of GHQ orders had gained the western bank of the Vistula, received another mission of smashing the enemy in East Pomerania.

During the East Prussian Operation the Soviet troops destroyed more than 25 enemy divisions (and other 12 enemy divisions lost from 50 to 75 per cent of their strength), liberated a part of Poland's northern territories and occupied the whole of East Prussia with the fortress town of Königsberg. By capturing East Prussia, the Soviet troops liquidated the bridgehead from which the German forces invaded Poland in 1939 and which in the past served as a springboard for the predatory campaigns against the Slav peoples.

The 4th Ukrainian Front was on the offensive in the Western Carpathians. Fighting in difficult mountain and forest terrain, it approached the upper reaches of the Vistula and liberated Poland's southern areas bordering on Czechoslovakia.

Thus, in the course of the January offensive the German forces were driven out of key economic regions of Central, West and South Poland with Lodz, Cracow, Warsaw, Katowice, Bydgoszcz and other important industrial centres. Military operations shifted to German territory, and the tip of the huge wedge which the Soviet troops drove into enemy positions reached the western bank of the Oder only 60 kilometres from Berlin.

4. POLAND IS FREE

POLAND REGAINS HER BALTIC
SEABOARD

The Soviet Army's January offensive seriously altered the strategic situation along the entire Soviet-German Front, especially in the Berlin sector, where the Soviet troops directly threatened Germany's vital regions and her capital. Extremely alarmed by the situation on the Eastern Front, the German Command did its best to halt the Soviet offensive against Berlin. In the first place it bolstered defences along all lines and brought up reinforcements from other fronts. At the same time it planned to attack the 1st Byelorussian Front from East Pomerania, rout it north of the Warta and thus be able to put up a lasting defence at the approaches to Berlin. For this purpose it formed Army Group Wisla in East

Pomerania. According to the testimony of the former chief of staff of the German High Command, Keitel, the plan was to undertake a counter-operation from the Pomeranian springboard against the Soviet troops driving on Berlin in February and March 1945. Accordingly, Army Group Wisla entrenched in the area of Grudziaz (Graudenz), was to break the Soviet front, reach the valley of the Netze and Warta and come out to Küstrin from the rear. The Soviet intelligence learned about these plans in good time and they were taken into account by GHQ.

By February 10, 1945 the German Command had concentrated the 2nd and 11th armies consisting of 16 infantry, four panzer and three motorised divisions, four brigades, eight combat groups and five fortress garrisons, in East Pomerania. Overhanging the 1st Byelorussian Front from the north, the East Pomeranian group was a serious threat which could not be ignored. It was most important, therefore, that the Soviet troops should wipe it out as quickly as possible before undertaking any other operations. The first to go into action was the 2nd Byelorussian Front. Its mission was to assume the offensive on February 10 west of the Vistula, capture the area of Danzig (Gdansk) and Gdynia and clear the Baltic coast of the enemy right up to the mouth of the Oder.

At the beginning of the operation the Front had five field armies, one of which, the 19th, was committed from the GHQ reserves. The land forces were covered by the 4th Air Army. Three field armies and one tank army which were operating in East Prussia were assigned to the 2nd Byelorussian Front. Not counting the 19th Army (nine divisions) the 2nd Byelorussian Front had 36 divisons, three fortified areas, three tank, one mechanised and one cavalry corps.

The German force consisted of the 2nd Army which had fought in East Prussia. It had about 22 divisions, including 13 infantry and two panzer divisions, two brigades, six combat groups and three large fortress garrisons.

Having no time thoroughly to prepare the operation, the 2nd Byelorussian Front attacked on February 10 from the Graudenz-Sempolno line. The offensive made slow headway and in ten days the Soviet troops advanced from 40 to 60 kilometres in isolated sectors. Realising that the 2nd Byelorussian Front alone would be unable to rout Army Group Wisla, GHQ in the nick of time committed the 1st Byelorussian Front, too.

On February 16 two panzer and one infantry corps totalling 14 divisions, one brigade, several separate panzer and assault gun battalions with strong air support delivered a series of powerful blows at the Soviet troops in the areas of Stargard, Arnswalde (Choszczno), Reez and Kalisz and in the course of two or three days managed to push back the right wing of the 1st Byelorussian Front some 8-12 kilometres.

The Soviet troops taking part in the operation against the enemy forces in East Pomerania were to deliver two powerful blows, reach the Baltic coast, split up the German grouping, whose strength had been augmented to 29 infantry, three panzer and three motorised divisions, three brigades and a considerable number of separate units, and destroy it piecemeal.

With the arrival of the 19th Army the 2nd Byelorussian Front resumed its offensive and dealt the main blow out of the Sempolno area at Köslin (Koszalin).

Having repulsed the counterblows of the East Pomeranian grouping, the 1st Byelorussian Front went over to the offensive on March 1. The Front, which also included the Polish 1st Army, delivered its main attack at Kolberg (Kolobrzeg) from the area of Arnswalde.

On March 5, the both fronts reached the Baltic coast at Köslin and Kolberg, splitting the enemy forces in Pomerania. In order to wipe out the Pomeranian group GHQ turned the main forces of the 2nd Byelorussian Front against the Danzig-Gdynia group of the enemy, and to exploit the offensive of its left wing reinforced the front by the 1st Byelorussian Front's 1st Guards Tank Army, which included the Polish 1st Tank Brigade.

By the end of March the 2nd Byelorussian Front smashed the main forces of the German 2nd Army, liberated Danzig and Gdynia, clearing the Baltic coast of the enemy between the mouth of the Vistula and Kolobrzeg.

In the meantime the right-wing armies of the 1st Byelorussian Front reached the Oder on a wide frontage extending from its mouth to the town of Schwedt and drove the enemy

out of a part of East Pomerania west of the Neustettin (Szcze-
cinek)-Kolberg line.

The capture of Danzig marked the successful culmination
of the East Pomeranian Operation in the course of which the
Soviet Forces routed 21 divisions and eight brigades, including six divisions and three brigades, which were completely
wiped out, took more than 91,000 prisoners, captured 900
panzers, 5,600 guns and mortars, 431 aircraft and large quantities of other equipment. Sealed up north of Gdynia, the
remnants of the German 2nd Army were mopped up and
taken prisoner on May 4, and enemy units trapped on the
Hel Peninsula and in the Vistula delta surrendered on May 9.

By routing the East Pomeranian grouping, the Soviet forces
frustrated the flanking blow the Germans intended to strike
at the Soviet divisions which had reached the immediate approaches to Berlin, and improved the conditions for an offensive on the German capital.

As a result of the East Pomeranian Operation the Soviet
forces liberated and returned to Poland her ancient lands on
the Baltic coast between the Vistula and the Oder.

For meritorious action in the operation the Soviet Command awarded the Order of the Red Banner to the Polish 1st
Tank Brigade and attached the name Kolberg to a number
of units.

THE LIBERATION OF SILESIA

While the Byelorussian fronts were fighting in East Pomerania, the 1st Ukrainian Front which was liberating Poland's
southwestern regions conducted the Upper and then the Lower Silesian operations.

With the completion of the Vistula-Oder Operation any
delay in exploiting the success would have given the German
Command a breathing spell, enabling it to bring up reserves,
reorganise the divisions which had been smashed during the
Soviet Army's winter offensive, and hold on firmly to the
defences along the Oder.

In order to frustrate these plans, the commander of the
1st Ukrainian Front, with GHQ approval, decided to begin
a fresh operation in the Berlin direction, and in a very short

space of time the Front's main forces were shifted from its left wing in the Silesian industrial region to its right wing.

On February 8, the 1st Ukranian Front's right-wing and central armies (3rd and 5th Guards, 13th, 52nd and 6th armies, and the 3rd and 4th Guards Tank armies) struck out from bridgeheads on the western bank of the Oder. They quickly overran enemy defences and smashed his reserves and by February 15 surrounded the fortress town of Breslau with a 40,000-strong garrison and Glogau whose garrison consisted of 18,000. Continuing the offensive the Soviet troops reached the Neisse from its mouth to Penzig. In this operation the Front's right-wing armies liberated the whole of Lower Silesia, entered the province of Brandenburg in Germany and came up abreast of the 1st Byelorussian Front. In this way both fronts were in a favourable position for pursuing an offensive and delivering the final blow at the enemy at Berlin. At the same time the 1st Ukrainian Front enveloped the enemy forces in Upper Silesia which were to be routed in the forthcoming Upper Silesian Operation. This operation had to be conducted because the Front's left wing was lagging far behind and its lines were greatly stretched. Taking this into account, the Front Commander planned an operation, in the course of which the Front's left wing (the 5th Guards, 21st, 59th, 60th armies and the 4th Guards Tank Army which had been transferred to the area) were to deal two converging blows, encircle and reduce the enemy in the area of Oppeln and enter the foothills of the Sudeten.

The operation was mounted on March 15. Breaking up the enemy defences and pushing rapidly on Neustadt, the Soviet forces on March 18 encircled five enemy divisions southwest of Oppeln and destroyed them two days later. Pressing forward in the face of mounting resistance, the Soviet troops reached the foothills of the Sudeten and took up temporary defence.

In this operation the Soviet troops averted the threat of an enemy blow at the left wing of the 1st Ukrainian Front, liberated Upper Silesia and deprived the Germans of any chance of relieving the surrounded Breslau garrison.

During the fighting in Silesia the 1st Ukrainian Front inflicted another heavy defeat on the 4th Panzer and the 19th armies of Army Group Centre: 15 divisions and three brigades lost from 50 to 70 per cent of their manpower and nine divisions were completely wiped out.

True to its line of rendering fraternal assistance to the Polish people, the Soviet Government established a department for the administration of Silesian coal basins. Headed by Lieutenant-General M. P. Milovsky who had all the necessary machines and equipment and a staff of Soviet specialists at his disposal, the department was established to help rehabilitate the Upper and Lower Silesian coal basins and ensure the supply of coal to frontline and nearby railways. Pooling their efforts Soviet and Polish citizens rehabilitated the Silesian coal basins, thus making an important contribution to Poland's economic revival.

The liberation of Poland within her present borders was completed in the course of the Berlin and Prague operations. The Prague Operation completed the liberation of Silesia, and the Berlin Operation resulted in the liberation of Stettin (Szczecin) and Swinemünde (Swinoujiscie), which, in keeping with decisions of the Berlin (Potsdam) Conference of the leaders of the USSR, the United States and Britain, were subsequently turned over to Poland.

The Soviet Army liberated Poland in the course of almost nine months of extremely bitter fighting. With the help of Wojsko Polskie it inflicted crushing defeats on large enemy forces—Army Groups A, Centre, North Ukraine, North and Wisla, routing more than 170 divisions, of which about 100 were completely wiped out.

About 600,000 Soviet officers and men fell in battle for the liberation of Poland. The Polish 1st Army lost about 10,000 officers and men in killed, 27,000 in wounded and more than 6,000 as missing.

In recognition of their courage and heroism in the fighting in Poland, the Presidium of the USSR Supreme Soviet conferred the title of Hero of the Soviet Union to 1,382 officers and men. The Soviet Government awarded orders and medals to more than 5,000 soldiers of Wojsko Polskie; the names "Praga", "Warsaw", "Pomerania", "Kolberg" were added to the names of 34 Polish units; 29 Polish units were decorated with the orders of the Red Banner, Kutuzov, Alexander Nevsky and Red Star, and the Tadeusz Kosciuszko Polish 1st Army was decorated with two Soviet orders.

Paying tribute to the Soviet troops which had fought in Poland, the Government of People's Poland and the High Command of Wojsko Polskie awarded orders and medals to 36,000 Soviet servicemen. The highest decorations of the Polish Republic were awarded to Marshals G. K. Zhukov, I. S. Konev and K. K. Rokossovsky who commanded the Soviet troops which drove the Germans out of Poland, and also to General N. A. Bulganin, the Soviet representative with the Polish Committee of National Liberation.

5. RESULTS OF THE STRUGGLE FOR POLAND'S LIBERATION

The complete liberation of Poland by the Soviet troops and their presence on her territory created favourable conditions for a relatively peaceful development of the revolution in the country. This fettered the internal reaction, averted civil war, frustrated the efforts of British and US imperialists openly to support the reaction and restore the old bourgeois order in the country, and opened the way for an all-out struggle to build a new life in the country first along democratic and then along socialist lines.

From the first days of the country's liberation the popular authorities in the Polish Republic under the guidance of the Polish Workers' Party started work to overcome the consequences of German occupation. They initiated an agrarian and other democratic reforms and abolished the economic domination of the wealthy bourgeoisie by nationalising key branches of industry. The landlords and the wealthy and middle bourgeoisie deprived of their power, the welfare of the masses was gradually improved. In addition to these measures the Provisional Government tackled the very difficult task of settling and developing the recovered western territories which gave Poland access to the sea through the ports of Gdansk and Szczecin.

Radical democratic changes were also taking place in the social and political life of the country.

In view of the vicious resistance of internal reactionaries backed by imperialists in the United States and Britain, democratic reforms in new Poland could not be carried out without the effective assistance of the Soviet Union and the Soviet Army.

The Soviet Army's swift offensive prevented the nazis from turning Poland into scorched earth zone. In the course of their drive the Soviet troops took steps to prevent the destruction of power stations, factories, mills, telephone exchanges, warehouses and banks.

Under an agreement signed in January 1945 the Soviet Union granted Poland credits to the value of 50 million rubles and another $10 million for the needs of her foreign trade. At the end of February the Soviet Union sent more than 45,000 tons of coal, about 3,000 tons of kerosene, 280,000 tons of fuel oil, 6,000 tons of salt and 60 tons of tea to Poland. In April the same year it sent 150,000 head of cattle and sheep, 8,000 tons of meat and a thousand tons of fats to Poland. On top of that it delivered 20,000 tons of textile raw materials and 100,000 hides on the condition that 50 per cent of the finished product would be turned over to the USSR.

On July 7, 1945 the Soviet Union and Poland signed a trade treaty and agreement on mutual goods deliveries. Under the terms of the agreement which was concluded in Moscow the Soviet Union undertook to supply Poland in the latter half of 1945 with 250,000 tons of iron, 30,000 tons of manganese ore, 25,000 tons of cotton, 3,000 tons of tobacco, 2,400 tons of flax, 40,000 tons of apatites and other commodities. The deliveries of Soviet raw materials for the Polish industry and the conclusion of a trade treaty between the countries helped reduce unemployment in the country.

The USSR favoured the establishment of a strong and independent Polish state which would maintain friendly relations with the USSR and consistently upheld Poland's sovereignty and independence in the international arena. Thanks to the Soviet delegation's firm stand the Crimea Conference of the Heads of Government of the USSR, the USA and Britain held in February 1945 adopted decisions that were favourable for Poland. In particular, the conference agreed that the Polish-Soviet border should basically run along the Curzon Line. The conference was unable to determine Poland's western border in view of the sharply negative stand of the British and American delegations. The leaders of the three states returned to this question at the Berlin Conference in July-August 1945. In keeping with the wishes of the Polish people and the proposal of the Soviet Union, the conference adopted a just decision concerning Poland's western and northern borders. Indigenous Polish lands, formerly seized by Germany and then reunited with the country as a result of Soviet war victories, were officially returned to Poland which also received the territory of East Prussia, with the exception of Königsberg and the adjoining regions. The return of Poland's western lands considerably increased her natural and raw material resources.

The decision adopted at the Crimea Conference concerning the Polish government was preceded by a sharp political struggle. American and British representatives tried hard to establish a reactionary government in Poland headed by Mikolajczyk but failed to do so in the face of resolute objections of the Soviet delegation. The conference decided to establish a Polish Provisional Government of National Unity which, upon the insistence of the Soviet delegation and contrary to the wishes of American and British delegations, would have the Provisional Government as its core. All attempts by the American and British representatives to replace the Provisional Government with a one consisting of representatives of Polish reactionary circles in circumvention of the Crimea Conference decisions were resolutely opposed by the USSR.

The Polish Provisional Government of National Unity was set up in Warsaw on June 28, 1945 and included members of the former Provisional Government, democratic elements inside Poland and Poles living abroad. It was recognised by the USSR, USA, Britain, China and other countries and, at the insistence of the Soviet Union at the Berlin Conference, Britain and the United States agreed to terminate diplomatic relations with the Polish government in London.

On April 21, 1945 a new chapter was opened in Soviet-Polish relations. On that day the two countries signed a treaty of friendship, mutual assistance and post-war co-operation in Moscow, in which both sides pledged to join efforts in fighting the war to a victorious conclusion, do everything in their power to prevent a repetition of aggression and not to participate in coalitions directed at the other side. The treaty also provided for the establishment of broad economic and cultural co-operation and mutual assistance in economic rehabilitation. It put an end to the old, unfriendly relations between the two countries and created a basis for goodneighbourliness and lasting friendship between the Soviet and Polish peoples. International imperialism was forced to abandon its plans of reviving its anti-popular policy of establishing a *cordon sanitaire*.

Assessing the treaty's significance the Polish newspaper *Glos Ludu* in an editorial on April 22, 1945 wrote: "An act of the greatest historical significance has taken place. The Polish-Soviet treaty which was signed yesterday expresses the unflinching will of our people to build its future on the basis of a permanent alliance and friendship with the mightiest bulwark of freedom and democracy—the Soviet Union. The Polish people regard this alliance, this friendship as the foundation of its strength, its development and its security."

In furtherance of the Soviet-Polish treaty of friendship and mutual assistance, the USSR and Poland on August 16, 1945 signed a treaty on the Soviet-Polish border. It was agreed that the Soviet-Polish border would follow the Curzon Line with deviations at some points of five to eight kilometres in favour of Poland. In addition the Soviet Union turned over to Poland territory south of Krylov and a part of the Bialowieza Forest. The Soviet-Polish border on the territory of East Prussia was also fixed with part of East Prussia south of the Goldap-Braunsberg (Braniewo) line and also the territory of the former free city of Danzig turned over to Poland. At the same time the two sides signed an agreement on compensation for the damage caused to Poland by the German occupation. The Soviet Government renounced in Poland's favour all its claims to German property and other assets throughout Poland, including that part of Germany which was being ceded to Poland, and also agreed to turn over to Poland 15 per cent of the share of reparations accruing to it. The Soviet-Polish agreements were yet another manifestation of the fraternal assistance of the Soviet peoples to the people of Poland.

In memory of the immortal feat of the Soviet Army, which brought freedom and independence to Poland, the Polish people built obelisks and monuments to Soviet soldiers in

Warsaw, Czestochowa, Lodz, Kolobrzeg, Lublin and many other cities.

The Polish people will always remember the internationalist stand of the Soviet Government on the question of Poland's independence proclaimed in the decree of the Council of People's Commissars of August 29, 1918. Article 3 of this decree which was signed by Lenin reads: "All the treaties and acts concluded by the government of the former Russian Empire and the governments of the Kingdom of Prussia and the Austro-Hungarian Empire concerning the partitions of Poland are hereby irrevocably abrogated because they contradict the principle of the self-determination of nations and the revolutionary awareness of justice of the Russian people which recognises the Polish people's inalienable right to independence and unity."

After the war in Europe the Polish people under the leadership of the Polish Workers' Party and with the fraternal assistance of the countries of the socialist community, the Soviet Union in the first place, made great progress in socialist construction. On the ruins of the old bourgeois and landlord Poland arose a new, free, independent, democratic Poland, a strong and viable state with broad prospects of further development and prosperity.

Within three decades Poland developed into one of the world's economically advanced states. She is playing an important role in further strengthening the socialist community and consolidating the unity of the international communist movement, of all the anti-imperialist forces.

The years of socialist construction were characterised by dynamic economic development and radical changes in the country. Poland owes her rapid economic growth to the dedicated efforts of her people and also to the fact that Soviet-Polish economic ties are based on principles of socialist internationalism, full equality, respect for sovereignty and national interests, mutual advantage and comradely mutual assistance.

Dwelling on Poland's relations with the Soviet Union, First Secretary of the Central Committee of the Polish United Workers' Party, Edward Gierek, noted at the Sixth Congress of the Party in 1971 that the fraternal relations with the Soviet Union "created historical opportunities for restoring the

Polish state within just and favourable frontiers, reliable guarantees of the independence and security of the Polish people.
We associate Poland's future with the strengthening of
friendship, alliance and co-operation with the USSR.

"The prospects for Poland's further development, the opportunities of realising the chief aspirations of our people,
the young generation in the first place, can be fully insured
only in co-operation with the Soviet Union and as a result
of this co-operation. This is the key principle of our national
policy. We are effecting it in an atmosphere of friendship
and fraternity of the Polish people with the Russian people,
with all the peoples of the Soviet Union."

As the Polish People's Republic develops and strengthens
so do its Armed Forces which together with their loyal
comrades-in-arms, the armies of the Warsaw Treaty countries, stand guard over the great achievements, peace
and security of the peoples building socialism and communism.

Communists and the working people of the Soviet Union
and the Polish People's Republic are linked by firm and
tested bonds of friendship; they are inspired by a great and
common aim—the formation of the most humane and just
society. Extensive and many-sided links in political, economic, cultural and scientific fields are developing between
the Soviet Union and the Polish People's Republic from year
to year.

Fulfilling the history-making decisions of the 24th CPSU
Congress, Soviet Communists will continue to do their utmost
consistently to promote Soviet-Polish co-operation, and
strengthen the fraternal alliance of our countries for the sake
of the Soviet and Polish peoples, for the sake of peace, progress and socialism.

1. ON THE EVE OF LIBERATION

COLLAPSE
OF THE ANTI-SOVIET POLICY
OF THE RUMANIAN RULING CIRCLES

The third year of the Great Patriotic War was drawing to an end. The Soviet troops were irresistibly pushing westwards. In the winter and the spring of 1944 they launched a sweeping offensive in the south of the USSR. It was the first offensive of such scope and scale ever to be conducted in the history of wars in conditions of spring thaw and lack of roads, and it showed once again that the Soviet Army could conduct successful campaigns in any season.

At the end of March 1944 the 2nd Ukrainian Front under Marshal I. S. Konev reached the Soviet-Rumanian border. Moscow saluted this victory with 24 salvoes from 320 guns.

The Soviet troops considered it their internationalist duty to help the Rumanian people get rid of the nazi bondage which had been their lot for many years. It was an exceptionally difficult task; in order to accomplish it they had to liberate a country which had participated in the nazi aggression against the Soviet Union and was still at war with it.

Drawn into the war against the Soviet Union by the fascist government which came to power in September 1940 with the support of the leaders of the bourgeois and landlord parties who disregarded the country's national interests, Rumania became nazi Germany's satellite, a source of cannon fodder and raw materials for the Third Reich. This was a logical outcome of the entire pre-war anti-Soviet policy of monarchial Rumania whose ruling circles, manoeuvring as they did between different groups of imperialist states, strove to carry through the aggressive plans of creating a "Great Rumania". At first they pinned their hopes on the British, French and American imperialists and played a prominent role in the anti-Soviet *cordon sanitaire*. But when the Second World War broke out and Germany appeared to be the winning side, they decided to enter into an alliance with her. General Antonescu said as much during his conversation with Mussolini and Ciano in Rome in November 1940. With cynical arrogance he declared that compared with Germany and Italy, France and Britain proved to be weak partners who in actual fact resembled "a circus performer lifting enormous though hollow dumbbells in front of the spectators" and that the developments of 1940 proved this point. In the hope that aided by the Axis Powers they would be able to carry through their aggressive plans, the Rumanian ruling circles subjugated the country to nazi Germany. Rumania signed a fettering economic agreement with Germany and on November 23, 1940 officially joined the fascist bloc. After that German troops and advisers flooded the country.

Refusing to co-operate with the Soviet Union and turning down its sincere offers of assistance, the Rumanian leaders took to the path of national betrayal. "When the Anglo-French 'Munichites' yielded the 'sphere of influence' in this part of Europe to Hitler," it was noted in the Political Report of the Central Committee to the First Congress of the Rumanian Workers' Party, "the then ruling classes swiftly changed their course and began to serve Hitler and German big capital with the same slavish zeal with which they earlier served British, French and American reactionaries and capitalists."[1]

This was a fresh corroboration of Lenin's words to the effect that the bourgeoisie of the small countries which orientates itself on an alliance with the imperialist powers is incapable of pursuing an independent policy: "...they strive to come to terms with one of the rival imperialist powers for the sake of implementing their predatory plans (the policy of the small Balkan states, etc.)."[2]

The class hatred for the Soviet people and thirst for territorial aggrandisement impelled the Rumanian exploiter classes to embark on anti-Soviet ventures. The Rumanian fascists dreamed of creating a "Greater Rumania" at the expense of Soviet Moldavia and the Ukrainian lands extending to the Dnieper. To achieve these aims the Rumanian rulers

---

[1] Gheorghe Gheorghiu-Dej, *Articles and Speeches*, Vol. I, Moscow, 1965, p. 125 (Russian edition).

[2] V. I. Lenin, *Collected Works*, Vol. 22, p. 148.

sent about 30 divisions and brigades to the Soviet-German front and placed the country's entire military and economic potential at Hitler's service. The further the fascist armies advanced to the east the greater became the appetite of the Rumanian fascists. For example, in October 1942 when the enemy was standing at the walls of Stalingrad and the nazi leaders and their collaboraters were visualising the enslavement of the whole of the USSR, the Rumanian newspaper *Viata* demanded that the Rumanian border be shifted to the east, right up to the Urals.

On the occupied territories of Moldavia and the Ukraine the Rumanian fascists instituted a reign of terror, plunder and violence. Together with the nazis the Rumanian fascists exterminated hundreds of thousands of Soviet people. In Odessa Region alone they killed up to 200,000 civilians, about 64,000 in Moldavia and more than 16,000 in Chernovtsy Region.

While the Rumanian Army fought on Soviet territory for the interests that were alien to the Rumanian people, the Germans plundered and oppressed Rumania.

In the war against the Soviet Union the Rumanian Army lost more than 600,000 officers and men, of whom 400,000 were killed.

The damage sustained by Rumania's economy during the war was estimated at 10,000,000 million lei. This sum was equal to her budget allocations for more than 12 years (in the 1945 currency). The country was on the brink of an economic collapse.

The anti-Soviet plans of the Rumanian fascists fell through. By the spring of 1944 the Rumanian armies had rolled back to the lines from where they attacked the USSR. It also proved to be impossible to mislead the Rumanian working people who wrathfully condemned the anti-Soviet war. At the head of the anti-fascist movement in Rumania stood the Communist Party, the only Party which from the very outset of the war against the USSR denounced its predatory aims and summoned the popular masses to fight for Rumania's withdrawal from the war on nazi Germany's side, for the overthrow of the fascist regime and for the victory of the Soviet Union, which was liberating the peoples from the nazi yoke.

In June 1943 the Communist Party succeeded in uniting the country's anti-fascist forces into a single Patriotic Front. The chauvinistic fever induced by fascist propaganda and temporary military successes at the beginning of the war began to subdue under the impact of the Soviet victories and the courageous struggle of the Rumanian Communists. There was growing discontent with the fascist regime and German occupation in the country and the Resistance Movement gained in scope and scale. The most widespread forms of struggle were industrial sabotage, subversion and strikes, draft evasion and anti-Hitler activity. Early in 1944 the guerrilla movement began to spread in the country. Secretary of the Ilf Committee of the Communist Party Petre Gheorghe, Vasile Tudose, Ioja Bela, Suzana Pirvulescu, Filimon Sirbu and many others fell in the struggle against the fascist regime and the German occupation. More than 3,600 anti-fascists were sentenced to prolonged imprisonment and thousands were thrown into concentration camps. But nothing could force the anti-fascists to abandon their courageous struggle.

THE BEGINNING
OF RUMANIA'S LIBERATION

The Soviet people and its Armed Forces came to the assistance of the Rumanian people in its hour of need. On the night of March 26, 1944 the 2nd Ukrainian Front crossed the Prut. At the time the Rumanian Army had 31 divisions, including an armoured division. Seven divisions were in the Crimea, eight faced the 1st, 2nd and 3rd Ukrainian fronts and 16 were deployed in Rumania. Army Group A which covered the Balkan theatre at the end of March consisted of 64 divisions out of the 250 that were deployed on the Soviet-German front.

Lieutenant-General S. G. Trofimenko's 27th Army entered Rumania first. It was followed by the 40th Army under Lieutenant-General F. F. Zhmachenko. The right-wing units of Lieutenant-General K. A. Koroteyev's 52nd Army also crossed the Prut. The enemy put up a stubborn resistance.

By mid-May the Soviet troops had advanced more than 100 kilometres into Rumania, and reached the foothills of the Carpathians and the town of Jassy.

The working people in the liberated areas warmly welcomed the Soviet troops who, as they could see for themselves, were fulfilling a noble mission.

On April 2, 1944, in connection with the entry of the Soviet troops into Rumania, the Government of the USSR issued a statement which said that it did not intend to take over any part of Rumanian territory or alter the existing state system in Rumania, and that the entry of the Soviet troops into Rumania was dictated solely by military necessity and the continuing resistance of the enemy forces.

The main points set forth in the statement were expounded in a resolution passed by the State Defence Committee on April 10, 1944, instructing the Military Council of the 2nd Ukrainian Front to issue an address to the Rumanian people reaffirming the main points of the Soviet Government's statement of April 2. The resolution demanded that all existing Rumanian organs of power, the entire administrative, economic and political system and religious rites be left intact. It designated the procedure for the establishment of the Soviet Military Administration and specified its functions in the liberated areas. The State Defence Committee ordered the Front's Military Council to assume general supervision over the establishment of civilian administration and control its activity throughout the liberated areas of Rumania.

These documents enabled Rumania to withdraw from the unjust war and regain her freedom and independence.

The Soviet Military Administration in the liberated areas closely co-operated with the local organs of power. Transport was rehabilitated and communal services, industrial enterprises, schools and offices resumed work. Friendly relations were established between the Soviet troops and the population.

At the same time Rumanian patriots in the occupied parts of the country intensified their operations. Through the underground press the Communist Party of Rumania explained the substance of the Soviet statement to the population and called upon the toiling masses to intensify their struggle

against fascism and demand the cessation of the war against
the USSR.

Giving in to popular pressure Rumania's ruling circles
asked the Soviet Government about the terms on which Rumania could withdraw from the war. The armistice terms
which were presented to the Rumanian representative in
Cairo, Count Barbu Stirbey, on April 12 once again evidenced
the Soviet Union's desire to see Rumania regain her sovereignty. They envisaged: 1. Complete break with the Germans and joint struggle of the Rumanian troops and the
Allied troops, including the Red Army, against the Germans
with the view to re-establishing Rumania's independence and
sovereignty. 2. Re-establishment of the Soviet-Rumanian border in keeping with the terms of the 1940 treaty. 3. Reparations for direct damage caused to the Soviet Union by Rumania's military actions and occupation of Soviet territory.
4. Return of all Soviet and Allied prisoners of war and in-
ternees. 5. The Rumanian Government was to create conditions enabling the Soviet troops and also other Allied forces
to more freely in any direction on Rumanian territory if the
military situation made this necessary, and facilitate their
movement by placing all available land, water and air transport facilities at their disposal. 6. Agreement of the Soviet
Union to declare the Vienna award on Transylvania null and
void and to help liberate Transylvania.

Contrary to common sense the Antonescu government rejected these terms. It tried to conceal them from the knowledge of the people and decided to continue the war on nazi
Germany's side. Antonescu proclaimed yet another total mobilisation and fresh forces were hastily dispatched to the
front. Called out of the reserve, the Rumanian 4th Army
was rushed to Jassy where it joined the German 8th Army
in defending the line, Straz-Pascani—north of Jassy.

Determined to hold on to Rumania as a satellite and a
key strategic spring-board covering the Balkans, the German
Command strove desperately to push the Soviet troops out of
her northeastern areas and reduce the bridgeheads captured
by the 3rd Ukrainian Front on the west bank of the Dniester.
The Soviet Command, on its part, decided not only to hold
on to these bridgeheads, but also to enlarge them in preparation for a devastating blow that would smash the

southern wing of the Wehrmacht, force Rumania to withdraw from the war and also liberate the other Balkan states.

In the spring of 1944 the Soviet Command concentrated a powerful group consisting of the 40th, 27th, 52nd and 7th Guards Field armies, and a part of the 2nd and 6th Tank armies on a small area. The Germans, who had assembled a strong force against the 2nd Ukrainian Front holding dominating heights north of Jassy, unleashed a series of counterattacks, but sustained heavy casualties in manpower and equipment.

Especially heavy battles took place in May and early June when the German Command mounted an offensive in an attempt to hurl the Soviet troops back across the Prut. It concentrated a powerful force of 10 divisions, including four panzer divisions, at Jassy. On May 30 after a strong artillery barrage and a massive air strike the Germans attacked the 52nd and 27th armies. Fierce battles raged for seven days, in the course of which the Soviet troops displayed incredible staying power in the face of powerful panzer attacks.

The enemy failed to achieve his objective. At the cost of heavy casualties his troops managed to press the Soviet troops slightly back in some sectors. From May 30 to June 5, the enemy lost more than 27,000 officers and men, over 500 panzers and assault guns, and 366 aircraft. The heaviest losses were incurred by the 14th, 23rd and 24th Panzer divisions, the 3rd, 11th and 79th Infantry divisions, the 18th Jager Division and Das Grossdeutschland Motorised Infantry Division.

An important role in the liberation of Rumania was played by the 3rd Ukrainian Front, commanded by General R. Y. Malinovsky, which captured the key positions from which it subsequently mounted an offensive against the enemy's Jassy-Kishinev grouping.

By the middle of June 1944 the front's southern wing had stabilised along the Straz-Pascani north of Jassy-Orgeyev-Dubossary-Bendery line and then along the Dniester to the Black Sea, and remained that way until August 20, 1944.

THE SITUATION
ON THE BALKAN THEATRE
BY THE MIDDLE OF AUGUST 1944

The Soviet Army reached the main routes leading to the
Balkan states which for a long time were regarded as Europe's powder keg and a region where political relations
were among the most complicated in the world.

During the Second World War the situation in the Balkans became aggravated to the extreme. Having occupied
the region, nazi Germany instituted a regime of terror,
plunder and violence. The Balkans became a crucial source
of strategic raw and other materials for her armed forces.
A special role was played by Rumania which was Germany's
principal source of oil. From 1939 to 1944 she delivered 13.3
million tons of petroleum products to the Third Reich.[1] Hitler
said at a meeting in 1944 that he would rather lose Byelorussian forests than Rumanian oil. Moreover, Rumania supplied Germany with other products, including 1,378,000 tons
of grain, 75,147 tons of meat, 126,605 tons of vegetables and
fruits and 428,522 tons of timber.[2] It should also be borne
in mind that owing to their terrain and natural conditions
Rumania and other Balkan states were an important strategic theatre with good conditions for organising defence. The
German Command realised that with the fall of Rumania
Germany would also lose her Bulgarian and Hungarian allies. Therefore, it was determined to hold on to this region
at any cost, and build up a large force consisting of Army
Groups South Ukraine, F and E which totalled more than 80
divisions there.[3]

British and American imperialists also had predatory
plans regarding the Balkan states, intending to use them as
a *cordon sanitaire* against the Soviet Union. There is docu-
mentary proof that US representative Allen Dulles at the
secret separate talks at the end of 1943 in Switzerland with

---

[1] See *Dezvoltarea economică a Rumaniei 1944-1964,* Bucharest, 1964,
p. 12.

[2] *Analele institutului de istorie a partidului de pelinga C.C. al
P.M.R.* (further *Analele...*) No. 6, 1963, pp. 89-91.

[3] On August 1, 1944 Army Group South Ukraine had 56 divisions
and Army Groups F and E had 25.5 divisions.

Hitler Germany's representative Prince Hohenlohe said that it was necessary to support the creation of a *cordon sanitaire* against Bolshevism and Pan-Slavism by expanding Poland eastwards and preserving Rumania and a powerful Hungary.

In the opinion of Britain and the United States it was of utmost importance to enter the Balkans before the Soviet Army, whence they intended to move their troops northwards to bar the way for the Soviet Army to the countries of Central and Southwest Europe, prevent the victory of people's democratic revolutions, preserve the reactionary regimes in these countries and secure important positions for future military ventures. British Prime Minister Winston Churchill wrote in his memoirs that prior to the Allied landing in Sicily he had sent a cable to General Alexander imperatively demanding that he should prepare his troops for the seizure of the Balkans.

But the realisation of the imperialist plans was blocked by the growing might of the USSR, the major successes of the Soviet Army, the growth of the national liberation movement of the Balkan peoples and the flexible and yet determined foreign policy of the Soviet Union.

In the course of their offensive operations in the spring and early summer of 1944 in the south of the USSR the Soviet troops occupied an advantageous position vis-à-vis the enemy group in the Jassy-Kishinev area. The 2nd Ukrainian Front had enveloped the main forces of Army Group South Ukraine from the north, while the 3rd Ukrainian Front threatened them from the east. In June, July and August 1944 the Soviet forces in other sectors of the Soviet-German front carried out the large-scale Vyborg, Svirsk-Petrozavodsk, Byelorussian and Lvov-Sandomierz offensive operations. In the central, Warsaw-Berlin sector, Soviet forces advanced far to the west early in August and reached the Vistula on a wide frontage, smashing Army Groups Centre and North Ukraine, two of the four German army groups on the Soviet-German front. The Soviet Army ground down large enemy forces, including reserves transferred from Germany, the occupied countries of Europe and the neighbouring army groups, and greatly worsened the position of Army Group South Ukraine covering the Balkans. To strengthen Army Groups Centre and North Ukraine the German Command transferred 12 divisions, including a motorised division and six panzer divisions, from Army Group South Ukraine. The 4th Ukrainian Front which on August 5 went into action in the Carpathians between the 1st and 2nd Ukrainian fronts also tied down large enemy forces.

The loss of the Crimea had an extremely negative effect on the position of the German forces on the southern flank of the Soviet-German front. The Soviet Black Sea Fleet which had redeployed to Sevastopol and Odessa posed a serious threat to the Rumanian coast and interdicted the movement of enemy ships through the Bosporus and the Dardanelles.

Inspired by the Soviet Army's victories the Balkan peoples intensified their anti-fascist struggle and turned to more resolute actions. In Rumania the Communist Party succeeded in uniting the national liberation forces into a single front for struggle against Antonescu's fascist regime and for the liberation of their country. In May 1944 a united front of Communists and Social Democrats was formed and on June 20 an agreement was reached on the formation of a national democratic bloc which, in addition to the Communist Party of Rumania and the Social Democratic Party, included the bourgeois National Peasant and National Liberal parties. In other Balkan countries the Resistance Movement also gained in scope.

2. ROUT OF THE GERMAN
JASSY-KISHINEV GROUPING.
END OF THE FASCIST REGIME
IN RUMANIA

THE MILITARY AND POLITICAL
OBJECTIVES
OF THE JASSY-KISHINEV OPERATION

The Jassy-Kishinev Operation, one of the biggest operations of the Second World War, was carried out by the 2nd Ukrainian Front under General R. Y. Malinovsky[1] and the 3rd Ukrainian Front under the command of General F. I. Tolbukhin. It was supported by the Black Sea Fleet,

---

[1] He was appointed to this post on May 22, 1944.

the Danube Military Flotilla, long-range aviation and the partisans of Moldavia, and co-ordinated by GHQ representative Marshal S. K. Timoshenko.

General Friessner's Army Group South Ukraine which faced the Soviet forces was divided into two combat groups, Wöhler and Dumitrescu. The first group entrenched along a 270-kilometre front from Straz to the Prut consisted of the German 8th and the Rumanian 4th armies and the German 17th Corps. The second group consisting of the German 6th and the Rumanian 3rd armies was on the defensive along a front of 310 kilometres from the Prut to the Black Sea. All in all, the enemy had 47 divisions (25 German and 22 Rumanian), five Rumanian brigades, 15 separate regiments and 32 separate battalions. Army Group South Ukraine had more than 7,600 guns and mortars, over 400 panzers and assault guns. It was supported by 810 aircraft of the 4th Air Fleet and a Rumanian air corps, and its total manpower including the logistical units was over 900,000, of whom 565,000 were Germans. Besides, seven Rumanian divisions and about 60,000 German occupation troops were deployed inside Rumania. In case of need the German Command intended to throw Bulgarian and Hungarian troops into action on the southern wing of the Soviet-German front. The main German forces were assembled in the centre—in the Kishinev salient.

The enemy had a powerful defence system of several lines, each from 8 to 15 kilometres, and in the most vulnerable sectors up to 20 kilometres deep. In the Jassy sector, for instance, there were four defence lines extending to a depth of 80 kilometres. The first line passed along the heights north of Jassy, the second followed the Bahlui river, the third ran along the Mare Ridge and was called the Trajan Line. The fourth covered the 80-kilometre passage, called the Focsani Gate, between the Carpathians and the Danube. It consisted of 1,700 permanent emplacements, a ramified system of trenches, minefields, anti-tank blocks and ditches. Many inhabited localities were turned into strong-points. There were powerful defences also along the Dniester.

The Soviet Command took all these factors into account and prepared the operation most thoroughly. In July 1944, the commanders of the 2nd and 3rd Ukrainian fronts were summoned to GHQ where the concept and the plan of the operation were considered. Its military and political objective was to rout Army Group South Ukraine, complete the liberation of Moldavia and force Rumania to quit the war as Germany's ally. This would radically alter the military and political situation in the Balkans and create favourable conditions for liberating the countries of Southeastern Europe.

In keeping with the plan, the 2nd and 3rd Ukrainian fronts were to break through the enemy defences in two sectors far removed from each other (northwest of Jassy and south of Bendery) and then, developing the offensive along lines converging on the Husi-Vaslui sector, surround and wipe out the main forces of Army Group South Ukraine. After that an offensive was to be launched into the interior of Rumania.

In fulfilment of the general concept of the operation, and the tasks set by GHQ, the command of the 2nd Ukrainian Front decided to strike the main blow with its 27th, 52nd and 53rd Field armies, the 6th Tank Army and the 18th Tank Corps from an area northwest of Jassy in the direction of Vaslui and Falciu, and an auxiliary blow with the 7th Guards Army and a mechanised cavalry group (the 5th Guards Cavalry and the 23rd Tank corps) in the southerly direction along the Siret to cover the right flank of the strike group. By the end of the fifth day these forces were to reach the Bacau-Husi line, link up with the 3rd Ukrainian Front and together with it surround the enemy grouping at Kishinev. After that the Front's main forces, numbering more than 30 infantry divisions, two tank, one mechanised and one cavalry corps, were to push ahead on Focsani, forming the outer ring around the trapped enemy; the Front's left wing (17 infantry divisions and a tank corps) were to form the inner ring and together with the 3rd Ukrainian Front reduce the encircled enemy. The Front's flank armies also received their assignments: the 40th Army was to strike out in the direction of Tupilati and Piatra following the entry of the 7th Guards Army into the Tirgu-Frumos area, and the 4th Guards Army, after the 52nd Army liberated Jassy, was to open an offensive along the east bank of the Prut on Ungeny to cut off the enemy from river crossings. The 5th Air Army supported the land troops.

The command of the 3rd Ukrainian Front decided to launch its main attack from the Kitskan bridgehead south of Bendery. It was to be delivered by the 37th, 46th and 57th Field armies and the 4th Guards and the 7th Mechanised corps at the junction of the German 6th and the Rumanian 3rd armies, in the general direction of Husi where, after linking up with the troops of the 2nd Ukrainian Front, they were to close the ring around the enemy grouping at Kishinev. An auxiliary blow was to be dealt by the 46th Army's left wing in conjunction with the Danube Flotilla across the Dniester lagoon at Akkerman (Belgorod-Dniestrovsky). Once the strike group reached the Leovo-Tarutino-Moldavka line, the Soviet troops were to mount an offensive on Izmail and Reni to prevent the enemy from retreating across the Prut and the Danube. Seventeen infantry divisions, a mechanised corps and a tank brigade were detached for joint action with the 2nd Ukrainian Front on the inner ring of encirclement, and another 10 infantry divisions and three brigades were detached for action on the outer ring.

The 5th Strike Army was given a special assignment. Being on the defensive, it was to simulate preparations for an offensive in order to divert the German forces to Kishinev sector of the front and tie them down there. After the enemy began to withdraw, the army was to pursue him and liberate Kishinev. The 17th Air Army was to support the operations of the ground forces. An important role was to be played by the Black Sea Fleet which was ordered to cut the enemy's sea communications, land a task force at Akkerman and attack the ports of Sulina and Constanta.

It was an original plan that mirrored the enhanced level of Soviet military art. The directions of the main blows ensured a rapid breakthrough of the enemy defences and the fragmentation and encirclement of the German forces. The attack to be delivered by the 2nd Ukrainian Front was directed at the weakest spot in the enemy lines, avoiding fortified areas. As a result the Soviet troops were able to break up the enemy defence in a very important sector, cut off the German 6th Army from the 8th and bypass the rugged East Carpathians from the south. The echeloned order of battle of the Soviet divisions made it possible to build up the strength of the blows, rapidly push into the enemy defences,

smash his reserves and surround the grouping. The decision
to strike with the 3rd Ukrainian Front at the junction of
the German and Rumanian troops allowed the 3rd Ukrainian Front, together with the 2nd Ukrainian Front, to split
up Combat Group Dumitrescu and wipe out the German
6th Army and then rout the Rumanian 3rd Army in co-operation with the Black Sea Fleet.

It was planned that during the offensive the infantry
would advance from 20 to 25 kilometres and the mobile units
from 30-35 kilometres daily. This high pace would enable
the troops to capture the Focsani Gate on the eighth or ninth
day and then push swiftly into the central regions of Rumania. From there they could take the shortest route to the
Bulgarian and Yugoslav borders and also enter the Hungarian Plain in the rear of the enemy Carpathian group.
Skillful camouflage largely contributed to the success of the
operation which was prepared with such secrecy that the
enemy knew nothing about it until August 18.

Large forces—13 armies, including two air and one tank
—were assembled for the operation. The two fronts had over
90 divisions, six tank and mechanised corps, three fortified
areas and three brigades. The 2nd Ukrainian Front included
the Rumanian Tudor Vladimirescu Volunteer Division and a
Yugoslav brigade. The two fronts had 930,000 combatant
troops (1,250,000 including logistical units), 16,000 guns and
mortars (upwards of 76 mm calibre), more than 1,870 tanks
and self-propelled guns, and about 2,200 aircraft (including
naval aviation). The 2nd Ukrainian Front which was to play
the main role in the operation had 50 per cent more manpower and means than its neighbour on the left. A part of
the Black Sea Fleet and the Danube Military Flotilla commanded by Rear Admiral S. G. Gorshkov, which was under
the fleet's operational control, were also involved.

The Soviet Command had a 1.8-fold superiority in the
number of divisions, 1.4-fold in manpower, more than two-
fold in artillery and aircraft, and 4.5-fold in tanks. The superiority of the Soviet forces in the breakthrough sectors was
even greater, from four to six times.

Serious political and educational work was carried on
among the Soviet troops who had to fulfill the very difficult
task of crushing powerful defences and fighting on the terri-

tory of a state whose army continued to take part in the war against the USSR. On the eve of the offensive the Military Council of the 2nd Ukrainian Front issued a directive which said: "It should be explained to the troops that we are now fighting on alien territory and that every officer and man should display a high degree of vigilance and discipline and resolutely suppress any manifestations of negligence, gullibility and indiscipline. The Rumanian civilian population should be treated with dignity and not be subject to any arbitrary actions." The Military Council of the 3rd Ukrainian Front issued a similar directive. The commanders, political officers and Party and Komsomol organisations explained to the men that the Soviet Army was fulfilling its internationalist mission by liberating Rumania and described the just, liberatory aims pursued by the Soviet Union in the war.

While preparations for the operation were in progress, membership of the Party organisations in companies increased considerably. A total of 38,355 men were accepted to full and probational Party membership in the troops of the 3rd Ukrainian Front alone.

Thoroughly prepared, the operation was carried out in strict conformity with the plan.

THE BREAKTHROUGH
AND THE ENCIRCLEMENT
OF THE ENEMY JASSY-KISHINEV GROUP

The two fronts went into action in the morning of August 20. Thousands of guns and planes pounded enemy positions. On the first day the 2nd Ukrainian Front pierced the enemy's tactical defence zone in the direction of the main attack to a depth of 16 kilometres, reached the third line of defence and routed up to five enemy divisions. The 3rd Ukrainian Front completed the breakthrough of the enemy's main defence line to a depth of 10-12 kilometres and in places wedged into the second line of defence, routing four divisions.

The enemy sustained serious casualties. The heavily mauled Rumanian army was staggered. Commander of Army Group South Ukraine General Friessner admitted that the results of the fighting on August 20 were catastrophic. "In Combat

Group Dumitrescu," he wrote, "the two Rumanian divisions (4th Mountain Infantry and 21st Infantry) of the 29th Army Corps completely disintegrated. Five Rumanian divisions of Combat Group Wöhler were totally smashed."[1] The German Command made a futile attempt to stop the Soviet drive by transferring one panzer and three infantry divisions to the Jassy area. The Soviet Command moved large tank units into the breach which exploited the success and initiated pursuit of the battered enemy units which were retreating in disorder. A vast number of Soviet infantry, a thousand tanks, three thousand guns and mortars, hundreds of rocket launchers supported by attack aircraft, bombers and fighters swept to the south.

The mass heroism of the Soviet troops confirmed Lenin's words that realisation of the just character of the war raised the morale of the soldiers and enabled them to endure incredible difficulties.

By nightfall on August 21 the enemy defence had been overrun. The 2nd Ukrainian Front widened the breach up to 65 kilometres along the front and 40 kilometres in depth, overcame three defence lines, captured Jassy and Tirgu Frumos and reached an area which gave them greater operational freedom. The troops of the 3rd Ukrainian Front sliced the enemy defence to a depth of 30 kilometres, widened the breach up to 95 kilometres and created conditions for cutting off the German 6th Army from the Rumanian 3rd Army.

The land forces had the effective assistance of the 5th and 17th air armies whose pilots made 6,350 sorties in two days. The Black Sea Fleet's air army attacked enemy ships and bases, dealing especially heavy strikes at Constanta.

The German Command failed to alter the course of events to any substantial degree, although it exhausted all its operational reserves in the first two days. As regards the commanders of the 2nd and 3rd Ukrainian Fronts they still had 25 uncommitted infantry divisions at their disposal. As a result, the Soviet troops were in an advantageous position to surround the enemy in the Kishinev salient. Therefore, in the evening of August 21, GHQ ordered the front commanders to close the ring of encirclement at Husi without delay

---

[1] Hans Friessner, *Verratene Schlachten*, Hamburg, 1965, p. 69.

and thus open the road for the Soviet troops to the key economic and political centres of Rumania.

In these circumstances on August 22 Hitler sanctioned the withdrawal of his troops from the Kishinev salient to the line between Mare Ridge and the river Prut. The Soviet Army, however, interfered with the orderly withdrawal. By nightfall on August 22 the 2nd and 3rd Ukrainian fronts reached the Prut ahead of the enemy forces and almost completely encircled them at Husi. On the same day the sailors of the Danube Flotilla jointly with a commando party of the 46th Army performed a heroic exploit. They forced the 11-kilometre wide Dniester lagoon, liberated Akkerman and thus helped to encircle the Rumanian 3rd Army.

The successful actions of the Soviet troops on August 22 had a major impact on the development of the entire operation. On that day the enemy's resistance was finally crushed and he was no longer capable of restoring the situation. In three days the Soviet troops smashed 11 Rumanian and four German divisions and shot down 114 enemy aircraft. The 2nd Ukrainian Front advanced 60 kilometres, widened the breach up to 120 kilometres and liberated more than 200 large inhabited localities. The 3rd Ukrainian Front pushed ahead 70 kilometres and widened the breach up to 130 kilometres. A complete encirclement of the enemy forces was now inevitable. On August 23, the enemy grouping was on the whole trapped. Former commander of Army Group South Ukraine, General Friessner, wrote that by nightfall on August 23 the encirclement of the German 6th Army was an accomplished fact.[1] The Soviet troops liberated Birlad and Roman and came up to Bacau. The 3rd Ukrainian Front enlarged the breach up to 350 kilometres along the front and up to 110 kilometres in depth.

By the evening of August 24 the ring was tightly sealed around the enemy Kishinev group at Husi. Eighteen enemy divisions were trapped. The Rumanian soldiers who refused to fight for interests alien to them surrendered en masse. The remnants of the Rumanian 4th Army were retreating in disorder to the south, while the Rumanian 3rd Army consisting of four divisions and one brigade was encircled and laid down

---

[1] Hans Friessner, *op. cit.*, p. 84.

arms. The investment of a large enemy group brought to an end the first phase of the Jassy-Kishinev operation.

The excellent work of the staffs headed by Colonel-Generals M. V. Zakharov and S. S. Biryuzov played an exceptionally important role in ensuring the success of the entire operation.

THE OVERTHROW OF RUMANIA'S
MILITARY FASCIST REGIME
AND HER WITHDRAWAL
FROM THE WAR
AGAINST THE SOVIET UNION

By routing Army Group South Ukraine, the Soviet Army deprived the nazis and the fascist regime in Rumania of their military support in the country. This created favourable external conditions for overthrowing the fascist regime and pulling Rumania out of the war. Internal conditions for this were also maturing. Antonescu regime's anti-Soviet policy placed the country on the verge of catastrophe; the contradictions between the working people and the fascist regime became aggravated to the extreme, and discord among the ruling circles heightened. This was most vividly manifested in the desire of the palace circles and the leaders of bourgeois and landlord parties to dissociate themselves from the policy of the fascist regime. The king and his courtiers came to realise that the only way out of the crisis was to get rid of the Antonescu clique and thus avoid sharing its fate, and were forced to agree with the plan for an armed uprising worked out by the Communist Party of Rumania.

At first, in connection with the beginning of the Soviet offensive, representatives of the palace circles and the Communist Party of Rumania at a secret meeting on August 20 decided to begin the uprising on August 24-26. But the events at the front created favourable conditions for launching it on August 23. "The Central Committee of the Party," said Gheorghe Gheorghiu-Dej, "chose the moment for overthrowing Antonescu's fascist dictatorship and involving Rumania in a just war against fascist Germany in connection with the favourable conditions created by the Soviet troops in the Jassy-Kishinev sector."[1] Therefore, when the Communist

[1] G. Gheorghiu-Dej, *op. cit.*, p. 222.

Party leadership learned that the head of the fascist government, Ion Antonescu, intended to visit the king on August 23 to seek his support in continuing the war against the Soviet Union, it was decided to arrest him and launch the uprising.

The anti-fascist uprising began on August 23, 1944 in Bucharest under the leadership of the Communist Party of Rumania and resulted in the overthrow of the Antonescu dictatorship.

Under a pre-arranged plan agreed with the Communist Party the royal guard arrested Antonescu and his associates in the palace and turned them over to an armed detachment of the Communist Party which kept them in custody pending their handing over to the Soviet Command. The palace circles and leaders of bourgeois parties formed a new government with General Constantin Sanatescu at the head. Most of the members were reactionary-minded officers and civil servants, while the parties of the National Democratic Bloc had only one representative each who were given the post of ministers without portfolios.

The new government announced Rumania's withdrawal from the Axis, and its acceptance of the armistice terms and ordered Rumanian troops to cease operations against the Soviet Army.

Scared of the possible results of an armed uprising the king and his courtiers wanted to limit the August 23 action to a change of government and prevent the participation of the broad masses in the uprising. But their hopes were dashed when the arrest of the Antonescu government set off the armed uprising. In response to the Communist Party's appeal armed detachments of patriotic workers and units of the Bucharest garrison on the night of August 24 occupied government buildings and strategic points in the capital and then began to disarm the German troops in the city. The fascist regime crumbled before it could organise resistance. Gheorghe Gheorghiu-Dej pointed out that the decisive factor of the overthrow of the Antonescu regime on August 23, 1944 was the breakthrough of the German front in Moldavia and the Soviet Army's fast advance on Bucharest.[1]

Upon receiving news about the events in Bucharest Hitler ordered the German troops to crush the uprising, arrest the

[1] See Gheorghe Gheorghiu-Dej, *op. cit.*, p. 347.

king and the nobility and set up a government headed by a general friendly to Germany. Criminal plans were being hatched against the Rumanian people. Reporting to Hitler about Rumania's withdrawal from the Axis, Field-Marshal Keitel and General Guderian proposed that everything should be done "that Rumania should disappear from the map of Europe and that the Rumanian people should cease to exist as a nation."[1] The commander of Army Group South Ukraine was given extraordinary powers for action in Rumania. In the morning of August 24, 1944 the Luftwaffe bombed Bucharest. At the same time a hastily assembled group of 6,000 German troops mounted an offensive on Bucharest with orders to link up with the German units stationed in the city and unleash bloody reprisals against the population. General Gerstenberg was put in command of the operation to crush the uprising.

At first the balance of forces was in favour of the Germans who had about 8,000 troops in the city and about 6,000 in its suburbs. The patriotic forces taking part in the uprising consisted of approximately 7,000 armymen and 50 armed workers' groups.[2] The German Command intended to transfer a part of the 25,000-strong force stationed in Ploesti and also troops from other parts of the country to Bucharest and pinned great hopes on the para-military organisations of Rumanian Germans which had about 40,000 members.[3] It also planned to bring in troops from Yugoslavia and Bulgaria. But as more and more Rumanian troops arrived in the city, the balance of forces began to change in favour of the insurgents. By August 28 the number of Rumanian troops in Bucharest reached 39,000 and the total strength of the patriotic detachments rose to 2,000.[4] Repulsing the attacks of the German forces, units of Bucharest garrison and the patriotic detachments attacked and routed the German garrison. By August 29 the Rumanian patriots had cleared the city with its environs of the enemy and held it until the arrival of the Soviet Army. In the course of the fighting the

[1] *Analele...* No. 4, 1964, p. 31.
[2] See *Romania in razboiul antihitlerist*, Bucharest, 1966, p. 68.
[3] *Ibid.*, p. 45.
[4] *Ibid.*, p. 87.

Rumanian patriots took prisoner about 7,000 German officers and men, including their commander General Gerstenberg. There were armed clashes with the German forces in Ploesti, Brasov and in a number of other cities and regions.

At this historical turning point, when the anti-fascist uprising broke out in Bucharest, the Soviet Union and its army came to the assistance of the Rumanian people. Immediately upon being informed of the events of August 23, the Soviet Government broadcast a statement reaffirming its stand towards Rumania proclaimed on April 2, 1944. The statement noted that the USSR had no wish to take over any part of Rumanian territory or change the existing state system in the country, and that it wanted to restore Rumania's independence jointly with the Rumanians and to liberate the country from the nazis. The statement went on to say that if the Rumanian troops ceased operations against the Soviet Army and pledged to wage a war of liberation against the nazi invaders side by side with the Soviet forces, the Soviet Army would not disarm them, but would allow them to keep all their arms and do everything in its power to help them fulfil this honourable task.

This statement proved to be of great help to the Rumanian people in their fight against the nazi invaders. It indicated a realistic path leading towards the country's swiftest liberation and provided the Rumanian people and its army with an opportunity to play their part in routing nazi Germany.

The Soviet Union's principled stand was a blow at the plans of the Rumanian reactionary circles which hoped to prevent the country from joining the war against nazi Germany and come to an agreement with the German Command on a "free" withdrawal of its troops from Rumanian territory.[1]

---

[1] In the evening of August 23 King Michael invited the German Minister in Rumania Killinger and informed him that Rumania was withdrawing from the Axis. He also assured him that he did not want to wage a war against Germany and that the German troops were free to withdraw from Rumania without hindrance on the part of the Rumanian Government (A. Hillgruber, *Hitler, König Carol und Marschall Antonescu*, Wiesbaden, 1954, pp. 217-18).

Serious tasks faced the Rumanian people: it had to withstand the onslaught of the German forces holding hinterland areas, consolidate the victory of the uprising, protect the country's borders against an invasion by German and Horthy's troops and jointly with the Soviet Army drive the nazis out of the country. These tasks were all the more difficult because the main forces of the Rumanian Army were demoralised by their defeat in the Jassy-Kishinev operation and were unable effectively to assist the insurgents at the crucial period of the struggle against the Germans.

In this complicated situation it was most important that the Soviet Army should act with the utmost determination against the Wehrmacht to frustrate the German Command's efforts to put down the uprising of the Rumanian people. First and foremost, the Soviet Command took steps to complete the rout of the German Army Group South Ukraine within the shortest possible time and liberate the whole of Rumania from the nazi invaders.

LIQUIDATION
OF THE ENCIRCLED ENEMY,
LIBERATION OF CENTRAL
AND SOUTHERN RUMANIA

Having surrounded the Jassy-Kishinev group, the 2nd and 3rd Ukrainian fronts began to reduce it, using a part of their forces, while the rest launched a swift offensive into the interior of Rumania, liberating her from the Germans. The second phase of the Jassy-Kishinev operation began.

For five days from August 25 to 29 the Soviet troops were locked in bloody battles with the surrounded enemy. The German Command made a desperate effort to pull out its 6th Army which was trying to reach the crossings on the Prut at any cost. But it was a hopeless venture, for its way was barred by the 37th Army under Lieutenant-General M. N. Sharokhin. The command and HQ of the 6th Army abandoned their troops and fled to the Carpathians. It is possible to judge of the intensity of the fighting by the fact that on August 25 alone, the 3rd Ukrainian Front wiped up to 30,000 and took prisoner more than 20,000 German officers and men. The enemy group surrounded west of the

Prut was destroyed by the end of August 27. Only a small part of the enemy forces managed to cross the Prut. This force, however, was also surrounded and by nightfall on August 29 it was wiped out by the 2nd Ukrainian Front at Husi, west of the Prut. Scattered enemy groups which had remained in the forests and managed to cross the Siret were mopped up in the next few days.

The German troops who had broken out of the encirclement were wiped out with the participation of the Rumanian Tudor Vladimirescu 1st Volunteer Division under Colonel Nikolai Cambrae, which went into battle for the first time on August 29 south of the Vaslui. The Rumanian troops killed 300 and took prisoner more than 400 German officers and men, losing only 26 of their own men.[1]

By September 4 the remnants of the enemy group surrounded at Jassy and Kishinev had been completely wiped out. It was a great victory for the Soviet arms and a major defeat for the Wehrmacht. Eighteen out of the 25 divisions of Army Group South Ukraine were surrounded and destroyed.

While a part of the troops of the 2nd and 3rd Ukrainian fronts were fighting against the invested enemy troops at Kishinev, their main forces were driving into the interior of Rumania in three prongs towards the Carpathians, Focsani and the sea.

Events which proved to be of decisive importance for Rumania developed in the Focsani sector.

Putting up fierce resistance in deliberate defence lines the Germans made desperate efforts to slow down the pace of the Soviet offensive and win time to reconstitute the front. In its directive of August 26, the German High Command ordered General Friessner to build and hold defences along the Eastern Carpathians-Focsani-Galati line, defend the area of Galati, the Danube south of Bucharest, Bucharest, Ploesti, Braila and regain control of the Danube between Galati and the mouth of the river. This was an unrealistic task, for the Command of Army Group South Ukraine lacked the necessary strength, commanding only the remnants of seven German divisions. Deployed along the Hungarian-Ru-

---

[1] *Romania in razboiul antihitlerist*, pp. 138-39.

manian border, mainly facing the right wing of the 2nd
Ukrainian Front, were nine frontier and 20 Transylvanian
battalions of the Hungarians, while the remnants of retreating units and elements and also the logistical units of the
army group and separate German garrisons in Rumania were
facing the left flank of the 2nd Ukrainian Front and the
3rd Ukrainian Front.

The left-wing armies of the 2nd Ukrainian Front, fighting in the main Focsani-Bucharest sector, were rapidly pushing to the south, crushing individual strong-points in the
enemy defences. Having smashed the German troops holding defences along the Focsani fortified line, the 6th Tank
Army on August 26 liberated the town of Focsani. On August 27 it drove the enemy out of Rimnicu Sarat and came
up to Buzau. The enemy defended Buzau with exceptional
stubbornness, since it opened the way for the Soviet troops
to Ploesti and Bucharest. With the fall of Buzau the position of the enemy forces retreating to the southwest deteriorated to a still greater extent, for they intended to use this
route to withdraw into Transylvania. On August 29 the 6th
Tank Army reached Ploesti and units of other Soviet
armies entered Tulcea, Galati, Piatra, Sulina, Braila and
Constanta.

A very difficult task was assigned to the 2nd Ukrainian
Front's right-wing armies operating in the Carpathians where
the retreating divisions of the German 8th Army took advantage of the mountainous and wooded terrain to put up
a furious resistance. Nevertheless, the Soviet troops managed
to cross the Eastern Carpathians and on August 27 General
S. I. Gorshkov's mechanised cavalry task force reached the
pass.

In the south of Rumania the 3rd Ukrainian Front, advancing along the Danube, routed scattered groups of German troops preventing their transfer to Bucharest.

Thus, the Soviet Army's swift actions thwarted the German Command's attempts to assemble sufficient forces to
suppress the uprising. "The powerful offensive launched by
the Soviet Army on August 20 in the Jassy-Kishinev sector,
which resulted in the defeat of the main grouping of nazi
forces in the country and the development of a liberatory
offensive," Rumanian historians note, "placed the German

Command in a position in which it was unable to draw off forces from the front and throw them against the insurgents."[1]

An important factor contributing to the success of the Rumanian insurgents was the defeat of the enemy forces at Ploesti and the entry of the Soviet troops into Bucharest. At Ploesti the Soviet troops and the Rumanian patriotic forces had to batter down the obstinate resistance of the German forces whom the Führer ordered "at all costs" to hold on to this key oil region and communications centre. The Soviet-Rumanian comradeship-in-arms manifested itself vividly in the battles for the liberation of Ploesti, the second largest centre of insurrection after Bucharest. On the night of August 23 detachments of armed workers and units of the local garrison drove the German guards from the oilfields in the city's suburbs. The Germans blockaded the city and prepared to take it by assault. They had a considerable numerical superiority over the insurgents and more than 100 aircraft, tanks, an armoured train and much artillery at their disposal.[2]

The Soviet Command took all measures to prevent the Germans from smashing the Rumanian insurgents and wrecking oil industry enterprises thus causing enormous harm to the uprising and the Rumanian economy, and ordered the 6th Tank Army to liberate Ploesti by a swift thrust.

Using anti-aircraft guns against the Soviet tanks, the Germans tried to stop the Soviet forces at the distant approaches to the city. Their resistance, however, was swiftly crushed and by the morning of August 30 the 5th Guards Tank Corps and the 3rd Guards Airborne Division operating in conjunction with elements of the Rumanian 18th Infantry Division which had withdrawn from the front and the Rumanian units sealed in the city, routed the enemy at Ploesti. The Soviet and Rumanian troops overpowered the enemy grouping and liberated the entire oil-bearing province which was placed under the protection of the Soviet 180th Infantry Division.

---

[1] Popesku-Putzuri (et al.), *Rumania in the Second World War*, Bucharest, 1964, p. 88.

[2] *August 1944-Mai 1945*, Bucharest, 1969, pp. 67, 69.

Commenting on the fall of Ploesti, the former nazi General Buttlar wrote that from the military-economic point of view it was the heaviest and perhaps even the decisive blow for Germany. Moreover, it lifted the threat to Bucharest from the north.

As a part of the Soviet forces attacked Ploesti, the 6th Tank and the 53rd armies made a spurt to Bucharest thus directly assisting the insurgent Rumanian patriots.

On August 30 and 31 the Soviet troops and the Rumanian Tudor Vladimirescu Division entered Bucharest already liberated by the Rumanian patriots. The capital's population gave them a joyous welcome.

The entry of the Soviet forces into Bucharest consolidated the victory of the armed uprising in Rumania and dashed the hopes of the reactionary elements for a landing of Anglo-American paratroops in Bucharest to support their fight against the country's democratic forces. By the beginning of September a large part of Rumania had been cleared of the German invaders by the combined efforts of the Soviet troops and the Rumanian patriots.

THE RESULTS OF THE JASSY-
KISHINEV OPERATION

Taking into account its strategic, military and political results, the Jassy-Kishinev Operation was one of the most important campaigns carried out by the Soviet Army in the Great Patriotic War.

It ended in the rout of the large strategic Army Group South Ukraine, eighteen of whose divisions were encircled and wiped out. The shattering defeat sustained by the Wehrmacht sharply altered the entire strategic situation on the southern wing of the Soviet-German front and led to the collapse of the German defences in the Balkan strategic sector. The Soviet troops were now in a position to envelop the nazi Germany's entire southern strategic flank, and also to destroy in conjunction with the 4th Ukrainian Front the enemy forces in Transylvania.

The operation with especial clarity manifested the interconnection between politics and strategy. By solving strategic tasks the Soviet troops attained crucial political objectives. They completed the liberation of Soviet Moldavia, created conditions for the victory of the anti-fascist uprising in Rumania, her withdrawal from the war on the side of the fascist bloc and liberation from the German invaders. The Soviet Army could now advance towards the borders of Bulgaria, Yugoslavia and Hungary and assist them in casting off the fascist yoke. As a result of the victory of the people's uprising, Rumania not only withdrew from the fascist bloc but turned her guns against nazi Germany.

Shortly after the August armed uprising and the entry of the Soviet troops into Bucharest, a Rumanian government delegation arrived in Moscow where on September 12, 1944 it signed an armistice agreement with the USSR, the USA and Britain. By signing this agreement the Soviet Government displayed a basically new approach to a defeated country. It was guided not by a feeling of revenge towards a country which had taken part in aggression against the Soviet Union, but by principles of proletarian internationalism and the desire to help her people. The main terms of the agreement envisaged the speediest liberation of the country from the nazi invaders, victory over nazi Germany, weeding out of fascism in Rumania and the creation of conditions for her democratic and independent development. The Rumanian Government undertook to put up not less than 12 divisions for action against nazi Germany. The agreement reaffirmed the inviolability of the Soviet-Rumanian border established by the 1940 Treaty. An Allied Control Commission consisting of Soviet, American and British representatives was set up in Rumania to observe the fulfilment of the terms of the argeement.

The Rumanian people and world democratic forces welcomed the terms of the armistice agreement proposed by the Soviet Union. The *Rumania libera* wrote on September 20, 1944: "...the armistice agreement reasserts the fact that the Soviet Union is pursuing a policy of rendering fraternal assistance to the peoples in their struggle for independence, for creating a better life for the toiling people in the struggle against all exploitation and oppression." Even the bourgeois newspaper *Semnalul* in an article published on the same day noted that the Soviet Union "in spite of its strength did not demand annexations and in no way insulted" the Rumanian people, that "it respects our territorial integrity" and that "friendship with it means life and freedom" for Rumania. The democratic forces headed by the Communist Party of Rumania began a campaign for Rumania's active participation in the war against nazi Germany together with the Soviet Army so as to hasten her liberation from the German invaders.

3. RUMANIA IS FREE

THE BIRTH OF SOVIET- RUMANIAN
COMRADERSHIP-IN-ARMS

Now that the Rumanian Army had turned its guns against nazi Germany, the Soviet Command had to take practical steps to promote the comradeship-in-arms of the Soviet and Rumanian troops. This co-operation was built on the principles of friendship, equality, mutual assistance and respect for national customs and features, on the basis of the community of tasks in the joint struggle against the nazi invaders, for Rumania's freedom and independence.

The first sprouts of this co-operation appeared in the period of the Jassy-Kishinev Operation. In the beginning it involved the Tudor Vladimirescu 1st Volunteer Division, followed by individual units of the Rumanian Army which after the August armed uprising established contact with the Soviet Army in order to conduct joint operations against the Wehrmacht. The 3rd Frontier Regiment under Colonel N. Teodorescu was the first unit of the Rumanian royal army to begin acting in co-operation with the Soviet troops. On the night of August 23, it contacted the Soviet Command and as part of the 40th Army of the 2nd Ukrainian Front went into action in the East Carpathians. The Rumanian 103rd Mountain Infantry Division commanded by Brigadier General Ilie Cretzulescu went over to the side of the Soviet 7th Guards Army. From August 26 to 28 the commanders of a number of Rumanian Army units expressed their desire to fight against the German troops. The bulk of the Rumanian troops in the field, however, was demoralised and unfit to participate in the fighting against the German troops in the first days of uprising. Practical co-operation with the main forces of the Rumanian Army was only established at the beginning of September.

The Soviet Command had to contend with very considerable difficulties inasmuch as it had to organise co-operation between a socialist army and a royal army most of whose divisions had been fighting against the Soviet forces right up to August 23 and included a large number of pro-fascist officers. What made things still more difficult was that the Soviet and Rumanian troops were in direct contact with the enemy.

Nevertheless, the co-operation between the Soviet and Rumanian troops was established within a fairly short space of time. While the Soviet forces were pursuing the remnants of the routed Army Group South Ukraine retreating to the west, the main forces of the Rumanian Army covered Rumania's western and northwestern borders. The ten Rumanian divisions and separate frontier units that were deployed north of the passes in the Southern Carpathians had orders to hold on to these passes.[1]

The German Command, which had assembled the remnants of the retreating units of Army South Ukraine in Transylvania, tried to reconstitute the front and together with Horthy's troops strike a blow at the Rumanian Army, rout it and capture the important passes in the Southern Carpathians prior to the arrival of the Soviet forces. On August 29 the German General Staff ordered General Friessner's army group to re-establish the strategic front. The Germans wanted to link up the southern flank of Army Group South Ukraine with Army Group F in Yugoslavia and thus establish a continuous front along the Eastern and Southern Carpathians and the Western Balkans. The German General Staff also instructed the German units which had been transferred to Transylvania to take over the passes immediately.

Having mustered a fairly large force, the Germans launched an offensive against the Rumanian troops. At dawn on

---

[1] At the beginning of September the Rumanian Army had nine battleworthy divisions, the remnants of seven crippled divisions which had returned from the front and 21 training divisions. The army was short of artillery and had almost no tanks.

December 5 six German and Hungarian divisions supported by armour and aircraft struck out from Cluj at the Rumanian 4th Army which had just reached the pre-war northern border and had no time to organise defence. On the first day the enemy advanced 20 to 30 kilometres. The Rumanian Command tried to deploy the army's main forces along the river Mures but the enemy forestalled this move and in the next two days managed to advance another 20-25 kilometres. Simultaneously the Germans launched an offensive against the Rumanian 1st Army which covered the northwestern border. On September 6 they crossed the Danube at Bela Crkva and at a point 32 kilometres south of Turnu Severin, and pressed back the Rumanian 1st Army and captured several inhabited localities, including the towns of Beius, Arad and Ineu, threatening Timisoara and the industrial centre of Resita.

In this difficult situation it was necessary to put the Soviet and Rumanian troops under a single command. On September 6 with the agreement of the Rumanian Government the Rumanian 1st and 4th armies, the 4th Separate Army and the 1st Air Corps, an infantry brigade and an armour group, 20 divisions in all, were subordinated to the commander of the 2nd Ukrainian Front. The Rumanian divisions had 138,000 officers and men armed with 8,159 submachine guns, 6,500 machine guns, 1,809 mortars, 611 guns and 113 combat-worthy aircraft.[1]

THE COUNTERBLOW IS FOILED.
LIBERATION
OF RUMANIA'S WESTERN
AND NORTHWESTERN REGIONS

The Jassy-Kishinev Operation over, GHQ on August 29 ordered the Soviet troops to complete the rout of the German forces in Rumania. The left wing of the 2nd Ukrainian Front (the 27th and 53rd field armies, the 6th Tank Army

---

[1] Figures quoted according to data furnished by the Rumanian General Staff to the Soviet Command. In the latter half of October another two infantry divisions were placed under the control of the 2nd Ukrainian Front. From September 20 to October 5 the 2nd Ukrainian Front had 23 Rumanian divisions, including the Tudor Vladimirescu Division, an air corps, an infantry brigade and a tank group in its composition.

and the 18th Army Corps) operating in the main direction was to push forward to Ploesti, Slatina and Turnu Severin and reach Rumania's border with Bulgaria along the Danube between Turnu Severin and Giurgiu. The front's right-wing 40th Army, the 7th Guards Army and General Gorshkov's mechanised cavalry task force were to advance in the Eastern Carpathians and reach the line Bistrita-Cluj-Aiud-Sibiu by mid-September. After that, under the cover of the main forces of its right-wing armies, the front was to strike out in the general direction of Satu Mare to help the 4th Ukrainian Front cross the Carpathians and reach Uzhgorod and Mukachevo. The 3rd Ukrainian Front was to co-operate with the Danube Flotilla, liberate Northern Dobruja, cross the Danube and reach the Rumanian-Bulgarian border. The Front fulfilled the assignment and by nightfall on September 5 its troops reached the Rumanian-Bulgarian border between Giurgiu and the Black Sea.

The offensive of German-Hungarian forces against the Rumanian troops and the slow progress of the right wing of the 2nd Ukrainian Front made it necessary to change the direction of the Front's main attack. On September 5 GHQ ordered the Front's main forces to turn abruptly to the north and northwest and, striking out from the south through Brasov and Sibiu in the direction of Cluj, and from the area of Slatina at Petroseni and Deva, cross the Southern and Eastern Carpathians and in co-operation with its right-wing forces advance deep into Northern Transylvania. In this way they would assist the Rumanian troops which were repelling the enemy's offensive, and also the 4th Ukrainian Front which was advancing across the Carpathians into Slovakia where a popular uprising against the German invaders flared up on August 29. After that the Front's main forces were to reach the Tisza between Nyiregyhaza and Szeged. The defence of the Danube between Turnu Severin and Giurgiu was entrusted to the 75th Infantry Corps of the 53rd Army and the Rumanian 4th Army Corps.

Turning sharply to the north, the 27th Army and the 6th Tank Army moved to the assistance of the Rumanian 4th Army, while the 53rd Army and the 18th Tank Corps pushed ahead to help the Rumanian 1st Army. The 5th Air Army supported the land forces pushing ahead in difficult mountain terrain. The Luftwaffe incessantly bombed the narrow mountain roads. The tanks negotiated the heights with difficulty. Every yard of mountain roads in the Southern Carpathians was drenched with the sweat and blood of the Soviet troops.

And yet they were in time to help the allied Rumanian armies. It is recorded in the diary of the Rumanian 4th Army that the Soviet Army arrived at the most crucial moment of the fighting and Soviet armour helped to beat off the ferocious attacks of the enemy who strove to seize the passes in the Southern Carpathians.[1] On September 7 the 6th Tank Army successfully crossed this mountain range and reached Sibiu. Combining their efforts, the Soviet and Rumanian forces stopped the enemy drive. Repulsing a renewed series of powerful attacks, the 6th Tank and the Rumanian 4th armies went over to an offensive and drove the Germans back. The heaviest fighting took place at Turda where the 6th Tank Army lost more than 2,000 men in killed and wounded.

By nightfall on September 15, the Soviet 27th Army and the 6th Tank Army and the Rumanian 4th Army threw the enemy back to his September 5 positions and reached his main defence line along the Mures and the Ariesul. In ten days the 2nd Ukrainian Front's assault group advanced 180 to 250 kilometres.

Even General Friessner noted that the Soviet troops acted skilfully and swiftly. "The Soviet Command," he wrote, "realised the danger threatening its troops in the passes. It rapidly turned a field army, some of whose units had already reached Turda, in a new direction and also pulled up its 6th Tank Army through the Vulkan and Red Passes to the battle zone. As a result of increased enemy resistance, our counter-offensive petered out already on the following day."[2]

The 53rd Army and the 18th Tank Corps, which came to the assistance of the Rumanian 1st Army at Resita, in the Crisul Alb Valley, at the approaches to Timisoara and elsewhere, likewise acted with courage and speed.

---

[1] Nicolae Ciachir, Leonida Loghin, *Fratia de arme romino-sovietica*, Bucharest, 1959, pp. 71-72.
[2] Hans Friessner, *op. cit.*, pp. 113-14.

Soviet and Rumanian forces jointly repulsed enemy attacks on the large industrial centre of Timisoara. "The arrival of the Soviet troops considerably strengthened the defence of this industrial centre and the Banat railway junction. After the Soviet troops had replaced the Rumanian forces the enemy launched several more attacks, all of which were beaten off."[1]

By rapid and skilful actions the Soviet troops prevented the enemy from seizing the passes in this area. Fighting courageously side by side with the Soviet Army, the Rumanian forces retained their hold of the passes in the Southern Carpathians, thus enabling the Soviet troops to pull through the passes in good time and come to their assistance.

The broad manoeuvre of the 2nd Ukrainian Front's main forces across the Southern Carpathians not only overturned the German Command's plans of smashing the Rumanian troops and capturing the passes, but made the entire German-Hungarian grouping vulnerable to a smashing outflanking blow.

It was only in the middle of September that the German Command, for the first time after the defeat at Jassy and Kishinev, managed to put up a defence line before the 2nd Ukrainian Front.[2] The Germans concentrated up to 27 divisions, including six panzer and motorised divisions of the Hungarian 2nd and 3rd and the German 8th armies.

Throughout the latter half of September there was heavy fighting in this sector of the front, particularly in Northern Transylvania. Having strengthened his forces in the Cluj-Turda area with four divisions, the enemy undertook a series of powerful counterattacks against the 27th Army, the 6th Tank Army and the Rumanian 4th Army and brought the Soviet advance in the area to a halt. The Front's left-wing forces were more successful. Acting in co-operation with the Rumanian 1st Army, the 53rd Army, driving in the north-westerly direction, liberated Arad and Beius and on Septem-

---

[1] I. Kupsha (and others) *Rumania's Part in Routing Nazi Germany*, Moscow, 1959, p. 154 (in Russian).

[2] The continuous frontline was established along the line running from Vatra Dornei to area west of Toplita-Tirgu Mures-Turda and then from Beius to Arad, area west of Timisoara and to the Danube.

ber 24 reached the Rumanian-Hungarian border at the Hungarian town of Mako.

Thus, in the course of September, the 2nd Ukrainian Front in co-operation with the Rumanian 1st and 4th armies advanced from 300 to 500 kilometres to the west and northwest, prevented the German Command from stabilising the frontline along the Southern Carpathians, completed the liberation of Rumania within her 1940 borders and freed a part of Northern Transylvania.

THE LIBERATION
OF NORTHERN TRANSYLVANIA

Rumania was fully liberated in the course of the Debrecen Operation carried out by the 2nd Ukrainian Front between October 6 and 28 in Northern Transylvania and Eastern Hungary.[1]

Fighting for the liberation of Northern Transylvania was exceptionally bitter and stubborn. Taking advantage of the difficult terrain which was suitable for defensive actions and also the fortifications built by the Horthy government in Transylvania between 1940 and 1944, the German Command tried at all costs to stop the offensive of the 2nd Ukrainian Front and prevent it from entering Hungary. It also intended to use the Carpathian salient as a springboard for dealing another blow from the Turda area in the southerly direction in order to seize the passes in the Southern Carpathians in fulfilment of the September 30 directive of the General Staff of the Land Forces (OKH), ordering the German troops to secure a line for the winter which could be manned by insignificant forces, in other words, to padlock all exits into Northern Transylvania. The German Command assigned a large part of the forces of Army Group South to attain this aim.[2]

The German 8th and the Hungarian 2nd Army deployed in Rumania at the time were on the defensive along the line Reghin-area west of Turda-area south of Oradea and Salon-

---

[1] Details of the Debrecen Operation are given in Chapter VII.

[2] Army Group South was formed on September 23, 1944, to replace Army Group South Ukraine.

ta and offered very stubborn resistance to the 2nd Ukrainian Front's right-wing armies (7th Guards, 40th and 27th armies, Rumanian 4th Army and General S. I. Gorshkov's mechanised cavalry task force). The enemy put up an especially tenacious resistance at Cluj.

In this situation the successful offensive of the Front's forces in Eastern Hungary had a decisive effect on the outcome of the battles waged by Soviet and Rumanian troops in Transylvania.

The break-through of the Front's strike forces into the area of Debrecen, deep behind German lines, posed a threat of encirclement before the entire Transylvanian grouping. To avert this the Germans began to withdraw on October 9. The right wing of the Front immediately launched a pursuit and on October 11 the 104th Infantry Corps of the 27th Army with the support of Rumanian units liberated Cluj. By nightfall on the following day the 40th Army came up to Bistritsa and the 7th Guards Army reached Dej.

The liberation on October 12 of Oradea, a key strongpoint in the enemy defences in Northern Transylvania, paved the way for further successful military operations. The town was taken by Lieutenant-General I. A. Pliyev's mechanised cavalry task force in conjunction with the 33rd Infantry Corps which included the Rumanian 3rd Mountain Infantry Division and the Tudor Vladimirescu Division.

In the next few days the Soviet and Rumanian troops repulsed powerful infantry and panzer counterattacks and liberated Dej, Baia Mare, Zalau, Simleul Silvaniei, Sighet and a number of other towns.[1]

The mass heroism of the Soviet troops in the battles for Rumania's liberation inspired the Rumanian officers and men and the courageous struggle of the Soviet and Rumanian armies ended in complete victory. On October 25 units of the 40th Army and the Rumanian 4th Army captured Satu Mare and Carei, the enemy's last resistance points in Rumania.

In the coming months the Rumanian forces fought together with the Soviet Army, playing their part in ensuring victory over nazi Germany.

---

[1] Sighet was liberated by the 40th Army in conjunction with the 138th Infantry Division, 17th Infantry Corps, 4th Ukrainian Front.

4. RESULTS OF THE STRUGGLE
FOR RUMANIA'S LIBERATION

The overthrow of the fascist yoke created favourable conditions for Rumania's democratic and independent development. Headed by the Communist Party of Rumania the popular masses in an acute class struggle defeated fascism. But the reactionary bourgeoisie and the landowners tried to seize the fruits of their victory. The bourgeois governments of Generals Sanatescu and Radescu which remained in power until March 1945 tried to inhibit the democratisation of the country and the army, and did their utmost to sabotage the armistice terms and prevent the Rumanian Army from participating in the war against nazi Germany. They intensified their subversive activity to an even greater extent after the liberation of Northern Transylvania, spreading the view in the army that since Transylvania had been liberated there was no reason for it to continue the fight and if there was any fighting to be done it was the Soviet Union which had to do it.

Bands of reactionaries bearing the name of Maniu, leader of the National Peasants' Party, were formed in Northern Transylvania. They terrorised the Hungarian population, disrupted the logistics of the Soviet and Rumanian troops and also committed terroristic acts against the country's democratic forces. The General Staff of the Rumanian Army under the most diverse pretexts delayed the dispatch of troops and reinforcements to the frontlines. On February 10, 1945 the Rumanian units in the field were short of 80,382 men. While the two Rumanian armies which were in action against the Germans had only eight tanks, there were 211 tanks in Bucharest.

The reaction concentrated troops in the rear in an effort to suppress the revolutionary movement of the masses and establish a military dictatorship in the country. In February 1945 the new Prime Minister General Radescu even went so far as to order the troops to open fire on a peaceful demonstration. Nevertheless, the presence of the Soviet Army in Rumania and the determined struggle of the Rumanian democratic forces frustrated the attempts of Rumanian and international reaction to provoke a civil war which was to serve as a pretext for an Anglo-American intervention in the country. The popular masses overturned Radescu's reactionary government and on March 6, 1945 a people's democratic government headed by Petru Groza came to power. A people's democratic system was established in the country.[1] Following the assumption of power by a people's democratic government the Rumanian army changed its attitude to the war and became more active in the struggle against nazi Germany.

The Soviet Union and the Soviet military authorities in Rumania (Soviet representatives on the Allied Control Commission, military commandants and so forth) rendered the Rumanian people fraternal assistance and support in normalising economic and political activity in the country.

Of exceptional importance was the Soviet Union's principled and friendly stand in upholding Rumania's sovereignty and national independence and its role in frustrating the efforts of the Anglo-American imperialists to interfere in Rumania's internal affairs and impose on her their onerous terms of post-war peace.

The Soviet Union also rendered Rumania effective economic and technical assistance in rehabilitating her ruined economy. Under the economic agreements signed in Moscow on May 8, 1945, the Soviet Union supplied Rumania with cotton, non-ferrous metals, coke, coal, equipment for the timber and paper industries and so forth. The aid in food which the Soviet Union rendered the Rumanian people to offset the serious crop failure of 1945 was indeed an act of exceptional friendliness, selflessness and proletarian internationalism. Short of food itself, the Soviet Union, nevertheless, loaned her 300,000 tons of grain. Assessing Soviet assistance and support the newspaper *Scinteia* wrote on September 15, 1945: "The unexampled generosity of the Soviet Government dispelled the clouds looming over Rumania. The policy of respect for national independence and effective assistance to all democratic and freedom-loving peoples on the part of the USSR have once again been brilliantly expressed in the new agreement with Rumania."

---

[1] On December 30, 1947 the monarchy was overthrown and Rumania was proclaimed a republic.

Soviet armymen in Rumania established very friendly relations with the Rumanian working people. They helped them to restore transport and industrial enterprises, took part in field work and in the fight against a typhus epidemic. Soviet troops helped to repair 380 kilometres of railway trunklines, more than 1,000 bridges and 16 tunnels, dozens of oil wells and industrial enterprises. In October 1944 they helped cultivate 16,000 hectares of landed estates, repaired 100 flour mills and hundreds of farm machines, and took an active part in the 1945 spring sowing campaign. For example, using their own vehicles, the Soviet troops brought 15 railway cars of seeds and tractor fuel from Craiova to the surrounding villages. In the district of Radauti the Soviet Army turned over eight railway cars of seeds to the peasants. Army units detailed tractors and supplied the fuel to help the sowing. They took part in mine-clearing operations on land and on the Danube, and so on.

The Soviet Union also assisted the Rumanian authorities in democratising the army and raising new armed forces. The Soviet Command transferred to the Rumanian Army all the weapons and materials with which the two Rumanian volunteer divisions activated in the Soviet Union had been equipped.

Fulfilling their mission of liberation in Rumania, the Soviet troops acted with courage and heroism. They shed their blood in Rumania for the great and noble cause of liberating her people from fascist bondage and safeguarding its freedom and sovereignty. In the battles for Rumania's freedom the Soviet Army lost 286,000 officers and men, including 69,000 in killed, 2,083 guns and mortars, 2,249 tanks and self-propelled guns and 528 aircraft.[1]

For courage and heroism in the battles for the liberation of Rumania more than 50,000 Soviet officers and men were awarded government decorations in August to October, and many were made Heroes of the Soviet Union. More than 150 units were named after the towns they had liberated: Braila, Galati, Cluj, Constanta, Ploesti, Sulina, Focsani, Tulcea, Jassy and others.

---

[1] Between August 23 and October 30, 1944 the Rumanian Army lost 58,330 officers and men in killed, wounded and missing.

On its part the Rumanian Government decorated more than a thousand Soviet officers and men with orders and another 36,000 with medals; 1,216 Soviet citizens were decorated with orders and medals in connection with the 25th anniversary of Rumania's liberation from fascist oppression. Many Rumanian officers and men were decorated with Soviet orders and medals.

A high assessment of the Soviet Army's role in liberating Rumania is given in the documents of the Communist Party of Rumania. "The Rumanian people," reads the resolution of the Central Committee of the Communist Party of Rumania, the State Council and the Council of Ministers on the celebrations of the 25th anniversary of Rumania's liberation, "highly values the decisive role played by the Soviet Union, the Red Army in smashing fascism and fully liberating Rumania."[1]

These facts overturn the efforts of the falsifiers of history to belittle the Soviet Army's role in liberating Rumania. Against the background of these historic facts the assertion of the French General Cossé and Lieutenant-Colonel Paque that "the Soviet Army marched through Rumania with arms shouldered" on its way to Bulgaria and Hungary sounds strange, to say the least.

After the liberation of Rumania a firm basis for post-war Soviet-Rumanian co-operation was established for the benefit of the great cause of socialism and communism.

---

[1] *Scinteia*, March 12, 1969.

1. ON THE EVE OF LIBERATION

BULGARIA IS DRAWN INTO THE WAR
ON THE SIDE OF THE AGGRESSORS

Contrary to the will and interests of the Bulgarian people Bulgaria's royal fascist rulers turned her into an accomplice in the aggressive war of the fascist bloc. In Vienna on March 1, 1941, Prime Minister Bogdan Filov signed a protocol on Bulgaria's accession to the Tripartite Pact and on the following day German troops moved into Bulgaria, whence they attacked Yugoslavia and Greece. On Hitler's demand Bulgarian troops occupied a part of Yugoslav and Greek territory, making it possible for the German Command to shift a considerable portion of its troops to other fronts. On November 25, 1941 Bulgaria acceded to the Anti-Comintern Pact.

In December 1941 the Bulgarian Government declared war on the United States and Britain, but refrained from declaring war on the Soviet Union lest this move should fully discredit it in the eyes of the Bulgarian people, who entertained sincere feelings of respect and affection for the Russian people who had liberated Bulgaria from five centuries of Turkish domination. Nevertheless, the nazi clique with the consent of Bulgaria's royal fascist government attacked the Soviet Union from Bulgaria's Black Sea ports of Varna and Burgas and the port of Ruse on the Danube.

The war imposed a heavy burden on the Bulgarian people. In the summer of 1944 Bulgaria was gripped in a grave economic and political crisis. That year her military expenditures increased almost 10-fold compared with 1938 and made up almost 60 per cent of the state budget. According to Bogdan Filov, in 1944 alone Bulgaria spent 3,600 million levs on the upkeep of the German troops stationed in the country.

On top of that nazi Germany's leaders mercilessly plundered Bulgaria and on the basis of a clearing agreement shipped raw materials and food out of the country. As a result,

Germany owed Bulgaria 75,000 million levs, several times greater than Bulgaria's annual budget. Compared with 1939 direct taxes rose more than five times and indirect 2.4 times. The working people were in a difficult situation. Prices, including those of limited consumer goods and foodstuffs, rose 2-3.5 times during the war. The people were starving.

The Bulgarian people was enslaved both economically and politically. The Gestapo and its local henchmen instituted a reign of terror; more than 64,000 persons were subject to repressions between January 1942 and September 1944 alone. Fascist court martials passed 1,590 death sentences, and 40,000 anti-fascist fighters were thrown into jails and concentration camps.

Ingratiating itself with Hitler and helping nazi Germany, the Bulgarian Government as far back as 1943 conducted secret talks first in Istanbul and then in Cairo with British and American representatives on the possible occupation of Bulgaria by Anlgo-US forces with the view to preventing the entry of the Soviet Army into the country and preserving her reactionary regime. London and Washington drew up the terms of an armistice agreement with Bulgaria which were presented in Cairo to the Bulgarian representative S. Moshanov at the end of August 1944; they provided for the occupation of Bulgaria by Anglo-American troops and Turkish and Greek forces.

HEROIC STRUGGLE
OF THE BULGARIAN PEOPLE

Nazi Germany's attack on the USSR roused the indignation of the Bulgarian people. On June 22, 1941 the Central Committee of the Bulgarian Workers' Party appealed to the Bulgarian people to launch a determined struggle against the German invaders and internal reaction.

On the initiative of the Bulgarian Workers' Party a communist-led Fatherland Front uniting all the patriotic progressive forces of Bulgaria was formed in 1942. It included the Bulgarian Workers' Party, the left wing of the Bulgarian People's Agrarian Union, the Left wing of the Social Democratic Party and the Zveno Union (anti-German officers and bourgeoisie) and also a section of the anti-fascist intellec-

tuals. On July 17, 1942 the Khristo Botev Radio Station operating from Soviet territory broadcast the Front's first programme containing demands that were close to the hearts of
the Bulgarian people, namely, that Bulgaria should make a
complete break with Germany and other Axis powers, drive
out the German invaders, establish friendship and co-operation with the Soviet Union, withdraw her troops from territories which they had occupied and establish friendly relations with all the neighbouring countries. The immediate aim
of the Fatherland Front was the overthrow of the royal-fas-
cist regime and the formation of a people's democratic government.[1]

In August and September 1943 the National Committee
of the Fatherland Front was set up on the initiative of the
Bulgarian Workers' Party. It included representatives of the
Bulgarian Workers' Party, the Bulgarian Agrarian People's
Union (the Pladne wing), the left wing of the Social Democratic Party and the Zveno Union and one independent representative. The Committee demanded that all power in
the country be turned over to the Fatherland Front. On August 26, 1944 the Central Committee of the Bulgarian Workers' Party issued a directive (Circular No. 4) directing all
local Party organisations to start preparations for an armed
uprising.[2]

In their fight against the German invaders and the reactionary royal fascist system the Bulgarian people were guided
by the Bulgarian Workers' Party, a Marxist-Leninist Party
of the working class steeled in class battles. It was led by
Georgi Dimitrov, a fearless anti-fascist fighter and one of
the most prominent figures of the world communist movement, and his closest associate Vasil Kolarov. In 1944 the
Party had 25,000 members. Its staunch supporter was the
30,000-strong Workers' Youth Union.

The defeat of the Germans in Rumania had a decisive
influence on the state of affairs in Bulgaria whose people now

---

[1] See Georgi Dimitrov, *Fatherland Front Programme*, Selected Works,
Vol. II, Moscow, 1957, pp. 5-7 (in Russian).
[2] See *The Work of the Bulgarian Communist Party in the Army*
(1941-1944), Documents and Materials, Sofia, 1959, pp. 482-85 (in Bulgarian).

realised that the Soviet Army would come to their assistance, too.

The Bulgarian anti-fascists used to the full the new, favourable situation to intensify their struggle against the internal and foreign enslavers. On September 1, 1944 the Central Committee of the Bulgarian Workers' Party called upon the working people to organise meetings at all enterprises, declare a general strike, still further stimulate the insurrection movement and strengthen the militant alliance between the partisans and the army.

The partisan movement embraced virtually all parts of the country. By September 9, 1944 one partisan division, 13 brigades, 40 detachments, six soldiers' battalions and hundreds of combat groups had been in action in the country. They had 48,000 men, of whom up to 30,000 were members of combat groups. The partisans relied on the entire people and above all on the almost 200,000 supporters who provided them with hiding places and took part in their operations. By fighting against the gendarmes and army units, the People's Liberation Insurgent Army created a real internal front which tied down 11 divisions (seven Bulgarian and four German). The enemy was forced to throw against the partisans 30,000 policemen, 15,000 gendarmes and 8,000 riflemen of the forest guard. In the course of the difficult struggle the fascists, according to the newspaper *Narodna Armiya*, killed 9,140 partisans and 20,070 supporters.

The Gestapo and the internal reactionaries concentrated their efforts primarily at the Communists standing at the head of the Bulgarian people's heroic struggle. The fascists delivered their first blow at the Communist political emigres who had illegally returned to Bulgaria to help the Bulgarian Workers' Party and the people in the fight against the German invaders and the internal royal fascist reaction. They executed General Vladimir Zaimov, Ret., a great patriot and true friend of the Soviet Union.

The Bulgarian Workers' Party suffered the heaviest losses in 1942. On July 23, six Central Committee workers, including a Central Committee Secretary, Anton Ivanov, were executed by a firing squad and three days later the fascists shot another 18 patriots, including the head of the Central Military Commission of the Central Committee of the Bulgarian

Workers' Party, Tsviatko Radoinov. At the end of the year the fascists shot the Secretary of the Central Committee of the Workers' Youth Union, Adalbert Antonov. Many other true sons and daughters of the Bulgarian people were also killed.

In spite of all this the Bulgarian Workers' Party continued to act. Step by step it was gaining control of the army thanks to the dedicated efforts of Party members and members of the Workers' Youth Union, many of whom were serving their term of military duty.

Underground revolutionary soldiers' committees were established in army units. Soldiers deserted to join the partisans. In 1944 alone, according to the fascist military counter-intelligence, 966 groups of Bulgarian soldiers went over to the partisans. The 1st Sofia People's Liberation Division which was raised on the eve of the uprising on instructions from the Central Committee of the Bulgarian Workers' Party had 650 soldiers in its ranks. Subsequently a battalion of the 25th Infantry Regiment deserted and joined the division.

On the eve of the armed uprising, a number of revolutionary units commanded by their soldiers' committees and patriotic officers went over to the side of the people. On September 8 an artillery coastal defence regiment in Burgas refused to obey its fascist commanders and rallied to the banner of the Fatherland Front. The 1st Battalion of the 4th Frontier Regiment in Varna also joined the partisans.

The Bulgarian Workers' Party launched intensive preparations for establishing local organs of the new, people's government. Fatherland Front committees were being set up; by September 9, there were 670 of them with a membership of 3,637, in the country.

The approach of the Soviet Army and the intensified struggle of the Bulgarian people forced the government of I. Bagryanov, which had fully discredited itself in the eyes of the people, to resign on September 1. On the following day the Regent's Council formed a new government headed by Kosta Muraviev, a politician whose views were as reactionary as those of his predecessor. On September 4, the new government announced its domestic and foreign policy programme. Muraviev's government pledged to "restore all democratic freedoms and rights of the Bulgarian people" and "observe strict, unconditional and trustworthy neutrality". In effect, however, it allowed the units of the routed Army Group South Ukraine to withdraw from Bulgaria and continued secret separate talks with British and American representatives in Cairo aimed at preventing the entry of Soviet troops into the country. And when the Fatherland Front approached the government with the request to permit the activity of the Front's parties, Muraviev replied that he would not permit them to engage in "any political activity".

It was no longer possible to bear with the situation and on September 5, 1944 the Soviet Government sent a note to the Bulgarian Government stating that since it no longer considered it possible to maintain relations with Bulgaria it was breaking all relations with Bulgaria and declared that not only Bulgaria was in a state of war with the USSR, because in effect she was already in a state of war with the USSR, but that henceforth the Soviet Union would also be in a state of war with Bulgaria. This step put an end to the talks in Cairo and served as a signal for the Bulgarian anti-fascists to begin the uprising.

Taking advantage of the favourable situation, the Bulgarian Workers' Party stepped up preparations for the armed uprising. The Party's Central Committee and the National Committee of the Fatherland Front called upon the people to organise meetings and mass demonstrations. On September 5, the Political Bureau of the Party Central Committee and the Main Headquarters of the People's Liberation Insurgent Army completed their work on the plan of the uprising.

In response to the appeal of the Bulgarian Workers' Party and the Fatherland Front, powerful anti-fascist demonstrations were held in all parts of the country, including Sofia, Plovdiv, Varna, Pleven, Sliven and other towns. On September 6, the police attacked the demonstrators and the streets in many towns were drenched with the blood of the working people. But nothing could crush the will of the people.

On September 7, the working people of Pleven stormed and captured the local jail and freed political prisoners. On September 8, a nation-wide strike broke out. Units of the People's Liberation Insurgent Army went over to the offensive and in some parts of the country partisan detachments and brigades with the support of combat groups entered villages and without waiting for official permission established the rule of the Fatherland Front on the spot.

2. THE LIBERATION
OF BULGARIA

SOVIET TROOPS ENTER BULGARIA

In these circumstances, the Soviet Government decided to hasten to give assistance to the Bulgarian people in the struggle for its national and social liberation.

The liberation of Bulgaria was entrusted to General F. I. Tolbukhin's 3rd Ukrainian Front which included the 37th, 46th and 57th Field armies totalling 28 infantry divisions, the 17th Air Army and the 4th Guards and the 7th Mechanised corps. The Front had about 258,000 troops, 6,305 guns and mortars of all calibres, 470 tanks and self-propelled guns and 726 combat aircraft. A part of the ships of the Black Sea Fleet under Admiral F. S. Oktyabrsky and the Danube Flotilla commanded by Rear-Admiral S. G. Gorshkov also took part in the operation.

Fulfilling the instructions of the Soviet Government, the Military Council of the 3rd Ukrainian Front jointly with Deputy Supreme Commander-in-Chief Marshal G. K. Zhukov drew up a plan for the liberation of Bulgaria and on September 4, 1944 submitted it to GHQ which approved it on the following day.

A blow was to be delivered by the three armies (27 infantry divisions) and two mechanised corps supported by all reinforcing units on a 20-kilometre sector. They were to advance 210 kilometres in the general direction of Aitos and Burgas, capture the ports of Varna and Burgas, reach the line running from Giurgiu to Popovo, Kotel, Karnobat and Cape St. Agalina and seize the German and Bulgarian fleets concentrated in Varna and Burgas.

The Soviet Command took into account the revolutionary situation which had taken shape in Bulgaria at the beginning of September, and that explained the relatively simple objectives of the operation.

In its appeal "To the Bulgarian People. To the Bulgarian Army" the Military Council of the 3rd Ukrainian Front said:

"the Red Army has no intention of fighting the Bulgarian people since it regards the Bulgarians as a fraternal people. The Red Army has the only task, that of smashing the Germans and hastening the establishment of peace."

The Military Council urged the Bulgarian people to take an active part in the struggle against the German invaders and render all possible assistance to the Soviet Army. In its instructions to the troops, the Military Council pointed out that close, age-old ties of friendship linked the Bulgarian people with the Russian people and reminded the men: "Do not ever for a moment forget your noble mission of soldier-liberator.... We do not intend to impose our laws and order on Bulgaria. Let the Bulgarians themselves decide the question of their country's internal organisation...."

The Soviet troops were determined to liberate the Bulgarian people as quickly as possible and to help it to throw off the yoke of the internal reaction. The leading role among the Soviet troops was played by communists and Komsomol members. A large portion of political work among the Soviet forces involved explanation of the Soviet Government's note of September 5, 1944. Army and divisional newspapers published Sovinformbureau reports, the note of the USSR People's Commissariat of Foreign Affairs and also articles on Bulgarian-Soviet relations.

At the start of the Soviet Army's operations in Bulgaria there were 30,000 German troops in the country. At the time the Bulgarian Army had five field armies and two separate corps totalling 23 divisions and two brigades (not counting the border-guards). It had a total of more than 500,000 men (including air and naval personnel) and its weapons were about 5,000 guns and mortars of various calibres, 135 tanks, 556 aircraft and 80 warships (figures at mid-October 1944).

By its dedicated efforts the Bulgarian Workers' Party had gained strong positions in the army, with the result that the majority of its men did not want to fight against the USSR and impatiently waited for the Soviet troops to arrive.

The first Soviet units to enter Bulgaria were Major-General I. A. Maximovich's 34th Guards Infantry Division of the 46th Army, the 57th Army's 73rd Guards and 353rd Infantry divisions under Major-General S. A. Kozak and Co-

lonel P. I. Kuznetsov, and Colonel G. I. Kolyadin's 244th
Infantry Division of the 37th Army.

Encountering no resistance from the Bulgarian troops, the
advance Soviet units covered 65-70 km in the first day and
reached the line Tutrakan-Sakallii-Krasen Dol-Emirkei. The
31st Guards Infantry Corps under Major-General S. A. Bob-
ruk liberated Rushchuk (Ruse) and Tutrakan. The forward
detachment of the 7th Mechanised Corps commanded by
Major-General F. G. Katkov entered Shumen at 20.00 hours,
and the 4th Guards Mechanised Corps under Major-General V. I. Zhdanov entered Varna at 15.30 hours. At 12.00
hours the aircraft of the Black Sea Fleet landed a marine
task force in Varna.

The 17th Air Army conducted reconnaissance and
dropped leaflets with an address of the Soviet Command to
the Bulgarian people and army. In it the Military Council of
the Front said that the Red Army entered Bulgaria "in order
to help the Bulgarian people to liberate itself for all time
from the German yoke and bring a just and stable peace to
Bulgaria and all the Balkan nations. . . . The Red Army has
entered Bulgaria not as a conqueror but as a liberator. . . .
Just as 67 years ago Russia helped Bulgaria to cast off foreign
yoke, so now, too, the Soviet Union is helping Bulgaria to
regain her independence."

In view of the situation which took shape in Bulgaria, the
Soviet Command ordered the 3rd Ukrainian Front to co-
operate with the Black Sea Fleet in capturing Burgas and
Aitos on September 9, 1944 and reaching the line Rushchuk-
Razgrad-Tirgoviste-Karnobat. After that it was to halt.

It was clear to all patriotic working people of Bulgaria
that the Soviet Union had declared war not on the workers,
peasants and working intellectuals, but on the exploiters, the
royal fascist regime and on all reactionaries who in defiance
of the will of the working people had involved Bulgaria into
the Second World War on the side of nazi Germany. The
Bulgarian people regarded the Soviet troops as their liberators from the German invaders and the royal fascist tyranny.

On September 7, Kosta Muraviev's government was forced
to break off diplomatic relations with Germany and seek an
armistice with the Soviet Union.

THE UPRISING
OF SEPTEMBER 9, 1944

In connection with the entry of Soviet troops into Bulgaria the Political Bureau of the Bulgarian Workers' Party Central Committee and the Main HQ of the People's Liberation Insurgent Army in the morning of September 8 decided to begin the uprising in the night of the same day and strike the final blow at the enemy.

The heaviest blow at the royal fascist regime was to be delivered in the capital, Sofia, where key administrative, political and economic bodies, communications and the bulk of the Bulgarian army units which had gone over to the side of the Fatherland Front were concentrated. The 1st Sofia Infantry Division on whose support the reactionaries pinned their greatest hopes was neutralised on September 8 after talks between the Main Headquarters of the People's Liberation Insurgent Army and the divisional command.[1]

By a decision of the Political Bureau of the Central Committee of the Bulgarian Communist Party and the Main Headquarters of the People's Liberation Army the uprising was to be launched by an armoured regiment, the 1st Battalion of the 1st Infantry Regiment, a military school training company, an engineer assault battalion of the High Command, an engineer assault battalion of the 1st Engineer Regiment, a searchlight group of an anti-aircraft battery of the High Command, the Chavdar Partisan Brigade under D. Djurov and Commissar S. Halachev and a partisan element.

A special role was assigned to the 1st Sofia People's Liberation Division which was armed with the latest Soviet weapons dropped by parachute. Its task was to advance from the area of Kaln across Tryn on Sofia. A part of its forces were to assist the miners of Pernik in liberating the inmates of a concentration camp and seize power in the city.

The armed uprising in the country was led by the Political Bureau of the Central Committee of the Bulgarian Workers' Party and the Main Headquarters of the People's Liberation Insurgent Army in Sofia with the active participation of T. Zhivkov, B. Bylgaranov, A. Yugov, D. Ganev, D. Ter-

---

[1] See: Voin Bozhinov, *Political Crisis in Bulgaria in 1943-1944*, Sofia, 1957, pp. 128-29 (in Bulgarian).

peshev, T. Dragoicheva, G. Chankov, B. Ivanov and others. A special bureau consisting of Todor Zhivkov (head), I. Bonev-Vitan, S. Todorov and V. Bonev was set up to supervise the preparations for the uprising.[1]

According to plan the uprising in Sofia was started at 2.00 hours on September 9, 1944. The insurgents disarmed the guard at the war ministry where the royal fascist government was in session, occupied all exits and arrested the ministers, top officials and the reactionary officers of the General Staff.

Led by the Bulgarian Workers' Party the country-wide uprising of the Bulgarian people ended in victory and the royal fascist regime was replaced by the Fatherland Front Government which included four communists. In a radio broadcast early in the morning Prime Minister Kimon Georgiev informed the people of his government's programme. The Fatherland Front Government made a complete break with Germany and proclaimed war on her, established close contact with the Soviet Government and began to carry out democratic reforms.

Warmly welcomed by the Bulgarian working people the Soviet troops on September 9 advanced up to 120 kilometres and reached their designated line. On September 9 and 10, the radio and all central newspapers in the Soviet Union made public the order of the Supreme Commander-in-Chief J. V. Stalin commending the troops of the 3rd Ukrainian Front and the sailors of the Black Sea for liberating the Bulgarian towns of Ruse, Shumen, Varna and Burgas and for helping the Bulgarian people in its fight against the German invaders. The order also pointed out that "as a result of the successful actions of our troops the purpose of our operations has been attained: Bulgaria has broken off with Germany and declared war on her. In this way Bulgaria has ceased to be a bulwark of German imperialism in the Balkans as she had been in the course of the past thirty years".

As they advanced across Bulgaria the troops of the 3rd Ukrainian Front tried to prevent the Wehrmacht forces from pulling out of country and in every way assisted the toiling

---

[1] See *A History of the Bulgarian Communist Party*, 1970, p. 487 (in Bulgarian).

masses in their struggle against foreign and internal enslavers. But by connivance of Bulgaria's former fascist government the bulk of the enemy forces (with the exception of 3,750 German officers and men who had been earlier interned near Razgrad) managed to slip out of the country unharmed and withdraw to the northwest.

Following the victory of the armed uprising, the formation of the Fatherland Front Government and its declaration of war on Germany, there was no need for the Soviet troops to continue operations in the country. Therefore, GHQ ordered the 3rd Ukrainian Front and the Black Sea Fleet to cease operations in Bulgaria at 22.00 hours on September 9.

Brought up by the Communist Party in the spirit of proletarian internationalism, the Soviet troops fulfilled their internationalist duty with honour by helping the working people of Bulgaria to bring their struggle against the reactionary royal fascist regime to a successful conclusion.

However hard the fascist leaders tried and whatever hopes they cherished, they failed to poison the Bulgarian people with the venom of nationalism and get them to break their ties with the Soviet Union. As the Bulgarian historian S. Petrova wrote, "belief in 'Grandfather Ivan's' liberatory mission for five centuries sustained the Bulgarians in their fight against the Turkish enslavers. In 1878 the Russian troops liberated Bulgaria at the cost of 200,000 lives. The Bulgarians have a deeply ingrained feeling of gratitude to the Russian people, a feeling which has found its expression in numerous monuments with which they have perpetuated its glory".

The enthusiastic welcome accorded by the Bulgarian people inspired the Soviet troops to further exploits for the sake of freedom and independence of both fraternal peoples, for the sake of victory over the sinister forces of fascism and reaction.

Colonel G. K. Tsinev, chief of the Political Division of the 57th Army, wrote at the time that the entry into Bulgaria turned the troops into a festive mood: they marched through villages with their banners unfurled and bands playing; both officers and men displayed high discipline, taking all care not to upset the usual order of things in the Bulgarian towns and villages.

Although Bulgaria had in effect pulled out of the war on

nazi Germany's side and declared war on her, the first hours after the Fatherland Front Government had come to power were characterised by an abnormal situation when Bulgaria was still formally in a state of war with the Soviet Union, Britain and the United States, the leading states of the anti-Hitler coalition. To put an end to this, Georgi Dimitrov, who was still in Moscow at the time, at night of September 9, 1944 requested that a delegation from the Fatherland Front headed by D. Ganev, member of the Political Bureau of the Central Committee of the Bulgarian Workers' (Communist) Party, should be received at HQ of the 3rd Ukrainian Front.[1] The delegation gave a detailed account of the armed uprising and asked General F. I. Tolbukhin to conclude an armistice. It also expressed concern about Sofia's security and requested the Front HQ to organise the co-operation of the Bulgarian troops with the Front's operations. The Soviet Government immediately terminated the state of war with Bulgaria and communicated the Bulgarian Government's request to Britain and the United States.

Following the termination of the state of war with Bulgaria, some changes took place in the composition of the 3rd Ukrainian Front. By a GHQ directive of September 10, the 46th Army, which had three infantry corps, the 7th Mechanised Corps and the 7th Assault Artillery Division were incorporated into the 2nd Ukrainian Front whose offensive zone had been expanded.

THE COMPLETION
OF BULGARIA'S LIBERATION

Naturally, the withdrawal of two of nazi Germany's satellites—Rumania and Bulgaria—from the fascist bloc alarmed the leaders of the Third Reich.

As the position of the German troops in the Balkans took a sharp turn for the worse, the German Command became most concerned with preserving the communications linking its troops in Greece with those in southeast Yugoslavia. And

---

[1] After the armed uprising of September 9, 1944 the Bulgarian Workers' Party began to call itself the Bulgarian Workers' (Communist) Party. In December 1948 its Fifth Congress renamed it the Bulgarian Communist Party (BCP).

when the Soviet forces reached the line Ruse-Tirgoviste-Burgas some 300 kilometres from Sofia and 360-400 kilometres from the Bulgarian-Yugoslav border, the Germans started to disarm the Bulgarian forces carrying occupation duty in Yugoslavia.

In view of these developments Turkey began to show signs of activity and concentrated up to 20 divisions, three cavalry brigades, an armoured brigade and other units along Bulgaria's southern border in Thrace. Since Churchill was stubbornly upholding the so-called Balkan variant of the second front, and the US and British governments and Bulgaria's former royal government were involved in prolonged diplomatic backstage bargaining, the Soviet and Bulgarian governments had every reason to suspect that on instructions from the Anglo-American imperialists Turkish troops could be thrown into action against Bulgaria, under one pretext or another.

Taking all these factors into account, GHQ on September 13, 1944 ordered Commander of the 3rd Ukrainian Front Marshal F. I. Tolbukhin[1] to send Colonel-General S. S. Biryuzov as his deputy to Sofia to control the operations of the Soviet troops, including the air force, and to organise co-operation with the Bulgarian forces through the Bulgarian General Staff. S. S. Biryuzov arrived in Sofia on the following day, and at 19.15 hours on September 15, the 5th Guards Motorised Infantry Brigade and the 53rd Motorcycle Regiment entered the Bulgarian capital.

To guarantee the city's security, the following units were assembled by September 18 on GHQ orders at Sofia: the 34th Infantry Corps, the 5th Guards Motorised Infantry Brigade, the 53rd Separate Motorcycle Regiment, the 4th Guards Mechanised Corps, the 9th Anti-tank and the 96th Tank brigades, the 61st Rocket Launcher and the 384th Anti-Aircraft-Artillery regiments.

For the same purpose the Soviet Command on September 9 began to transfer a task force headed by commander of the 9th Mixed Air Corps, 17th Air Army Lieutenant-General O. V. Tolstikov to the Sofia airfield. By September 16, the

---

[1] F. I. Tolbukhin was promoted Marshal of the Soviet Union on September 12, 1944.

288th Fighter and the 306th Attack Aircraft divisions and an airfield maintenance battalion had been transferred to Sofia. On September 19, the 306th Attack Division had 134 aircraft, including 130 IL-2 attack planes. Fifty-seven planes of the 244th Bomber Division were also stationed on airfields around Sofia.

The formation of a new, Bulgarian People's Army began immediately after the victory of the armed uprising, and since the greater part of the old army went over to the side of the people there was no need to disband it completely. It was in the interests of the struggle against the German invaders to reorganise the army as quickly as possible. Yet the experience of political struggle and its political perception told the Bulgarian Workers' Party that it would be a mistake to preserve the old bourgeois army intact. In addition to the mass of revolutionary soldiers and progressive officers, it also had a fairly large number of royalists, some of whom were high-ranking officers.

Within a short period of time nine infantry divisions, or 41 per cent of the total number of divisions of the old army, were disbanded, and a large number of members of the partisan movement were assigned for service in the other divisions. On September 11, 1944 partisan detachments were united in the People's Guard, and the 1st Sofia Guards Infantry Division and the 13th Guards Infantry Regiment were formed. Guards battalions were attached to other divisions to bolster the revolutionary spirit of the troops.

All told, approximately 35,000 commanders, Guardsmen and volunteers with a high level of political awareness and considerable experience of revolutionary struggle were drawn into the ranks of the new Bulgarian People's Army. As a result it became a genuinely popular army both as regards its composition and objectives. On September 22, 1944 the Bulgarian Workers' (Communist) Party decreed that commanders of all units have deputies on political affairs, who enabled the Party to influence army life at all levels. A large part of the commanders, especially senior officers, were replaced by officers from among the Party workers, partisans and officers who had fought against the royal regime and the German invaders. All pro-fascist officers, who had taken part in repressions against the people, were court-martialled.

By order of the War Minister of September 11, 1944, about 800 men of the People's Liberation Insurgent Army were assigned to officers' posts. Several of them were given the rank of colonel-general and lieutenant-general, seven were made major-generals, 21 colonels, 28 lieutenant-colonels, 58 majors, 105 captains, 193 lieutenants and 298 sublieutenants.

A large number of officers whom the old royal regime had transferred to the reserve and who had taken part in the struggle for the victory of the new power were called up for service. Some, including generals Stoichev, Lekarski, Toshev and Trendafilov, were assigned to top command posts. Many steeled revolutionaries, heroes of the September 1923 uprising, commanders of international brigades in Spain and political emigrants also joined the new Bulgarian Army, among them Georgi Damyanov, Ivan Mikhailov, Ivan Kinov, Zakhari Zakhariev, Petr Panchevsky, Ferdinand Kozovski and Ivan Vinarov.

On September 17, 1944 the Fatherland Front Government took a decision to place the divisions designated for action against the German invaders under control of the commander of the 3rd Ukrainian Front.

The very first joint actions of the Soviet Army and the Bulgarian People's Army were characterised by fraternal and very close co-operation.

To improve co-ordination between Soviet and Bulgarian troops a military mission headed by Major-General Asen Krystev of the Bulgarian Army High Command was assigned on December 3 to the HQ of the 3rd Ukrainian Front. This mission ensured contact on all issues between the Fatherland Front Government, the War Minister, the General Staff and HQ of the Bulgarian 1st Army, on the one hand, and the Command of the 3rd Ukrainian Front, on the other.

Soviet military advisers rendered considerable assistance in the formation of the new Bulgarian Army.

On September 20, 1944 GHQ ordered the 3rd Ukrainian Front to move its 57th Army, consisting of two infantry corps (six infantry divisions), to the line Brusartsi-Medkovets-Vratsa-Mezdra by September 30 for action in the westerly direction.

The 37th Army which had three infantry corps (nine infantry divisions) was to occupy the line Kazanlik-Stara Zagora-Nova Zagora-Yambol-Burgas and be ready to strike out in the southerly direction. The group of forces at Sofia under General S. S. Biryuzov was placed under the direct control of the Front. The 4th Guards Mechanised Corps was to concentrate in the area of Yambol by September 24. The Bulgarian 1st, 2nd and 4th armies, totalling 13 divisions, were to take up positions along the Bulgarian-Yugoslav border from Chuprene to the Bulgarian-Greek border.

After redeployment the 3rd Ukrainian Front could advance into Yugoslavia and protect Bulgaria's southern borders. On September 19, 1944 the commander of the 3rd Ukrainian Front placed all anti-aircraft units in Sofia under one commander to ward off possible enemy air strikes on the Bulgarian capital.

The 57th Army, which was advancing towards Bulgaria's western borders, on December 27 engaged small German covering units which reeled under its pressure to the west. The Bulgarian 2nd Cavalry Brigade and some units of the Bulgarian 2nd Infantry Division held their ground against enemy counterattacks in the Strumica-Dabilia-Muratino sector. By nightfall on September 28, 1944, Soviet and Bulgarian forces reached the Bulgarian-Yugoslav border (the 57th Army between Negotin and Belogradchik, and the Bulgarian 1st, 2nd and 4th armies, between Belogradchik and the border with Greece).

3. BULGARIA TAKES A NEW ROAD

FRATERNAL ASSISTANCE
TO THE BULGARIAN PEOPLE

In a mere 20 days following the armed uprising enormous changes took place in Bulgaria. Everywhere organs of power of the Fatherland Front strengthened their positions. But in spite of the truly deep-going revolutionary changes which had occurred in the country, the new power first in one place and then in another encountered the opposition of the anti-national forces endeavouring to frustrate the policy of the Bulgarian Workers' (Communist) Party and the Fatherland Front.

Soviet military commandants' offices very effectively assisted the Bulgarian people and the local organs of power of the

Fatherland Front. There were 53 commandants' offices, all headed by politically experienced officers. Working in close contact with the local authorities, they helped normalise economic and political activity, uphold revolutionary order and fight against the reactionary elements.

The Soviet Army's friendship with the Bulgarian People's Army and the local population strengthened and expanded. On its part the local population and organs of power of the Fatherland Front did their best to help the Soviet Army.

In the meantime questions connected with the conclusion of an armistice were being gradually solved. It should be noted, however, that Britain and the United States did not hasten to reply to the request of the Fatherland Front Government, and gave it only on October 11, 1944. Evidently the Anglo-American reactionaries were displeased with the changes in Bulgaria that had overturned their calculations. Speaking in the House of Commons on September 28, 1944, Winston Churchill said: "The Soviet intervention in this theatre was at once startling and effective. Their sudden declaration of war against Bulgaria was sufficient to induce her to turn her caitiff armies against the German intruders."[1] The British Premier maliciously attacked not only the Bulgarian Government, but also the Bulgarian people.

Fulfilling its internationalist duty, the Soviet Union, besides rendering purely military assistance to the Bulgarian people in driving the German invaders out of the country, also gave it substantial economic and military-technical aid.

In March 1945 the USSR and Bulgaria signed a commodity exchange agreement, under which Bulgaria received 102,000 tons of petroleum products from the USSR, about 46,000 tons of ferrous and non-ferrous metals, 96,000 tons of textile raw materials, chemicals, railway cars and locomotives, automobile tyres, farm machines, dyes, paper and other commodities to the sum of 15,000 million levs.

The Soviet Union turned over to Bulgaria free of charge 1,302 tons of meat, 7,186 tons of wheat, 1,635 tons of rye, 2,695 tons of flour, 998 tons of beans, 590 tons of peas, 468 tons of sugar, 227 tons of sunflower oil, 1,240 tons of pota-

---

[1] Winston S. Churchill, *War Speeches 1941-1945*, London, 1946, p. 206.

toes, 2,455 tons of oats and barley and 1,707 tons of maize.[1]

The volume of military assistance was especially large. By the end of October 1944 the Soviet Union supplied the Bulgarian People's Army with 595 tons of fuels and lubricants. In October and November 1944 the Bulgarian People's Army received 100 million rounds of ammunition for submachine guns, rifles and machine guns, about 1,600,000 shells for field guns and mortars and 650,000 hand grenades.[2]

In January and February 1945 the 3rd Ukrainian Front turned over to the Bulgarian People's Army 10,000 pairs of footwear and 20,000 metres of cloth, and later gave the Bulgarian 1st Army 200 light machine guns, 600 submachine guns and 480 anti-tank rifles. Beginning with February 1, 1945, when the Bulgarian 1st Army was placed under the control of the 3rd Ukrainian Front, the latter supplied it with 600 tons of petrol, petroleum and oils each month. It also received hundreds of captured enemy motor vehicles, motorcycles, a large quantity of spare parts, many automobile tyres and so forth. All told, the Soviet Command spent 1,334 million levs for the maintenance of the Bulgarian 1st Army. From December 1944 to the end of the war the Bulgarian troops received from Soviet depots about 38 million rounds of small-arms ammunition, more than 700,000 artillery and mortar shells, 342,000 hand grenades, sapper equipment, etc.[3]

By order of the State Defence Committee of the USSR of March 14, 1945 the Bulgarian People's Army received 334 aircraft (Yak-9—120, IL-2—120 and PE-2—94), 65 T-34 tanks, 410 field guns, 153 anti-aircraft guns, 370 mortars, 18,880 rifles, 9,615 submachine guns, 1,270 light machine guns, 420 heavy machine guns, 40 large-calibre anti-aircraft machine guns, 280 anti-tank rifles, 369 radio stations, 2,572 telephones and 370 motor vehicles from the USSR. Most of this military equipment was delivered prior to August 1945. With the assistance of the USSR five infantry divisions, an air division and a tank brigade were re-equipped in 1945.

These measures strengthened Bulgaria's domestic and in-

---

[1] *The Patriotic War in Bulgaria (1944-1945)*, Vol. III, Sofia, 1966, p. 270 (in Bulgarian).

[2] See *The Patriotic War in Bulgaria...*, Vol. II, pp. 337-38.

[3] *Ibid.*, Vol. III, pp. 270, 271.

ternational situation and made it possible to mobilise the Bulgarian people for the struggle against the German invaders and the internal reaction.

THE HISTORIC SIGNIFICANCE OF BULGARIA'S LIBERATION

The Soviet Army completed its march of liberation into Bulgaria, meritoriously fulfilling its internationalist duty.

On the eve of the 30th anniversary of the Soviet Army and Navy, Georgi Dimitrov wrote that the Bulgarian people had special reasons to be very grateful to the Soviet Army and the Soviet people as a whole. "In spite of the malicious intrigues of the imperialists and their agents in our country," he wrote, "the Bulgarian people will always remember that the Russian troops first liberated it from Turkish pashas and beys. . . . It will always remember that the brave sons of the Russian and other peoples of the Soviet Union helped it to liberate itself for the second time from foreign conquerors, this time for good, and for ever take their destiny into their own hands. . . ."[1]

The Soviet and Bulgarian peoples cemented their friendship with blood shed in battles against the German invaders and their allies. Bulgaria lost about 32,000 people in the war against nazi Germany.

In tribute for the Soviet Union's part in liberating the Bulgarian people, the Government of Bulgaria decorated 350 Soviet officers and men with orders and more than 50,000 with the "Patriotic War 1944-1945" medal. On its part the Soviet Government awarded orders to 360 and the medal "For Victory over Germany in the Great Patriotic War of 1941-1945" to 120,000 Bulgarian officers and men in recognition of their heroism in the joint struggle.

---

[1] G. Dimitrov, *Selected Works*, Moscow, Vol. II, 1957, pp. 499, 500 (in Russian).

1. SOVIET TROOPS REACH
YUGOSLAVIA'S BORDERS

THE HEROIC STRUGGLE
OF THE YUGOSLAV PEOPLES

In September 1944 furious battles were fought all along the Soviet-German front. On its southern wing the Soviet Army routed large enemy forces in a series of brilliant victories, liberated Bulgaria, and was completing the liberation of Rumania. The military and political situation in the Balkans took a decisive turn in favour of the Soviet Union and the Balkan peoples themselves.

As the Soviet troops swept across Bulgaria and Rumania, Germany's former satellites, towards Yugoslav and Hungarian borders, it became obvious that the German defences in the eastern part of the Balkans had started to crumble. In view of the direct threat to its forces in Albania and Germany, the German Command ordered them to withdraw to the north.

The heroic struggle of the Yugoslav peoples against the German intruders had a tremendous impact on the situation in that part of Europe. Formerly encircled by nazi Germany's satellites, Yugoslavia now found herself in totally different conditions. Bulgaria, after the victory of the popular revolution, went over to the side of the anti-Hitler coalition and her troops were fighting side by side with the Soviet Army against the Germans. The Rumanian troops joined the war against the German invaders following the overthrow of the fascist dictatorship and the establishment of a new government. But the most important thing was that the Soviet forces had reached Yugoslavia's northeastern borders and could directly help the Yugoslav people in their struggle for liberation from the nazis.

Units of the 2nd Ukrainian Front were the first to reach the Yugoslav border. On September 6, 1944 a motorcycle regiment of the 6th Tank Army reached the Danube bend at Turnu Severin. It was a momentous day for the peoples of the Soviet Union and Yugoslavia. On September 7, 1944 the High Command of the People's Liberation Army of Yugoslavia wrote in the order of the day that the great hour which the Yugoslav fighters had been looking forward to in the course of three and a half years of heavy struggle had arrived and that a great ally, the Soviet Army, had reached the Yugoslav border to help the peoples of Yugoslavia drive the invaders out of their country.

The troops of the 2nd Ukrainian Front and the men of the 14th Corps of the People's Liberation Army of Yugoslavia quickly established direct contact. This important news swiftly spread in all units of the Liberation Army and evoked tremendous enthusiasm among the Yugoslav troops and people.

For over three years the two fraternal armies fought against the common enemy and had only one goal—to destroy fascism. That was why their link-up proved to be the only one of its kind throughout the Soviet Army's march of liberation.

The Yugoslav peoples did not lay down their arms. The armed struggle against the German intruders in Yugoslavia was well organised. It was conducted on a broad scale and was headed by the Communist Party.

The Yugoslav people achieved major successes in the fight against the German oppressors; the People's Liberation Army grew and hardened in the trials of the war. According to official Yugoslav figures, when the Soviet Army reached the Yugoslav borders, the People's Liberation Army and the partisans had about 400,000 men in their ranks. The Army had 15 corps (50 divisions), two combat groups (each consisting of two brigades), 16 separate infantry brigades and 130 partisan detachments.

Revolutionary changes were taking place in the internal life in Yugoslavia. The people's war against the invaders was closely intertwined with the class struggle in which the Yugoslav people attained important results. The balance of political power inside the country tipped in favour of the communists, and organs of people's rule were established.

The Anti-Fascist People's Liberation Veche (Assembly) of Yugoslavia was proclaimed the country's highest legislative and executive organ, and the National Committee of Liberation of Yugoslavia headed by Supreme Commander-in-Chief of the People's Liberation Army Josip Broz Tito was established as the country's Provisional Government. The emigre government was deprived of all rights. It was decided that the new state structure of Yugoslavia would rest on democratic and federal principles and a community of equal peoples. Local organs of the new power, People's Liberation Committees, were set up in the regions liberated by the patriotic forces.

Besides fighting against the Germans, the Yugoslav patriots fought against the units of the traitors Pavelic, Nedic, Mihajlovic and Rupnik who collaborated with the invaders and championed the old reactionary regime.

Thanks to the successes of the People's Liberation Army in the struggle against the nazi invaders and the establishment of central and local organs of power of new Yugoslavia the liberation struggle of the Yugoslav people won international recognition. At the end of 1943 British and American governments had no choice but to concede that the national liberation movement was the decisive political and military force of Yugoslavia. At the same time, however, they continued to support the Yugoslav reactionaries and strove to influence the operations of the People's Liberation Army and restore the bourgeois-royal regime in the country.

Pursuing this line, Winston Churchill at a meeting in Naples in August 1944 tried unsuccessfully to persuade the National Committee of Liberation of Yugoslavia to enter into negotiations with King Peter and General Mihajlovic. He sought Yugoslav co-operation in the landing of British troops on the Istria Peninsula so as to move them into Hungary and Austria. It was clear that the presence of British troops in Yugoslavia boded nothing good for her people.

The Soviet Government consistently supported the leaders of the liberation struggle in Yugoslavia in political matters, including the solution of acute questions connected with the emigre circles. The agreement on co-operation reached in the course of the talks between the National Committee and the new head of the emigre government I. Subasic signified that the emigre government recognised the revolutionary changes in Yugoslavia and the temporary rule of the revolutionary organs of power in the country.

The swift advance of the Soviet troops to the Yugoslav borders decisively contributed to the defeat of the invaders and the liberation of the country.

When the Soviet Army's advance units reached the Yugoslav borders the Supreme Commander-in-Chief of the People's Liberation Army of Yugoslavia requested the USSR State Defence Committee to send Soviet troops into Yugoslavia since the People's Liberation Army had no heavy artillery and tanks and was unable to smash the German troops in the country or prevent their withdrawal from Greece to the north.

The Soviet drive towards the Yugoslav borders boosted the morale of the Yugoslav people who extended the scope of their liberation struggle. The People's Liberation Army intensified its operations against the invaders. As regards the organisational structure of its troops and headquarters, methods of armed struggle and high morale the army was a formidable military force employing partisan tactics. It consisted of divisions and corps formed predominantly on a national and territorial principle. As a rule, a division had three brigades and support elements, and its strength ranged from two to twelve thousand men. A corps consisted of several divisions, joined by partisan detachments, operating within their own territories.

Although controlled from a central HQ, the army was scattered throughout the country and its divisions and corps usually employed partisan tactics.

The Supreme Headquarters of the People's Liberation Army was in direct command of five corps (18 divisions), and the Main HQ of Serbia had seven divisions. All the other units were under the command of the Main HQ of Macedonia (five divisions), Croatia (14 divisions), Slovenia (five divisions) and Vojvodina (one division).

The divisions and partisan detachments were armed chiefly with small arms (rifles, submachine guns and light machine guns) and a small number of light cannons and mortars. They had no aircraft, tanks, anti-aircraft weapons or heavy artillery and were always short of weapons, ammunition, clothes and food.

The People's Liberation Army was unable to maintain a continuous defence line and carry out major offensive operations. In September 1944, when the Soviet troops were hastening to the assistance of the fraternal Yugoslav people, it mounted active operations in the country's eastern and southern regions and in the direction of Belgrade. By the end of the month its 1st Proletarian and the 12th Assault corps which had been shifted to the Belgrade sector liberated almost the whole of Western Serbia and a considerable portion of Sumadija. Another group of forces consisting of the 13th and 14th corps and the 2nd Proletarian Division liberated a large portion of Eastern Serbia and was menacing from the rear the German forces defending the Bulgarian-Yugoslav border and also enemy units retreating from Greece.

The German forces in the Balkans held key positions in Albania, Greece and Yugoslavia. Their Commander-in-Chief Field-Marshal Weichs was in charge of Army Groups E and F stationed in Greece, Albania and Yugoslavia. In Yugoslavia the Germans had 270,000-strong Army Group F, consisting of the 2nd Panzer Army, Combat Group Serbia and separate units totalling 14 full-strength and eight under-strength German divisions and a large number of separate battalions and regiments. The Army Group had more than 200 aircraft. Five Hungarian divisions and several small units, a total of about 30,000 men, were stationed in Vojvodina, in the north-east of the country. Besides, there were 270,000 nationals serving in puppet units commanded by Nedic, Pavelic, Rupnik and Mihajlovic.

By the end of September 1944 the enemy had a total of 570,000 men in Yugoslavia. Armed with heavy artillery, panzers and aircraft, the enemy was superior to the People's Liberation Army both in manpower and weapons. The Germans occupied most of the large towns and industrial centres, controlled key strategic points, railways, waterways and the main highways.

In spite of the difficult situation, German Command was confident of its strength and intended to continue defensive operations in the Balkans. But the Soviet Army's rapid advance in the Balkans forced it to introduce serious changes into its plans.

Army Group E was ordered to begin a gradual withdrawal from Greece to the north. The 2nd Panzer Army was to enter the northeastern parts of Yugoslavia, take up defences facing east and link up on its left with Army Group South which was on the defensive against the 2nd Ukrainian Front. Combat Group Serbia was to organise defences along Yugoslavia's eastern border and reliably cover the evacuation of the German forces from the Balkan Peninsula. The remaining forces of Army Group F were to continue operations in central and western Yugoslavia.

The Soviet Government rendered continuous political, military and material support to the Yugoslav fighters.

To study the possibility of rendering all-round assistance to the People's Liberation Army and the partisans, a Soviet military mission headed by Lieutenant-General N. V. Korneyev arrived in the liberated areas of Yugoslavia on February 23, 1944, at a time when the Soviet Army was still some 1,200-1,300 kilometres away.

The mission was to organise material assistance to the Yugoslav troops which were desperately short of weapons, ammunition and food. The Soviet Government took steps to furnish this assistance, in spite of the difficulties it faced in supplying its own troops. In May 1944 a base was established in the small town of Kalinovka, Vinnitsa Region, from which the aircraft of the 5th Long-Range Air Division regularly flew to Yugoslavia.

Disregarding the difficult natural conditions and the enemy's powerful anti-aircraft defence, Soviet pilots flew thousands of missions delivering hundreds of tons of various supplies to the liberated parts of Yugoslavia.

At the end of May the German Command initiated yet another large-scale offensive against the patriotic forces. The main attack was aimed at the area of Drvara where the Supreme HQ of the People's Liberation Army was located. Here the Yugoslav forces routed an enemy force of 700 paratroops. But with the arrival of enemy panzers and motorised units the Supreme HQ was forced to abandon the area. In early June members of the Political Bureau of the Communist Party of Yugoslavia and most of the Supreme HQ staff were flown in a Soviet plane to Bari, Italy, and then to the island of Vis. The German attempt to deprive the people's liberation movement in Yugoslavia of its leadership failed.

In order to render more effective assistance to the Yugo-slav patriots the Soviet Government with the agreement of the British and Americans set up a Soviet air base at Bari, with transport planes and the latest combat aircraft piloted by Soviet fliers. From there the Soviet aircraft flew round-the-clock missions delivering supplies to the People's Libera-tion Army, evacuating the wounded and transferring fight-ing units on instructions from the Yugoslav Command.

Between May and September 1944 Soviet aircraft delivered 920 tons of weapons, ammunition, clothes, footwear, commu-nication facilities and medicines to the Yugoslav patriots. In August and September more than 80 Soviet doctors and nur-ses and 80 Soviet-trained Yugoslav radio operators with ra-dio equipment were flown to Yugoslavia via the Bari base and when Belgrade was liberated all the Bari-based aircraft were handed over to the People's Liberation Army of Yugo-slavia free of charge.

When the Soviet forces entered Rumania and Bulgaria and reached the Yugoslav border, the Soviet Command hastily established large supply bases in the Rumanian town of Craiova close to the Yugoslav border and in Sofia, capital of Bulgaria, and thus sharply increased deliveries to Yugosla-via. And when the Soviet troops entered Yugoslavia all the necessary freight was delivered to the People's Liberation Army and the partisans by motor transport.

2. THE BELGRADE OPERATION

PREPARATIONS FOR THE OPERATION

Laying the groundwork for the rout of the German troops in the Belgrade sector, the governments of the Soviet Union and Yugoslavia first agreed on a number of important mili-tary and political questions. At the end of September 1944 Marshal Tito arrived in Moscow to establish still broader political and military co-operation between the USSR and new Yugoslavia and coordinate joint operations.

During the talks the two sides agreed that the Soviet Army would enter Yugoslavia. They also resolved all questions concerning the joint actions of the Soviet and Yugoslav troops in liberating Eastern Serbia and Belgrade and all issues bearing on Soviet material and technical assistance to the People's Liberation Army. The Soviet Government declared that as soon as they accomplish their military tasks the Soviet troops would be withdrawn from Yugoslavia and that the civil administration in areas where the Soviet troops were temporarily deployed would remain in the hands of the organs of the National Committee of Liberation. For the peoples of Yugoslavia this was fresh proof of the Soviet Union's respect for their sovereign rights.

By officially announcing the agreement, the Soviet Government reaffirmed that it regarded the National Committee of Liberation as the sole lawful government of Yugoslavia and was prepared to give it full political support and all military and economic assistance.

Preparing for action in Yugoslavia, the Soviet Command took into account the strategic importance of Serbia and Belgrade through which passed the key routes between Central Europe and the southern part of the Balkan Peninsula.

The plan of the Belgrade Operation was in the main worked out by the command and HQ of the 3rd Ukrainian Front in conformity with the general plan of military operations of the Soviet Armed Forces on the southern wing of the Soviet-German front.

On September 20, 1944, GHQ ordered Commander of the 3rd Ukrainian Front Marshal F. I. Tolbukhin to deploy the 57th Army consisting of two corps (six infantry divisions) on the Bulgarian-Yugoslav border south of the Danube not later than September 30 and keep it on the alert for operations in the southerly direction. The Front command promptly launched preparations for the operation.

The Soviet troops in Bulgaria had to cover great distances and launch an offensive in difficult mountainous and wooded country. This required a high level of organisation and precision on the part of the commanders, all staffs and headquarters, the political apparatus and logistical service and also tremendous physical and moral exertion by the men in order to be able to take up assault positions on schedule.

On September 22, 1944 the troops of the 3rd Ukrainian Front began to move towards the Bulgarian-Yugoslav border, receiving reinforcements and new weapons, replenishments and ammunition en route. At the end of September and the beginning of October GHQ supplied the front with about 800 guns and mortars, nearly 1,300 machine-guns, 20,000 rifles and submachine guns and 546 tanks and self-propelled guns. When the operation was launched it had adequate stocks of ammunition and rations.

At the end of September the command of the 3rd Ukrainian Front completed its work on the plan of the Belgrade Operation, which was approved by GHQ on October 1. For the first time in the war it envisaged the joint actions of three armies—Soviet, Yugoslav and Bulgarian. The Soviet Command drew up a comprehensive plan coordinating the military operations of these armies whose troops were deployed over a large area.

The Soviet troops taking part in this operation were as follows: the 57th Army (64th, 68th and 75th Infantry corps), the 4th Guards Mechanised Corps, the 236th Infantry Division, the 5th Separate Guards Motorised Infantry Brigade, the 1st Guards Fortified Area, the 17th Air Army, the Danube Flotilla (all of the 3rd Ukrainian Front), the 10th Guards Infantry Corps, 46th Army, and a part of the 5th Air Army of the 2nd Ukrainian Front.

The Soviet forces which were to advance into Yugoslavia totalled 19 infantry divisions, one mechanised corps, 13 air divisions, three assault artillery divisions, five anti-aircraft artillery divisions, up to 50 artillery and mortars regiments and other units. The 57th and 46th armies had nearly 190,000 men. The Yugoslav forces taking part in the operation had four army corps totalling 17 divisions. The Bulgarian 1st, 2nd and 4th armies numbering 13 divisions and brigades under the operational control of the commander of the 3rd Ukrainian Front were to take part in liberating Yugoslavia's eastern regions.

In the course of the Belgrade Operation the Soviet, Yugoslav and Bulgarian troops were to destroy Combat Group Serbia, liberate eastern Yugoslavia and the city of Belgrade, establish a continuous front and seize key road junctions, cutting off the retreat routes of the German forces from the southern part of the Balkans to the north.

To achieve these objectives the Soviet and Bulgarian troops

were to attack the Germans from the east and the Yugoslav forces were to strike from the west, smash the enemy force and reach the line Danube-Obrenovac-Kragujevac-Cicevac-Knjazevac, advancing to a depth of 250-300 kilometres.

The main attack was to be delivered by 3rd Ukrainian Front's 57th Army and the 4th Guards Mechanised Corps. Their task was to crush the enemy's resistance in the East Serbian Mountains, move into the Morava valley and strike out at Belgrade. The 46th Army advancing on the right, north of the Danube, had orders to smash the enemy in Vojvodina and advance with its left-flank divisions to Belgrade, in the area of Pancevo. The Bulgarian 2nd Army, on the left of the 57th Army, was to deprive the enemy of the possibility of using the Salonika-Belgrade highway for shifting his troops out of Greece to the north. The Bulgarian 1st and 4th armies were to tie down the enemy forces south of the Bulgarian 2nd Army. The 17th Air Army received orders to attack enemy manpower and weapons in support of the land troops. The Danube Flotilla was to support the land forces advancing along the Danube with commando raids and artillery fire and also to transport troops and weapons to the Belgrade sector.

The co-operation of the 3rd and 2nd Ukrainian fronts, with the Yugoslav and Bulgarian armies was based on the operational plan drawn up by the Soviet Command. The joint actions of the three armies on Yugoslav territory were agreed with the Yugoslav Command in Moscow and in the Rumanian city of Craiova at the end of September and beginning of October 1944.

On October 1, GHQ ordered the commander of the 3rd Ukrainian Front to submit all the details of the operational plan to the Yugoslav Command. The head of the Soviet Military Mission in Belgrade was ordered to inform the headquarters of the People's Liberation Army that in order to secure the co-operation of the Soviet troops with the troops of the People's Liberation Army of Yugoslavia GHQ considered it necessary to set the following task to the forces of the People's Liberation Army operating in the Belgrade-Nis area: prevent the enemy troops from reaching the Kragujevac-Krusevac-Knjazevac line from the south and from the area of Nis, and if the situation developed favourably, capture Nis, and by conducting active operations south and southwest of Belgrade tie down the detachments of Nedic and Mi-hajlovic. Operations were to begin on October 9 or 10.

Key questions of the co-operation of the three armies on Yugoslav territory were settled by Soviet, Yugoslav and Bulgarian representatives at a meeting in Craiova on October 5. The sides exchanged information on manpower and weapons they had assigned for the operation and agreed on its most important aspects. At GHQ instructions, chief of staff of the 3rd Ukrainian Front General S. S. Biryuzov expounded the plan of the operation.

"The plan," he wrote, "encountered no objections. The meeting was also unanimous in its decision to use the Bulgarian troops in this operation.... Our talks ended in a day. By night we had signed an agreement on military co-operation in the struggle against the common enemy. We firmly decided that the Armed Forces of the Soviet Union, Yugoslavia and Bulgaria would immediately establish the closest co-operation, while remaining independent armies of sovereign states. Any hegemony was completely out of the question."

The Yugoslav-Bulgarian declaration that was signed on the same day said in part: "1. Military co-operation in the struggle against the common enemy—the German invaders; 2. That all questions pertaining to the relations between the allies and friendly co-operation between Bulgaria and Yugoslavia will be resolved in the spirit of fraternal and common interests of the peoples of Yugoslavia and the Bulgarian people."[1]

Extensive political work was conducted among the troops of the 3rd Ukrainian Front during preparations for the operation under the supervision of experienced Party organisers—member of the Front Military Council General A. S. Zheltov, Chief of the Front Political Department General I. S. Anoshin and member of the Military Council of the 57th Army L. P. Bocharov. The purpose was to instil the troops with a feeling of profound respect for the Yugoslav people and desire to help the Yugoslav soldiers and partisans in the fight against the common enemy. The soldiers were taught to fight in mountainous and wooded country and during assaults on large cities; they were briefed on the na-

---

[1] See A. Djonlagic (and others), *op. cit.*, p. 180.

tional-liberation struggle of the Yugoslav people, on the courage and heroism of its sons who heroically fought against the German intruders.

It was brought to the knowledge of all troops that at the beginning of September 1944 the USSR Supreme Soviet had awarded the highest Soviet orders to 46 officers of the People's Liberation Army of Yugoslavia for skilful command of the troops in the operations against the common enemy, and courage and fortitude in action.

Brought up in the spirit of proletarian internationalism the Soviet troops were resolved to fulfil their mission of liberation in Yugoslavia. All of them had heard of, and were inspired by, the daring exploits of Oleko Dundic, a hero of the Civil War in Russia. With many other Serbs and Croats he defended the gains of the October Revolution, fighting bravely against the enemies of Soviet Russia. Grateful Soviet people built an obelisk in his memory in Rovno where he was buried.

The sons of the Russian and Yugoslav peoples were determined to smash the enemy as quickly as possible and liberate Yugoslavia.

THE ROUT OF THE GERMAN TROOPS
IN THE EASTERN PARTS
OF YUGOSLAVIA

The Soviet offensive in the Belgrade sector was scheduled to begin on October 13 or 14, but in view of the changing situation it was started much earlier.

In the middle of September 1944 the Soviet Command learned that the Germans were withdrawing from the south of the Balkan Peninsula to the north. To frustrate their orderly retreat GHQ decided to use the air force on a large scale. In difficult weather the attack aircraft and bombers of the 17th Air Army commanded by General V. A. Sudets delivered day and night attacks at troop trains and motor convoys transporting men and equipment. Between September 13 and 30 Soviet aircraft flew 1,437 sorties, damaging or destroying 24 locomotives, 291 railway cars, 11 aircraft, and 121 motor vehicles and wrecking many bridges and other objectives. Traffic on the main highways in Serbia and Macedonia was largely paralysed.

In the meantime the 75th Infantry Corps under Major-General A. Z. Akimenko on September 22 crossed the Danube, entered Yugoslavia and opened an offensive in the great bend of the river west of Turnu Severin. In the course of very heavy fighting the Germans threw major forces into action in an attempt to retain the Iron Gate on the Danube. But the Soviet troops held on to the bridgehead until the main forces arrived.

GHQ kept a careful watch on the fighting and in view of the difficulties encountered by the corps ordered the 57th Army whose advance units reached the Yugoslav border on the night of September 27 to deploy on a line closer to the bend. Considerable enemy forces being tied down by the 75th Infantry Corps, Marshal F. I. Tolbukhin and commander of the 57th Army General N. A. Gagen decided to begin the offensive without waiting for all the troops of the army to assemble. On the night of September 27, the 3rd Ukrainian Front crossed the Bulgarian-Yugoslav border.

Fighting flared up along a 600-kilometre front in Yugoslavia's border areas. The Germans fell back before the pressure of the Soviet and Bulgarian troops, and on September 30 the 68th Infantry Corps and Rear-Admiral S. G. Gorshkov's Danube Flotilla liberated Negotin, a major strong-point which barred the way to the Soviet troops into Yugoslavia. The inhabitants of this town greeted their liberators enthusiastically.

On October 3, the enemy was driven out of Bor, the centre of Yugoslavia's gold and copper mining industry.

In the face of stubborn resistance the 57th Army continued to push deeper into Yugoslavia. The 75th Infantry Corps was advancing on the army's right flank along the right bank of the Danube in the general direction of Pozarevac; in the centre, the 68th Infantry Corps under Major-General N. N. Shkodunovich was driving on Petrovac and on the left flank the 64th Infantry Corps commanded by Major-General I. K. Kravtsov was bearing down upon Kraguevac and Krusevac.

In the course of the fighting the Soviet forces established direct co-operation with the Yugoslav troops. The headquarters of the 57th Army and the Yugoslav 14th Corps agreed on joint actions and worked out plans of using Soviet motor vehicles to bring in supplies for the Yugoslav troops. Between September 28 and October 4, the 57th Army acting in conjunction with the People's Liberation Army liberated 3,200 square kilometres of territory and a large number of towns. The enemy's losses were 8,000 officers and men, of whom 2,680 were taken prisoner.

Supported by the 17th Air Army the 3rd Ukrainian Front between September 28 and October 10 advanced 130 kilometres in the direction of the main blow and smashed the main forces of Combat Group Serbia. It crossed the East Serbian mountains, descended into the Morava valley, crossed the river in its stride and gained a bridgehead at Velika Plana. The best progress was made by the 68th Infantry Corps and the 5th Separate Guards Motorised Infantry Brigade. Committed from the Army Reserve to increase the momentum of the attack, the 5th Brigade executed a 120-kilometre approach manoeuvre in difficult terrain in 24 hours and by nightfall on October 8 was the first to break into the Morava valley. The enemy tried to retreat to the west and southwest but came under an attack by the People's Liberation Army and sustained heavy casualties.

During the crossing of the East Serbian Mountains, the advancing troops relied heavily on the Front's engineers commanded by Colonel-General L. Z. Kotlyar who together with the local population and labour battalions of the People's Liberation Army built and repaired bridges, cleared obstacles and demined and repaired roads. As a result of their efforts not only the infantry formations were able to cross the East Serbian Mountains between October 3 and 10 but also a motorised infantry brigade, a mechanised corps, an artillery division, three artillery brigades, 16 heavy artillery regiments and nearly 80 other combatant and logistical units. The advancing forces were supplied with 17,000 tons of ammunition, fuel and other military material.

General I. T. Schlemin's 46th Army advancing north of the Danube also achieved major successes. Upon entering Yugoslavia it established close contact with the Yugoslav units under the command of the Vojvodina Main HQ of the People's Liberation Army. Their joint actions in the Vrsac area were co-ordinated at a meeting of representatives of the Soviet and Yugoslav headquarters. Together with the

Rumanian 1st Army, which was under its control, and in conjunction with the People's Liberation Army, the 46th Army towards the end of the day on October 8 liberated Yugoslav territory between the Hungarian border and the mouth of the Tisza with the large towns Vrsac and Petrovgrad. The Soviet troops crossed the Tisza and secured important bridgeheads at Senta and Mol. The 10th Guards Corps under Lieutenant-General I. A. Rubanyuk captured Poncevo and reached the Danube along a 40-kilometre frontage. On the night of October 9, it crossed the river at Starcevo and captured a bridgehead on its right bank. Following a swift advance, the 46th Army approached Belgrade from the northeast. The troops of the 1st Guards Fortified Area under Major-General S. I. Nikitin and the Bulgarian 2nd Army commanded by General K. Stanchev also took part in heavy engagements. Supported by Soviet aircraft they were advancing towards Nis in co-operation with the 13th Corps of the People's Liberation Army of Yugoslavia and covering from the south the Soviet and Yugoslav troops converging on Belgrade.

While the Soviet troops and the Yugoslav 14th Corps advanced from the east, the 1st Corps Group of the People's Liberation Army[1] drew towards the Yugoslav capital from the south and southwest. In the morning of October 10 the Supreme Commander-in-Chief of the People's Liberation Army ordered the commander of the 1st Corps Group to link up at Palanca and Velika Plana with the troops of the 3rd Ukrainian Front which had crossed the Morava not later than October 11 and together with them advance on Belgrade.[2]

The entry of the 57th Army into the Morava valley created favourable conditions for committing the 4th Guards Mechanised Corps which was to launch a direct attack on the Yugoslav capital. This corps had covered a great battle road —from the banks of the great Russian river Volga to the banks of the Danube and the Morava. And now, together

---

[1] On October 5 the Group had 10 divisions numbering 32,080 men armed with small arms and supported by four artillery battalions. By October 10 the Group's numerical strength had risen to 40,000.

[2] See *Oslobodilacki rat naroda Jugoslavije 1941-1945*, Vol. 2, Belgrade, 1965, pp. 311-12.

with the 57th Army, it was waging battles for the liberation of Yugoslavia. The strike group of the 3rd Ukrainian Front was raised for attack on Belgrade 125-150 kilometres away.

Displaying mass heroism in the ferocious battles for the liberation of East Serbia, Soviet and Yugoslav troops lost about 3,500 men in killed and 4,500 in wounded. The common graves in Zajecar and Pozarevac alone hold the remains of 1,706 Soviet troops.

THE LIBERATION OF BELGRADE

Now that the Soviet troops were in the Morava valley and the Yugoslav 1st Corps Group had reached the south-western outskirts of Belgrade it was time to strike a direct blow at the capital. The enemy was determined at all costs to hold out in the face of assault by the Soviet and Yugoslav troops, bring in his main forces to Belgrade and ensure the withdrawal of the bulk of Army Group E from Greece.

After a thorough assessment of the situation it was decided to prevent the retreating enemy forces from entering the Yugoslav capital, since that could have considerably reinforced Belgrade's garrison and resulted in drawn-out street fighting, heavy damage to the city and numerous casualties among the civilian population. In the opinion of the Military Council of the 3rd Ukrainian Front the enemy's main forces had to be destroyed at the approaches to Belgrade and not in the city proper.

Only mobile forces could prevent the retreating enemy units from entering the city; this mission was assigned to the 4th Guards Mechanised Corps advancing from the southeast and to the Yugoslav 1st Corps Group pushing from the southwest and south. The Yugoslav troops looked forward impatiently to linking up with the Soviet Army.

Attaching great importance to the operations of the 4th Guards Mechanised Corps, the Soviet Command reinforced it with artillery and provided it with a powerful air cover. Its manpower strength was brought to 17,000, with 180 tanks and self-propelled guns, 324 guns and mortars and 21 rocket launchers.

The corps crossed the Morava, and in the morning of October 12 struck out against Belgrade. The enemy met it with heavy fire from artillery, panzers, assault guns and other weapons. But nothing could stop the Soviet armour. On the first day of its offensive the corps linked up with the 21st Serbian Division of the Yugoslav 1st Corps at the village of Natalinci, 12 kilometres east of Topola, and then pressed on Belgrade with a battalion of Yugoslav infantry riding the armour. The Soviet tanks captured Topola and Mladenovac, cutting an important highway leading from Belgrade to the south.

In Topola the Soviet troops linked up with the 10th Brigade, 5th Striking Division, of the People's Liberation Army. With Yugoslav troops riding on their tanks and in trucks, the Soviet units pressed on forward. In two days of heavy fighting on water-bogged terrain the corps advanced 120 kilometres and by the night of October 13 reached Belgrade at Mount Avala, now the site of the tomb of the unknown soldier, where the Soviet troops linked up with the main forces of the Yugoslav 1st Corps Group. From the mountain top they had a good view of Belgrade.

The appearance of Soviet troops at Belgrade spread panic in the enemy garrison. Nedic's puppet government in Belgrade fled to Vienna and the German Command proclaimed a state of siege in the capital. Losing no time, the Soviet and Yugoslav units stormed the outer ring of fortifications and in the evening of October 14 attacked the enemy in the city's southern outskirts.

The breakthrough to Belgrade by the 3rd Ukrainian Front from the south and east, the 2nd Ukrainian Front from the northeast and units of the People's Liberation Army from the southwest and south, resulted in the encirclement of a 20,000-strong enemy grouping southeast of Belgrade. The combined efforts of the Soviet, Yugoslav and Bulgarian troops hurled the strong enemy force, retreating from the Balkans, to the north into the mountains. The 68th Infantry Corps of the 57th Army reached Kraguevac, and the 64th liberated Krusevac; the Bulgarian 2nd Army, the Yugoslav 13th Corps and the Soviet 1st Guards Fortified Area on October 14 drove the enemy out of Nis and straddled the Athens-Belgrade railway at a number of points.

The heaviest fighting in the final phase of the Belgrade Operation took place in the city proper, southeast of it and at Kraguevac. Belgrade, which the enemy had prepared for defensive operations, had a garrison of more than 20,000 men, 40 panzers and about 170 guns and mortars. By putting up a stiff resistance, the German Command hoped to tie down as many Soviet and Yugoslav troops as possible, thus facilitating the withdrawal of the units of Army Group E and saving them at the expense of the Belgrade garrison. This plan, however, fell through. The German troops which had pulled out from the south of the Balkans were either wiped out or taken prisoner by the People's Liberation Army after the liberation of Belgrade. This was confirmed by former chief of staff of Army Group E Erich Schmidt-Richberg in his book *Das Ende auf dem Balkan*.

The overwhelming offensive of the Soviet, Yugoslav and Bulgarian troops in Yugoslavia forced the Germans to split up their forces which subsequently were routed piecemeal.

Meanwhile preparations were in progress for an assault on Belgrade. In view of the situation, the attack had to take the enemy by surprise. It was to be carried out by the 4th Guards Mechanised Corps, the 73rd Guards and the 236th Infantry divisions, three artillery brigades, 13 artillery and mortar regiments, three self-propelled artillery regiments, an anti-aircraft division, three anti-aircraft artillery regiments (all of the 3rd Ukrainian Front), the Danube Flotilla and the 109th Guards Infantry Division of the 46th Army, 2nd Ukrainian Front, and also eight divisions of the Yugoslav 1st Proletarian and 12th corps. Air cover was to be provided by the 3rd Ukrainian Front's aviation.

On the Soviet side preparations for the assault and the organisation of co-operation with Yugoslav forces were conducted by General S. S. Biryuzov and commander of the Front artillery General M. I. Nedelin; the Yugoslav side was represented by the commander of the People's Liberation Army's 1st Army Group, General Peko Dapcevic. Agreement was reached on all questions of the joint action of Soviet and Yugoslav troops. The leading role in the attack which was set for the afternoon of October 14 was assigned to the 4th Guards Mechanised Corps and a powerful Soviet artillery group of 600 guns and mortars.

Some time earlier the Command of the People's Liberation Army asked the Military Council of the 3rd Ukrainian
Front to give the Yugoslav units the opportunity to enter
their country's capital first. When after a powerful artillery
bombardment the Soviet and Yugoslav forces surged forward, men of the Yugoslav 1st Proletarian Division boarded
Soviet tanks so that Soviet and Yugoslav troops entered the
city simultaneously.

To save the city from being heavily damaged and to reduce civilian casualties the Soviet Command ordered the
troops to use their powerful weapons very carefully and for
the most part they used grenades, machine and submachine
guns and bayonets.

By nightfall on October 15, a large part of Belgrade was
free. The troops of the two fraternal armies fought shoulder
to shoulder in street battles, clearing the enemy out of every
house and every floor.

Despite the fairly great success of the first two days of the
assault, fighting in Belgrade became drawn out because considerable forces were assigned to deal with 20,000 enemy
troops who were sealed off in the southeast of the capital
and were making desperate attempts to break through to the
west. Fighting southeast of Belgrade ended on October 19
only. The enemy group was almost completely wiped out
with the effective assistance of the 17th Air Army.

The Germans had heavily mined the city, and the Military Council of the 3rd Ukrainian Front on October 14 ordered the troops to begin mine clearing as soon as they liberate it. This job was assigned to seven engineer battalions
whose first task was to remove mines from buildings to be
occupied by Yugoslav government agencies and the Supreme
HQ of the People's Liberation Army. They removed mines
from 845 structures, including 85 administrative buildings,
rendering harmless 3,179 mines, 3,540 explosive charges
weighing 28,656 kilos, 12 booby traps and seven HE dumps,
and saving the city from enormous damage.

The Yugoslav people paid tribute to the heroism of the Soviet soldiers who did not spare their lives in preventing heavy
damage being done to the city and its inhabitants injured.

R. Colakovic, who observed columns of Soviet troops moving along the liberated streets of Belgrade during the last

days of the assault, subsequently wrote: "The people wave to them. They give them bread and tobacco. As soon as a column stops, the townsfolk come up to the soldiers, shake their hands and even kiss them to express their thanks and to welcome their arrival."

In the morning of October 20, after an artillery bombardment, Soviet and Yugoslav troops attacked and captured the ancient Kalemegdan Fortress, the last nazi stronghold in Belgrade. Here General V. I. Zhdanov and Yugoslav general Peko Dapcevic, who commanded the operations in Belgrade, met and hugged each other in a brotherly embrace. By nightfall the Yugoslav capital was completely cleared of the enemy. In the street fighting Soviet and Yugoslav troops killed 15,000 and took prisoner 9,000 enemy officers and men.

Having liberated Belgrade, Soviet and Yugoslav troops continued to press the Germans to the west and by November 9 reached their fortified positions situated between Ilok and the confluence of the Drina and the Sava. On this line, lying approximately 100 kilometres west of Belgrade, the front was temporarily stabilised.

While heavy fighting was in progress for Belgrade, the 68th and 64th Infantry corps operating far to the south and southeast of the city pushed steadily forward. By nightfall on October 21 they reached the line Aranjelovac-Gornji Milanovac-Kraguevac-Kralevo-Krusevac, thus ensuring the successful outcome of the offensive of the 3rd Ukrainian Front's main forces and helping to liberate Yugoslavia's eastern regions. At the same time the Bulgarian armies and the Yugoslav 13th Corps advanced to the west and southwest of Nis and Leskovac, reached the line Kursumlia-Vrane-Kocano and covered the Front's flank and rear from attacks by enemy divisions retreating from the south of the Balkan Peninsula.

North of Belgrade the 46th Army was liberating Vojvodina. At the end of October it liberated Novi Sad and Subotica in co-operation with Yugoslav units and crossed the Danube into Hungary.

The Belgrade Operation was a decisive phase in the fighting for the liberation of the whole of Yugoslavia. In his order of the day of October 20, 1944 Supreme Commander-in-Chief J. V. Stalin commended the troops of the 3rd Ukrainian Front and the People's Liberation Army of Yugoslavia which had liberated Belgrade, and a 24-salvo salute from 324 guns was fired in Moscow in their honour. Twenty units which had distinguished themselves in action had the title "Belgrade" attached to their names and 30 received combat orders. On June 19, 1945 the Presidium of the USSR Supreme Soviet instituted a medal, "For the Liberation of Belgrade", which was awarded to all the troops which had participated in the operation. Three hundred officers and men of the People's Liberation Army of Yugoslavia were decorated with Soviet orders and medals.

For courage and valour in the fighting for the freedom of Yugoslavia and her capital, the Presidium of the Anti-Fascist People's Liberation Veche of Yugoslavia conferred orders and medals on 794 men of the People's Liberation Army and more than 2,000 Soviet officers and men, thirteen of whom were made People's Heroes of Yugoslavia.

The people of Yugoslavia will always remember the courage of the Soviet troops and the losses they sustained in the common struggle against fascism. In the Belgrade Operation alone, according to incomplete figures, the Soviet Army lost more than 30,000 troops in killed, wounded and missing.

The Belgrade Operation executed by the combined efforts of the Soviet Army, the People's Liberation Army of Yugoslavia and the Bulgarian Army had a very important impact on political and military developments. It ended in the rout of Combat Group Serbia and the defeat of a part of Army Group E. In the fighting against the 3rd Ukrainian Front approximately 100,000 enemy officers and men were killed or taken prisoner. The Germans were driven out of the eastern part of Yugoslavia and her capital. Belgrade became the site of the central bodies of the political and military leadership of new Yugoslavia. The enemy troops in this sector of the Balkan Peninsula had been thrown back some 300 kilometres to the west. Large enemy forces were deprived of the opportunity of pulling out from the south of Balkans along convenient routes. They were compelled to take to difficult mountainous and roadless regions only to come under heavy blows delivered by units of the People's Liberation Army.

With the liberation of the eastern parts of the country the Yugoslav people and its army acquired a stable home front with large manpower and material resources essential for the complete liberation of the country. The People's Liberation Army could now establish a continuous front, and, relying on the liberated part of the country, take its place in the common struggle against nazi Germany.

3. YUGOSLAVIA IS FREE

THE INVADERS ARE EXPELLED

The battle for Belgrade over, the Soviet troops, having fulfilled their mission, were leaving the friendly country. This was in keeping with a GHQ directive of October 15, 1944 to Marshal F. I. Tolbukhin saying that after capturing Belgrade the 3rd Ukrainian Front was to consolidate itself on captured ground and "not to advance any further into Yugoslavia".

Now the Soviet troops had to drive the nazis out of Hungary and Austria. To support the further operations of the Yugoslav forces against the Germans, a Soviet air group under General A. N. Vitruk was ordered to remain in the country. The 68th Infantry Corps and the 1st Guards Fortified Area were also to remain in Yugoslavia for a time to cover Belgrade from the southwest against possible attacks by enemy forces withdrawing from Greece.

The 57th Army which was shifted to the Hungarian sector of the front crossed the Danube at Batina and Apatin and in November 1944 in the course of heavy battles liberated a considerable part of Yugoslavia between the Danube and the Drava.

Early in December the Soviet 68th Infantry Corps arrived in the combat area of the People's Liberation Army at Ilok. Co-operating with the Yugoslav 1st Proletarian Corps and the Danube Flotilla, the 68th Corps waged offensive operations in the general direction of Osijek and on December 25 handed over their positions to the Bulgarian 1st Army and headed for Hungary. In the south of Yugoslavia, the units of the People's Liberation Army of Yugoslavia and the Bulgarian troops in the middle of November liberated Skopje, the capital of Macedonia, and continued to drive the Germans out of the south of the country. At the end of 1944, the Bulgarian 1st Army was transferred to Hungary and the remaining Bulgarian forces began gradually to return home.

By the end of the year Serbia, Montenegro and Macedonia were completely cleared of the Germans, but almost the whole of Bosnia, Hercegovina, Croatia and Slovenia were still occupied. Large forces of the People's Liberation Army were engaged there. In the first months of 1945 there were no major changes in the situation, decisive events only developing in March.

All the most important political and military changes in Yugoslavia at the time were effected under the overwhelming influence of the Soviet Army's victories on the southern wing of the Soviet-German front and the Soviet Government's measures designed to uphold the national aspirations of the Balkan peoples.

The political situation steadily shifted in favour of the patriotic forces which determined the country's further development and attained major results. In spite of the intrigues of the emigre circles, a united Yugoslav Government headed by Josip Broz Tito, with members of the National Committee of Liberation as its core, was formed early in March.

The advance of the Soviet troops in Hungary impelled the German Command to speed up the withdrawal of its troops from Yugoslavia. This sharply reduced the strength of the Germans in Yugoslavia, and after the defeat at Lake Balaton, they virtually ceased all resistance in Yugoslavia and in great haste retreated to the western areas of Hungary and Austria.

In the course of preparations for the final operations the Yugoslav Command coordinated its plans with the commander of the 3rd Ukrainian Front which was poised to attack Vienna. This attack enabled the Yugoslav Army to continue its successful advance.

In the middle of April 1945, the Soviet Army reached the line Vienna-Bruck-Graz, virtually cutting off the German troops in Croatia and Slovenia from Germany and dooming them to defeat. The enemy kept up his resistance during the last weeks of the war not in an attempt to retain the captured territory, but in the hope of holding out long enough to surrender to the Anglo-American forces.

In the last days of the war the Yugoslav troops supported by Soviet combat aircraft drove the enemy out of Croatia and Slovenia and on May 8 freed their capitals Zagreb and Ljubljana.

The whole of Yugoslavia was liberated within a week after the Soviet troops had smashed the Germans at Berlin and Prague. On May 15 the Yugoslav Army routed and captured a German grouping in the extreme northwest of the country from where it tried to retreat to the west. Yugoslavia was free.

FRATERNAL ASSISTANCE

During the struggle against the German invaders Yugoslavia received enormous political, military, material and technical assistance from the Soviet Union.

On September 7, 1944, the USSR State Defence Committee decided to provide training facilities in the USSR for 500 armour officers of the People's Liberation Army. The formation of a Yugoslav armoured brigade consisting of 895 men and 65 T-34 tanks was completed by March 1945, and shortly afterwards it was dispatched to the front.

Early in October 1944, when the Soviet troops were already fighting in Yugoslavia, the Yugoslav 1st Infantry Brigade which had been raised, equipped and trained in the USSR was transferred to the Command of the People's Liberation Army which incorporated it into the group of Yugoslav troops advancing on Belgrade.

In response to a request from the Yugoslav Command the Soviet Government on November 15, 1944 placed under its operational control the 10th Guards Attack and the 236th Fighter air divisions, the 9th Air Base, 15 liaison and several transport aircraft. As a result, the People's Liberation Army acquired an air group of about 350 aircraft under Major-General A. N. Vitruk of the Soviet Union.

Under an agreement between the Soviet and Yugoslav governments, the USSR supplied Yugoslavia with weapons and equipment for 12 infantry and two air divisions. They were delivered at the end of 1944 and early in 1945 and went to re-equip units of the People's Liberation Army fighting in Serbia and Vojvodina.

During the war Soviet arms supplies to Yugoslavia totalled 155,300 rifles and carbines, over 38,000 submachine guns,
more than 15,500 machine guns, 5,800 guns and mortars,
69 tanks and 491 aircraft.

The USSR played a considerable role in training and re-
organising the Yugoslav forces into a regular army. Soviet
military advisers and instructors were posted with the
People's Liberation Army at the request of the Yugoslav
Command.

The Supreme HQ of the People's Liberation Army began
the re-organisation of its troops after the Belgrade Operation, and so the Soviet Command transferred to the Yugoslavs captured enemy equipment and weapons, besides large
quantities of its own material.

In keeping with instructions of the Supreme HQ of the
People's Liberation Army, the 1st, 2nd and 3rd armies were
activated on January 1, 1945, and the 4th Army on March 1.
On March 3 the People's Liberation Army was renamed the
Yugoslav Army and the Supreme HQ was re-organised into
the General Staff.

At the beginning of 1945, the Yugoslav Army had 59 divisions numbering approximately 800,000 men. But since they
were short of weapons the USSR State Defence Committee
on February 10, 1945 decided to supply the Yugoslav army
between March and September 1945 with enough weapons
and other war material to arm 20 infantry divisions, three
artillery brigades, two armoured brigades, and one mixed and
one transport air division.

Soviet airmen played an important role in the formation
of the Yugoslav air force. In addition to flying combat missions, General Vitruk's Air Group trained 4,516 specialists,
including attack and fighter pilots, in something like six
months. The Group's Command helped the Yugoslavs to establish the headquarters of an air corps and two air divisions,
build 24 air strips and repair another 14.

When withdrawn from Yugoslavia in May 1945, the Air
Group on orders from the Soviet Command transferred its
aircraft to the Yugoslav Army. In June 1945 two Yugoslav
air regiments activated and trained in the USSR were transferred to Yugoslavia.

The various assistance furnished by the Soviet Union to

Yugoslavia during their joint struggle against the common enemy, at a time when the USSR was experiencing grave economic difficulties, manifested the lofty internationalist feelings of the Soviet people.

At the request of the Yugoslav leadership the Soviet Government supplied Yugoslavia with 50,000 tons of grain and flour which were urgently transported to the liberated towns by water (Danube), rail and road. By December 7, 1944 all the grain and flour was delivered. In a talk to Harrison of Reuter's agency at the end of November 1944 Josip Broz Tito said that thanks to the Soviet Government and the efforts of Soviet officers 50,000 tons of grain were being delivered to Yugoslavia at a great risk; 17,000 tons of this grain being supplied to Belgrade. This quantity, he said, would keep the city's population supplied with bread for five or six months on the basis of 400 grammes of flour a day per person. When measures were taken to supply Belgrade with fuel, the Soviet Army once again provided the transport to deliver it to the population and the army.

On April 11, 1945 a Soviet-Yugoslav treaty of friendship, mutual assistance and post-war co-operation was signed in Moscow. By its terms the two countries undertook to continue the joint struggle against Germany to the victorious conclusion and to assist each other in this struggle with all the means at their disposal. It was also envisaged that the two sides would act in the spirit of friendship and co-operation after the war with the view to developing and strengthening the economic and cultural ties between their peoples. By signing this treaty the Soviet Union gave the Yugoslav people very effective moral and political support. It was an important political act which strengthened Yugoslavia's position in the world to a still greater extent.

The Soviet-Yugoslav Trade Agreement which was signed in Moscow two days later envisaged the deliveries of Soviet commodities essential for Yugoslavia's war effort and the needs of her civilian population.

The Soviet Union took part in rehabilitating railways and waterways in the liberated areas of Yugoslavia. Sailors of the Danube Flotilla helped clear mines and make the Danube navigable again.

4. THE RESULTS
OF THE STRUGGLE
FOR THE LIBERATION
OF YUGOSLAVIA

The USSR played a most important part in helping the peoples of Yugoslavia win national independence in their long and difficult fight against the German invaders. Thanks to the victories of the Soviet Army, the peoples of Yugoslavia, like other Balkan peoples, could independently tend to their domestic affairs and take the path of democratic development.

Acting in close co-operation with the People's Liberation Army the Soviet Army smashed powerful enemy forces and liberated large parts of the country, and its swift offensive towards Budapest and Vienna paved the way for a complete liberation of Yugoslavia.

Two Soviet field armies and one air army fought side by side with the Yugoslav forces. Twenty Soviet infantry divisions, one mechanised corps, more than 10 air divisions, the Danube Flotilla and several dozen artillery units took part in the fighting in Yugoslavia.

In the course of their offensive operations in Yugoslavia, the fraternal armies routed the main forces of Army Group F (13 divisions and brigades) and up to six divisions of Army Group E transferred from Greece and Albania.

A million and seven hundred thousand Yugoslavs lost their lives in the long struggle against fascism. The losses sustained by the People's Liberation Army and the partisans were 305,000 in killed and 425,000 in wounded. These casualties would have been even greater if the Soviet Army did not extend a helping hand to the Yugoslav people. Soviet troops did not spare their lives for the sake of their lofty cause and their losses in the battles in Yugoslavia amounted to 8,000 dead.

During the war and in the post-war years the Yugoslav people, its political and military leaders, spoke of the decisive role played by the Soviet Army in the country's liberation. The newspaper *Borba*, organ of the Central Committee of the Communist Party of Yugoslavia, wrote on February 23, 1945: "We are absolutely certain that the participation of the Red Army in the war against fascism was the principal factor that ensured our victory in the struggle for national liberation. The participation of the Red Army in the fight against Germany and Italy made our national uprising possible. Without this participation our partisan war would have been impossible. Without the struggle of the Soviet Union and its Red Army against the fascist enslavers our uprising would have been doomed to failure."

The struggle against the nazis which was brought to a successful conclusion with the help of the Soviet Army, opened a new chapter in the history of the Yugoslav people. A major political victory was scored over domestic reactionary forces and a people's democratic government was established in the country. In November 1945 Yugoslavia was proclaimed a Federal People's Republic, and the Constitution adopted in January 1946 confirmed the political and social gains of the working people of the Federal People's Republic of Yugoslavia and became the legal basis for its development along the socialist path.

Cemented by the blood shed in the war the friendship between the peoples of the USSR and Yugoslavia is developing for the benefit of peace and world progress.

Chapter VI

FINLAND WITHDRAWS
FROM THE WAR.

LIBERATION
OF NORWAY'S NORTHERN REGIONS

The countries of the Scandinavian Peninsula—Norway and Sweden—and the Soviet Union's northern neighbour Finland occupied an important place in nazi Germany's aggressive plans in the Second World War. Overhanging Europe, they reliably covered nazi Germany's northern strategic flank and were a convenient springboard for military operations both against the Soviet Union and Britain, and offered advantageous naval bases for operations in the North Atlantic. On top of that the Scandinavian countries were of considerable economic importance for nazi Germany.

Neutral Sweden, with her developed industry and vast iron ore resources, became Germany's economic appendage. One out of three German panzers was made out of Swedish iron ore.

Having occupied Norway in the spring of 1940, the Germans used her for invading the Soviet Arctic regions, and turned her numerous ice-free ports into their naval bases. They also exploited Norway's economy, annually shipping out 25,000 tons of copper, 30,000 tons of aluminium and 75 per cent of the molybdenum and 100 per cent of the sulphur used in Germany. Millions of tons of Swedish iron ore were shipped through the Norwegian port of Narvik.

Finland attracted the attention of the German aggressors by the proximity of her borders to Leningrad and the profascist sentiments of her government. The foreign policy of the Finnish government at the time was characterised by Pehr Evind Svinhufvud, one of the Soviet Union's most diehard enemies, who said: "...any enemy of Russia must always be a friend of Finland."[1]

---

[1] *Documents on German Foreign Policy 1918-1945*, Series D (1937-1945), Vol. V, London, 1953, p. 536.

1. FINLAND WITHDRAWS
FROM THE WAR

FINLAND, AN ALLY
OF NAZI GERMANY

Finland declared war on the Soviet Union in June 1941.
Dazzled by Germany's victories in Western Europe, the Finnish reactionaries imagined that they would have no trouble
in realising their expansionist plans. Finnish President Ryti
started to bargain with Germany over Finland's claims to
the Kola Peninsula and other parts of the Soviet Union.
Field-Marshal von Mannerheim declared that the present
battle was the continuation of the war of 1918 for the establishment of Greater Finland extending to the Urals.

But the course of developments dashed the hopes of the
Finnish reactionaries. The war immediately acquired a sanguinary and protracted character. From 1941 to 1943 the
Finnish Army lost 37,000 officers and men in killed.[1] The
country's economy was beset by grave difficulties as each
month of the war cost her huge sums, and already in 1943
the more far-sighted Finnish politicians began to think
seriously about ways of pulling Finland out of the war.
The Soviet Army's successful offensive in the winter of 1944
at Leningrad and Novgorod, which ended in a crushing defeat for the German troops and in the liberation of the greater
part of Leningrad Region, sharply aggravated Finland's military and political position. The Finnish Command was
fully aware of this fact. General Erfurth, German liaison officer with Mannerheim's headquarters, noted in his diary in
January of 1944 that for the first time he heard Finnish General Staff officers speaking of the possibilities of a separate
peace, since no one any longer believed in the possibility of
a German victory.[2] Yet many people still believed that a
military conflict between the USSR and its Western Allies
in the anti-Hitler coalition was "inevitable".

Anti-war sentiments gripped ever larger sections of the

---

[1] See *Finland, a Democracy of the North*, Helsinki, p. 61.
[2] C. Leonard Lundin, *Finland in the Second World War*, Blooming-
ton, 1957, p. 193.

civilian population and there were increasing cases of desertion from the Finnish Army. The illegal Communist Party of Finland intensified its efforts to rally together the supporters of Finland's withdrawal from the war. "The Communists," wrote Ville Pessi, General Secretary of the Communist Party of Finland, "set up secret groups in various parts of the country which worked among the population for Finland's withdrawal from the war and for the restoration of peace. At the final stage of the war an anti-war opposition which included members of various parties appeared in the Seim."

In these circumstances Finland's ruling circles were forced to enter into negotiations with the USSR. In the middle of February 1944 Soviet Minister in Stockholm Alexandra Kollontai met the representative of the Finnish Government, Juho Paasikivi, who had instructions to find out the terms of Finland's withdrawal from the war.

Desiring to attain peace and save human lives, the Soviet Government shortly presented the following preliminary armistice terms: rupture of relations with Germany and the internment of her troops in Finland; renewal of the Soviet-Finnish treaty of 1940; return of Allied prisoners of war and civilians. In many countries these terms were assessed as generous and moderate.[1]

But the nazis did all they could to postpone the collapse of the Axis. Goebbels' propaganda tried to frighten the Finns with "Bolshevisation" and "exile to Siberia", and when on April 19 Hitler ordered an embargo on supplies of weapons and food to Finland, her reactionary ruling circles rejected the Soviet armistice terms. Taking this step, the Finnish Government relied heavily on powerful defensive lines on the Karelian Isthmus and also on the political support from the United States which maintained diplomatic relations with Finland.

During the three years of war the Finnish troops built a powerful defence system, taking advantage of the inaccessible terrain. It was especially well organised on the Karelian Isthmus where it had three defensive lines extending to a depth of more than 100 kilometres, and the Finnish Command considered that the Karelian Wall would prove too great an obstacle for the Soviet troops.

[1] See *The Times*, London, June 13, 1944.

Taking stock of the situation, the Soviet Government decided that in order to chase the Finnish invaders out of the USSR and hasten Finland's withdrawal from the war it had to resort to active military operations.

THE PLANS
OF THE FINNISH REACTION
FALL THROUGH

The Soviet Command was faced with a difficult task. The military operations which took place on the Karelian Isthmus in late 1939 and early 1940 showed that overcoming heavily fortified positions and a large number of natural obstacles required enormous effort. At the time it took the Soviet troops three and a half months to break through the Mannerheim Line and take Vyborg. Now they had to overrun the Karelian Wall with the utmost speed and with the least possible losses. The operation had, therefore, to be prepared with exceptional thoroughness.

The plan was to liberate Vyborg and Petrozavodsk, rout the enemy's main forces on the Karelian and Onega-Ladoga isthmuses, drive them out of Soviet territory and restore the state border with Finland. This was to be achieved by two successive blows delivered by the right wing of the Leningrad Front in co-operation with the Baltic Fleet, and by the left wing of the Karelian Front with the support of the Onega and Ladoga Flotillas. The first blow was to be struck by the Leningrad Front and the second, 11 days later, by the Karelian Front. The assault was to be preceded by mass strikes at key military targets in Finland by long-range bombers.

Accordingly the 21st and 23rd Field armies of the Leningrad Front (commander Marshal L. A. Govorov) in conjunction with the 13th Air Army and the Baltic Fleet were to direct their main attack along the coast of the Gulf of Finland, pierce the Finnish defences and capture Vyborg, the strategically important strongpoint and main communications hub of the Karelian Isthmus.

The 7th Army of the Karelian Front (commander General of the Army K. A. Meretskov) was to strike out from the river Svir in the general direction of Sortavala, and the 32nd Army out of an area north of Lake Onega at Medvezhyegorsk and in co-operation with the 7th Air Army and the Ladoga and Onega flotillas liberate the occupied regions of Karelia as far as the state border with Finland.

North of Lake Onega, in Southern Karelia and on the Karelian Isthmus in the zone of the Leningrad and Karelian fronts the enemy had 15 divisions and six brigades, a total of about 268,000 officers and men, with 1,930 guns and mortars, 110 tanks and about 250 combat aircraft. A considerable number of warships were operating in the Gulf of Finland, and lakes Ladoga and Onega. The Finnish naval aviation had 100 aircraft.

Taking into account the enemy strength, the impregnability of his fortified positions and the difficult terrain, the Soviet Command assembled considerable forces in Southern Karelia and on the Karelian Isthmus.

When the two fronts launched the offensive, they had 1.6-fold superiority in manpower, 3.3 times as many guns and mortars, 3.2 times as many tanks and self-propelled guns and six times as many aircraft as the enemy had.

In the morning of June 9, 1944 the artillery of the Leningrad Front and the Baltic Fleet opened fire on the first line of the enemy defences. For 10 hours 240 guns of calibres ranging from 122 mm to 406 mm kept up murderous fire, while the air force dealt concentrated strikes. According to commander-in-chief of the Finnish Army Marshal Mannerheim the artillery fire and the air strikes were so powerful that they were "heard even in Helsinki, 270 kilometres from the front line."[1]

On the same day the Soviet troops conducted reconnaissance in force along the entire front. The Finnish Command took it for the beginning of the offensive and hastily moved its tactical reserves to the first line of defence. At 6.00 hours on the following day the artillery bombardment was resumed in the zone of Colonel-General D. N. Gusev's 21st Army.

On June 10, after artillery and arial softening up, the army assumed the offensive. On the same day it crossed the Sestra, ploughed through the first line of the enemy defence along a 19-kilometre sector and pushed along the Vyborg Highway to a depth of 14 kilometres. Effectively supporting the advancing infantry, the 13th Air Army under Lieutenant-

[1] G. Mannerheim, *Minnen. Del. II, 1939-1946*, Helsinki, 1952, p. 382.

General S. D. Rybalchenko carried out almost 900 sorties during the day.

On the second day the 23rd Army under Lieutenant-General A. I. Cherepanov was moved into the breach. The resistance of the Finnish troops was crushed and by nightfall on June 11, the troops of the Leningrad Front had captured more than 80 inhabited localities and, in effect, reached the second, main line of defence. On the same day GHQ ordered the army to continue the offensive, vigorously pursue the enemy and capture the area of Vyborg on June 18-20.

The enemy, however, managed to hold on to the main line of the defence and organise fierce resistance with the result that on June 12 the troops of the 23rd Army advanced only 2-6 kilometres. The Commander of the Leningrad Front regrouped his forces and committed the second echelons of his infantry corps. At 8.00 hours on June 14 the Soviet troops started another powerful artillery bombardment. For 90 minutes heavy shells pounded the defenders' concrete pillboxes. There were up to 250 guns and mortars per kilometre of the front line in the sector of the main attack. At the same time the 21st Army shifted the direction of its main attack to the maritime sector, catching the Finnish Command completely by surprise.[1] Although the Finns resisted desperately they fell back to the third line of defence by June 17.

The Finnish Army found itself in a critical situation. On June 19 Marshal Mannerheim appealed to the Finnish troops to stop the Soviet advance before the last defence line. A day earlier the Finnish Command requested help from nazi Germany and the German Command urgently transferred by sea the 122nd Infantry Division, the 303rd Assault Artillery Brigade and an air squadron from Combat Group Narva. But German reinforcements could not stem the Soviet advance on Vyborg. At 11.00 hours on June 20 the 108th Infantry Corps under Lieutenant-General I. F. Tikhonov broke into the town's southern outskirts and by nightfall Vyborg was free.

On June 21 GHQ once again altered the tasks of the Leningrad Front, indicating that its main forces should strike out at Lappeenranta and a part should advance on Elisenvaara and drive the enemy out of the northeastern sector of the Karelian Isthmus.

---

[1] *Kansan Uutiset*, June 10, 1964.

On the same day the 7th and 32nd armies of the left wing of the Karelian Front, after a more than three-hour long artillery bombardment, went over to the offensive in the direction of Svir and Petrozavodsk. During the day Lieutenant-General A. N. Krutikov's 7th Army crossed the Svir, cut through the enemy's main defences along a 12-kilometre front and advanced 5-6 kilometres; the 32nd Army under Lieutenant-General F. D. Gorelenko advanced from 14 to 16 kilometres. The enemy's stubborn resistance, however, soon slowed down the Soviet advance.

To break enemy resistance, GHQ on June 23 ordered the Front to act with greater determination and fixed the time when its troops should reach specified enemy lines. The advancing troops were effectively supported by the Ladoga Flotilla under Rear-Admiral V. S. Cherokhov. It landed a task force in the rear of the enemy defending Olonets. Retreating to the northwest the Finns erected road blocks and blew up roads and bridges. On June 24 the Soviet troops liberated Medvezhyegorsk and on June 28 Petrozavodsk. The Finnish Army was on the brink of disaster.

In these circumstances the Finnish Government once again asked the Soviet Government for its armistice terms. But on June 22, Ribbentrop unexpectedly arrived in Helsinki, as the nazi clique undertook yet another attempt to keep Finland harnessed to its war-chariot. He demanded that the Finnish Government commit itself unequivocally to alliance with nazi Germany. Although it was absolutely clear that in view of the situation Finland had to quit the war without any further delay, President Ryti (he was tried as a war criminal after the war) decided to submit to nazi Germany's demands and continue senseless bloodshed. In a letter to Hitler of June 26 he pledged not to conclude a separate peace with the USSR without Germany's consent.

It was obvious to the Finnish people that the war had been lost. The Finnish troops, who had suffered 44,000 casualties on the Karelian Isthmus alone and about 90,000 in killed during the whole war,[1] were hurled back almost to the state border. In the course of the offensive from June 21 to August 10 the Karelian Front advanced 160-180 kilometres and its right-

---

[1] See C. Leonard Lundin, *op. cit.*, p. 221.

wing armies reached the border with Finland. The Soviet Army continued to attack along the entire Soviet-German front. The Finns were aware that further resistance would be senseless. The morale of the Finnish troops declined and desertions increased, and anti-war sentiments grew in the country. And so the Finnish rulers once again approached the USSR with a request for a cease-fire. On August 1 President Ryti retired in order to free himself from his commitment to Germany and was replaced by Marshal Mannerheim. The new government headed by Antti Hackzell declared that it did not consider itself bound by the former president's commitment to Hitler.

On September 4 the Finnish Government accepted the preliminary Soviet armistice terms and declared that it was ceasing hostilities.

At 3.00 hours on September 5 GHQ sent the following directive to the commanders of the Leningrad and Karelian fronts: "In view of the fact that the Finnish Government has met the demands of the Soviet Government to break off relations with Germany and disarm the German troops, GHQ orders the troops of the Karelian and Leningrad fronts to cease hostilities against the Finnish forces at 8.00 hours on September 5, 1944."

The armistice agreement between the Soviet Union and Britain on one side, and Finland, on the other, was signed in Moscow on September 19, 1944. Although more than six months had elapsed since the first ceasefire talks and many Soviet and Finnish soldiers had been killed due to the stand of the Finnish ruling circles, the Soviet Government concerned with establishing goodneighbourly relations with the Finnish people presented the same mild armistice terms. The Soviet Union was sympathetic to Finland's difficult situation, and although the original armistice terms envisaged reparations to the sum of $600 million payable over a five-year period, the Armistice Agreement cut this sum by half to be paid within six years later extended to eight years. This sum was only a fifth of the damages inflicted by the Finnish troops on the Soviet people.

Late President Juho Paasikivi said: "...it should be remembered that the Soviet Union in the autumn of 1944, just as in the winter of 1940, could have continued the struggle inflicting fresh heavy defeats on Finland, and could have crushed Finland completely if it wished. . .".[1] But, he said, "in many cases the Soviet Union displayed sympathetic feeling towards Finland", to the "amazement" of the Western countries.[2]

From the point of view of the norms governing relations between imperialist states, the Soviet attitude to Finland was bound to evoke surprise in the West. As regards nazi Germany, Finland's former ally, her attitude to Finland after September 19, 1944 changed completely. Retreating from northern Finland, the German troops burned down about 16,000 houses, 125 schools, 165 churches and other public buildings, and demolished 700 out of 900 biggest bridges. The damage was estimated at more than $120 million. They frequently provoked armed clashes, killing 800 and wounding 2,900 Finnish soldiers.[3]

Far from giving thought to revenge, the Soviet Union based its relations with Finland on principles of socialist humanism and the desire for peace and the establishment of goodneighbourly ties. That was why it did not move troops into Finland, reduced reparations and met the Finnish Government's request for help in food, although it was experiencing great difficulties in feeding its own population.

A NEW STAGE IN THE LIFE OF THE FINNISH PEOPLE

The Armistice Agreement put an end to Finland's dependence on Germany and restored her national independence and sovereignty. Yet the Finnish reactionaries, in the hope that the Western powers would start a war against the USSR, planned to seize power and begin a partisan war; they delayed the fulfilment of the agreement on the arrest of war criminals and the disbandment of fascist and para-military organisations.

Secret arms caches were established in various parts of

---

[1] *Paasikiven Linja,* Juho Kusti Paasikiven, Puheita vuosilta, 1944-1956, Helsinki, 1956.

[2] *Ibid.*

[3] *Finland, a Democracy of the North,* p. 63.

the country. President Mannerheim tried to preserve the army whose strength exceeded the pre-war level by 75 per cent and was not in a hurry to expel the German troops. Fascist elements terrorised democratic organisations and parties, which had just emerged from the underground and were still weak, and on several occasions attacked Soviet representatives. The working class and the democratic sections of the people were alarmed by the situation. Therefore Finland's progressive circles supported the firm and consistent stand adopted by the Allied Control Commission in Finland under the chairmanship of Member of the Military Council of the Leningrad Front Colonel-General A. A. Zhdanov in fulfilling the armistice terms, dissolving the fascist organisations and trying war criminals — which all created favourable conditions for the country's further development along democratic lines.

In October 1944 a Democratic Union of the People of Finland was formed on the initiative of the Communist Party of Finland just emerged from the underground. Five months later this Union won 25 per cent of the votes in the parliamentary election. Wide sections of the population upheld many of the ideas put forward by the Communists, particularly the demand to build Finnish-Soviet relations on the basis of friendship and non-enmity. The most notable event engendered by the new situation in the country was the spontaneous re-birth of the Finnish-USSR Society whose membership at the end of October 1944 was 3,000 and 170,000 a year later.

The rout of nazi Germany and reactionary elements in Finland and the observance of the armistice terms opened great prospects for Finland's democratic development. In its time the 1917 October Revolution brought national liberation to Finland, and now the rout of the Wehrmacht enabled the Finnish Republic to preserve and strengthen its independence. A peace treaty was signed between the Soviet Union and Finland in 1948. True to its Leninist policy of respect for the rights of nations, the USSR did not take a single step to curtail Finland's national independence.

The goodneighbourly relations which have developed between the two countries in the post-war period stimulated Finland's economic growth, raised her people's welfare. The

Finnish Government's consistent policy of friendship and co-operation with the USSR and other states has won Finland great international prestige.

2. LIBERATION OF NORWAY'S NORTHERN REGIONS

GERMANY ATTACKS NORWAY

In the small hours of the morning on April 9, 1940 German warships appeared unexpectedly at Norway's key ports, shelled them and landed troops. By mid-day German soldiers were marching in the streets of the Norwegian capital Oslo and the country's biggest towns Trondheim, Bergen, Kristiansand, Stavanger, Narvik and Orendhal.

Norway's former Defence Minister Vidkun Quisling, whose name is now synonymous with national betrayal, largely helped the Germans to carry out their plans of invading Norway.

At first the German occupation authorities resorted to economic bribery. In preparation for attacking the Soviet Union they launched military construction in Norway, attracting local manpower by paying relatively high wages.

In the meantime the war brought disheartening news for the Norwegians as the nazis scored successive victories over their Western adversaries.

ON THE EVE OF LIBERATION

The entry of the Soviet Union into the war stimulated the Resistance Movement in Norway to a considerable extent. Seeing that the Soviet Army had stopped the nazi war machine and dispelled the myth about its invincibility the Norwegian people became confident that the nazis could be defeated.

The Norwegian Resistance Movement acquired yet another dimension. The first strike since the country's occupation broke out in Oslo on September 10, 1941, involving 25,000 industrial workers. Hitler's governor in Norway, Josef Terboven, proclaimed a "state of emergency" in Oslo, and together with Quisling's political police the Gestapo carried out arrests, directing their main blow at the Communist Party.

The patriots increased acts of sabotage at industrial enterprises and military installations. For instance, they carried out a series of subversive acts against the hydropower station in Glomfjord, blew up a mine in Fosdalen, damaged a transformer substation at Bordshaung and tried to blow up the German battleship *Tirpitz*. A group under the command of the famous Norwegian frogman Max Manus using magnetic mines sunk the German transports *Ortelsburg*, *Tugela* and *Donau*. The Norwegian patriots also took part in the raid against a heavy-water factory in Rjukan. As a result 1.5 tons of heavy water was blown up.

Early in 1944, in compliance with Hitler's demand, Quisling began hastily activating Norwegian divisions for action on the Eastern front. It was planned to call up five age groups, or approximately 75,000 men.

Under the guidance of the Communist Party and other patriotic organisations the Norwegian working people urged the population to boycott the mobilisation. The nazi authorities and Quisling responded by resorting to mass repressions, and a fresh wave of arrests swept across the country. Nevertheless, only 300 persons, instead of 75,000, turned up at the induction centres. Not only was this an expression of the increasing hatred of the Norwegian patriots for the German invaders and the quislings, but also an indication of their profound respect for the Soviet people and its army. In February 1944 the Norwegian Embassy in Sweden, which was best informed about the events and sentiments in occupied Norway, reported to its Government in London: "It is impossible to describe the admiration for the Russians. All sections of the population have placed their hopes on the Russians. These sentiments are especially strong among the working class. There is also widespread disenchantment with the British and Americans. Many people believe that Britain and America want to weaken the Russians, but not many think that this is possible. It is said that if it were not for the Russians, democracy in Europe would have been in danger. Admiration for the Russians is particularly great among the young people."[1]

[1] *Regjeringen og Hjemmefronten under krigen*, Aktstykker utgitt av Stortinget, Oslo, 1948, Doc. No. 201, p. 368.

The help which the Norwegians rendered to Soviet prisoners of war, of whom there were about 100,000 in Norway, was yet another manifestation of the growing sympathies for the Soviet people and its army. The nazis kept the Soviet prisoners of war in terrible conditions and mostly at hard labour. As a result of the deliberate policy of exterminating Soviet people conducted by the German Command, more than 10,000 Soviet citizens perished in nazi camps in Norway.

Many Soviet prisoners of war who managed to escape from nazi concentration camps actively participated in the struggle against the German invaders in Norway.

The Soviet Army's victories and Finland's withdrawal from the war created favourable conditions for rendering fraternal assistance to the Norwegian people. By liberating Karelia and driving the Germans away from the Kirov Railway and the White Sea-Baltic Canal, the Soviet troops improved the supply of the Karelian Front and the fleet operating inside the Arctic Circle, thus enabling the Soviet Army to begin an offensive in the Far North. But the Germans did not want to withdraw from the Arctic where next to the Soviet-Norwegian border, there were nickel mines, the only source which supplied the nazi war machine with this crucial raw material. German warships were based in Norway's ice-free ports on the Barents and Norwegian seas. After Germany had lost her naval bases in France and partly on her own territory, the greater part of German warships were shifted to bases in Norway, especially in her northern areas. The loss of Northern Norway would have, therefore, deprived her of her naval bases there and also considerably weakened her control over the North Sea. Moreover, German troops in the north had their main ammunition, arms and food depots in the area of Kirkenes.

Hitler issued strict orders to hold on to the Arctic regions and dispatched troops specially trained for action in the north.

The German 20th Army deployed between the Barents Sea and Ukhta had about 200,000 officers and men. Its 19th Mountain Infantry Corps, with 53,000 men and more than 750 guns and mortars supported by approximately 160 combat aircraft, was on the defensive in the Petsamo-Kirkenes sector. German naval strength in the area totalled about 200 vessels of various types. All in all the German Command assembled approximately 350,000 officers and men in the north.

By October 1944 the Germans had established a powerful defensive belt in the Petsamo-Kirkenes sector consisting of resistance centres and strong-points adapted to perimeter defence. The trenches were reinforced with concrete and some strong-points had connecting tunnels hacked in the rocks. There were from 15 to 20 pillboxes per kilometre of the frontage and the entire defence system consisted of three lines.

THE SOVIET ARMY
ASSISTS THE NORWEGIAN PEOPLE

The Karelian Front began preparations for the offensive in the Petsamo-Kirkenes sector on September 26, 1944, upon receiving a GHQ directive that a blow be delivered at the Germans in the Petsamo area by the 14th Army reinforced by the 31st Infantry Corps and some of the Front's elements. In keeping with a plan designed by the front's HQ the 14th Army under the command of Lieutenant-General V. I. Shcherbakov was to deliver the main attack from an area south of Lake Chapr to the northwest in the general direction of Luostari and Petsamo. The blow was to be struck by the 31st, 99th and 131st infantry and 126th and 127th light infantry corps. Two infantry corps were assigned to break through the tactical defence zone, and an infantry corps was to envelop the enemy positions from the south, thus covering the operations of the striking group in that direction.

Acting in conjunction with the Northern Fleet under Admiral A. G. Golovko, the 14th Army was to smash the main forces of the German 19th Mountain Infantry Corps, capture Nikel and Salmijarvi and by reaching the border with Norway completely liberate the Petsamo area. The Northern Fleet had orders to blockade the ports of Petsamo and Kirkenes, while marine units advancing from Sredni Peninsula were to land commandos in the enemy rear to ensure the success of the 14th Army's operations. Air support was to be provided by the 7th Air Army and the fleet's air arm, about 1,000 combat aircraft all told. The plan of the operation took account

of all specific conditions. The main blow was to be delivered
at the weakest sector in the enemy defences so that the Soviet
troops could strike at the enemy's main forces from the rear.
The breakthrough was to take place simultaneously with the
envelopment of the enemy fortifications by the light infantry
corps. A second echelon consisting of two infantry corps was
assigned to consolidate the success of the operation.

On September 29, GHQ approved the plan with a few al-
terations and ordered the operation to begin on October 5-7,
1944.

At the beginning of the offensive the 14th Army comprised
nearly 50 per cent of the Front's effective strength. It had
97,000 men, over 2,100 guns and mortars, and 126 tanks and
self-propelled guns. The Soviet troops had a 1.8-fold superiority over the enemy in manpower, a 2.7-fold superiority in artillery and a 6.1-fold superiority in aircraft.

The morning of October 7 dawned. The sky was heavily
overcast. At 8.00 hours a fearful thunder shattered the silence
as the Soviet artillery opened up. The barrage lasted for 2
hours and 35 minutes, in the course of which about 100,000
shells pounded enemy trenches, pillboxes and fire emplacements. The 131st Infantry Corps under Major-General
Z. N. Alexeyev attacked in the wake of the artillerly barrage
so as to give the enemy no respite.[1] By 15.00 hours the 14th
Infantry Division had pierced the main line of resistance and
reached the Titovka River. Two battalions of the division's
95th Regiment forded the river, and seized a bridgehead on
its west bank. The 10th Guards Infantry Division also broke
through the main line of resistance.

The 99th Infantry Corps under Major-General S. P. Mikul-
sky operating on the left flank was less successful.[2] It failed to
take the enemy defences in its stride and was pinned to the
ground in front of the wire entanglements surrounding Mount
Bolshoi Karikvaivish turned by the enemy into a powerful
strong-point. The fighting went on throughout the night and
it was only on the second day that the Soviet troops finally
broke the enemy resistance and wiped out the garrison.

---

[1] The 131st Infantry Corps consisted of the 14th Guards and 10th
Guards Infantry divisions.

[2] The 99th Infantry Corps consisted of the 65th, 1144th and 368th
Infantry divisions.

On the far left flank of the 14th Army, the 126th Light Infantry Corps commanded by Colonel V. N. Solovyev[1] had to
fight in the marshes where the Germans had no fortified positions considering the terrain impassable. But the Soviet troops
passed. Each man carried the necessary equipment on his
shoulders, only the artillery and mortars being packed on
horses and reindeer. Carrying a load of 40 kilogrammes,
wading chest-deep through the marshes the soldiers made
their way into the enemy rear to outflank his defences and
cut the crucial Luostari-Ahmalahti-Nikel road.

Having covered 70 gruelling kilometres of marshland, the
corps came out to the road by 8.00 hours on October 10.
Abandoning their heavy weapons the Germans fled in panic.
The road was straddled and the enemy was deprived of the
possibility of bringing up reserves to Luostari from Ahmalahti
and Nikel. For two successive days the corps's 31st and 72nd
brigades beat back fierce attacks of the Germans who strove
to recapture the crucial road, losing more than 1,200 officers
and men in killed and wounded.

Sensing the threat of encirclement, the German Command
began to withdraw its 19th Corps to Petsamo. To frustrate
its organised retreat the Northern Fleet in the night of October 9 landed the reinforced 63rd Marine Brigade under
Colonel A. M. Krylov on the southern shore of the bay of
Mativuono.

In the morning of October 10 the brigade came out into
the flank and rear of the enemy's defences along the Musta
Tunturi Ridge. Meanwhile the 12th Marine Brigade on the
defensive on Sredny peninsula surged against the enemy defences after a 90-minute artillery bombardment. Overcoming
the enemy's stubborn resistance, the brigade cut through his
defences by mid-day, crossed the ridge and linked up with
the 63rd Brigade which was attacking the enemy's positions
from the rear. To avoid encirclement the German forces retreated from Rybachi Peninsula towards Petsamo.

In order to cover the withdrawal of the routed units to
Northern Norway, the nazi command concentrated its efforts
on holding the town and port of Petsamo. But the command
of the Northern Fleet forestalled the Germans: on the night

---

[1] The corps consisted of two brigades.

of October 11 a detachment of torpedo boats landed a party of sailors under Major I. A. Timofeyev directly on the docks of Linahamari. Without waiting for daybreak they attacked the heavily fortified strong-point which covered the firing position of a 210-mm battery.

The Germans counter-attacked at sunrise. Although the battle broke up into hand-to-hand fighting they were thrown back and by noon the Soviet forces captured the strong-point and the battery. On receiving reinforcements the Germans resumed their counter-attacks. Things became very difficult for the sailors. But just then Soviet planes delivered a powerful blow. The German resistance collapsed and the port of Linahamari was liberated.

On October 12, the 99th Infantry Corps and the 7th Guards Tank Brigade attacking from the east and the southeast and the 126th Light Infantry Corps pushing from the southwest with air support knocked the enemy out of Luostari, a key strong-point which covered the approaches to Petsamo and the nickel mines. On October 15, the Soviet troops gained possession of the old Russian town of Pechenga (Petsamo), an important naval base and powerful strong-point in the German defences in the Arctic. Reeling under the blows of the Soviet troops, wrecking and burning everything in their path, the main enemy forces hastily withdrew to prepared positions in Northern Norway.

LIBERATION OF NORTHERN NORWAY

The Soviet troops entered Norway under the Argeement of May 16, 1944 between the governments of the USSR, USA and Great Britain, on the one hand, and the Government of Norway, on the other. At that time the Norwegian Government expressed the wish that Norwegian units stationed in Britain take part in liberating Norway together with the Allied forces. J. V. Stalin made a similar proposal during his talks with Winston Churchill in Moscow in September 1944. But Churchill turned it down, and the Soviet Army had to fight on its own in Norway because the Norwegian units were unable to arrive in Northern Norway in time.

In the circumstances the Front Commander set the 14th Army a fresh task which was approved by GHQ on October 16. With the support of the Northern Fleet, the army was to continue the offensive in the northwesterly and southwesterly directions, complete the liberation of the Petsamo area, capture Kirkenes and Neiden and reach the Nautsi area, carrying its operations to a depth of 45-65 kilometres. Committing its second echelon (31st Infantry and 127th Light Infantry corps) at 9.00 hours on October 18, the army resumed its offensive. Its main forces continued to drive along the Luostari-Ahmalahti and Luostari-Nikel roads, while the light infantry troops advancing on the flanks covered it from the north and the south.

One of the first to enter Norway on October 18 was the 1st Battalion of the 253rd Infantry Regiment, the 45th Infantry Division. At 13.50 hours it forced the Jakobselven River, crossed the Norwegian border and, encountering only weak resistance of a small enemy group, reached the eastern bank of the Banebekken, by the end of the day.

In the small hours of October 22, the 45th and 14th infantry divisions reached the first Norwegian inhabited locality, Tarnet, one of the most powerful resistance points on the left flank of the Kirkenes fortified zone. Here the Germans decided to stop the Soviet advance and established a "dead area" around it.

The retreating enemy burned and wrecked most of the buildings, bridges and other structures in Finnmark. At the same time the nazis and the local traitors launched a vicious anti-Soviet campaign frightening the population with alleged "brutality" of the Soviet Army. If the Russians arrived, declared the German and collaborationist authorities in an address to the population of Northern Norway on October 18, 1944, "murder and plunder, terror and arbitrary rule, violence and immorality will reign supreme."[1]

The entire population of Northern Norway was ordered to evacuate. The reactionary propaganda began to spread rumours alleging that the population in the areas liberated

---

[1] *Norges krig 1940-1945*, Vol. III, p. 573; S. Hartmann, *Nytt lys over*, Oslo, 1965, pp. 185-86.

by the Soviet troops was driven to Siberia and the men were forcibly inducted into the Red Army.[1] Despite anti-Soviet propaganda, the bulk of the local population trusted the Soviet Union and its mission of liberation. Under the most diverse pretexts the Norwegians defied evacuation orders and hid in the mountains and mines pending the arrival of the Soviet Army.

The Norwegian working people joyously welcomed the entry of the Soviet troops. In those days the Communist Party newspaper *Friheten* wrote that the arrival of the Soviet Army created unprecedented enthusiasm among the Norwegian people. The whole people realised, it underlined, that freedom and victory and the termination of the occupation was a matter of the near future.

Expressing the sentiments of the country's patriotic forces the Central Committee of the Norwegian Communist Party on October 24, 1944 called upon the Norwegian Government in London and the central leadership of the Norwegian Resistance to help stimulate the subversive activity of the Norwegian guerrillas throughout the country and thus assist the advancing Soviet Army.[2] While guerrilla detachments and underground patriotic organisations intensified their sabotage against the German occupation forces and the collaborationists, the emigre government in London and the reactionary bourgeois elements in the leadership of the Resistance movement did not support the Communist Party's appeal. The very fact that the Soviet troops had entered Norway and the presence of thousands of Soviet war prisoners in the country who were in contact with the local population and wanted to take part in the fighting alarmed the reactionary circles. In October 1944, the bourgeois leaders of the Resistance movement advised the emigre government in London to ensure that the German Command continue to bear responsibility for guarding the Soviet POW camps even after Germany's surrender. Later some leading Norwegian statesmen admitted that they were pleased that the Russians "went only as far as Kirkenes and not deeper into Norway". In its turn the Anglo-Ameri-

---

[1] *Friheten*, September 25, 1950.
[2] *Vart Partis politikk under krigen. Krigspolitikken*, Oslo, 1945, p. 137; *Friheten*, October 23, 1964.

can Command "ordered the authorities concerned not to take part in stimulating the Resistance in Norway."[1]

In the meantime, the 14th Army continued to batter the Germans in Norway: the 131st and 99th Infantry corps advanced along the roads leading to Kirkenes; the 127th Light Infantry Corps and part of the 31st Infantry Corps pursued the enemy in the southwesterly direction along roads following the Norwegian border to Nautsi.

The 126th Light Infantry Corps was ordered to cross Lake Fossvan, execute a cross-country march and cut the crucial Kirkenes-Svanvik road. Entrenched in strong-points and taking advantage of terrain the Germans put up fierce resistance and in a single engagement in the night of October 23 the corps' 31st Brigade lost 142 officers and men in killed and wounded. Two days later the corps managed to straddle the road at the cost of 113 men in killed and 199 in wounded. German casualties were 500 men in killed and wounded. At dusk on October 22 the 45th and 14th infantry divisions captured Tarnet and reached the Storbukt-Karpbukt line, and on October 24 engaged the enemy at the approaches to the fortress town of Kirkenes.

In the night of October 23, the 61st Infantry Regiment, 45th Infantry Division, crossed the Jarfjord on amphibian vehicles and captured a bridgehead on its western shore. By nightfall on October 24, the 45th Division extended the bridgehead and seized the inhabited localities of Munkgord, Bagen, Haga, Sleten and Elvenes and reached the eastern coast of the Bekfjord. The local inhabitants turned over all available crossing means to the Soviet troops. The Northern Fleet landed two battalions of the 63rd Marine Brigade to assist the 14th Army in capturing a town in Holmengro Fjord. The marines seized a hill on its coast and locked the enemy's sea route out of Kirkenes.

At 5.00 hours on October 25, following a 20-minute artillery softening up, the 45th and 14th infantry divisions began to cross the Bekfjord. Lighting up the fjord with hundreds of flares the Germans met the Soviet troops with a squall of machine-gun and artillery fire. The first attempt to force a crossing was foiled. After regrouping and another artillery

---

[1] *Norges krig*, Vol. III, p. 629.

barrage, they made another attempt to reach the opposite shore. The local fishermen ferried the Soviet soldiers in their boats. When, for instance, German artillery demolished a pontoon crossing, the Norwegians steered their boats to save the Soviet soldiers drowning in the middle of the fjord.

The enemy fell back and by 9.00 hours the 14th and 45th divisions reached Kirkenes. At the same time the 24th Infantry Regiment, 10th Guards Infantry Division and the 73rd Guards Tank Regiment also approached Kirkenes after crushing the Germans at Sulheim.

Realising the hopelessness of the situation the Germans began a barbarous destruction of the town which was virtually engulfed in flames and the smoke of explosions. Out of a thousand houses only 28 were left standing. More than 3,500 citizens, together with sheep, cows, horses and fowl sought safety in an underground tunnel at the railway station near the town. The walls and ceiling of the tunnel where people suffered from foul air shook from the explosions as heavy fighting raged in and around Kirkenes.

Learning that the Germans intended to blow up the tunnel together with the people in it as they retreated from the town, the Norwegians appealed to the Soviet Army for assistance. Under the cover of darkness Hugo Ensen slipped past German outposts to the Soviet positions and told about the tragic plight of the Kirkenes inhabitants. Immediately a reconnaissance platoon under Lieutenant Bakhteyev of the 65th Infantry Division was sent to their help. It smashed the Germans in a surprise attack at dawn on October 25 and captured the station. The Norwegians, many of them women and children, with tears in their eyes embraced and kissed their liberators. In the meantime the 14th, 45th and 16th Guards Infantry divisions and the 73rd Guards Tank Regiment were knocking the enemy out of shelters and ruins and by 13.00 hours the 5,000-strong German garrison was smashed.

On October 25 Moscow saluted the Karelian Front and the Northern Fleet for meritorious action in the Arctic.

Shortly afterwards the 14th Army liberated Naiden and Nautsi. Having lost about 30,000 men in killed alone from October 7 to November 9, the German 19th Mountain Infantry Corps hastily retreated to the west.

The Germans also sustained considerable casualties at sea where the warships and aircraft of the Northern Fleet sank 156 enemy warships and vessels in the same period.

In view of the crushing defeat which deprived it of its main supply bases in Kirkenes, the German Command was compelled to withdraw its forces hastily into the interior of Norway.

By capturing Kirkenes and Naiden, reaching the shore of Korsfjord and completely liberating the Petsamo region, the troops of the Karelian Front fulfilled their assignment; so on November 9, 1944 GHQ ordered the 14th Army to assume the defensive.

FRATERNAL ASSISTANCE

The population of the liberated areas warmly welcomed the Soviet troops. Denouncing the fabrications of the occupation regime and the reactionary elements about "Bolshevik atrocities" the underground newspaper *Siste Nytt* which was published in southern Norway wrote: "Kirkenes has returned to life... The liberators were welcomed with great joy. Excellent relations have been established between the Russians and Norwegians."

On November 9 a Norwegian military mission headed by Colonel A. D. Dahl left Murmansk for Northern Norway. At the same time a Norwegian military detachment numbering 234 men arrived in Northern Norway from Britain, and two police platoons totalling 307 men arrived from Sweden.

But the civilian population in the liberated areas began to form military units even before the arrival of these troops. On October 29, the Norwegian Government published an appeal urging the population to join these units. The Command of the 14th Army and the Karelian Front rendered all possible assistance to the Norwegian authorities, and Norwegian military units were regularly supplied from the 14th Army's stocks.

From February to April 1945 more Norwegian units arrived from Britain and Sweden and by the end of the war there were 2,735 Norwegian troops in Northern Norway. The Soviet Union supplied them with 685 submachine guns, 40 machine-guns and ammunition, motor vehicles, carts and horses, medical equipment and so forth. In 1944-1945 the Soviet Union spent more than 27.5 million rubles on the maintenance of the Norwegian troops. But they took no part in any major operations against the Germans and were used chiefly for patrol duty in Northern Norway after the withdrawal of the German forces.

At the height of the rigorous Arctic winter the population of the liberated areas found itself in a very difficult situation: many were homeless and there was no food, fuel and transport. Epidemics broke out. "But the Soviet Army", wrote a leading member of the Norwegian Communist Party, Just Lippe, "proved in practice that it entered Norway not only as a military force, but also as a true friend of the Norwegian people."

And again the Soviet Command came to assistance of the population by taking urgent measures to feed the people in the liberated parts of Finnmark. According to the Norwegian Military Mission, each Norwegian was entitled to a weekly ration of 1,600 grammes of bread and 200 grammes of fats and sugar. In the small town of Svanvik which was short of food because winter seriously handicapped deliveries the Soviet soldiers shared their rations with the local inhabitants.

The Soviet Command also took resolute steps to put down epidemics of diphtheria and dysintery. Six additional hospitals were opened for Norwegians and the most serious cases were treated at a Soviet army hospital.

The housing problem presented the greatest difficulties. Kirkenes was burnt down, and 50 per cent of the housing was destroyed in Ser-Varanger, 65 per cent in Vadsö and 85 per cent in Vardö. In the circumstances the Soviet Command decided not to occupy the undamaged buildings. The Norwegian Minister of Justice, Terje Wold, who visited the liberated areas at the time reported to his government in London that the Soviet troops lived in the open field. "At night," he wrote in his report, "we could see hundreds of small fires with soldiers sleeping around them. There were few tents. Thanks to this amazing display of endurance the Soviet troops enabled the Norwegian population to take shelter in the few houses that survived the general destruction." Of course, it was not only a matter of the exceptional endurance of the Soviet officers and men mentioned by the Norwegian minister, but rather their awareness of their internationalist duty, for the sake of which they were not only prepared to sleep in the snow on Norwegian territory they had liberated, but also to die for it. In the course of the Petsamo-Kirkenes operation 15,773 Soviet officers and men were killed or wounded, 2,122 of them in Norway.

Under an agreement with Norway, the Soviet Command had full power in the zone of military operations in the liberated part of Norway and its relations with the Norwegian administration were most cordial.

In March 1945 all Swedish newspapers carried an interview given by a Norwegian Archbishop Arne Fjellbu immediately upon returning from a trip through the liberated areas of Northern Norway. "Many people want to know," he wrote, "whether the Russians interfere with church activity. I can say that the Russians were not only tactful but obliging as well; they willingly helped us. . . . When there was no room where I could read my sermon, they provided me with one. . . . This happened in other places, too."

The Soviet Command took steps to bring life back to normal in the liberated areas. Soviet engineer units quickly repaired the docks at Kirkenes, Tarnet, Jakobsnes, Vadsö and Botsfjord. In Kirkenes they repaired the water supply system and the telephone exchange, and removed 15,000 mines from dwellings, docks and industrial enterprises. The civilian population was invited to lectures and films, and Soviet soldiers took part in amateur art performances which became very popular among the Norwegians.

In September 1945, shortly after the end of the war, Soviet troops, having fulfilled their mission of liberation, withdrew from Northern Norway. "The Russians," wrote the Norwegian bourgeois newspaper *Aftenposten*, "were the first to come to us and they were the first to leave us. The Norwegians will always remember what the Russians had done for them and for the common victory over the enemy."

In those trying years Norwegian statesmen justly and highly assessed the Soviet Union's great contribution to the common cause of smashing nazi Germany and liberating a part of Northern Norway. In July 1945 King Haakon VII of Norway said: "The Norwegians enthusiastically observed the

heroism, courage and the powerful blows which the Red
Army dealt the Germans. . . . The war was won by the Red
Army on the Eastern front. It was this victory which led to
the liberation by the Red Army of Norwegian territory in the
north. The Norwegian people welcomed the Red Army as
its liberator."[1]

The Norwegian press noted that "Red Army soldiers . . .
evoke a sense of gratitude and admiration among the Norwegians".[2]

But there are people in Norway who would have liked to
obliterate the kind memories of the Soviet troops in the country. This applies above all to those who support Norway's
participation in NATO. They are very anxious to make the
Norwegians suspicious of the Soviet soldier and to glorify
the nazi cutthroat. That has been the objective of the former
head of the Norwegian Military Mission in Northern Norway,
Colonel A. D. Dahl, one of the authors of the large three-
volume edition of *Norges krig 1940-1945*. In this work of
2,500 pages a mere two pages are devoted to the Soviet
Army's operations in the Arctic. Dahl says nothing at all
about the unexampled march of the 126th and 127th light
infantry corps to Naiden and Nautsi across roadless country and marshes, and the Soviet assistance to the Norwegian
population.

He claims that the Soviet Command created "difficulties"
for the Norwegian authorities[3] and at the same time speaks
with admiration about the German 20th Army. Paying little
heed to the atrocities committed by the German soldiers during their retreat and the crushing defeat sustained by the 20th
Army, he focuses the reader's attention on what he calls its
"brilliant" retreat. "This retreat," he writes, "was a fantastic
achievement in the way it was planned and executed. It was
a military exploit which not many armies could have accomplished".[4]

---

[1] *Pravda*, July 5, 1945.

[2] *Friheten*, August 31, 1950.

[3] A. D. Dahl, "Frigjoringen av Finnmark", *Norges krig 1940-1945*,
Vol. III, Oslo, 1950, p. 580.

[4] A. D. Dahl, "Krigsbegivenhetene i Lappland og Frinnmark
1944-1945. Rendulics memoarer." *Norsk Militart Tidsskrift*, Oslo, 1957,
No. 5, p. 298.

The working people of Norway, however, have not forgotten the sacrifices made by the Soviet troops for the sake
of liberating humanity, including the Norwegian people, from
fascist bondage. The words "Norway thanks you" are in-
scribed on monuments to Soviet soldiers in Oslo, Kirkenes,
Budö, Faüske, Elvenes and other Norwegian towns.

1. IN THE CLUTCHES
OF THE HORTY REGIME

ON THE ROAD TO WAR

In order to understand what plunged Hungary, allied
with German nazism, into a national catastrophe, it is necessary to examine the events which took place from October
1944 to April 1945, and also the developments preceding
them.

The darkest chapter in Hungary's latest history began after
the fall of the Hungarian Soviet Republic, when, with the help
of international reaction, a fascist dictatorship headed by
Admiral Horthy was established and "constitutionally" consolidated in the country.

The foreign policy of the Horthy government was wholly
orientated on the achievement of imperialist, expansionist
aims. Either in collaboration or with the support of other
aggressive Western countries, the Horthy regime intended
to seize the territories of a number of neighbouring countries
in the interests of Hungary's capitalists and the landlord
oligarchy. Having come to power Horthy immediately
launched a broad programme of Hungary's militarisation with
especial emphasis on ideologically indoctrinating the population in the spirit of "national unity" with the help of chauvinistic slogans about the "chosen mission" of the Hungarian
race, its "cultural superiority" and about a "Great Hungary"
dominating the Carpathian region. Schoolchildren were
taught to hate the neighbouring nations, the Slavs in the first
place. Revanchism was elevated to the status of official policy.

Striving to enlarge Hungary's territory by annexing the
lands of her neighbours, the Hungarian rulers sided with the
nazis long before Germany's attack on the USSR. For many
years they distorted Hungary's history in order to show that
Hungary and Germany had a common destiny. They became most anxious to get on the good side of nazi Germany
after her invasion of Czechoslovakia in the hope of laying
their hands on a part of Czechoslovakia.

Meeting the imperialist ambitions of the Hungarian ruling circles and at the same time furthering its own far-reaching plans of enslaving all the Danube countries, the nazi leaders in the autumn of 1938 incorporated the southern part of Transcarpathian Ukraine and Slovakia into Hungary and in March 1939 the entire Transcarpathian Ukraine became a part of Hungary. This enabled Hitler firmly to harness Hungary to his war chariot. Characteristically, the British Government adopted a "sympathetic" attitude towards the Horthy clique and the United States showed "lack of interest" in this question.

Seeing that as a result of the Munich deal the Western powers gave Hitler full freedom of action in southeast Europe, the Horthy clique decided to place its main stake on German nazism. In February 1939 Hungary joined Hitler's anti-Comintern pact, and at the end of August 1940 in keeping with the decisions of the Second Vienna Arbitration, Hungarian troops occupied Northern Transylvania which was a part of Rumania. In November 1940 Hungary joined the Tripartite Pact (nazi Germany, fascist Italy and militarist Japan) and thus became nazi Germany's loyal satellite and a weapon of her expansionist policy.

At first nazi Germany used Hungary as a springboard for invading Yugoslavia and then, on April 10, 1941, in violation of the "treaty of eternal friendship" of December 1940, Hungary attacked Yugoslavia and occupied a part of Vojvodina, thus becoming Hitler's active military ally.

Betraying the national interests of the Hungarian people and creeping into the good graces of nazi Germany, Hungarian ruling circles gradually involved their country in the Second World War. The Hungarian capitalists and landlords managed to steep the minds of a considerable part of the population, especially the young people, in the venum of chauvinism and plunge the country into the war against the USSR.

The Soviet Government made every effort to avert an armed clash with Hungary. In the spring of 1941, the USSR took part in the Budapest industrial fair where the Soviet pavilion became very popular with the visitors. At about the same time the Soviet Government returned the banners of the Hungarian units which fell into the hands of Russian troops in 1849. It also urged the Hungarian Government to remain neutral, but Horthy and his associates ignored this sensible proposal which was also a warning.

HUNGARY, NAZI GERMANY'S ALLY

On June 27, 1941 Hungary declared war on the Soviet Union, using a provocative raid of German aircraft on Kosice which had been organised by the nazis and Horthy clique as a pretext. At the end of June and early July 1941, the Hungarian Government dispatched to the Soviet-German front a mobile corps (two mechanised and one cavalry brigade), the 1st mountain construction and the 8th frontier brigades, totalling about 44,500 officers and men, and 42 aircraft. From September to December of the same year the Hungarian 102nd, 105th, 108th, 121st, 124th and 201st light infantry divisions were moved to the Ukraine and Smolensk and Bryansk regions to fight the partisans and guard German supply routes there. At the beginning of 1942 there were nearly 100,000 Hungarian troops on the Eastern front.

After the defeat of the Wehrmacht at Moscow, the Hungarian 2nd Army consisting of nine divisions, an armoured brigade and supporting units arrived at the Soviet-German front in April to June 1942. It had about 180,000 men and later was reinforced by another 50,000.

As the Soviet Army was nearing the Hungarian border, the 110,000 strong 3rd Army was activated in September 1944 and deployed along the Hungarian-Rumanian border.

The Hungarian economy was geared to meet the needs and demands of Germany which began to receive trainloads of Hungarian industrial and agricultural products. The German Minister in Budapest reported to Berlin in 1943 that 60 per cent of Hungary's war industry was working on German orders. As regards food products, in 1941 and 1942 Hungary provided Germany with one million tons of wheat, 23,000 tons of flour, 19,000 tons of fats, 483,000 hogs and a large quantity of other products. And this at the time when food rations in Hungary were much smaller than in Germany. In 1942, the daily ration of bread in Hungary varied from 160 to 200 grammes, while in Germany the lowest ration was 340 grammes. Other food rations in Hungary were from 20 to 30 per cent smaller than in other nazi bloc countries. The Hungarian working people lived on a starvation diet.

From the first days of the anti-Soviet war the outlawed Communist Party launched an active struggle to stop it, overthrow the Horthy regime and establish an independent democratic Hungary. A considerable part of the population continued to give credence to the chauvinistic propaganda of the Horthy clique and followed its lead. Nevertheless, Hungarian workers devised ways of sabotaging government instructions and frontline soldiers intensified their covert resistance to military orders. The Hungarian reaction retaliated by intensifying the persecution of progressive elements fighting against fascism and war. The situation became especially difficult for the Communists and all Hungarian patriots in the spring of 1944.

Horthy and his associates adhered to their line of continuing the war in alliance with the Axis powers and at the same time took steps to win the patronage of Britain and the United States should it become necessary to end the war "not at will" but as a result of nazi Germany's defeat, in which case the possibility was envisaged of Hungary being occupied by US and British troops. In pursuing their double-faced policy Horthy and his clique strove at all costs to prevent the Soviet Army from entering the country. But while London and Washington approved the Hungarian Government's balancing act, Berlin would not tolerate the duplicity of its Hungarian satellite. No longer trusting the ability of the Hungarian leaders to ensure their country's further participation in the war on Germany's side Hitler decided to occupy her. The Hungarian Government knew of the nazi plan and Hitler had a private agreement with Horthy on this score. Viewing the Soviet Army's swift advance towards Hungary's borders with increasing anxiety the Horthy clique took no steps to prevent the German troops from entering Hungary on March 19, 1944.

A puppet government with former Hungarian Minister in Berlin Döme Sztojay at its head was formed on Berlin's instructions. Sztojay enjoyed the trust of Horthy and the nazis. On March 22 the new government to one man pledged allegiance to nazi Germany.

Thus, with the help of the Hungarian fascists Hitler turned Hungary into a German colony whose manpower and material resources were widely used in the war. Budapest was occupied by SS units which started reprisals against the patriots, and that on top of the reign of terror unleashed by the Horthy clique. The economic plunder of the country increased to a still greater extent.

The Hungarian Communist Party called on the people to fight resolutely against fascism. It put out a leaflet which said: "In this hour of mortal danger the entire nation must unite into a single Hungarian front and take part in the common struggle." Armed groups of young workers and employees which were raised on the initiative of the Communist Party were active in various parts of the country including Budapest and its suburbs. A group established by the Budapest Communists was best known for its activity. Armed struggle, however, was on a limited scale, and the working people resisted fascism and war mainly by sabotage.

In a statement on May 13, 1944, the Soviet, British and US governments summoned Hungary, Rumania, Bulgaria and Finland immediately to stop fighting on Germany's side. Horthy and his clique, however, decided to continue their collaboration with Germany, for a break with her would have been tantamount to an admission of their responsibility for involving Hungary in a criminal and ruinous war. Realising that the Soviet Army's victories along the entire Soviet-German front and Rumania's declaration of war on Germany hastened the downfall of the Horthy regime the Hungarian reactionaries feverishly searched for a way out of the situation.

On August 25, 1944 the Hungarian Government debated the question whether it should break relations with Germany or continue to hold her side. There were two points of view, one favouring continuation of the war on Germany's side, and the other advocating the occupation of the country by the British and American troops. "It is a fact," it was stated at this meeting, "that the Anglo-Saxons do not want the Russians to occupy Hungary. They would have liked the Hungarians to hold up the Russians until the Anglo-Saxons occupy Hungary." It was also put on record that the Government considered it necessary not only to protect the borders of the northern part of Transylvania, but also to occupy her southern part, all the more since this decision dovetailed with the plans of the German Command.

On September 5 Hungarian and German forces launched an offensive into the southern part of Transylvania. It proved to be a futile undertaking. This circumstance, and above all the successful Soviet offensive, still further aggravated the political crisis in Hungary.

At its meeting on September 7 the Crown Council under Horthy noted: "In the last 24 hours the military situation in Southern Hungary has worsened catastrophically.... The road to Budapest is open.... The removal of this threat and salvation... are possible only if Germany gives prompt and sufficiently effective support...." On the next day the Hungarian Government adopted a resolution which said in part: "The Council of Ministers is unanimous in its decision that if the Germans fulfil their promise and furnish assistance within two days and if the Germans provided guarantees of their promises, Hungary will agree to continue the struggle for the time being and will not hasten to approach the allies with a request for an armistice."

At a crucial moment, when Hungary had every opportunity to end the destructive war, break with Germany and turn against her, the Hungarian Government continued to fight on the side of nazi Germany. This policy was doomed by the Soviet Army's victorious offensive on the southern wing of the Soviet-German front where the 2nd Ukrainian Front fighting in Northern Transylvania was approaching Hungary's southeastern frontiers.

Consequently Horthy had to take practical steps to pull Hungary out of a war that was clearly lost. On his instructions Colonel-General Naday flew to the Allied Headquarters in Casertao near Naples to persuade the British forces to land at Rejeka and from there break through into Southern Hungary via Zagreb. He passed Horthy's message to the representative of the Allied Command, General Wilson, in which the dictator asked Britain and the USA to prevail on the Soviet Union not to send troops into Hungary.

No talks were held, however, for Churchill and Roosevelt did not want to begin negotiations which were doomed to failure from the very outset, with the Soviet Army already fighting in Hungary. After the unsuccessful trip of his representative, Horthy had no other option than turn to the Soviet Union—and on October 1 a Hungarian delegation headed by Colonel-General Faragno arrived in Moscow.

In a letter to J. V. Stalin brought by the Hungarian delegation Horthy asked for the cessation of hostilities, unimpeded withdrawal of the German troops from Hungary and the participation of the British and Americans in the occupation of the country. These were the principal conditions which Horthy instructed the delegation to secure in Moscow. The delegation was not authorised to sign an armistice agreement, but only arrived for "agreeing" on its conditions.

Fully informed about the actual state of affairs in Hungary and the intentions of her ruling circles, the nazi leaders took steps to prevent their last ally from withdrawing from the war, one of which was to assemble major panzer forces at Budapest. Learning that the concentration of German forces at Budapest greatly alarmed the Hungarians, General Guderian wrote that the Chief of Staff of the German Land Forces could not afford treachery in the rear of the German troops fighting at the front. Noting that on four previous occasions Germany had to cope with similar situations, he said that this time the necessary preventive measures would be taken.

On their part Horthy and his associates were not seriously inclined to oppose the German measures. They were in mortal fear of the Soviet Army, its presence would encourage the workers and peasants to overthrow them. Horthy rejected the proposals of the Popular Front to establish an anti-Hitler government.

There was only one force in the country which could have changed the course of events, get Hungary to break with Germany and turn her guns against the nazis. This force was the Resistance Movement, the anti-fascist Hungarian Front. But the Social Democratic Party and the Smallholder Party continued their policy of temporising even after the establishment of the Hungarian Front in May 1944 and rejected the proposal of the Communists to organise a large-scale guerrilla movement. This was a serious shortcoming of the Hungarian anti-fascist Resistance. The guerrilla detachments raised on the initiative of the Foreign Bureau of the Hungarian Communist Party conducted operations mostly in the Transcarpathian Ukraine, east of Bratislava and in the northern regions of Transylvania. Their actions were limited in scope and when the Soviet Army reached the Hungarian borders they were unable to render it substantial support.

The policy of the Horthy clique caused extreme political instability in Hungary. It was obvious to the Soviet Supreme Command that only a swift and determined offensive would compel Hungary to withdraw from the war on Germany's side, help the Hungarian people to do away with nazism and Hungarian fascism and take the road of democratic development.

2. LIBERATION
OF EASTERN HUNGARY

ON THE EVE OF DECISIVE BATTLES

Continuing the offensive begun at Jassy and Kishinev, the 2nd and 3rd Ukrainian fronts in the latter half of September 1944 were preparing to strike fresh blows at the Germans entrenched in Czechoslovakia, Hungary and Yugoslavia. Pursuing the retreating forces of Army Group South Ukraine, the Soviet troops were approaching the Hungarian borders.

Having crushed powerful enemy resistance south of Oradea, the mobile units of the 2nd Ukrainian Front on October 5 captured Salonta a short distance from the Hungarian border. Somewhat earlier, on September 23, the 18th Tank Corps under Lieutenant-General P. D. Govorunenko and elements of the 243rd Infantry Division liberated the village of Battonia and two days later took Mako, the first Hungarian town to be freed by the Soviet troops. Retreating, the Germans blew up the bridges across the Maros, cutting off Mako from the surrounding homesteads. Life, however, quickly returned to normal in the town as the Soviet troops built a bridge across the river and helped to put the town's three small canneries back into operation. The workers elected factory committees which took change of production. The autumn field-work which was interrupted by the hostilities was resumed on nearby farms.

While the 2nd Ukrainian Front pushed ahead in Northern Transylvania, the 46th Army and the Rumanian 1st Army were advancing towards Hungary's southeastern border and Yugoslavia's northeastern border.

The Soviet Army's victories in southeastern Europe heightened the apprehensions of British and American ruling circles, whose prime concern was to bring their troops into the Balkans and Austria ahead of Soviet forces, thus making it possible for the reactionary regimes there to remain in power. "If the Germans either evacuated Italy or retired to the Alps," wrote Winston Churchill, "I much desire that Alexander should be able to make his amphibious thrust across the Adriatic, seize and occupy the Istrian peninsula, and try to reach Vienna before the Russians."[1]

This statement by the British Prime Minister disclosed the expansionist nature of the policy pursued by British ruling circles towards southeastern Europe. At the time when the Soviet Army was liberating the peoples of southeastern Europe from nazi slavery, British and American leaders were preoccupied with preventing the Soviet Union from carrying out its mission of liberation.

Developments on the southern wing of the Soviet-German front caused great anxiety among the nazi leaders. In order to prevent the Soviet troops from breaking into Hungary, to cover the main routes leading to Austria and Southern Germany and to ensure the withdrawal of their troops from Greece and Albania, the nazi leaders began urgently to build defences along the Rumanian-Hungarian and Bulgarian-Yugoslavian borders. In place of the routed Army Group South Ukraine Army Group South was formed under the command of Colonel-General Friessner whose troops had been smashed at Jassy and Kishinev. The Army group was replenished with manpower and material, and reserves were rushed to Hungary.

In their plans the nazi leaders accorded an important role to Germany's last satellite in Europe, Hungary, whose armed forces could still be of considerable help to the Wehrmacht. By the beginning of October 1944 the Hungarian Govern-

---

[1] Winston S. Churchill, *The Second World War*, Vol. VI, New York, 1962, p. 127.

ment had managed to increase the number of Hungarian troops to 22 divisions and five brigades. Besides, Hungary supplied the Wehrmacht with considerable quantities of oil, uniforms and food, and partly with weapons and ammunition, and delivered various raw materials to the German industry. For example, she annually supplied the German industry with nearly a million tons of bauxites essential for military production. With the loss of Rumanian oil, the Nagykanizsa oil-fields in Western Hungary and Zistersdorf in Austria became nazi Germany's last sources of natural fuel. "The retention of Hungarian territory," Hitler said in September 1944, "is of such vital importance for us that it simply cannot be overestimated."

On September 30, 1944 the General Staff of the Land Forces ordered Army Group South to hold up the Soviet offensive and then strike out from the area of Debrecen, smash the Soviet troops which had reached the Hungarian border between Oradea and Makó, and seize a line that could be defended by small forces till the end of winter. After that it intended to regroup the German forces in order to strike out from the area of Turda in the southerly direction and seize the exits from the Southern Carpathians.

Simultaneously with planning active operations, the German Command hastened to build fortifications in the sectors of a possible Soviet offensive. The local population and the German troops were building several defensive lines along the border, and inside Hungary. The first followed the border, the second was built on the west bank of the Tisza, and the third on the right bank of the Danube. The last line included the fortifications on the approaches to Budapest. Yet another defensive line called the Margaret Line was being built southwest of the Hungarian capital.

By the beginning of October 1944, Army Group South (German 8th and 6th armies,[1] and the Hungarian 2nd and 3rd armies) had 20 infantry, four panzer, two motorised and three cavalry divisions, three infantry and two panzer brigades. Moreover, three infantry divisions of Army Group F had taken up positions along the Yugoslav-Rumanian bor-

---

[1] The 6th Army was reconstituted after its defeat at Jassy and Kishinev.

der at Vrsac and further up to the bend of the Danube south of Orsova. On the whole the enemy had 3,500 guns and mortars and 300 panzers and was supported by the 4th Air Fleet numbering about 550 aircraft. Three quarters of the force, that is, 23 divisions and two panzer brigades, were on the defensive along the line running from the Prislop Pass in the Carpathians to Reghin, Turda and Oradea, their chief task being to cover Dej and Cluj.

Facing Army Group South along an 800-kilometre frontage from Prislop Pass to the great bend of the Danube south of Orsova, was Marshal R. Y. Malinovsky's 2nd Ukrainian Front. At the start of the operation it included the 40th, 7th Guards, 27th, 53rd, 46th, the 6th Guards Tank and the 5th Air armies, the 18th Tank Corps and two mechanised cavalry groups. All told, it had 40 infantry divisions, two fortified areas, three tank, two mechanised and three cavalry corps, one tank brigade, and the total of 750 tanks and self-propelled guns, 10,200 guns and mortars (upwards of 76 mm) and 1,100 aircraft. Besides, it had the Rumanian Ist and 4th armies totalling 17 divisions under its operational control.

In this period the 3rd Ukrainian Front was fighting for Belgrade in the south, and the armies of the 4th Ukrainian Front were engaged along the Soviet-Czechoslovak border, threatening the German-Hungarian forces from the north.

The plan of the Soviet offensive was based on a thorough appraisal of the general military and political objectives. The first objective was to rout the enemy in the Carpathians, at Belgrade and to the southeast of the Yugoslav capital. After that the Soviet troops were to turn against the enemy at Budapest. This operation was to be performed by three Ukrainian Fronts. The 4th Ukrainian Front, in conjunction with the 38th Army of the Ist Ukrainian Front, was to continue the offensive begun early in September, destroy the German Ist Panzer and the Hungarian Ist armies, cross the Ukrainian Carpathians and liberate the Transcarpathian Ukraine. The 2nd Ukrainian Front, striking its main blow from the south at Debrecen and Miskolc, was to rout the main forces of Army Group South, free Hungary's eastern regions and help the 4th Ukrainian Front to liberate the Transcarpathian Ukraine. After that it was to cross the Tisza and push on towards Budapest. The operations of the 4th and 2nd Ukrainian fronts were to be co-ordinated by Marshal S. K. Timoshenko. Meanwhile, the 3rd Ukrainian Front in co-operation with the People's Liberation Army of Yugoslavia was to liberate Belgrade.

ADVANCE ON DEBRECEN

The concept of the operation of the 2nd Ukrainian front which has gone down in the history of the Great Patriotic War as the Debrecen Operation was as follows: its main attack was to be dealt in the centre by the 53rd Field and 6th Guards Tank armies and General I. A. Pliyev's mechanised cavalry group from an area south of Oradea and north-west of Arada in the direction of Debrecen. The 40th Field and 7th Guards armies fighting in northern Rumania were to advance along a broad front and reach the Surdok-Apahida line. The 27th Army and the Rumanian 4th Army which were advancing on the left of the 40th and 7th armies were to capture Cluj and pursue an offensive in the general direction of Debrecen. The 46th Army and the Rumanian Ist Army were to continue the offensive in Yugoslavia.

The operation was boldly conceived: if the main attack was successful, that is, if the Soviet troops broke through to the north and west of Debrecen, they would threaten to surround the enemy forces in Transylvania and in the passes in the Eastern Carpathians.

The great length of the front line which extended for 800 kilometres, the almost 1,000-kilometre-long supply routes, and the railways that could not be used unless the width of the tracks was changed in Rumania and Hungary, created enormous difficulties for the Soviet troops during both the preparations for and the operation itself. Within a short period of time, not more than five or six days, the 2nd Ukrainian Front, however, was replenished with manpower and equipment, stocked with adequate quantities of fuel, lubricants and ammunition, made the necessary regroupings and built up a strike force in the sector of the main attack.

The strike force went into action in the morning of October 6, in the wake of an artillery and aerial bombardment, and sliced through the enemy defences. The best results were recorded in the zone of the 53rd Army under General

I. M. Managarov. General Pliyev's mechanised cavalry group consisting of the 7th Mechanised and the 4th and 6th Guards cavalry corps was rushed into the breach, and the infantry which followed the mobile units consolidated its success.

The German-Hungarian forces fought desperately but were unable to stop the mobile formations of the 2nd Ukrainian Front. Inflicting heavy casualties on the enemy, the 53rd Army and General Pliyev's group advanced 100 kilometres by the end of the third day right up to Karcag, a heavily fortified strong-point in the enemy defences.

The advancing forces were supported effectively by General Goryunov's 5th Air Army, its aircraft making more than 1,300 sorties in three days.

The Soviet drive, however, was not all a resounding success. The 6th Guards Tank Army which was short of tanks was forced to suspend its offensive south of Oradea, a major strong-point of the enemy. Without overpowering this strong-point the army could not advance swiftly in the northerly direction. Therefore, Marshal Malinovsky shifted a part of his Front's right-wing forces to the area and turned General Pliyev's group to the southeast, deploying it for a blow from an area northeast of Karcag at the rear of the enemy forces at Oradea. After that the Soviet offensive regained its momentum.

Oradea was liberated on October 12 by converging blows by General Pliyev's mechanised cavalry group and the 33rd Infantry Corps which included the Rumanian Tudor Vladimerscu and the 3rd Mountain Infantry divisions. By then the 6th Guards Cavalry Corps was nearing Debrecen.

The Soviet progress was relatively slow in the Cluj area where the enemy's determined resistance prevented the 40th and the 7th Guards armies from making any headway.

In the course of their offensive the Soviet troops crossed several small and big rivers, their opposite banks defended by heavily entrenched enemy's forces. The German Command built the most formidable fortifications along the Tisza, and was confident that it would take the Soviet troops a long time to cross this river. Nevertheless, the 53rd Army crossed to the opposite bank on the third day of the offensive.

By breaking towards Debrecen the Soviet forces threatened to cut the routes linking the enemy forces in Transylvania with Budapest. In the face of this threat Friessner began to disengage his troops from the 2nd Ukrainian Front's right-wing armies, and then from the sector facing the centre and the left wing of the 4th Ukrainian Front. Pressing home the offensive, the Soviet troops on October 11 liberated Cluj, the administrative centre of Transylvania, and Szeged, an important economic, political and administrative centre which was taken by the 46th Army's 320th Infantry Division in a night battle.

Continuing their advance, the mechanised cavalry groups under Generals Pliyev and Gorshkov,[1] in conjunction with General A. G. Kravchenko's 6th Guards Tank Army and General A. I. Semenov's 33rd Infantry Corps broke into Debrecen from several directions in the evening of October 19 and by the morning of the next day had fully cleared the town of the enemy.

The breakthrough of the 2nd Ukrainian Front into the Central Danube lowlands which became a scene of heavy fighting and the fall of Debrecen had a major impact on the further development of military operations.

Meanwhile, changes had also taken place in the internal political situation in Hungary. On October 11 the Hungarian delegation in Moscow accepted the preliminary terms of an armistice agreement between the Soviet Union and Hungary, under which Hungary was to pull back her troops to within her frontiers as they existed on December 31, 1937, completing their withdrawal within 10 days under the super-vision of an Allied Commission; Hungary was to sever forth-with relations with Germany and declare war on her. On its part the Soviet Government undertook to help Hungary fulfil these terms.

Having accepted these terms, the Hungarian Government, however, made no effort to honour them. It did not order its troops to cease fighting and continued to collaborate with the Germans.

The nazi leadership, however, were suspicious of Horthy's policy of manoeuvring between Germany and the countries of the anti-Hitler coalition and on October 15 Gestapo or-

---

[1] General S. I. Gorshkov's group included the 5th Guards Cavalry and the 23rd Tank corps.

ganised a coup in Budapest and installed the nazi hireling, Ferenc Szalasy, as head of the new government. On the following day Horthy officially transferred power to this even more rabid fascist, and sought asylum in the Third Reich. Thus ended the inglorious career of this hangman.

Fearing just retribution for its crimes, Horthy clique gave way to another fascist group which, in Berlin's opinion, was more capable of continuing the war on Germany's side.

Having liberated Debrecen, the 2nd Ukrainian Front pushed ahead at Nyiregyhaza and Szolnok. In the area south of Nyiregyhaza, an important railway and highway junction, the German Command delivered a powerful counter-blow. Smashing the enemy in a bitter engagement, the Soviet troops on October 22 liberated the town, General Pliyev's group immediately developing the offensive and shortly cutting the retreat routes of the German 8th Army north of Nyiregyhaza.

In an effort to save the army from encirclement and annihilation the German Command on October 23 counter-attacked in force at the flank and rear of General Pliyev's group north of Nyiregyhaza. Two infantry corps of the Soviet 27th Army failed in their effort to check the enemy's counter-attack north of Nagykallo. The mechanised cavalry group found itself in an extremely difficult situation when the enemy cut its communications north and northwest of Nyiregyhaza. For five days and nights the encircled group was fighting heavy battles against superior enemy forces which strove to wipe it out at all costs. The Commander of the 2nd Ukrainian Front took vigorous steps to help the encircled forces whose men were fighting with exceptional skill and courage. The 5th Air Army was ordered to cover the group from the air. Only a few Luftwaffe aircraft managed to break into the battle zone. Between October 21 and 28 the airmen of the 5th Air Army flew 1,500 missions, mostly in support of the troops in the Nyiregyhaza area and also those fighting on the Szolnok bridgehead.

On the night of October 25 Marshal Malinovsky ordered General Pliyev to launch a full-scale attack in the direction of Nagykallo and link up with General Trofimenko's 27th Army which was also advancing on Nagykallo. On October

27 the Soviet troops withdrew from Nyiregyhaza and fought their way out of the encirclement.

Furious battles raged in all sectors of the front. By dusk on October 28, the 53rd Army advancing towards Szolnok together with General M. S. Shumilov's 7th Guards Army, which had been transferred to the area, seized several bridge-heads on the western bank of the Tisza. This was a major success, for the enemy's defences on the river had been dis-rupted. On October 25 General F. F. Zhmachenko's 40th Army and the Rumanian 4th Army completed the liberation of northern Transylvania, crossed the Rumanian-Hungarian border and in the last days of October reached the Tisza at Chop. The 46th Army, operating on the Front's left wing, on October 21 liberated the towns of Baja and Sombor. Pushing ahead it secured a large bridgehead between the Tisza and the Danube by the end of the month and thus created favourable conditions for subsequent offensive opera-tions against Budapest.

As a result of the Debrecen Operation almost the whole of Hungary east of the Tisza was freed. The liberated area was about a third of the country's territory and accounted for a quarter of her entire population. The whole of North-ern Transylvania was also liberated. Advancing from 130 to 275 kilometres in 23 days, the Soviet troops reached the line Chop-Szolnok-Baja, crossed the Tisza and captured a large bridgehead between Polgar on the Tisza and Baja on the Danube.

The fascist regime was overthrown in the liberated regions of Hungary and in the northern part of Transylvania, where the presence of the Soviet Army drastically heightened the influence of the Hungarian progressive forces on the course and the results of the country's democratisation.

The successful operations of the 2nd Ukrainian Front over-turned the nazi leaders' plans of routing the Soviet troops at the Hungarian border and retaining defensive lines in east-ern Hungary. The conditions were now ripe for mounting an offensive against Budapest and threatening the communi-cations of the German forces in the southern Balkans.

The breakthrough of the 2nd Ukrainian Front to the supply routes of the enemy's Carpathian-Transylvanian forces com-pelled them to withdraw from the northern Carpathians.

RELATIONS BETWEEN
THE SOVIET UNION AND HUNGARY

On October 27, 1944 the USSR State Defence Committee issued a statement to the effect that the Soviet Army was entering Hungary not as a conqueror but as the liberator of the Hungarian people from nazi oppression, and that it had no objectives other than routing the German armies and overthrowing nazi Germany's rule in the occupied countries.

Supervision over the functions of local self-government bodies in Hungary's liberated areas was entrusted to the Front's Military Council which had instructions "not to break up the Hungarian order of things and not to introduce the Soviet order of things". The decisions of the State Defence Committee were to be carried into effect by military commandants' offices which were established in all major towns and inhabited localities.

For many years the Hungarian people were intimidated with fabrications about the "horrors of Bolshevism", particularly with the lie that with the arrival of the Soviet Army the entire able-bodied population would be banished to Siberia. Not all people believed these falsehoods, least of all the workers and the village poor, but many were taken in by them.

In these difficult conditions the Soviet troops had to be thoroughly acquainted with the Party's internationalist policy and learn to distinguish friend from foe. "It would be wrong to identify the working population of Hungary enslaved by German and Hungarian fascism with the criminal Hungarian Government," said the statement of the Military Council of the 2nd Ukrainian Front.

Gradually the Hungarian people realised that they had been misled by the fascist propaganda, for from the very first days the Soviet troops helped them to bring life back to normal.

The enormous explanatory work which was conducted among the population of the liberated areas stimulated the efforts of the Hungarian people to democratise the country. Legal organisations of the Communist Party were set up in the liberated parts of Hungary. On October 10 the Communist and Social Democratic Parties reached an agreement on unity of action which greatly invigorated the Resistance Movement.

Established in October and November in Szeged the Central Committee of the Hungarian Communist Party, consisting mainly of the members of the Communist Party Foreign Bureau, took charge of the activities of all Party organisations in the liberated areas.

At the time an underground Central Committee, including Antonal Apro and Janos Kadar, was active in Budapest, and it was not long before that contact was established between these two centres.

A large part of the population in the occupied parts of Hungary began to display increasing opposition to German rule.

The guerrilla struggle in the rear of the enemy gained in scope and scale. In order to help the Hungarian guerrillas the Soviet Command in 1944 sent 11 groups (about 280 people) of officers and experts mostly radio operators and demolition experts, across the frontline. And although guerrilla movement in Hungary did not develop into a nation-wide armed struggle, its results should not be underestimated. The Hungarian guerrillas carried on explanatory work among the population, exposed the treacherous policy of the Hungarian Government, campaigned for a national-liberation struggle against the German troops and the Hungarian oppressors, and called upon the population not to be afraid of the Soviet Army and join its fight against the common enemy, German nazism.

3. BATTLES FOR BUDAPEST

THE BATTLE IN THE AREA BETWEEN THE TISZA AND THE DANUBE

The German Command did its utmost to check the Soviet offensive against Budapest. On October 28 the commander of Army Group South ordered his troops to build stable defences along the Tisza and to wipe out the Soviet forces which had entered the area between the Tisza and the Danube using all their reserves to achieve this aim.

When the Soviet troops started their offensive against Budapest the main forces of Army Group South (24 divisions) were deployed in the Nyiregyhaza-Miskolc sector against the centre and the right wing of the 2nd Ukrainian Front. About seven Hungarian divisions, seriously depleted in preceding battles, were in action against the Front's left-wing troops southeast of Budapest, and other enemy forces were being shifted to the Budapest sector. All in all Army Group South had 35 divisions (including nine panzer and motorised) and three brigades.

Seven German divisions from Army Group F faced the 3rd Ukrainian Front in the Vukovar-Krusevac sector. Their orders were to hold up the Soviet advance to the southwest in order to retain the routes essential for evacuating German troops from Greece, Yugoslavia and Albania.

The 2nd Ukrainian Front had almost the same strength as at the end of the Debrecen Operation. Its main forces— 22 infantry divisions, three cavalry, one tank and one mechanised corps, two fortified areas and 10 Rumanian divisions— were engaged along a 200-kilometre line east and northeast of Budapest. To the southeast, 17 infantry divisions, two infantry and one Rumanian cavalry divisions were consolidating their positions along a 235-kilometre line. A tank army, two separate mechanised corps (2nd Guards and 4th Guards) which were shifted from the GHQ Reserve, and an infantry corps made up the Front Commander's reserve and were deployed behind the Front's central and left-wing forces. Separate units were in action between a point south of Baja to the Front's left boundary.

The disposition of the Soviet troops was not favourable for offensive action. Nevertheless, Budapest had to be taken without delay, for any loss in time incurred through redeployment would have only benefited the enemy. The 2nd Ukrainian Front, therefore, was ordered to launch an offensive on Budapest on October 29, i.e., on the second day after the end of the Debrecen Operation.

On the whole the 2nd Ukrainian Front had twice as much infantry as Army Group South, from four to four and half times as many guns (not counting anti-tank and anti-aircraft) and mortars, 1.9 times as many tanks and self-propelled guns, and 2.6 times as many combat aircraft.

In keeping with GHQ instructions the concept of the operation was as follows: the front's left-wing 46th Army, reinforced by two mechanised corps and supported by its right-hand neighbour, the 7th Guards Army, was to deal a frontal blow, slice through the relatively weak enemy defences southeast of Budapest and capture the city in a swift assault.

General I. T. Shlemin's 46th Army together with the 2nd Guards and 4th Guards mechanised corps[1] was to strike out in the general direction of Kecskemet and Budapest. The 7th Guards Army and its Rumanian divisions were to go over to the offensive on October 30 out of an area southeast of Szolnok, cross the Tisza and gain a bridgehead on its western bank. The 6th Guards Tank Army was also to go into action in the army's operational zone.

The 40th, 27th and 53rd armies and the Rumanian forces on the Front's right wing were to advance in the general direction of Miskolc, and tie down the enemy troops facing them to prevent them from being transferred to the Budapest area where the front was delivering its main blow.[2] General Pliyev's mechanised cavalry group was to go into action in the area of the 7th Guards Army and General Gorshkov's group, in the area of the 27th Army.[3] The 4th Ukrainian Front was to continue its drive into the interior of Czechoslovakia tying down the enemy forces there and preventing their transfer to Budapest. The 3rd Ukrainian Front continued to concentrate its main forces in the Yugoslav Banat. At the same time its advance units were to secure a bridgehead on the right bank of the Danube and, with the arrival of the main forces, join in the general offensive in Hungary.

The attack was launched on schedule, in the afternoon of October 29. Ploughing through the enemy defences, the 46th Army advanced 20-40 kilometres by the end of the second day and the 7th Army gained a bridgehead over 10 kilometres

---

[1] The 4th Guards Mechanised Corps was committed on November 1, 1944.

[2] These orders were issued on November 1, 1944.

[3] By that time General Gorshkov's mechanised cavalry group consisted of the 5th Guards Cavalry and the 7th Mechanised corps; General Pliyev's group had the 4th Guards and 6th Guards cavalry and the 23rd Tank corps.

deep and 30 kilometres wide on the west bank of the Tisza. The enemy failed to hold on to the Kecskemet strong-point although the 24th Panzer Division had been transferred to the area, and by the morning of November 1 the town fell to the Soviet troops. Later it came to light that the 46th Army's offensive caught the enemy by surprise.

The successful operations of the Soviet troops created a direct threat to Budapest.

On November 2, the 4th Guards and 2nd Guards Mechanised corps advanced 75 kilometres and on the following day occupied Alsonemedy 15 kilometres from Budapest. By then the Germans had shifted three panzer divisions and a motorised division to the Budapest area considerably strengthening their defences south of the Hungarian capital. The offensive of the 46th Army slowed down and the efforts of the 4th Guards Mechanised Corps to break into the city in its stride met with no success.

On November 4, GHQ pointed out to the Commander of the 2nd Ukrainian Front that an attack on Budapest carried out along a narrow front by only two mechanised corps with a small number of infantry could lead to unwarranted losses and expose the troops operating in this sector to a flanking blow from the northeast. It ordered him to speed up the transfer of the Front's central and right-wing forces to the right bank of the Tisza so as to pursue an offensive along a broad frontage and rout the enemy forces at Budapest by strikes from the north and the northeast in conjunction with the 46th Army and the two mechanised corps advancing on the city from the south. In fulfilment of these instructions the Front on November 11 launched an offensive which lasted 16 days.

In spite of their determined efforts the Soviet troops were unable to overpower the enemy grouping by splitting it up east of the city. The reason was the autumn slush, the almost unceasing rains, the interrupted delivery of ammunition due to stretched supply routes, and the fatigue of the men who had been attacking for more than three months on end. At his request the commander of the 2nd Ukrainian Front was allowed to make a pause in the offensive and resume it not later than December 5, after carrying out the necessary regrouping and preparations.

Under Marshal Malinovsky's decision the offensive against Budapest was to be undertaken by the Front's central and left-wing troops. The Hungarian capital was to be captured as a result of enveloping movement, one from the north executed by the 7th Guards Army, the 6th Guards Tank Army and General Pliyev's group, and the other from the southwest by the main forces of the 46th Army and the 2nd Guards Mechanised Corps, while the 53rd Army was to push northwards in support of the strike forces.

The Front's right-wing 40th and 27th armies were to strike at Miskolc, capture it and prevent the enemy from shifting his troops from this area to Budapest.

After five days of the offensive the 2nd Ukrainian Front cut the enemy's retreat routes from Budapest to the north, but failed to encircle the enemy at Budapest because the 46th Army lacked the strength to break through to Budapest from the southwest.

The second attempt to capture Budapest using the forces of the 2nd Ukrainian Front alone failed although, on the whole, the offensive had a measure of success. The Soviet troops liberated almost the entire area between the Tisza and the Danube bringing freedom to hundreds of thousands of Hungarians. The fascist regime was done away with over the larger part of Hungary.

While the 2nd Ukrainian Front was fighting for Budapest, the 3rd Ukrainian Front crossed the Danube and captured a bridgehead 50 kilometres wide and from 14 to 17 kilometres deep near Batina and Apatin on its right bank. Pushing to the north and the northwest, it began liberating Hungarian territory southwest of Budapest. By December 9 it had reached an area south of Lake Balaton, threatening the enemy group defending Budapest from the rear. In the latter half of November the 4th Guards Army, which arrived in Hungary and was incorporated into the 3rd Ukrainian Front, was committed on the right bank of the Danube.

Having captured ground northeast of Lake Balaton, the 3rd Ukrainian Front was poised, in co-operation with the 2nd Ukrainian Front, to invest and wipe out the German forces at Budapest.

THE ENCIRCLEMENT AND ROUT
OF THE GERMAN FORCES
IN BUDAPEST

On December 12, GHQ issued fresh orders: the 2nd and the 3rd Ukrainian fronts were to deliver combined blows from the northeast, east and southwest with the view to surrounding and smashing the enemy grouping at Budapest and capturing the Hungarian capital. This time two fronts were assigned to surround the Budapest group of forces.

When the offensive began on December 20, the 2nd Ukrainian Front had 39 infantry divisions, two tank, two mechanised corps, and two cavalry corps, two fortified areas and 14 Rumanian divisions; the 3rd Ukrainian Front consisted of 31 infantry divisions, a marine brigade, one fortified area, a tank, a mechanised and a cavalry corps. The Bulgarian Ist Army also took part in the Front's operations.

Facing the two fronts were 51 enemy divisions and two brigades, including nine panzer and four motorised divisions and a motorised brigade.

The 2nd Ukrainian Front was to deliver its main blow from Sahy in the general direction of Kebelkut, gain the Danube between Neszmei and Esztergom and thus sever the retreat routes to the northwest for the enemy forces in Budapest.

The 3rd Ukrainian Front and the attached 46th Army and the 4th Guards Mechanised Corps were to pierce enemy defences northeast and southwest of Lake Velencei, develop their offensive on Bicske, reach the Danube in the Esztergom-Neszmei sector and cut the retreat routes to the west for the enemy Budapest grouping. A part of the Front's forces was to advance on Budapest from the west and capture the city in conjunction with the left wing of the 2nd Ukrainian Front.

On the first day of the offensive both fronts cut through the enemy defences north and southwest of Budapest. Pursuing the offensive with tank and cavalry formations between the Ipoy and Hron rivers in the southerly direction and from the area of Lake Velencei to the north and northwest, the Soviet troops gradually tightened the ring around Budapest.

By nightfall on the first day of the offensive, the 7th Guards Army and the 6th Guards Tank Army of the 2nd Ukrainian Front, operating north of the city, burst into the valley of the Ipoy and pushed towards the Danube where they were to link up with the troops of the 3rd Ukrainian Front at Esztergom. To avert the threat of encirclement the Germans on December 21 delivered two converging counterblows from Szakalosi at Sahi, and from Nemcze to the south. Committing more than 200 panzers and assault guns, the German Command intended to cut off and destroy the 6th Guards Army.

Very heavy battles, most of them tank engagements took place between the rivers Ipoy and Hron. They lasted eight days and nights and ended in the victory of Soviet forces who wiped out or took prisoner more than 15,000 enemy officers and men, destroyed 150 panzers, 87 guns and a large quantity of other equipment. On December 26, the 7th Guards Army and the 6th Guards Tank Army reached the Danube north of Esztergom where they linked up with the troops of the 3rd Ukrainian Front, which entered the area from the south, to close the ring of encirclement around the enemy Budapest grouping consisting of seven infantry, two panzer, one motorised and two cavalry divisions, three artillery brigades, up to 30 separate regiments, battalions and diverse German and Hungarian combat groups totalling more than 188,000 officers and men.

Budapest was strongly fortified, its every street and block and even many buildings adapted for sustained defence. The enemy took special care to fortify Mount Sashegy, the Palace Hill and the railway station.

In an effort to avert casualties among the civilian population and destruction of the city, the Soviet Command offered the enemy to surrender. The truce envoy of the 2nd Ukrainian Front, Captain Miklos Steinmetz, was shot and killed. The truce envoy of the 3rd Ukrainian Front, Captain I. A. Ostapenko, delivered the ultimatum which the Germans rejected and then shot him in the back as he was returning to Soviet positions. The nazis violated international law guaranteeing the immunity of truce envoys. By killing them the German Command assumed full responsibility for the needless loss of human life and the destruction of the Hungarian capital. The GHQ ordered the 2nd and 3rd Ukrainian fronts to wipe out the encircled enemy forces.

The battle for Budapest was exceptionally stubborn, for the enemy was fully resolved to hold on to the city. The German troops at Budapest were told that Hitler had dispatched 12 divisions to the city with orders to burst through the Russian positions and restore the situation in Hungary. To emphasise the importance of a German victory at Budapest, Hitler himself directed the deblockading of the invested garrison.

In January 1945, having assembled several panzer divisions and powerful infantry and artillery forces the German troops with Luftwaffe support counter-attacked three times in a attempt to break the ring of encirclement around Budapest. On one occasion they even managed to reach the Danube and cut the 3rd Ukrainian Front in two. But in the course of a fierce battle the Soviet troops stopped the enemy pushing towards Budapest and hurled him back to his starting positions, thus enabling the 2nd Ukrainian Front to deal with the German garrison in the city.

This task was achieved in two stages: in the first stage from December 27, 1944 to January 18, 1945, the enemy garrison in the eastern part of the city, Pest, was destroyed, and in the second stage, which lasted from January 22 to February 13, in the western part, Buda. Pest was liberated by the 30th Infantry and the Rumanian 7th Army corps of the 7th Guards Army, and the 18th Separate Guards Infantry Corps. On January 12 they were united under the commander of the 18th Separate Guards Corps, Major-General I. M. Afonin, into the Budapest Group.

The closer the Soviet troops drew to Budapest, the more desperate the enemy resistance became. The Budapest suburbs of Veczes and Racoscaba were most heavily fortified. The advancing troops had to overcome a maze of trenches, wire entanglements, anti-tank ditches and concentrated fire from all weapons. They had to take almost each building by storm and blast their way through road blocks and barricades. The thunder of battle hung over the city day and night. Smoke obscured the sky during daylight hours and at night fires could be seen for kilometres around. The troops had difficulty in finding their bearing in the labyrinth of narrow streets; it was not easy to maintain radio contact and Soviet attack plane pilots flew almost at rooftop level so as not to mistake their own troops for those of the enemy.

On January 18, after 23 days of heavy fighting, the units of the Budapest Group completely liberated Pest, the eastern part of the Hungarian capital, in this period they killed over 35,000 enemy troops, took more than 62,000 prisoners, and destroyed or captured 291 panzers and assault guns, 1,419 guns and mortars, 222 armoured cars and personnel carriers, 784 machine guns, 20,140 rifles, 2,700 motor vehicles, 8,000 railway carriages, 96 locomotives and large quantities of other equipment. These figures show that the enemy had mustered very considerable forces in that part of the city.

Having wiped out the enemy in Pest, the Budapest Group was shifted to Buda, the city's western part, with the task of surrounding and destroying the enemy there. The Budapest Group[1] launched an offensive on January 20. On January 22 commander of the 53rd Army General I. M. Managarov replaced General Afonin who was wounded in the fighting as commander of the Budapest Group. Augmenting the power of its blows as troops kept arriving from Pest, the Group slowly pushed forward in the face of stubborn resistance. In 20 days of fighting it managed to free only 114 blocks of the 608 which were still in the hands of the enemy.

The enemy forces in the city were experiencing very serious difficulties. In February the soldiers received only 75 grammes of bread a day. There was no electricity and gas, and almost no water. Shops and bakeries were closed. Life was at a standstill. The streets were littered with corpses which no one bothered to remove, and after nightfall bands of marauders roamed the streets robbing and killing the helpless civilians.

On the night of February 11 the German Command undertook a final desperate effort to pierce the ring of investment around Buda, and break out of the city. It concentrated about 2,000 men on a narrow sector who cracked the lines of the 180th Infantry Division and pulled out more than 15,000 men through the corridor. By February 14, however, they

---

[1] By then the Budapest Group was reinforced by the 75th and 37th Infantry corps. The 30th Infantry Corps was withdrawn from it.

were destroyed by the 3rd Ukrainian Front. Scattered enemy forces which remained in Buda were also routed and taken prisoner. By 10.00 hours on February 13, 1945, the Hungarian capital was free.

A glorious page in the history of the battle for Budapest was written by the Danube Flotilla which landed troops in the rear of the enemy, helping the attacking forces.

On July 9, 1945 the Presidium of the USSR Supreme Soviet instituted the medal "For the Capture of Budapest" which was awarded to all the participants in the battle for this city. Many units were honoured with the title "Budapest" added to their name.

Hungarian soldiers took part in the fighting for Budapest together with the Soviet Army. At first they were companies incorporated into Soviet units, and they participated in the fighting for the Southern Railway Station, Mount Gellert and the fortress. Later these companies were merged into the Buda Volunteer Regiment under the command of Hungarian Lieutenant-Colonel Oszkar Varihazy. The regiment sustained heavy casualties in the fighting for Budapest, and its role in the liberation of the Hungarian capital had an important moral and political impact.

Risking their lives many Hungarian patriots helped the Soviet troops. Among them were the husband and wife Lajos and Lajosne Szabo and father and son Janos and Arpad Klein, who in November 1944 helped four Soviet war prisoners escape from the hospital of the Budapest jail.

During the fighting for Budapest, Soviet troops tried to cause as little suffering as possible to the civilian population and to avert large-scale destruction. The Germans, on the contrary, deliberately wrecked the city and blew up the bridges across the Danube.

The battle for the Hungarian capital lasted 108 days, from October 29, 1944 to February 13, 1945. It was exceptionally vicious and arduous due to the German Command's efforts to hold the city at whatever the cost. The Germans knew that the fall of Budapest would force Hungary to withdraw from the war and Germany would find herself completely isolated. From the strategic point of view, the enemy regarded Budapest as the key resistance centre in the entire system of defences blocking the road into western Hungary.

With Budapest liberated, considerable Soviet forces were transferred to other sectors of the front and the Soviet command could now turn to liberating the whole of Hungary and smashing the enemy forces in Austria by opening up offensive on Vienna.

THE POLITICAL SITUATION
IN HUNGARY AT THE BEGINNING
OF 1945

The enemy was still in Budapest when political life in Hungary entered a period of fundamental changes arising from Soviet victories and the anti-war, revolutionary struggle of the Hungarian Communist Party.

Early in December 1944, the Hungarian Front was transformed into the Hungarian National Front of Independence. Taken on the initiative of the Communists, this move was designed to strengthen the unity of all the anti-fascist forces in the struggle for the establishment of a democratic, independent Hungary. The Programme for Hungary's Democratic Restoration and Development worked out by the Communist Party became the political platform of the Hungarian National Front of Independence. It urged the Hungarian people to help the Soviet Army in completing the expulsion of the German invaders from Hungary, and also determined what had to be done to establish a new social order in the country. The Programme envisaged the establishment of local national committees vested with full powers and the convocation of a National Assembly to elect a Provisional Government.

The programme was approved at mass rallies of working people in Szeged and Debrecen. The national committees which were set up in these towns put in a lot of work to prepare and convene the Provisional National Assembly.

Held in Debrecen on December 21, 1944, the Assembly elected a Provisional Government headed by Colonel-General Bela Miklos, former commander of the Hungarian Ist Army, and included two representatives each from the Social Democratic and Smallholder parties, three from the Communist Party, one from the National Peasant Party and four "unaffiliated" members, i.e., Horthyites. The majority of

the government was not in favour of the Programme for
Hungary's Democratic Restoration and Development, but,
taking into account the revolutionary sentiments of the broad
masses, they did not venture openly to reject its demands at
the time.

With a part of Hungarian territory west of the Danube still
a battlefield, a new, free Hungary had already come into being. In compliance with the will of the broad masses, the
Provisional Government on December 28 severed diplomatic
relations with Germany and declared war on her.

An agreement concerning an armistice between the USSR,
Great Britain and the United States, on the one hand, and
Hungary, on the other, was signed in Moscow on January
20, 1945. Under one of the points of the agreement Hungary
undertook to commit not less than eight infantry divisions
against Germany.

In an appeal to the working people of Hungary, the Hungarian Communist Party noted that the armistice agreement
engendered the birth of a Hungarian people's army which
together with the victorious Soviet Army would take part in
routing nazism and avenge the suffering of the Hungarian
people.

Newspapers in the liberated areas of Hungary reported
many instances of Hungarian citizens volunteering for service in the new Hungarian armed forces.

The agreement also provided for the establishment of an
Allied Control Commission under the general guidance of
an Allied (Soviet) High Command in Hungary and enabled
the democratic forces to undermine the positions of internal
reactionary circles.

Budapest was returning to life. With lightning speed the
news spread among its war-weary, starving inhabitants that
the Soviet Union, whose population was short of food itself,
provided them with 33,000 tons of grain, 4,400 tons of meat,
3,300 tons of sugar and 180 tons of coffee.

At the request of Budapest Communists and local self-
government, bodies, the engineers of the 2nd Ukrainian Front
repaired the bridge across the Danube linking the capital's
eastern and western parts, removed mines from residential
houses and industrial enterprises, and provided technical assistance in rehabilitating and putting a number of factories

and mills back in operation. Fulfilling orders placed by the Soviet Command, workers of restored factories knew that they were contributing their share to the struggle against the nazi invaders.

Hungarians could now form their own opinion of the Soviet soldiers without being misled by the tales spread by Goebbels' and Horthy's propaganda. Wherever the Soviet soldier passed, fulfilling his mission of liberation, people began to lead a new life with only good prospects for the future.

Meanwhile, guns thundered far beyond the Danube in the West Hungarian Plain where the Soviet Army continued to maul the enemy forces.

4. LAST BATTLES IN HUNGARY

THE BATTLE AT LAKE BALATON

On February 17, 1945 GHQ ordered the 2nd and 3rd Ukrainian fronts to start preparations for an offensive on Vienna with the objective of completing the liberation of Hungary and smashing the German forces in the eastern part of Austria. It would have seemed that in the prevailing circumstances the German Command could do no more than organise a stubborn resistance in western Hungary, on the approaches to Eastern Austria and in the south of Germany. However, in February 1945 the German Command was directed by Hitler to get ready for striking a blow in the Lake Balaton area.

With the Soviet troops a mere 60 kilometres from Berlin, what made the Germans fight with such tenacity in order to hold on to the remaining part of Hungary and even bring in divisions from vulnerable sectors of the front?

The German Command decided to undertake a counteroffensive in the area of Lake Balaton in order to smash the troops of the 3rd Ukrainian Front, drive them out of the bridgehead on the west bank of the Danube and to stem the Soviet offensive in Southeast Europe. In this way the Germans hoped to retain possession of Hungary's oil-fields, remove the threat to industrial regions in Austria and Southern Germany, keep their last ally, Hungary, in submission and force the Soviet Command to shift its forces from the central sector to the south. After carrying out the operation the Germans intended swiftly to transfer their armoured divisions to the central sector of the Soviet-German front and consolidate their positions at Berlin.

To back the forthcoming offensive at Lake Balaton from the north o powerful enemy force, which included about 400 panzers, on February 17, four days after the fall of Budapest, dealt a heavy blow at the 7th Guards Army under General M. S. Shumilov deployed north of Budapest on the west bank of the Hron.

Taken by suprise, the 7th Guards Army, which had weak defences on the bridgehead, sustained heavy losses in manpower (about 8,800 officers and men) and weapons, and after eight days of fighting had to withdraw from the bridgehead and take up the defensive on the east bank of the Hron. The enemy broke off the offensive, which was merely a prelude to the forthcoming operations at Lake Balaton.

The Germans concentrated a powerful group for the counter-offensive at Lake Balaton. Early in March 1945 the 3rd Ukrainian Front on the sector Gant-Lake Balaton was opposed by the main forces of Corps Group Balk[1] and the SS 6th Panzer Army transferred from the Western Front. The Hungarian 2nd Army Corps was on the defensive on the northwestern shores of Lake Balaton; the German 2nd Panzer Army was operating on the sector between Lake Balaton and the Drava, and Army Group E defended positions further to the left, on the south bank of the Drava.

The Germans planned to attack the 3rd Ukrainian Front with a large force of 31 divisions, including 11 panzer divisions, three combat groups and a motorised brigade, totalling more than 430,000 effectives, more than 5,600 guns and mortars, about 900 panzers and assault guns and 850 aircraft.

Characteristically, the number of Hungarian divisions in the Wehrmacht dropped sharply due to political developments in Hungary, as a result of which Szalasy's army simply "melted away" in the preceding five months. Only nine Hungarian

---

[1] Combat Group Balk included the German 6th Army and the Hungarian 3rd Army.

divisions were left compared with 27 at the disposal of the German Command at the beginning of the Debrecen operation and 20 which were involved in the fighting for Budapest.

The 3rd Ukrainian Front had 37 infantry divisions and six Bulgarian infantry divisions, two tank, one mechanised and one cavalry corps. They had a total of nearly 400,000 officers and men, up to 7,000 guns and mortars, about 400 tanks and self-propelled guns and 700 aircraft. Except tanks, of which the Germans had twice as many, the opponents were almost equal in strength.

In the circumstances, the 3rd Ukrainian Front had to put up organised defence, repulse the enemy's counter-offensive and then mount an offensive towards Vienna.

Having entrenched themselves in fortified positions, the Soviet troops were fully prepared for the German offensive which began in the morning of March 6.

Eleven panzer divisions and infantry in personnel carriers supported by artillery and aviation descended on Soviet positions. The heaviest blow fell on General N. A. Gagen's 26th Army and General S. G. Trofimenko's 27th Army deployed between lakes Velencei and Balaton.

Guns thundered for ten days and nights as the two sides fought bitter battles involving more than 800,000 men, more than 12,000 guns and mortars, about 1,300 tanks and assault guns and more than 1,500 aircraft. Casualties were heavy on both sides. On several occasions the Germans committed up to 500 panzers simultaneously. It is difficult to describe the dramatism and intensity of the defensive battles waged by Soviet, Bulgarian and Yugoslav troops in the area of Lake Balaton and further south, on the banks of the Drava. Hundreds of Soviet soldiers and even whole units displayed heroism.

Thanks to the well-organised defences, skilful conduct of battle, combining rigid defence and broad manoeuvre, and also the courage of the Soviet troops frustrated the enemy's plans.

All those who took part in the fighting in Hungary in the spring of 1945 are grateful to the sailors of the Danube Flotilla commanded by Rear-Admiral G. N. Kholostyakov for their part in bringing in supplies and reserves from the east to the west bank of the Danube when ice floes had swept away the bridges.

Failing to achieve its aim, the German Command on March 15 ordered the battle weary, heavily mauled troops of Combat Group Balk and the SS 6th Panzer Army to halt their offensive and assume the defensive.

The Soviet forces and the Bulgarian and Yugoslav formations fulfilled their task. They repulsed the counter-offensive, retained the main lines of defence in their hands and paved the way for a Soviet drive towards Vienna. Between March 6 and 15 the enemy lost nearly 45,000 officers and men in killed and taken prisoner, more than 280 guns and mortars, some 500 panzers and assault guns, nearly 500 personnel carriers and over 1,300 motor vehicles. The 3rd Ukrainian Front, too, sustained heavy casualties.

TOWARDS THE AUSTRIAN BORDERS

After the defeat at Lake Balaton, the German Command hastened to evacuate its troops from Yugoslavia into the western parts of Hungary and Eastern Austria. Outflanked by the troops operating in the centre and the right wing of the 3rd Ukrainian Front the enemy force at Lake Balaton also found itself in a very disadvantageous position. Taking this factor into account, the Soviet Command decided to destroy it and after that initiate an offensive on Vienna.

On March 9, 1945, while the Balaton Operation was still in progress, GHQ issued the following instructions to the 2nd and 3rd Ukrainian fronts: in the course of defensive battles the 3rd Ukrainian Front was to wear down the enemy panzer forces attacking in the Szekesfehervar area, and not later than March 16 throw its right wing armies into attack, smash the enemy north of Lake Balaton and press forward in the general direction of Papa and Sopron. The 2nd Ukrainian Front was to push ahead towards Vienna, using only the 46th Army deployed south of the Danube. The 46th Army was to go over to the offensive on March 17-18, wipe out the enemy south of the Danube in conjunction with the 3rd Ukrainian Front and then press home the offensive in the general direction of Dyör.

Accordingly, GHQ concentrated the troops of the 3rd Ukrainian Front and the 46th Army of the 2nd Ukrainian Front for the operation in the course of which they were to rout the enemy forces south of the Danube, complete the liberation of Hungary and enter Austria.

After the collapse of the counter-offensive at Lake Balaton the enemy took urgent steps to reinforce the permanent defences between Esztergom and Szekesfehervar and build defences along the Szekesfehervar-Simontornial-Lake Balaton-Siofok line captured during the counter-offensive. The defences consisted of three belts and several intermediate lines. The main line of resistance passed north of the Danube along the west bank of the Hron, and south of the Danube along the slopes of the Verteshegyseg Mountains up to Szekesfehervar. It was 5-7 kilometres deep and fully manned.

In fulfilment of GHQ instructions commander of the 3rd Ukrainian Front, Marshal F. I. Tolbukhin, decided to aim the main blow at Varpalota and Veszprem with his right-wing 9th Guards and 4th Guards armies, pierce the enemy defence north of Szekesfehervar and, together with the 27th and 26th armies, encircle and destroy German forces between lakes Velencei and Balaton. Then the Soviet troops were to strike out in the general direction of Papa, Sopron, reach the Austrian border and prepare the ground for an offensive on Vienna.

The tasks of liberating Hungary's southwestern regions was assigned to General M. N. Sharokhin's 57th Army and the Bulgarian Ist Army under General V. Stoichev who were to rout the German forces at Nagykanizsa.

Lieutenant-General A. V. Petrushevsky's 46th Army reinforced by the 2nd Guards Mechanised Corps was under orders to disrupt enemy defences north of Csakvar and exploit their success in the general direction of Dad and Dyör. A part of the forces were to cut the enemy's retreat routes from an area southwest of Esztergom, press him to the Danube and, in co-operation with the Danube Flotilla, destroy him. So, the Soviet offensive was to take place on a front extending from the Danube to the Drava and result in the complete liberation of Hungary.

The 2nd Ukrainian Front's 7th Guards Army operating north of the Danube was to advance in the general direction of Bratislava.

When the 3rd Ukrainian Front began the offensive, which has gone down in history as the Vienna Operation, it had only a negligible superiority over the enemy in manpower and materiel. Overcoming certain difficulties connected with the preparations for the Vienna Operation, while the enemy counter-offensive was still going on, the 2nd and 3rd Ukrainian fronts succeeded most thoroughly to prepare for the forthcoming offensive.

The 3rd Ukrainian front opened its offensive on March 16, the day after the enemy halted his counter-offensive, and a day later the 2nd Ukrainian Front's 46th Army went into action.

The blow delivered by Colonel-General V. V. Glagolev's 9th Army and Lieutenant-General N. D. Zakhvatayev's 4th Guards Army, both of the 3rd Ukrainian Front, caught the enemy by surprise.

Armour was badly needed to exploit the success of the main blow; so, GHQ, on March 16, placed the 2nd Ukrainian Front's 6th Guards Tank Army, which had already assembled west of Budapest, under the control of the 3rd Ukrainian Front with orders to close the ring around the enemy forces operating southeast and southwest of Szekesfehervar.

Fighting for Szekesfehervar broke out on March 17. The Germans attached tremendous importance to keeping their hold on this town inasmuch as it barred the way for the Soviet troops attacking the rear and flank of the SS 6th Panzer Army's main forces.

The 6th Guards Tank Army which attacked in the morning of March 19 could not advance rapidly enough in the face of the stubborn resistance offered by the enemy southwest of Lake Velencei and very difficult terrain. Reconnaissance reported that the Germans had started pulling out of the area south of the lake in a westerly direction and, therefore, urgent measures had to be taken to encircle the SS 6th Panzer Army.

In the morning of March 20 the 27th and 26th armies struck at Polgardi and Lepsen. Having overwhelmed the resisting enemy, they reached Polgardi by nightfall on the following day. Meanwhile, the Front's strike group repulsed numerous counter-attacks as it reached Varpalota and south of it and was now 10 kilometres from Lake Balaton.

By nightfall of March 21, the Soviet troops had outflanked the main forces of the SS 6th Panzer Army south of Szekesfehervar. Some 24 hours later the enemy could retreat only along a narrow 2.5 kilometres wide corridor exposed to artillery and machine-gun fire. The German Command made every effort to withdraw its panzer army before the Soviet troops closed their ring of encirclement, and succeeded in doing so at a heavy cost in manpower and equipment.

The 46th Army's main forces attacked on March 17. Together with the 2nd Mechanised Corps they overcame the enemy defences along the Verteshegyseg Mountains within a few days, and by dusk on March 20 had advanced 40 kilometres to the west. By reaching the Danube north of Tovarosz, the 2nd Ukrainian Front's left-wing forces deeply outflanked the enemy Esztergom group of about four divisions from the south and severed its westward retreat routes. By the morning of March 27 the 46th Army and the Danube Flotilla had completed the rout of the enemy group which had been pressed to the Danube west of Esztergom.

Continuing their offensive in Western Hungary, the Soviet troops by March 25 had crossed the Bakony Hegyseg mountains and launched the pursuit of the enemy retreating to the defensive line along the Austro-Hungarian border.

To interfere with the Soviet advance the German Command began to reinforce its divisions in the Vienna sector with Volkssturm battalions, reserve units and divisions shifted from Italy. When the Soviet troops reached the Austro-Hungarian border, Hungarian units, no longer wishing to fight for alien interests, began to surrender. In three days the Soviet troops took prisoner 45,000 officers and men of the Hungarian army.

The successful operations of the right-wing forces of the 3rd Ukrainian Front and the left-wing forces of the 2nd Ukrainian Front in the Vienna sector, made it possible for the other troops of the 2nd Ukrainian Front north of the Danube, including the Rumanian 1st and 4th armies, to go over to the offensive.

In the morning of March 25, the 53rd Army, the 7th Guards Army and the 1st Guards Mechanised Cavalry Group[1]

---

[1] General Pliyev's mechanised cavalry group was named Guards on January 26, 1945. Its composition did not change.

18*

of the 2nd Ukrainian Front cracked the enemy defences along the Hron north of the Danube, their main forces pursuing the offensive along the left bank of the Danube in the general direction of Bratislava.

March was drawing to an end and so was the fighting for the liberation of Hungary. Setting out in pursuit of the enemy, the 46th Army, the 2nd Guards Mechanised and the 23rd Tank corps on April 2 captured the industrial centre and communications hub of Magyarovar and reached the Austro-Hungarian border between the Danube and Neusiedler See. On April 3 and 4, they continued to push ahead in the face of heavy fire and infantry and panzer counter-attacks, pierced the enemy's border defence line to its entire depth and reached the Kietsee-Bruck line. By nightfall on March 31 the troops of the centre and the right wing of the 3rd Ukrainian Front also came up to Hungary's western border south of Sopron and Kermend. The Soviet troops entered Austria.

The 57th and the Bulgarian 1st armies on April 1 liberated the oil centre of Nagykanizsa. On April 4 they completed the liberation of southwestern Hungary and entered Yugoslavia north of Varazdin.

So, on April 4, 1945 Soviet forces, including Bulgarian and Yugoslav units, liberated the whole of Hungary from the nazi invaders.

5. THE FINALE OF THE STRUGGLE FOR HUNGARY

The military and political results of the Soviet Army's operations in Hungary were most impressive.

They overturned the plans of the German Command to hold on to Hungary. Having sustained a crushing defeat, the large enemy grouping was unable to stop the Soviet advance in Eastern Austria, in the so-called Alpine Fortress. The Soviet troops routed 56 enemy divisions and three brigades, and completely wiped out 14 divisions and six brigades. Under the pressure of the 2nd and 3rd Ukrainian fronts in Hungary, the German Command was forced to speed up the withdrawal of Army Group E from the Balkans. Germany lost the oil-bearing province of Nagykanizsa, her last source of natural fuel, and her last European ally, Hungary, with her industrial and agricultural products.

The plans of Anglo-American imperialists to preserve the bourgeois system in Hungary by harnessing her to international imperialism fell through. Hungary became free and in a position to decide her future social system by herself.

What the young Soviet republic was unable to do in 1919, the USSR accomplished in the spring of 1945. Soviet people extended a hand of assistance to the labouring people of Hungary, translating into reality Lenin's internationalist ideas.

The fact that Rumanian, Bulgarian and Yugoslav units fought side by side with the Soviet troops in the plains and mountain passes of Hungary to liberate the Hungarian people was a factor of great significance for the course and the outcome of military operations, and chiefly, for the future military and political co-operation between the People's Democracies. Hungarian patriots, including officers and rank-and-file who went over to the side of the Soviet Army, actively helped the Soviet troops in the fighting for Budapest. The comradeship-in-arms of the Soviet troops and the troops of the emerging People's Democracies was born and strengthened in battles against the common enemy.

Shortly after Hungary's liberation the Hungarian Provisional Government moved from Debrecen to Budapest. A wave of meetings, at which the Hungarian people expressed their gratitude to the Soviet Union and its army, swept across the country.

The Soviet Army's offensive not only delivered Hungary from fascist slavery, but also stimulated the mass struggle of all her progressive forces for a democratic social order. Soviet forces which stayed on in Hungary did not interfere in her internal affairs, but their presence kept the reactionaries in check.

On the initiative of the Communist Party of Hungary, the Provisional Government on March 17, 1945 adopted a decree "On the abolition of large landed estates and allotment of land to peasants". It also introduced many other democratic reforms.

The revolutionary struggle of the Hungarian people encountered the resistance of internal reactionary elements which wanted to restore the old order in the country.

The establishment of people's rule in Hungary was a long process which took place in the complex conditions of class struggle, but which, nevertheless, ended in the complete victory of the labouring people.

"On April 4, 1945," noted the First Secretary of the Central Committee of the Hungarian Socialist Workers' Party Janos Kadar, "when the victorious Soviet Army drove the remnants of Hitler's hordes from the territory of our country, a new chapter was opened in our national history. On the anniversary of this day, we solemnly declare that a free and independent Hungary was born, that a wide road of social progress opened before us. . . ."[1]

The Presidium of the Hungarian People's Republic proclaimed April 4 a national holiday.

In the course of its liberation mission in Hungary the Soviet Army lost more than 140,000 officers and men.

The Hungarian people respect the memory of the Soviet troops who liberated Hungary. "Wherever you go in Hungary," said Janos Kadar, "you see graves... In them sleep heroes, Soviet soldiers, who gave their lives for the freedom of our people. Their memory is sacred to us and we promise that their graves will never be forgotten."

---

[1] *Pravda,* April 4, 1960.

1. UNDER HITLER'S HEEL

NAZI GERMANY SEIZES AUSTRIA

German imperialism always looked upon Austria as a key springboard for penetrating into the Danubian countries and intensified its policy of subjugating Austria when Hitler came to power. In the summer of 1936 Germany and Austria signed an agreement which became the first step towards Anschluss. Under this agreement Austria, while formally retaining independence, undertook to comply in her policy with the interests of nazi Germany. The Austro-Hungarian agreement increased the threat to Austria's independence. In a report to the People's Commissariat for Foreign Affairs the Soviet Ambassador in Vienna wrote: "...the agreement ... as Berlin understands it is an instrument for effectuating the Anschluss."

Formally independent, Austria found herself right in the centre of Hitler's foreign policy. It was the penetration of German monopoly capital into Austrian economy that unavoidably dragged Austria towards an Anschluss with Germany. This process reached its height in the thirties when about 25 per cent of Austrian enterprises were controlled by German capitalists.

Austria's policy culminated in a national catastrophe on March 12, 1938, the day she was invaded by the nazi forces and ceased to exist as an independent state. On March 13, Hitler's government promulgated a law incorporating Austria into the German Reich. At the end of 1937, the British and French governments, supported by the USA in their policy of connivance of aggression, conceded to the nazis seizing Austria in the hope of encouraging nazi aggression in Central and Eastern Europe and hastening the clash between Germany and the Soviet Union.

Hitler's decision to go on with the Anschluss was based on emphatic assurances by prominent statesmen and politicians of leading Western states that their governments would not oppose Germany's aggressive acts. Nine or ten days prior to Germany's invasion of Austria, the British Ambassador in Berlin, Henderson, assured Hitler that he favoured an Anschluss. At about the same time Hitler received similar assurances from the United States in his conversations with ex-President of the United States, Herbert Hoover, in Berlin. Italy adopted a similar stand. Although Mussolini himself was not averse to enriching himself at Austria's expense he felt that he was no match for Hitler.

The USSR condemned German aggression which deprived Austria of political, economic and cultural independence. On March 17, the Soviet Government proposed to the great powers that the situation be discussed at an international conference. In an official statement assessing Germany's acts of aggression, the Soviet Government drew the attention of the Western powers to their responsibility for the destiny of peace. The statement ended with the following words: "Tomorrow it may be too late, but today there is still time if all states, especially the great powers, would assume an unequivocal stand towards the problem of collectively saving the peace."

The Soviet Government was one of the few governments to voice protest in those tragic days of March 1938. This is a fact, which even those who would have liked to forget all about it cannot deny. "One of the few nations to protest Hitler's seizure of Austria was the Soviet Union," wrote William Lloyd Stearman in his book *The Soviet Union and the Occupation of Germany.*

The Western powers turned down the Soviet proposals and thus helped raise tensions in Europe.

Just as shameful was the stand of Austrian Right-wing socialists who openly upheld the nazis by collaborating with the invaders and betraying the national interests of their country.

The Communist Party of Austria most resolutely rejected the Anschluss and appealed to the Austrian people to fight for the re-establishment of Austria's national independence. The day the Wehrmacht entered the country the Central Committee of the Communist Party of Austria published an appeal which said: "Austrian people. Defend yourself. Resist."

At first the Second World War did not cause any major changes in British and American policy towards Austria. They were still influenced by the "Munich" line whose initial stage was the seizure of Austria, and the statement by the British Prime Minister on November 9, 1940 made it clear that Britain continued to regard Austria's future an open question. Naturally this stand was detrimental to the interests of the Austrian people who were struggling for their independence.

The Soviet Union alone firmly spoke up in defence of the right of the Austrian people to independent state existence. During the discussion of the Soviet draft treaty on post-war co-operation at the Soviet-British talks in December 1941, Soviet representatives demanded that it should envisage the re-establishment of all countries occupied by Germany and Italy within their pre-war borders. Austria and Albania, the draft said, should be re-established as independent states. But Britain had other plans which held no promise for the restoration of Austria's sovereignty.

THE MOSCOW DECLARATION
ON AUSTRIA

Serious diplomatic efforts were required on the part of the Soviet Union to prevail on Britain and the United States to agree to the re-establishment of independent Austria. British ruling circles planned to establish a so-called Danube Federation. At a meeting in Washington in May 1943 Churchill defended the need to set up such a federation after the war with its centre in Vienna. These plans were designed to thwart the national liberation struggle in Southeast Europe, including Austria, and to establish a *cordon sanitaire* to isolate the Soviet Union from Europe.

Early in June 1943 the Soviet Government once again enunciated its policy concerning Austria, emphasising that it could not accept the plans for the creation of various federations in Europe in general, and the inclusion of Austria into them, in particular.

An especially acute struggle for the independence of the Austrian people took place at the Moscow Conference of the

Foreign Ministers of the Soviet Union, United States and Britain in October 1943. The Soviet Foreign Minister strongly rejected British plans of uniting small European states in various groups either as federations or confederations.

The discussion ended with the adoption of the Declaration on Austria which said in part: "Austria, the first country to fall a victim to Hitler's aggression, shall be liberated from German domination." The three powers declared that they regarded the annexation imposed on Austria by Germany in 1938 as null and void.

They declared that they wished to see re-established a free and independent Austria and that she could ease her fate by actively struggling against Hitler fascism. This was one of the first documents in which the states of the anti-Hitler coalition declared officially the repeal of an act of Hitler's aggression, on the eve of the Second World War.

The Declaration on Austria became the foundation and point of departure for all the other Allied decisions on Austria. This important document incontrovertibly proved that the Soviet Union sincerely and consistently supported the independence and sovereignty of the Austrian state. Finally, both as a result of the resolute and purposeful policy of the Soviet Union and in view of the military and political situation, the Western Powers were compelled to condemn Germany's aggression against Austria, i.e., to do what they had categorically declined to do five years previously.

But even then neither Britain nor the United States acted fully in keeping with the Declaration. British Prime Minister Winston Churchill continued to nurse his plans of establishing British control in Southeast Europe pinning hope on assistance by reactionary elements among the Austrian bourgeoisie. It was only the entry of the Soviet Army into the countries of the Danube Basin and then the resolute efforts of the popular masses in the enslaved countries to achieve the establishment of democratic rule, that overturned the intention of British and US imperialism.

THE POLITICAL SITUATION
IN AUSTRIA

Having seized Austria, nazi Germany turned her into one of her basic arsenals. In the course of the Second World War Austrian industry and agriculture catered for Germany's military needs.

By 1945, there were 600 arms factories in Austria which annually manufactured 9,000 aircraft and 17,000 engines. Moreover, each month she produced up to 850 panzers and armoured vehicles, more than 1,000 artillery pieces and large quantities of military equipment and ammunition.

During the war more than 1,500,000 Austrians served in the Wehrmacht. Of the 35 divisions that were raised in Austria and in which Austrians accounted for 60-80 per cent of the manpower, 17 fought against the Soviet Army.

Nazi Germany and the Austrian reactionaries forced the Austrian people to the detriment of their national interests not only to work for Germany but also to furnish the cannon fodder in the war against the USSR and other countries.

Administratively, Austria was divided into seven Danubian and Alpine regions directly governed by Berlin. The word Austria was erased from the map of Europe. The nazis often contemptuously referred to the Austrians as "booty Germans" and rapaciously plundered Austria's material wealth, works of art, bullion and currency reserves.

In order to strengthen its hold on Austria and force the Austrians submissively to work for Germany, the German Command intensified chauvinistic nazi propaganda to brainwash them into believing that Austria was not a viable state and that they had no choice other than side with the Germans. The nazis had their own way of dealing with people who thought otherwise and stood up for what they believed in. Many thousands of Austrian patriots who opposed the nazi order ended their lives in death camps which were set up in the country.

But as the Germans suffered one defeat after another on the Soviet-German front, Austria's working people stiffened their opposition to the invaders, mainly through sabotage at industrial enterprises. The Austrian Resistance was further stimulated by the decisions of the Moscow Foreign Ministers'

Conference of the Three Powers in October 1943. At the same time the nazis hardened their reign of terror, especially against the Austrian Communists who led the patriots' struggle against German rule. Thousands of communists were clamped in prisons and 5,680 were either killed or committed to concentration camps so that at the end of 1943 the underground Central Committee of the Communist Party of Austria ceased to exist.

The stand adopted by Austrian social democrats tremendously injured the Resistance Movement in the country. Their opposition to the establishment of a single political and military guiding centre restricted the scope of the anti-fascist struggle which acquired considerable momentum only when the Soviet Army was already close to Austria's borders.

Subversion on communication lines and roads, at industrial enterprises and transport was the main form of activity of the small armed detachments which had been formed at the initiative of the Communist Party of Austria.

Two Austrian battalions were helping the partisans in Yugoslavia. Shortly before Soviet troops entered Austria a military organisation of the Resistance Movement headed by Major Karl Sokol was established in an Austrian army unit, but was betrayed before it had a chance to go into action.

The Austrian Communists appealed to the Austrian patriots to help the Soviet Army liberate the country, and on March 31, 1945 they set up a clandestine organisation called the Austrian Freedom Front.

Anti-fascist groups and centres appeared in some of the death camps, including Mauthausen. On February 3, 1945 its inmates mutinied, but only a few managed to escape. Others who took part in the mutiny were put to death. The nazis brutally killed General D. M. Karbyshev whom the Soviet Government posthumously made Hero of the Soviet Union.

Austria's progressive forces were much too weak, and the bulk of the population had been too thoroughly brainwashed by the nazi propaganda for Austria to throw off the nazi yoke and regain her state independence without outside help.

2. LIBERATION
OF EASTERN AUSTRIA.
VIENNA IS FREE

TOWARDS VIENNA

It was the last spring of the war. The days of nazi Germany were numbered. The Soviet troops operating in the southern sector of the Soviet-German front completed the liberation of Hungary, and at the end of March crossed into Austria. The 3rd Ukrainian Front's 4th, 9th Guards Field and the 6th Guards Tank armies, and 1st Guards Mechanised Corps were advancing on Vienna, enveloping it from the south and west; the 26th and 27th armies and the 18th Tank Corps were pressing on Bruck and Graz, and further south the 57th and the Bulgarian 1st armies and the 5th Guards Cavalry Corps were advancing towards Maribor. The 17th Air Army covered the operations of the land troops.

The 2nd Ukrainian Front committed its 46th Army, the 2nd Guards Mechanised Corps, the 23rd Tank Corps, which was brought up in the course of the fighting, and the Danube Flotilla.

The Soviet offensive in Austria took place in difficult conditions. The Germans blew up every bridge and river crossing and on top of that the mountainous terrain made it impossible for the Soviet troops to effect broad enveloping manoeuvres and forced them to keep to the roads most of the time. The German Command established numerous resistance points in mountain passes, defiles and on river banks. For this purpose combat groups were formed out of the retreating units and also out of the local detachments raised by provincial Gauleiters. For example, the commander of the 18th Defence District activated a mountain infantry corps out of reservists and military cadets who offered strong resistance to the 26th Army.

In spite of the fact that the greatly stretched supply routes and the lack of usable railways in the initial stage of the offensive seriously impeded the supply of ammunition, fuel and lubricants, the 3rd and 2nd Ukrainian Fronts kept pushing ahead day and night.

The Germans resisted with the greatest determination between Neusiedler See and the spurs of the Eastern Alps. There
was heavy fighting at the approaches to Vienna, east and
south of Wiener Neustadt, an industrial town and an important communications hub turned by the Germans into a powerful resistance centre. It was defended by a reserve infantry division, the Vienna Officers' School and other units and the Soviet troops failed to take it in their stride. The enemy retreated in haste only when the Soviet troops threatened the garrison from the rear. Wiener Neustadt was liberated on April 3.

Pursuing the German forces which were retreating to the
west, the 57th and the Bulgarian 1st armies, advancing on
the left wing of the 3rd Ukrainian Front, reached the crossings on the river Mur. The 46th Army of the 2nd Ukrainian
Front was fighting along the line extending from the Petron-
ell railway station to the northern shore of Neusiedler See.
The battered divisions of Army Group South were withdrawing to Vienna.

Soviet troops entered Austria, nazi Germany's ally in the
war against the USSR, not with a feeling of revenge, but
with a strong desire to hasten the end of nazism, liberate the
Austrian people from nazi oppression and create conditions
in which they would be free to determine the future of their
country. It was necessary to disprove the lies spread by nazi
propaganda which had brainwashed the Austrian population
into believing that the Soviet Army would kill all propriet-
ors, including petty merchants and middle peasants, demolish
churches, wipe out the clergy and introduce compulsory
atheism. Hitler's propaganda merchants mired the Soviet
Army with every imaginable infamy.

But within a few days after the Soviet troops had entered
the country the Austrian population came to realise how bas-
ely it had been deceived by nazi propaganda.

THE STORMING OF VIENNA

The fighting for Vienna, which was defended by eight
panzer divisions[1], one infantry, and up to 15 separate in-

---

[1] Those which had retreated from Hungary.

fantry battalions, lasted from April 5 to 13 and was extremely vicious. On the approaches to the city and in Vienna proper the German Command set up numerous defensive installations, including anti-tank ditches and various anti-tank and anti-personnel obstacles in the armour-prone sectors on its outer perimeter. There were barricades and road blocks made of logs, telegraph poles, tramcars and railway carriages, and fire emplacements in many stone and brick buildings. The German Command did all it could to turn Vienna into an impregnable fortress.

The German Command was very seriously concerned with retaining its hold on Vienna and its economic area. In an order of the day issued on April 6, 1945, Hitler wrote: "The oil-fields in the Vienna region are of decisive significance for the continuation of the war."[1] Vienna was the last bastion of the German defences covering the approaches to Germany's southern regions.

Following the defeat of Army Group South in Hungary and Slovakia, its commander General Wöhler was replaced by Lieutenant-General Rendulic, an expert in defensive operations. Soon the Group was renamed Austria.

According to the GHQ plan, Vienna was to be liberated by the right-wing forces of the 3rd Ukrainian Front (the 4th and 9th Guards armies and the 6th Guards Tank Army, the 1st Guards Mechanised and the 18th Tank corps) and by the left-wing forces of the 2nd Ukrainian Front (the 46th Army, and the 23rd Tank and the 2nd Guards Mechanised corps) supported by the 17th Air Army and part of the 5th Air Army. The Danube Flotilla was also to take part in the operation.

Commander of the 3rd Ukrainian Front Marshal F. I. Tolbukhin decided to capture the city by a multipronged blow. On April 6, in an effort to save the Austrian capital with its numerous monuments from destruction, he appealed to the Viennese to remain in their homes, do their best to prevent the nazis from wrecking the city and assist the Soviet Army in liberating it.

The 4th and 9th Guards armies attacked Vienna in the morning of April 6 from the east and south, while the 6th

[1] Theodor Rossiwal, "Die letzte Front". In *Die Wochenpresse* No. 12, Vienna, March 20, 1965, p. 10.

Guards Tank Army began to envelop it from the west in order to prevent the defenders from retreating in that direction. The tank forces had to cut across the mountainous and wooded terrain of the Vienna Forest. They performed this difficult manoeuvre in the face of desperate enemy resistance, outflanked Vienna and on April 7 reached the Danube thus cutting the enemy's retreat routes. The city was besieged on three sides.

On April 9, the Soviet Government published a statement which said: "The Soviet Government does not intend to take over any part of Austrian territory or alter the state system in Austria. The Soviet Government adheres to the views set forth in the Moscow Allied Declaration concerning Austria's independence and will implement its provisions. It will help abolish the regime of the nazi invaders and re-establish democratic order and institutions in Austria. The Supreme Commander-in-Chief of the Red Army has ordered the Soviet troops to help the Austrian population in this respect."

The Austrian people welcomed this statement with joy and hope.

The troops of the 3rd Ukrainian Front fought for every city block and at times for individual buildings which had been converted into strongpoints. As in Budapest, assault teams acted with great efficiency.

Capturing block after block, the Soviet troops split up the enemy garrison into isolated groups and began mopping up operations. Fighting went on night and day. On April 10, Soviet troops driving from the south and east linked up in the centre of the city with units fighting in this sector. The German garrison was enveloped by the 4th Army from the south and east, and by the 9th Guards Army and the 6th Guards Tank Army from the southwest and west, but continued to fight back with desperation. In the night of April 10, the 4th Guards Army began to cross the Danube Canal. Fighting for Budapest entered its last stage.

On April 13, the Soviet troops crushed the resistance of the Germans, gained full possession of Vienna and entrenched along the line extending from St. Poelten to the south. Soviet and Austrian flags fluttered in the streets of the Austrian capital.

Acting swiftly and resolutely, the Soviet forces prevented

the nazis from destroying one of Europe's loveliest cities and saved the lives of thousands of Viennese. Soviet armymen also saved many architectural monuments which the Germans had intended to blow up or which they had set on fire, including the St. Stephen Cathedral and the Town Hall.

More than 20 Soviet formations which had distinguished themselves in the fighting had the title "Vienna" attached to their names. The Soviet Government struck a medal "For the Capture of Vienna", awarding it to all those who took part in the fighting for the city.

Meanwhile the 3rd Ukrainian Front's central and left-wing forces continued to press forward in the general direction of Graz and by the middle of April reached an area east of Maribor.

The military operations of the left-wing of the 2nd Ukrainian Front undertaken for the purpose of cutting the retreat routes of the Vienna grouping to the north, ended on April 15 when the 46th Army reached the area of Korneuburg and Floridsdorf sector, thus hastening the liberation of Vienna. At the end of April, the Soviet troops fighting in Austria reached the Linz-Hiefletz-Klagenfurt line where they linked up with American troops.

On May 5 US reconnaissance tanks appeared at the Mauthausen death camp just when its inmates led by Soviet Major A. I. Pirogov and the Austrian political prisoner Colonel Kadre were fighting for their lives against the SS guard. Two days later, in the evening of May 7, US troops entered Mauthausen and helped the prisoners to wipe out the camp guard.

So, in April 1945, the Soviet troops liberated the sixth European capital, lovely Vienna, and the Austrian people from nazi bondage.

3. MILITARY AND POLITICAL RESULTS OF THE STRUGGLE FOR AUSTRIA'S LIBERATION

The Vienna Operation was not only a major victory of Soviet arms; it was also an event which produced major political repercussions. The Soviet Army crushed the entire southern wing of the Wehrmacht's strategic front. Army Group South ceased to exist as a fighting organism.

During their month-long offensive in Western Hungary and in Austria the Soviet troops smashed 32 enemy divisions and took more than 130,000 prisoners. The remaining German forces fled to the west where they surrendered to the US and British armies. The Soviet Army liberated 36,551 square kilometres of Austrian territory—the entire eastern part of the country—with a population of 4,500,000 out of a total of 6,800,000.

The efforts of the German Command to organise a stable defence in Austria's mountainous and wooded areas, Western Czechoslovakia and Southern Germany were in vain. The successful offensive of the Soviet troops on Vienna, south of the Danube, helped the 2nd Ukrainian Front capture Bratislava and open an offensive on Brno and deeper into Czechoslovakia, and reliably covered the Soviet troops operating in the central sector against possible enemy strikes from the south.

The Soviet advance on Vienna compelled the German Command to speed up the evacuation of its troops from Albania. Army Group E, which found itself in complete isolation in northwest Yugoslavia, began a general retreat. Taking advantage of the situation, the Yugoslav 1st, 2nd and 3rd armies supported by the Soviet Air Force started a close pursuit. Following Germany's unconditional surrender the remnants of Army Group E which had withdrawn from Greece, Albania and Yugoslavia, also downed their arms.

The Soviet Army delivered the Austrian people from nazi bondage and the Austrian national flag was raised over Vienna for the first time in seven years. The beginning was laid for the revival of Austria's statehood. It was the Soviet armymen who shouldered the main burden of the war, defeated a strong and experienced enemy and brought freedom to the Austrian and other European peoples.

Nearly 26,000 Soviet officers and men died in the battles for the liberation of the Austrian people.

A memorial to the Soviet troops who had fallen in the battles for Austria's liberation was erected in August 1945 in one of Vienna's main squares as a token of the Austrian people's high regard for the great exploit of the Soviet Armed

Forces and the numerous sacrifices suffered by the Soviet people for the sake of Austria's freedom and independence.

The Soviet Union and its Armed Forces not only drove the nazi invaders out of Austria, but also put in a great deal of effort to bring life back to normal in the country.

First and foremost, a provisional government had to be formed in Austria, and the Soviet Government, true to its policy of non-interference in the internal affairs of other countries, assented to the wish of the Austrian public to entrust its formation to the social-democratic leader, Karl Renner. On April 27, 1945, i.e., within a fortnight of Vienna's liberation, a Provisional Government consisting of representatives of the Communist, Socialist and People's parties was formed and began to discharge its functions.

Pending the final solution of the problem of post-war order in Europe, including the question of Austria's independence, and also in connection with the presence of Allied troops in Austria, the governments of the countries of the anti-Hitler coalition—USSR, USA, Britain and France—established four occupation zones in the country. An Allied Control Council of representatives of the four countries, who were called High Commissioners, was formed in Austria with the right to exercise supreme authority on all matters concerning Austria as a whole.

The Soviet representative and his staff had the exceptionally difficult task of solving a wide range of problems, of which the most important were those of providing all-round assistance to the Austrian people in establishing democratic rule and normalising economic life; repatriation of displaced persons and implementing the decisions of the Potsdam Conference.

Soviet troops repaired two of the most important bridges across the Danube in Vienna. The sailors of the Danube Flotilla cleared mines in the Danube within Austrian territory, salvaged 128 ships and repaired 30 per cent of cranes and other equipment in the Danube ports.

Soviet Army engineers helped the Austrian people to repair railways and highways in the Soviet occupation zone, including 1,719 kilometres of railway, 45 railway bridges, 27 depots, over 300 locomotives and about 10,000 freight cars. They repaired water supply, equipment in a number of factories, made the tramcar service operative, rehabilitated schools and hospitals and so forth.

By May 1, 1945, in keeping with the instructions of the Soviet Government the Military Council of the 3rd Ukrainian Front provided the Viennese with 7,000 tons of grain, 500 tons of corn, 1,000 tons of beans, 1,000 tons of peas, 200 tons of vegetable oil, 300 tons of meat, 200 tons of sugar, 200 tons of salt, 100 tons of oil crops, and large quantities of other foodstuffs.

On May 23, the State Defence Committee decided to furnish additional food supplies to the Viennese raising their average daily ration to 300 grammes of bread, 50 grammes of cereals, 30 grammes of meat, 10 grammes of fat, 20 grammes of sugar; besides each month they were entitled to 50 grammes of coffee and 400 grammes of salt.

In the course of five months following the liberation of the Austrian capital, the Viennese were only supplied from Soviet Army stocks. Within the first post-war year, the Soviet Union supplied Austria with 67,585 tons of flour, 16,375 tons of cereals, 5,436 tons of sugar, 33,162 tons of potatoes, 7,683 tons of meat, 1,937 tons of fats and 434 tons of coffee— all adding up to the impressive figure of 132,612 tons.

Let us note for comparison's sake that the USSR provided Austria with as much food as did the USA, Britain and France taken together, and did so without any strings attached.

Soviet troops in all parts of Eastern Austria worked to improve the conditions of the local inhabitants and helped them to return to peaceful labour activities.

The Austrian population, and especially the Viennese, were sincerely grateful to the USSR and its Army for their timely all-round assistance.

Chapter IX   FRATERNAL ASSISTANCE
TO THE PEOPLES
OF CZECHOSLOVAKIA

1. CZECHOSLOVAKIA
ON THE EVE OF LIBERATION

THE INTERNAL SITUATION
IN THE SPRING OF 1944

An old, fraternal friendship links the peoples of the Soviet
Union and Czechoslovakia. In the years preceding the Second
World War the Soviet Government displayed its determination to save Czechoslovakia from the nazi aggression. But
her leaders headed by President Benes turned down offers of
Soviet assistance with the result that Czechoslovakia came
under nazi Germany's heel. And when she was occupied by
the nazis the Soviet people did their best to help the Czecho-
slovaks in their grim struggle for freedom and independence.

It took a long time and a great deal of effort to turn the
prospect of liberating the Czechoslovak people from nazi
tyranny into a reality. Only as a result of the magnificent
victories of the Soviet Armed Forces, especially in the operations in the western part of the Ukraine and in the Lvov-
Sandomierz sector, did the Soviet troops draw close to the
borders of Czechoslovakia. This inspired the Czechs and Slovaks and prompted them to fight against the nazi invaders.
These developments characterised the internal situation in
the country at the time.

Although the nazis eliminated the Czechoslovak Republic
and dismembered its territory they were unable to break
the determination of the popular masses to fight against the
invaders and their bourgeois lackeys in Czechoslovakia. A
broad patriotic movement unfolded in the country as far
back as the tragic days of Munich and helped in the political
education of the masses. There was a further demarcation
of the class forces which laid bare the political insolvency of
the wealthy bourgeoisie and conciliatory reformist parties
supporting it. Of all parties the Communist Party alone consistently fought for the country's freedom and independence,
leading the patriotic movement in anti-fascist struggle.

The national-liberation movement developed in the frightful conditions of nazi occupation, brutal terror and repressions. The first period, which lasted from October 1938 to June 1941 in conditions of the most barbarous reaction, when the people were disunited by the dismemberment of the country and seriously demoralised by the Munich betrayal, in effect became a time for the renewed mobilisation of forces for the forthcoming battles against nazism. The second period began in the summer of 1941, when nazi Germany and her allies attacked the Soviet Union thus inveigling it in the Second World War, and lasted till early 1943; it was characterised by the rise and spreading of the partisan movement as the most effective form of struggle against the nazi invaders.

The victory of the Soviet Armed Forces at Stalingrad further invigorated the activity of the patriotic forces in Czechoslovakia. This was the third period. It ended in August 1944 and witnessed the consolidation of the unity of all patriots and large-scale development of the partisan movement.

In 1943 the Foreign Bureau of the Communist Party of Czechoslovakia instructed the Resistance Movement in Czechoslovakia to intensify partisan and other forms of struggle against the nazi invaders, establish a system of underground national committees and prepare a national armed uprising. With this end in view it dispatched two groups of experienced party workers, one to Bohemia headed by Rudolf Vetiska, and the other to Slovakia headed by Karel Smidke and K. Bacilek.

Considering that the national-liberation movement had already become particularly widespread in Slovakia, no time had to be lost in setting up a powerful party leadership there and concentrating the efforts of the entire Party on launching preparations for a nation-wide insurrection. This task was assumed by the underground Central Committee of the Communist Party of Slovakia which was established in August 1943 and included Karel Smidke, Gustav Husak and Lado Nowomesky.

The Central Committee of the Communist Party of Slovakia consistently and successfully fought against the sectarian trend in the Party and upheld the line of forming a broad national front. It re-established contacts with Party organisations and gradually created a new party leadership from top to bottom. On its initiative a Slovak National Council was formed in December 1943 to head the national liberation movement in Slovakia.

Dwelling on the situation in Slovakia at the time and the chief task which faced the Communists, Gustav Husak wrote: "We had to unite all the democratic and anti-fascist forces, all opposition trends, give them a single programme and aim, a single organisation and leadership, to search for the most acceptable and effective forms of struggle against nazism and co-ordinate the Resistance Movement of the Slovak people with the struggle of the European peoples, and first and foremost with the peoples of the Soviet Union."

In mid-December 1943 the Communist Party of Slovakia concluded a political agreement with other democratic forces and groups in the Resistance on joint struggle and the tasks of the Slovak National Council. In Slovakia, this agreement, the main document of the nation-wide Resistance Movement, was named the 1943 Christmas Agreement.

In fear of being thrown overboard, Czechoslovak emigres in London gave up their policy of undisguised anti-communism and passive temporisation. In December 1943 Benes visited Moscow where he and a delegation of the Foreign Bureau of the Communist Party of Czechoslovakia conducted talks on questions concerning the further guidance of the national liberation struggle. They agreed on general principles to be observed in the course of the introduction of initial provisional measures in the economic and social spheres, namely, the abolition of all property and other reforms forcibly promoted by the nazis, payment of compensation to the victims of persecution and institution of national control over large enterprises and joint-stock companies owned by the Germans and traitors. On the basis of the recommendations submitted by the Communist Party, agreement was also reached on the status of the German minority.

Finding it impossible to ignore the altered balance of forces on the fronts of the Second World War and the actual situation in Czechoslovakia where the national liberation struggle steadily increased in scope and scale, Benes had no choice but come to an agreement with the leadership of the Communist Party of Czechoslovakia at the talks in Moscow.

Nevertheless he, his government and the political and military circles connected with them subsequently changed their course and began to issue instructions to the Resistance fighters which were running counter to the terms of the agreement. Benes' representatives in Czechoslovakia made no secret of the fact that he did not recognise the Slovak National Committee which allegedly was not a representative body, and that a new organ headed by V. Srobar from which communists would be barred had to be established. Accordingly, Benes' supporters began to set up their own "national committees" on what they called a "mass scale" with the financial assistance of the Czechoslovak manufacturer Bata who placed five million crowns at Srobar's disposal.

Such was the true image of the Czechoslovak emigre circles in London which made every effort to take over the leadership of the national liberation struggle in Czechoslovakia and wage it in the interests of the bourgeoisie's class interests.

On May 8, 1944, when the Soviet troops were already standing at the Czechoslovak borders, an agreement was signed between the Soviet commander-in-chief and the Czechoslovak administration governing their relations following the entry of the Soviet troops into the country. It was recorded in the agreement that as soon as any part of Czechoslovakia ceased to be a zone of hostilities it would be placed under the control of the Czechoslovak Government which would render the Soviet Command every assistance through its civic and military agencies. The agreement was based on the principles of full recognition of Czechoslovakia's state sovereignty and seriously inhibited the expansionist designs of the US and British ruling circles which hoped to replace the nazi regime in the liberated countries of Europe with the Anglo-American occupation regime.

The agreement stimulated the national liberation movement in all parts of the country, especially in Slovakia. The increasing Soviet assistance produced an upsurge in the partisan struggle. At the request of the Czechoslovak leaders and in conformity with the Soviet-Czechoslovak agreement of friendship and mutual assistance, Czechoslovak and Soviet partisan groups were transferred from the USSR to Slovakia. A number of Soviet partisan detachments and large army formations were also transferred to Slovakia, where they were either joined by local inhabitants or merged with the Slovak partisan detachments.

The Communist Party of Czechoslovakia consolidated the forces of the people and guided them towards a historical turning point—the Slovak National Uprising. An important role in this uprising was assigned to the partisan movement and the Slovak Army whose numerous anti-fascist groups embraced the rank-and-file and some of the higher officers.

THE SLOVAK NATIONAL UPRISING

In the spring and summer of 1944 the rule of the Tiso-Tuka clique was overthrown in many parts of Slovakia and replaced by the rule of the Revolutionary People's Committees. In some areas power was assumed by the partisans. The strike movement of the working class gathered momentum and workers began to arm themselves. Anti-German sentiments were running high in the Slovak Army, some of whose units (65,000-70,000 men) were stationed in Slovakia proper. A considerable part of this force, mainly the East Slovak Corps billeted at Presov, could be drawn into the fighting against the Germans. The corps had two divisions totalling 24,000 officers and men, and 15,000 rifles, 1,250 machine guns and 270 guns and mortars. A factor of no small importance for the development of the people's resistance movement was that formally the Wehrmacht had not yet occupied Slovakia. There were large Luftwaffe units only in her western part and the Gestapo had its departments in towns and at key industrial enterprises.

The national liberation movement in Slovakia was approaching the stage of a national and democratic revolution whose culminating point was the Slovak Uprising which the Communist Party of Slovakia had been preparing both politically and organisationally for a long period of time.

On July 20, 1944 the Slovak National Council and a group of high-ranking officers of the Slovak Army held the last meeting before the uprising. It was attended by all the members of the Slovak National Council and four representatives of the Military Centre: J. Golian, Lieutenant-Colonel M. Ferencik, Major J. Marko and Captain M. Polak. Gustav Husak delivered the main report on the political situation and the progress of the preparations for the uprising, while J. Golian reported on the situation in the Slovak Army and the state of the military preparations for the uprising. The meeting drew up the uprising's final political and military plan.

The organisers and leaders of the Slovak Uprising emphasised that politically and militarily its preparation was orientated on the Soviet Union. Due to various considerations and with various amendments, this orientation was also accepted by the non-communists in the Slovak National Council and the Council's military leadership.

Only a group of Right-wing anti-communist politicians, comprising the emigre government in London, supported the political line of the British Conservative Government of knocking together a Polish-Czechoslovak Federation to serve as an anti-Soviet stronghold in Central Europe.

Unwilling to promote effective co-ordination between the operations of the Soviet Army and the forthcoming popular actions in Slovakia, Benes and his government kept the Soviet leaders uninformed about the political and military situation in Slovakia. As a result, the Soviet political and military authorities right up to August 1944 lacked adequate information about the preparations for an uprising in Slovakia. Such was the situation when the Slovak National Council sent K. Smidke and M. Ferencik to Moscow to co-ordinate all matters concerning the armed uprising in Slovakia with the Soviet Supreme Command.

Arriving in the USSR on August 5, the delegation had a meeting with commander of the 4th Ukrainian Front General I. Y. Petrov, and informed him about the purpose of the visit and the situation in Slovakia.

On the following day Smidke and Ferencik flew to Moscow where they were immediately received by high Defence Ministry officials to whom they handed over four important documents: an account of the preparations for the uprising, the military plan of the uprising, a memorandum of the National Defence Minister of the Slovak puppet government of Catlos and a political report concerning events in Slovakia.

In Moscow K. Smidke met K. Gottwald and other members of the Foreign Bureau of the Communist Party of Czechoslovakia. The leadership of the Communist Party of Czechoslovakia approved the ways and means of solving the tasks of the national liberation movement, the objectives, the concept and the concrete plan of the armed uprising of the Slovak people.

Shortly afterwards the Slovak National Council issued a directive demanding Slovakia's immediate withdrawal from the war on Germany's side; return to Slovakia of two Slovak divisions stationed in Rumania and Italy; cessation of all military movement through Slovakia; withdrawal of German troops from the occupied regions of Slovakia and the expulsion of all German representatives from Slovak territory; a halt to the export of foodstuffs and raw materials from Slovakia to Germany; the return of Slovak workers from Germany and an end to the further export of labour power to Germany.

Envisaging the possibility of Germany attempting a swift occupation of the whole of Slovakia to retain her territory as a theatre of operations, the directive provided for the immediate enforcement of a series of political, organisational and military measures and set forth two variants of the plan of the uprising.

In the event of a German attempt to occupy Slovakia, even with the consent of the Tiso government, the Slovak people would rise using all its forces and means, including the Slovak army. In that contingency the task would be to liberate and, if possible, to hold on to a large part of Slovak territory, establish a provisional people's government (the Slovak National Council) there, and wage partisan warfare on the territory still occupied by the invaders until the whole of Slovakia would be liberated with the assistance of the Soviet Army.

If the Soviet Army entered Slovakia, the directive stated, a national uprising would have to be launched which should lead to the overthrow of the Bratislava Government, the establishment of revolutionary organs of power (Slovak National Council), the expulsion, with the assistance of the Soviet Army, of German and Hungarian invaders, and the participation of the Slovak forces in the liberation of the rest of Czechoslovakia.

This document showed that in view of the situation in the country the Communist Party of Slovakia and the Foreign

Bureau of the Communist Party of Czechoslovakia concentrated on organising a popular uprising with the participation of the Slovak army, the partisans and armed groups of workers and peasants, and considered that assistance by the Soviet Army in the fight against the German invaders on Slovak territory was crucial for the success of the uprising.

The revolutionary build-up in Slovakia and the Soviet Army's successful offensive forced the nazis to stop feigning support for Slovakia's independence. On August 23 German divisions were moved in to occupy her. To counter the Soviet offensive the nazi command intended to establish a powerful defensive front along Slovakia's border to be manned by the East Slovak Corps as well as the German forces.

The threat of occupation aroused the indignation of the broadest sections of the Slovak people. Partisans and detachments of armed workers opened operations against Tiso's puppet authorities and the Germans. On August 25 and 26 the insurgents captured Ruzomberok, Poprad, Zvolen and some other towns. National Committees took power into their hands. A number of units of the Slovak Army and the garrisons of Sv. Turc, Martin, Banska Bystrica, Brezno and the Tri Duba Airfield near Zvolen went over to the side of the insurgents. On August 25 Golian ordered the Slovak army to resist the German forces. By August 29 the local anti-fascist actions developed into a national uprising, and towards nightfall on August 30 the insurgents and the partisans controlled two-thirds of Slovak territory. On the night of August 29 partisans entered Banska Bystrica which became the political centre of the uprising and the seat of the Slovak National Council, the Military Centre, the Central Committee of the Communist Party of Slovakia, various partisan headquarters and editorial offices of the newspaper *Prawda*, organ of the Central Committee of the Communist Party of Slovakia.

From the very first days the uprising acquired a nationwide character. On September 1, the Slovak National Council announced that it had taken legislative and executive power into its hands. The Council was headed by a Presidium consisting of four members of the Communist Party and four representatives of other parties, all enjoying equal rights. The Communist Party was represented by K. Smidke, G. Husak, L. Novomesky and D. Ertel; other political parties were represented by V. Srobar, J. Lettrich, J. Ursiny and J. Stych. K. Smidke and V. Srobar were Council Chairmen. The Council ordered the mobilisation of all men between 18 and 40 years of age which made it possible to replenish the military units which had gone over to the side of the people. By mid-September an Insurrection Army under the command of the Military Centre had been activated on the liberated territory of Slovakia.

The partisan formations and detachments were a serious force of the insurgent people. On September 16 a Main Headquarters of the Partisan Movement of Slovakia was established to co-ordinate partisan activity. It included K. Smidke (chief of staff), R. Slansky and Soviet colonel A. N. Asmolov (both deputy chiefs of staff).

On September 2 the Communist Party of Slovakia issued an appeal to the people urging them to make an all-out effort to smash the enemy.

The German Command moved major regular forces against the insurgents. It shifted part of an SS division from the West, and the 357th Infantry Division and a number of separate regiments and battalions from other divisions of Army Group A from the east. On August 29 German troops which had entered Slovakia from Moravia reached Zilina where Slovak patriots clashed in a first major battle with the invaders. The Slovak people responded to the invasion of the Wehrmacht by putting up a most determined armed resistance.

THE SITUATION
IN THE CARPATHIAN SECTOR
IN THE AUTUMN OF 1944.
PREPARATIONS FOR THE EAST
CARPATHIAN OPERATION

The Soviet Government and the Supreme Command learnt at the end of August about the uprising in Slovakia and that the insurgents had occupied a number of towns. On August 31, planes with Slovak officers carrying instructions to inform the Soviet Command about the uprising and establish contact with it landed in the zone of the 1st Ukrainian Front. On September 1, deputy commander of the East Slovak

Corps Colonel Viliam Talsky had a conversation with Marshal I. S. Konev, commander of the 1st Ukrainian Front, who reported on the conversation to the Supreme Commander-in-Chief, J. V. Stalin, by telephone, and on September 2 sent a written communication which said in part: "Colonel Talsky has said that in the event of a Soviet westward drive, the Slovak 1st and 2nd divisions deployed on the border... could advance eastward to link up with the Red Army.

"Our units in the area of Krosno are 30-40 kilometres from the Slovak border. Should you decide that we link up with the Slovak units and the partisan movement in Slovakia, it would be expedient to carry through a combined operation by the left flank of the 1st Ukrainian Front and the right flank of the 4th Ukrainian Front and enter the territory of Slovakia in the Stropkov-Medzilaborce sector.

"The 1st Ukrainian Front can commit four infantry divisions of the 38th Army and a Guards cavalry corps. The main blow could be delivered at Krosno, Dukla and Tyliava. It would be desirable to commit the Czechoslovak 1st Corps in this sector, too. The operation can be launched in seven days. Awaiting your orders on this question."

On August 31 Czechoslovak Ambassador in the Soviet Union, Zdenek Fierlinger, requested the Soviet Government to provide military assistance to the insurgents. On September 1 a similar request was presented to the Soviet Command by the head of the Czechoslovak Military Mission in Moscow, General G. Pika, on behalf of the Minister of National Defence of the Czechoslovak Republic and Chief of the Military Centre of the Slovak National Council.

The Soviet Government and the Supreme Command ordered the Soviet Army to help promptly the Slovak people in its fight against the German invaders. The most important role was to be played by a major offensive operation by the 1st and 4th Ukrainian fronts. The commanders of all the Soviet partisan units operating in Czechoslovakia were told that their basic task was to help the Slovak people fighting for an independent democratic Czechoslovakia.

On the night of September 4 nineteen transport aircraft of the Soviet 4th and 5th Long-Range Air divisions delivered the first consignment of weapons and ammunition to the Tri Duba airfield held by the insurgents. Between September

5 and 17 they airlifted to the airfield 603 submachine guns, 329 machine guns, 174 anti-tank rifles, 1,300,000 rounds of ammunition and 1,096 kilogrammes of TNT.

The situation in the Carpathian sector at the beginning of September 1944 was as follows. The 38th Army of the 1st Ukrainian Front and the 4th Ukrainian Front were facing Army Group Heinrici (the German 1st Panzer Army and the Hungarian 1st Army) totalling 20 divisions with about 300,000 men, 3,250 guns and mortars, up to 100 panzers and assault guns and nearly 450 aircraft.

In connection with the outbreak of the popular uprising in Slovakia and the request from the insurgents for assistance GHQ examined and approved the proposals of the command of the 1st Ukrainian Front. On September 2 it ordered the Front to prepare and execute an operation at the junction of the 1st and 4th Ukrainian fronts. The Soviet troops were to strike out from the Krosno-Sanok sector in the general direction of Presov, reach the Slovak border and link up with the Slovak patriots. Permission was given to use the Czechoslovak 1st Corps in the operation and Soviet troops were ordered to co-operate with the Slovak forces deployed at Presov.

On September 3 the Military Council of the 1st Ukrainian Front submitted the operational plan to GHQ. The attack was to be delivered by the 38th Army, consisting of three infantry corps, a tank corps and a cavalry corps, and also by the Czechoslovak 1st Corps. The operation was to be completed within five days, in the course of which the Soviet troops were to advance to a depth of 90-95 kilometres and reach the Star-Lubovna-Lubotin-Presov line. The 1st and 2nd Infantry divisions of the East Slovak Corps and partisan detachments were to support the offensive by attacking the enemy rear positions in Slovakia and capturing the mountain passes for the Soviet forces.

At the same time the Military Council of the 1st Ukrainian Front requested GHQ to commit four right-wing divisions of the 4th Ukrainian Front, or assign them to the 1st Ukrainian Front. Approving the plan on September 3, GHQ ordered the 1st Ukrainian Front to assume the offensive not later than September 8. On the same day it issued the following instructions to the 4th Ukrainian Front: "On September

8 the Front's right flank (one infantry corps) will mount an offensive from the Sanok area in the direction of Komanca (5 km north of Radosice), reach the Slovak border and link up with the Slovak troops and partisans fighting against the German invaders. You shall co-ordinate your actions with those of the 38th Army of the 1st Ukrainian Front."

On September 5, 1944, GHQ issued an order to the 2nd Ukrainian Front which read: "By striking out from the south through Brasov and Sibiu at Cluj and committing the 40th Army and the 7th Guards Army to an offensive from the east the Front troops shall cross the Transylvanian Alps, the southern part of the Carpathian Range and reach the Satu Mare-Cluj-Deva-Turnu Severin line.

"Upon reaching Satu Mare the Front shall help the 4th Ukrainian Front cross the Alps and capture the area of Uzhgorod, Chop and Mukachevo.

"Subsequently, the Front shall develop the offensive, reach the Tisza on the Nyiregyhaza-Szeged sector with its main forces, supported by friendly forces extending from Szeged to Turnu Severin."

At the end of August the 3rd Mountain Infantry Corps of GHQ reserve was incorporated in the 4th Ukrainian Front. Its three divisions had fought in the mountains of the Caucasus and the Crimea and had special equipment. The Front was also reinforced with four mountain pack mortar regiments, two tank brigades, two self-propelled artillery regiments and two mountain engineer brigades.

On August 31 and September 1, the 2nd and 3rd Guards and the 5th and 6th Long-Range Air corps were ordered to redeploy to the areas of Proskurov (Khmelnitsky), Brodov, Tarnopol and Lvov.

On September 11, in order to ensure contact with the partisans operating in Slovakia, the staff of the representative of the Ukrainian Partisan Movement HQ with the Military Council of the 1st Ukrainian Front was placed under the control of the Military Council of the 4th Ukrainian Front.

Within four days, from September 4 to 7, a great deal of work was done to plan and organise the operation, and prepare and supply the troops.

At the end of August and in early September, after considerably augmenting his forces, the enemy initiated an offensive

March 1944. The Soviet
troops have reached the
USSR state border

The 1st Byelorussian Front
Units crossing the Vistula
south of Warsaw

Review of the Tadeusz
Kosciuszko Polish Ist In-
fantry Division. 1943

Soviet armour heading to-
wards Berlin

Buzuluk, 1943. Men of the
Czechoslovak Battalion before departure for the front

Major-General G. N. Zakharov, Commander of the 303rd Air Division, assigns a combat mission to the commander of the Normandie-Nieman Air Regiment

The Yugoslav Brigade marching towards the front-line, 1944

Crimea Conference, 1945. Right to left: Joseph Stalin, Franklin Roosevelt and Winston Churchill

General of the Army I. D. Chernyakhovsky, Commander of the 3rd Byelorussian Front, and his Chief of Staff Colonel-General A. P. Pokrovsky. 1944

Soviet and Polish soldiers during a lull in the fighting. 1944

Military Council of the 3rd Byelorussian Front. Left to right: Member of the Military Council Lieutenant-General V. Y. Makarov, Front Commander Marshal of the Soviet Union A. M. Vasilevsky and Chief of Staff Colonel-General A. P. Pokrovsky

October 1944. A trainload of food from the Soviet Union. A gift to the Polish people

Memorial to Soviet and Polish soldiers killed in the battles for the liberation of Warsaw

Commander of the Baltic Fleet Admiral V. F. Tributs (centre), Members of the Fleet Military Council Rear Admiral N. K. Smirnov (right) and Major-General A. D. Verbitsky

Military Council of the 2nd Ukrainian Front. Left to right: Member of the Military Council Lieutenant-General M. M. Stakhursky, Chief of Staff Colonel-General M. V. Zakharov, Front Commander Marshal of the Soviet Union R. Y. Malinovsky, Member of the Military Council Colonel-General (Armour) I. Z. Susaikov. 1944

On the eve of the Jassy-Kishinev Operation. Left to right: Commander of the 37th Amry Lieutenant-General M. N. Sharokhin, Commander of the 46th Army Lieutenant-General I. T. Shlemin, GHQ reprentative Marshal of the Soviet Union S. K. Timoshenko, Commander of the 3rd Ukrainian Front General of the Army F. I. Tolbukhin, Commander of the 57th Army Lieutenant-General N. A. Gagen and Commander of the 5th Striking Army Lieutenant-General N. E. Berzarin

Battleship *Sevastopol*, 1944. Right to left: Commander of the Black Sea Fleet Admiral F. S. Oktyabrsky, Vice-Admiral S. G. Gorshkov and Vice-Admiral N. Y. Basisty

August 31, 1944. Bucharest welcomes Soviet troops

Rumanian forces on their way to the frontline for joint actions with Soviet Army units

Bucharest. A memorial to
Soviet soldiers

into the liberated regions of Slovakia. By September 8 the Germans had captured Poprad, Ruzomberok, Zilina, Trencin and a number of other towns, thus considerably worsening the position of the insurgents who were forced to withdraw into the mountains from several important valleys.

In the meantime events took place in the East Slovak Corps which very seriously affected the course of the uprising and the forthcoming operation of the Soviet troops. The regiments of the corps were billeted at a considerable distance from one another. When the uprising erupted, many of its senior officers, including deputy corps commander Colonel Talsky behaved in a faint-hearted manner, with the result that the units proved unfit for action. Just then the Germans shifted strong forces to the area. On September 1 and 2 the Germans disarmed the corps, and only very few of its men managed to make their way to the partisans.

So, on September 2 the East Slovak Corps, which had been set the very important task of seizing the Dukla and Lupkow passes to open the way for the Soviet troops into the interior of Slovakia, ceased to exist. The Soviet Command which still knew nothing about this ordered the 1st and the 4th Ukrainian fronts to begin the East Carpathian Operation.

2. LIBERATION OF SLOVAKIA

ASSISTANCE
TO THE SLOVAK NATIONAL UPRISING
AND THE LIBERATION
OF THE TRANS-CARPATHIAN UKRAINE

The Soviet offensive in the Carpathians got under way on September 8, with the 38th Army under General K. S. Moskalenko as its spearhead. On the following day General A. A. Grechko's 1st Guards Army went into action. Right up to September 14 the Soviet troops waged heavy battles to pierce the enemy's first line of defence in the Carpathian foothills. After seven days of fighting in heavy rain on difficult mountainous terrain, they managed to advance not more than 12-23 kilometres and merely wedged into the enemy's defence. Neither army fulfilled its task on schedule.

Meanwhile the Germans brought up eight divisions, including the bulk of the forces which had been thrown against the Slovak insurgents, into the area of the Soviet penetration. The new balance of forces compelled the Soviet Command to alter the plan of the East Carpathian Operation. The main effort in the sector of the 1st Ukrainian Front was shifted from the right to the left flank of the 38th Army in order to break into the rear of the enemy on the defensive at Dukla. Two tank corps and two infantry divisions drawn from the Front's reserve were included into the 38th Army which on September 15 resumed operations after having re-arranged its order of battle. In the course of the heavy fighting which lasted till September 24 it advanced another 20 kilometres and reached the immediate approaches to the Main Carpathian Range.

In those days, in addition to the 1st Guards Army, the 18th Army under General Y. P. Zhuravlev and the 17th Guards Infantry Corps went into action in the sector of the 4th Ukrainian Front.

On September 20 the 1st Guards Army reached the Polish-Czechoslovak border. The first to enter Czechoslovakia were General V. B. Lisinov's 242nd Mountain Infantry Division and General T. U. Grinchenko's 129th Guards Infantry Division. By September 30, the 38th and the 1st Guards armies had reached the Main Carpathian Range along its full length and crossed it at several points.

In the latter half of September the enemy continued to bring up reinforcements to avert the threat of a Soviet breakthrough into Slovakia. From September 15 to 30 approximately four divisions were transferred to the zone of the 38th Army and the 1st Guards Army.

Tying down increasing numbers of the enemy troops, the Soviet offensive staved off a concentrated blow at the insurgents in Slovakia and facilitated their operations against the invaders. The Slovak uprising gained in strength and scope as more and more people joined the insurgents.

At the end of September Jan Sverma, member of the Foreign Bureau of the Communist Party of Czechoslovakia, arrived in the area of the uprising. He did much to organise correct Party guidance of the insurrection and the activity of the Party organisations, strengthen the Party's bonds with the masses and give greater impetus to the partisan movement. Jan Sverma was co-opted into the Military Council under the Main Headquarters of the Partisan Movement of Slovakia.

By the beginning of October three partisan divisions, six brigades and twenty separate detachments, totalling 15,845 men, were fighting in Slovakia. A part of the partisan units was fighting in the enemy's rear, while another part was defending the liberated areas of Slovakia where units of the Slovak army under General J. Golian, who was later replaced by General Rudolf Viest,[1] were also in action.

The Soviet Government and the Supreme Command continued to assist the insurgents with ammunition, weapons and medicine. On GHQ instructions a Czechoslovak fighter regiment consisting of twenty La-5's was redeployed to the Tri Duba airfield in Slovakia and the Soviet 5th Long-Range Air Corps began to airlift the Czechoslovak 2nd Airborne Brigade to Slovakia. Soviet bombers attacked key railway junctions in the rear of Army Groups A and South.

In the beginning of October the advancing troops of the 1st and 4th Ukrainian fronts had to cope with an even more difficult task, since nothing short of an exceptionally powerful assault could dislodge the enemy from the top of the Main Carpathian Range and break up his defences with their formidable permanent installations.

On September 26 the commander of the 38th Army decided to deliver the main blow in the direction of Msana and Zborov, using the 101st and 67th infantry corps and the Czechoslovak 1st Corps, with the 52nd Infantry Corps supporting their operations on the right flank. On September 29, 1944 the command of the 4th Ukrainian Front also decided to continue the operation and to shift the Front's main efforts somewhat further south, to the adjoining flanks of the 1st Guards and 18th armies.

The 38th Army reopened its offensive on September 30, in spite of the rains which resumed on September 27, creating still greater difficulties for the attacking forces.

On October 1 the 67th Infantry Corps crossed the Polish-

---

[1] General Viest arrived in Slovakia from London via Soviet territory in early October 1944, with powers of a representative of the emigre government.

Czechoslovak border five kilometres northwest of the Dukla Pass and entered Czechoslovakia. To exploit the success in the area the commander of the 38th Army moved the 31st Tank Corps into the zone. The 359th Infantry Division and General Svoboda's Czechoslovak 1st Corps, after executing a series of redeploying movements, increased their pressure on the enemy in front. On October 6 the Czechoslovak 1st Corps with the direct assistance of the 67th Infantry and the 31st Tank corps captured the Dukla Pass and entered their homeland. The slogan "Forever with the Soviet Union" was born in the fighting for Dukla Pass. October 6 was subsequently proclaimed Czechoslovak People's Army Day.

Having captured Dukla Pass, the 38th Army and the Czechoslovak 1st Corps continued their drive and by October 28 had advanced 15 to 20 kilometres west and southwest of the pass. At that point their offensive was halted.

The 4th Ukrainian Front resumed its offensive on October 3. Pushing ahead on a wide front towards the passes of the Main Carpathian Range, the 1st Guards and the 18th armies and the 17th Guards Infantry Corps dislodged the enemy from intermediate positions and on October 14 completed the liberation of the Transcarpathian Ukraine.

Pressing forward, the 1st Guards Army by October 18 had crossed the Main Carpathian Range on a 30-kilometre front and captured the Russky Pass. On the same day the 18th Army also crossed the range along the full width of its zone, captured the Uzhoksky and Veretsky passes and advanced from 5 to 18 kilometres to the south.

During the heavy battles for the passes the 4th Ukrainian Front shifted its main effort from the right wing to the centre, attaching primary importance to the Uzhgorod and Mukachevo sectors, where the Soviet troops made the biggest gains in the first half of October. This was due in the first place to the fact that by committing large forces against the 38th Army and the 1st Guards Army, the Germans had weakened their defences on the left wing of the 4th Ukrainian Front. The enemy was forced to do this also as a result of the operations of the 2nd Ukrainian Front whose swift drive in the northwesterly direction created a threat to the supply lines and rear of the Hungarian 1st Army whose command had been gripped by a grave crisis.

Realising the futility of fighting any longer on Germany's side, its commander, Colonel-General Bela Miklos, and his chief of staff on October 18 went over to the side of the Soviet troops with the intention of withdrawing the Hungarian 1st Army from the war against the USSR. But the German Command swiftly replaced the army's top-ranking officers with their own placemen, thus averting its disintegration.

Stiffened up with German units the Hungarian 1st Army offered stubborn resistance later on, but the very fact that its commanding officers had been replaced affected the morale of the Hungarian troops and eventually weakened their fighting efficiency.

In the latter half of October the 4th Ukrainian Front continued to shift its main efforts to the south, to the Uzhgorod and Mukachevo sector.

On October 25, the 18th Army liberated Mukachevo, a large town in the Transcarpathian Ukraine, and considerable territory east of the town. On October 27 it freed Uzhgorod and then concentrated on cutting supply routes and roads leading from the north, and also on stepping up the offensive at Presov and Kosice.

Thus, by the end of October the 1st and 4th Ukrainian fronts had crossed the East Carpathians and entered the valleys of the Wislok and Ondava rivers.

The Germans tried to regain Uzhgorod and Mukachevo with a series of powerful blows. And although they failed to do so, they did manage to halt the Soviet offensive on a permanent line of defence. The Soviet forces had made serious tactical gains, but they were unable to break through to the insurgents and had to revert to the defensive. They were exhausted in the heavy fighting during the crossing of the Eastern Carpathians and weakened by the losses. Moreover, their progress was impeded by pouring rain which turned the soil into quagmire and sharply raised the water level in numerous rivers and canals.

Meanwhile, the German Command intensified operations against the insurgents in Slovakia. After serious setbacks in Hungary and the Carpathians, the nazi leaders attached great importance to Slovakia and transferred fresh forces from the West to the region of the uprising. In the second half of

October the Germans concentrated four divisions, four combat groups and 10 security and police battalions there. On 18-20 October superior German forces began a fresh offensive against the liberated regions from all directions and made considerable headway despite the heroic resistance of the insurgent army and the partisans.

On October 22 General Rudolf Viest called a meeting of unit commanders who decided to stop defending the area of the uprising and thus placed the fighting patriots in an exceptionally difficult situation. On October 25 the insurgents' airfield near Zvolen was lost and on October 28 the Germans occupied Banska Bystrica. On the same day General Viest ordered the army to discontinue resistance and disband. This completely disorganised the defence of the uprising area. The insurgent army commanded by Generals Viest and Golian fell apart; the majority of its officers and men returned to their homes and only a small part of them took to the mountains.[1]

Nevertheless, the struggle did not come to an end with the fall of Banska Bystrica and the occupation of the liberated area by the Germans. Acting on orders from the Main HQ of the Partisan Movement, partisan detachments withdrew into the mountains.

Jan Sverma, Czechoslovakia's national hero, was killed on November 10 during the retreat of the Czechoslovak partisans into the mountains.

The 2nd Airborne Brigade withdrew into the mountains retaining its full fighting capacity. On October 25 the Czechoslovak 1st Fighter Air Regiment returned to the USSR.

The East Carpathian Operation of the 1st and the 4th Ukrainian fronts was initiated and executed in specific conditions and was designed to assist the Slovak National Uprising. Although the troops were unable to achieve all the set objectives, the offensive had a significant impact on military and political developments.

In the course of the heavy fighting in the Carpathians the Soviet forces inflicted a crushing defeat on Combat Group Heinrici. In September and October the 38th Army of the

---

[1] Generals Viest and Golian were taken prisoner by the Germans and shot.

1st Ukrainian Front and the troops of the 4th Ukrainian Front took 31,360 prisoners.

By defeating the enemy and surmounting the East Carpathians with their strong fortifications, the Soviet forces created a totally new situation in the area between the Carpathians and Prague. The Germans had lost an important strategic line which covered Czechoslovakia from the east and were compelled to transfer many troops there from Poland and Hungary, thus providing the Soviet Army with favourable prospects for continuing its offensive into Czechoslovakia from the east.

In the course of the operation the 1st and the 4th Ukrainian fronts liberated a considerable part of Slovakia and the whole of the Trans-Carpathian Ukraine. By drawing off large enemy forces, they directly assisted the Slovak National Uprising. Moreover, the Soviet Government and the military command helped the Slovak patriots with manpower, weapons, ammunition, medicine and communication facilities. Groups of organisers headed by Soviet partisan commanders and Czechoslovak patriots were sent into the enemy's rear. In September and October the Ukrainian HQ of the Partisan Movement dispatched 15 such groups numbering over 270 men. From September 5 to November 29, 2,050 rifles, 460 machine-guns, 1,702 submachine guns, 120 anti-tank rifles, 3,700,000 rounds of amunition and other equipment was delivered to Czechoslovakia.

Thanks to Soviet assistance Slovak insurgents were able to withstand the enemy onslaught for two months. The Slovak Uprising was the highest point of the anti-fascist struggle of the Czechoslovak people and the beginning of the national democratic revolution in the country. Its military consequences were also significant: more than 6,500 kilometres of roads were put out of order for two months, the Germans could not use the Slovak Army against the Soviet Army or draw upon the economic potential of Slovakia. At the same time the Slovak insurgents tied down approximately five enemy divisions and many separate units.

The Slovak Uprising, in which people of more than 30 nationalities took part, was a vivid manifestation of the international character of the anti-fascist movement. The heroic struggle of the insurgents attested to the further consolidation of Soviet-Czechoslovak friendship. Addressing a meeting in Banska Bystrica on August 29, 1969, First Secretary of the Central Committee of the Communist Party of Czechoslovakia, Gustav Husak, said: "The Slovak National Uprising placed the Czech and Slovak peoples into the ranks of the fighters against fascism. The uprising was a great event in our history for it put our peoples in this struggle next to the Soviet Union, the main force in the battle against fascism. And our peoples, the Czechs and Slovaks, consciously joined the front of the anti-fascist struggle. The Slovak National Uprising is a great uprising because in ·this world-wide struggle it was on the side of progress, on the side of the anti-Hitler coalition, on the side of the Soviet Union, the main force of the anti-fascist camp."[1]

The offensive in the Carpathians lasted through November and December. In this period the 2nd Ukrainian Front made the greatest gains. Shattering enemy defences along the Tisza it advanced from 90 to 160 kilometres to the northwest, reaching the Hron and the Danube at Esztergom. Its right-wing armies crossed the Hungarian-Czechoslovak border and liberated a considerable part of southern Slovakia.

During the offensive the Soviet troops gained complete control over the Lvov-Uzhgorod-Chop-Miskolc railway. This was a major success since it made it possible to organise the swift supply of both fronts as they developed their drive into the interior of Czechoslovakia.

THE CROSSING
OF THE WESTERN CARPATHIANS
AND BATTLES FOR THE LIBERATION
OF CZECHOSLOVAKIA'S
INDUSTRIAL AREAS

The Soviet offensive in Czechoslovakia in 1945 developed in different conditions. In January 1945 the Central Committee of the Communist Party of Czechoslovakia discussed the state and the tasks of the national liberation movement and, following the instructions from the Foreign Bureau, adopted and published an appeal to the people in the illegal *Rude*

---

[1] *Pravda*, August 30, 1969.

Pravo. Noting that the Soviet Union would undoubtedly free the enslaved peoples and restore their independence, the appeal added: "It cannot be tolerated that our people should passively look forward to being liberated by the Red Army, for this would leave an indelible stain on its honour.... The Czech people must participate in its own liberation.... Immediate preparations for military action is the demand of the day." This document played a decisive role rallying the masses for the struggle against the enemy.

In the winter of 1945 the partisans waged an active struggle against the German invaders in Czechoslovakia. The operations of the Soviet troops and the partisans were coordinated by the Partisan Movement HQ under the Military Council of the 4th Ukrainian Front. At the time the main partisan forces were active in the mountains and forests of the Western Carpathians.

The flames of the people's partisan war which flared up in Slovakia had spread to Moravia and Bohemia. On orders from the Main HQ of the Partisan Movement in Czechoslovakia groups and detachments of organisers were sent to the central and western regions of the country where they established contact with the local patriotic organisations, raised new partisan detachments and supported their operations against the German invaders.

Besides guiding the national liberation struggle and mustering the anti-fascist forces inside the country, the Communist Party of Czechoslovakia was drawing up a programme and conducting practical preparations for the postwar state and political organisation of the country. In its January decision the Central Committee of the Communist Party of Czechoslovakia said the following in this connection: "The primary objective of our struggle is the establishment of a democratic people's republic.... It will be a new republic. It will be a republic of working people in which the Czech people will be master in the Czech lands and the Slovak people in Slovakia. National Committees will assume full power immediately upon liberation and all their organs big and small, will execute the will of the working population."

Czechoslovak emigre circles in London, however, opposed the country's democratisation. They raised armed detachments of reactionary officers and infiltrated them into Czechoslovakia with instructions to take control of administrative bodies. With this aim in view, the Benes Government in London tried its best to preserve the underground bourgeois organisations operating in Czechoslovakia.

But the course of events overturned these reactionary plans. As a result of their dedicated struggle for the fundamental interests of the peoples, the communists became the most influential force in the country. In the circumstances, Benes could not turn down the offer of the Communist Party of Czechoslovakia to meet its leading members in Moscow to discuss the character of the state system in the liberated republic and the formation and programme of the National Front Government. The talks which were held in March 1945 ended in a victory for the line of the Communist Party. This was yet another major achievement of Czechoslovakia's progressive, revolutionary forces in their efforts to establish a people's democratic state. All these circumstances taken together created favourable conditions for the operations of the Soviet troops which were battering the German forces in Czechoslovakia.

In January and February 1945, the 4th and 2nd Ukrainian fronts launched a joint offensive operation to cross the Western Carpathians and reach the approaches to the Moravska Ostrava industrial region. Both fronts made considerable headway in January partly thanks to the fact that their offensive was timed with the general offensive opened by the Soviet Army in January along a front extending from the Baltic Sea to the Danube. January 15, 1945, when several Czechoslovak artillery regiments first took part in the fighting at the Polish town of Jaslo, was a memorable day in the offensive. Now January 15 is annually observed as Artillery Day of the Czechoslovak Army.

In February both fronts continued to advance in the area of Bielsko and along the Hron.

In the course of two months of battles in Czechoslovakia the 4th and 2nd Ukrainian fronts liberated the districts of Kosice, Presov and Banska Bystrica with a total population of 1,400,000. The 4th Ukrainian Front advanced from 180 to 220 kilometres, crossed the greater part of the Western Carpathians, and towards the end of the operation gained the upper reaches of the Vistula. There it engaged the enemy at the doorsteps of the Moravska Ostrava industrial region which played an important role in nazi Germany's war effort. The 2nd Ukrainian Front smashed the German troops in the Slovenske Rudohorie. In this period the Soviet forces routed about 18 enemy divisions and took nearly 140,000 prisoners. The Soviet losses were 16,000 killed and more than 50,000 wounded. The Czechoslovak 1st Corps incorporated in the 4th Ukrainian Front lost 209 men in killed and 777 in wounded.

The plan of the Moravska Ostrava Operation, to start not later than March 10, was approved by GHQ on February 17. The 4th Ukrainian Front was to smash the 1st Panzer Army, liberate the Moravska Ostrava industrial region and open the way for a drive into central Czechoslovakia. It was to co-operate with the 1st Ukrainian Front which was advancing in Upper Silesia, Poland. The 2nd Ukrainian Front's orders were to initiate an offensive north of the Danube, deliver the main attack in the direction of Nove Zamky, capture Bratislava and liberate Brno on the 20th day of the operation.

By the beginning of the spring offensive scheduled to get under way in the middle of March 1945, the 4th and 2nd Ukrainian fronts faced 22 enemy divisions totalling 350,000 men, 3,300 guns and mortars, 220 panzers and 270 combat aircraft.

The Soviet Army's offensive in Czechoslovakia in March and April was prepared and executed at a time when the Soviet Armed Forces were dealing the final blow at the enemy. The end of the war was in sight and all freedom-loving peoples were becoming increasingly preoccupied with problems of the post-war settlement.

The Czechoslovak people, who had been suffering the nazi "new order" longer than anyone else, strove to get rid of the oppressors as quickly as possible. The people in Slovakia, which had been liberated by the Soviet forces and the Czechoslovak 1st Corps, assumed power on its own initiative. People's organs of power—the national committees—were set up and state power in Slovakia passed into the hands of the re-organised National Council. The working class and the peasantry launched revolutionary reforms: the old fascist state machinery was abolished; a land reform began by decision of the Slovak National Council, and the army of the former Slovak state was disbanded.

The initiative in guiding the national liberation struggle and determining the future organisation of the entire state passed into the hands of the Communist Party of Czechoslovakia. On its suggestion a National Front of Czechs and Slovaks, with Klement Gottwald as its elected chairman, was established to improve the leadership of the anti-fascist movement in the country and unite the masses.

On February 28 Moscow and London broadcast an appeal of the National Front urging the Czech and Slovak peoples to launch an armed uprising at the final stage of the war to expedite their country's liberation. The working class at large industrial enterprises in occupied regions set up factory committees and formed workers' detachments under the guidance of the communists. Sabotage at factories working on war orders for the Wehrmacht became widespread.

In order to improve the leadership of the Resistance Movement in the occupied territory, the Central Committee of the Communist Party of Czechoslovakia and the Central Trade Union Council in February 1945 decided to establish its guiding centre—the Czech National Council—which included representatives of the Communist Party, underground trade unions, partisan detachments, peasants and intellectuals. Defying the Gestapo terror, the Council put in a great deal of work to organise the struggle of the working people of Czechoslovakia and guided partisan activity.

At the beginning of March 1945, the Partisan Movement HQ under the Military Council of the 4th Ukrainian Front claimed to have under its control 20 partisan formations, brigades and detachments numbering over 7,700 people fighting against the enemy in Czechoslovakia. Together with the underground organisations of the Communist Party, the partisans carried on extensive political work among the population.

Early in April 1945 another momentous event took place in the life of the Czechoslovak people: the country's democratic forces formed the first Government of the National Front with communists in key ministerial posts. The Programme of the National Front, which came to be known as the Kosice Programme, was read out on April 5 at the first session of the new government in Kosice. Drawn up by the Communist Party of Czechoslovakia, the Programme called for a range of socio-economic reforms whose realisation would open the road to socialism for the Czechoslovak people. It also set forth the principles of the formation of a new, genuinely democratic, anti-fascist Czechoslovak Army.

In connection with the formation of the government and the adoption of the Kosice Programme, the Communist Party of Czechoslovakia issued an appeal to the people which said: "Support our liberator, the Red Army, with all your strength and enlist into the new Czechoslovak Army. Restore railways, highways, bridges, telegraph and telephone services, that is, all that serves the front. . . ."

Under the plan of the spring offensive in Czechoslovakia the Soviet troops carried out two interconnected offensive operations—the Moravska Ostrava and the Bratislava-Brno operations. The first was executed by the 4th Ukrainian Front and the other by the 2nd Ukrainian Front. In March and April the Soviet forces advanced 150-350 kilometres, liberating the whole of Slovakia and a considerable part of Moravia, or 40,800 square kilometres of territory with a population of more than 4,300,000.

The country's key industrial centres, the Moravska Ostrava, Bratislava and Brno regions, were returned to the Czechoslovak people. Having liberated these regions the Soviet Army was poised for an advance into Austria and central Czechoslovakia.

3. LIBERATION OF BOHEMIA
AND THE CAPITAL
OF CZECHOSLOVAKIA

THE SITUATION
IN THE PRAGUE DIRECTION
AT THE BEGINNING OF MAY

The military and political situation in early May 1945 was most peculiar. The Soviet Army had just brilliantly completed the Bratislava Operation. The banner of victory had been raised over the capital of nazi Germany, Berlin. The Soviet and Allied troops had already linked up on the Elbe.

But the German Command still had considerable forces which continued to resist the Soviet Army. More than 160 enemy divisions (over 1,500,000 officers and men and about 2,500 panzers) were still fighting on the Soviet-German front and in Yugoslavia. Battleworthy German forces were also deployed in the north and south of Germany and in Italy.

With such numerically large forces at its disposal nazi Germany's new leadership was not disposed to recognise the futility of the further existence of the nazi regime.

The main German forces on the Eastern Front were deployed in the south of Czechoslovakia, Austria and Yugoslavia. Their best divisions were on the defensive in the area north of the Danube in Czechoslovakia and in northern Austria against the 1st, 4th and 2nd Ukrainian fronts. These were Army Group Centre (the 1st and 4th Panzer and the 17th armies), a part of Army Group Austria (the 8th Army and the SS 6th Panzer Army) and a large number of reserve units of all arms. From the west these forces were covered by the German 7th Army which on May 3 was incorporated into Army Group Centre. Deployed on a broad front along the Mulde River and the western border of Czechoslovakia, the army's five divisions were facing the US 3rd Army which had taken up positions there in the middle of April.

Commander of Army Group Centre Field-Marshal Schoerner and Reich Minister for the Affairs of the Protectorate of Bohemia and Moravia Frank thought that with the help of political manoeuvres they would be able to prevent the Soviet Army entering Bohemia. "In view of Germany's steadily worsening political and military situation," Frank admitted later, "I devised a plan which was to give the Reich a political advantage in the event of armistice or peace negotiations. Under this plan the Protectorate was to be turned over to the international control of a group of Western powers."

As regards the British and the Americans, their political calculations and military plans of the last weeks of the war were characterised by a desire to occupy Czechoslovakia and bring US troops into Prague. Winston Churchill was especially determined to attain this objective. In a letter to General Eisenhower of April 2, 1945, he wrote: "I deem it highly important that we should shake hands with the Russians as far to the east as possible...." His letter to

President Truman on April 30 was even more specific: "There can be little doubt that the liberation of Prague and as much as possible of the territory of Western Czechoslovakia by your forces might make the whole difference to the post-war situation in Czechoslovakia, and might well influence that in near-by countries. On the other hand, if the Western Allies play no significant part in Czechoslovakian liberation that country will go the way of Yugoslavia.

"Of course, such a move by Eisenhower must not interfere with his main operations against the Germans, but I think the highly important political consideration mentioned above should be brought to his attention."[1]

Field-Marshal Montgomery also had hopes of occupying Prague and the whole of Western Czechoslovakia. "The important point," he wrote, "was... to ensure... a political balance in Europe which would help us, the Western nations, to win the peace. That meant getting possession of certain political centres in Europe before the Russians—notably Vienna, Prague and Berlin."[2]

The US Command tried to occupy Czechoslovakia and her capital, Prague. On April 30 General Eisenhower informed the Soviet Command that he intended to establish demarcation lines in the north and south of Germany, cross the Czechoslovak border and occupy the country up to the line running from Karlovy Vary to Plzen and Ceske Budejovice.

In his letter Einsenhower said that while the American positions in the centre were being established as agreed along the rivers Elbe and Mulde, operations were being undertaken to cross the middle reaches of the Elbe with the view to establishing a stable front approximately along the Wismar, Schwerin, Doemitz line. He indicated that beginning from the upper reaches of the Mulde American troops would occupy positions at Erz Gebirge and the Bohemer Forest approximately following the 1937 Czechoslovak border. Conditions permitting, these troops would probably advance to Karlsbad (Karlovy Vary), Plzen and Budejovice.

The Soviet Command accepted this proposal and halted

---

[1] Winston Churchill, *The Second World War*, Vol. VI, "Triumph and Tragedy", New York, 1962, pp. 400, 433.

[2] *The Memoirs of Field-Marshal the Viscount Montgomery of Alamein*, Cleveland and New York, 1958, p. 296.

the movement of its troops towards the Lower Elbe along the Wismar, Schwerin, Doęmitz line. Despite this agreement General Eisenhower in a letter of May 4 to the Chief of the Soviet General Staff, General A. I. Antonov, said the US Command intended to occupy the whole of Western Czechoslovakia, including the country's capital, Prague.

Since this plan went against the agreement reached on May 5 General A. I. Antonov through the British and US military missions forwarded the reply of the Soviet Supreme Command which said that the Soviet Command had already begun the planned operation to clear both banks of the Vltava of the enemy. To avoid a possible intermixing of the troops, the Soviet Command asked General Eisenhower not to move the US troops into Czechoslovakia east of the initially designated line, i.e., Ceske Budejovice, Plzen and Karlovy Vary.

Eisenhower had to agree. "On the morning of 6th May," wrote British historian John Ehrman, "Eisenhower... ordered Twelfth Army Group not, after all, to move beyond the line Karlsbad-Pilsen-Budejovice. 'Presume,' he added when informing Moscow of this decision, 'Soviet forces can advance rapidly to clear up the situation in centre of the country.' "[1]

Nevertheless, reactionary circles in the United States and Britain did not abandon the thought of occupying Prague and the whole of western Czechoslovakia. A group of German forces numbering almost a million men continued to wage a stubborn struggle against the Soviet Army. The group's command and the Doenitz government took all possible steps to withdraw these forces to the west, behind the lines of the Allied troops and surrender to the Americans.

In these circumstances a task of great political importance confronted the Soviet Supreme Command, that of routing and taking prisoner a large enemy group and completing the liberation of Czechoslovakia and her capital Prague. By fulfilling it with utmost dispatch, the Soviet troops would tear the net of intrigues which the leaders of nazi Germany and the reactionary circles in the USA and Britain were weaving around Czechoslovakia, and Prague in particular.

---

[1] John Ehrman, *History of the Second World War. Grand Strategy*, Vol. VI, London, 1956, pp. 159-60.

Georgi Dimitrov talking with
Marshal of the Soviet Union
F. I. Tolbukhin (right) and
Lieutenant-Colonel S. S. Bi-
ryuzov (centre)

Soviet and Bulgarian of-
ficers

Bulgarian partisans. Commander of the Chavdar Partisan Brigade D. Djurov (right)

Sofia, capital of Bulgaria,
welcomes Soviet troops

Sofia. Memorial to the Soviet troops

Yugoslav partisans pledge to fight to the last drop of blood

Commander of the 4th Guards Mechanised Corps Lieutenant-General (Armour) V. I. Zhdanov and Commander of the Yugoslav 1st Proletarian Corps Colonel-General P. Dapcevic congratulating each other on the liberation of Belgrade

Memorial to Soviet and Yo-
goslav troops in Murska So-
bota

Moreover, the need for a fresh offensive operation was also dictated by the internal situation in Czechoslovakia where preparations for a popular armed uprising were being conducted throughout her territory, including Prague.

Patriots in Bohemia were swiftly arming themselves. National Committees operating under the leadership of the Communist Party of Czechoslovakia were getting ready to take over power; in areas controlled by the partisans power was already in their hands. A nation-wide uprising was gaining momentum. The towns were first to rise on May 1 and 2, and on May 4 the uprising had embraced the whole of Central Bohemia. On the night of May 4 the workers of Kladno, one of the country's biggest industrial areas, rose in an uprising, and on May 5 power in the area passed into the hands of the National Committees, and armed clashes took place between the population and the German troops. On the same day an uprising broke out at the Skoda factories in Plzen which was liberated by the Czech patriots. On May 6 US troops entered the town and prevented its citizens from coming to the assistance of the insurgents in Prague. On May 5 the uprising enveloped the whole of Bohemia and western Moravia.

The armed uprising which began in the Czechoslovak capital lent these actions a nation-wide character. It marked the beginning of the May People's Uprising whose leading force was the Communist Party of Czechoslovakia.

At 12.33 hours on May 5, Prague Radio gave the signal for the uprising to begin in the capital whose citizens began to disarm German troops stationed in various parts of the city. Meeting in full under the chairmanship of Dr. A. Prazak, the Czech National Council, the guiding centre of the uprising, issued an appeal to the people on behalf of the Kosice Government of the National Front which proclaimed the abolition of the Protectorate and the assumption of power in Bohemia by the Council. An ultimatum was broadcast over the radio demanding the immediate and unconditional surrender of the German troops in Prague.

On the first day the insurgents occupied key buildings and installations, including the post and telegraph offices, the central telephone exchange, radio station, railway stations, the city power station and most of the bridges across

21—1719

the Vltava. To crush the uprising the German Command rushed troops from Army Group Centre to reinforce the Prague garrison which included a large number of SS units. In an effort to win time Frank, the nazi governor in Prague, entered into negotiations with the insurgents. At the same time commander of Army Group Centre Schoerner ordered his troops to crush the Prague uprising with all the means at their disposal. Panzer divisions were rushed to the city and all units billeted there were alerted. Schoerner ordered the Luftwaffe to bomb the city. Faced with the prospect of a long and difficult struggle the people of Prague urgently needed effective assistance.

Taking all these factors into account, the Communist Party advised the Czech National Council to appeal to the inhabitants of near-by towns and villages for assistance and also to the Allied armies, the Soviet Army in the first place. On the night of May 5 Prague Radio broadcast the following appeal: "Request of the city of Prague to all Allied armies. The Germans are advancing on Prague from all directions. German panzers, artillery and infantry are in action. Prague urgently needs assistance. Send planes, tanks and weapons. We need help immediately."

At 15.00 hours on May 6 chief of the Czechoslovak Military Mission in the USSR, Brigadier-General G. Pika, arrived at the Foreign Relations Department of the USSR Commissariat for Defence, carrying an official account of the events in Prague addressed to General A. I. Antonov and requested the Soviet Supreme Command "to render assistance at this historical and decisive moment for the Czech people".

The Soviet Command began to prepare an offensive which was to liberate the Czechoslovak capital as speedily as possible, even before it was informed about the situation in Prague, having taken this decision when it planned the final blows at the German Army. It was clear that, having taken Berlin and Vienna, the Soviet troops would have to launch powerful and swift attacks on Prague from the north and south.

At the end of April, when the Soviet forces involved in the Berlin Operation had linked up with the US forces on the Elbe and closed the trap round the enemy troops in Berlin, Supreme Commander-in-Chief J. V. Stalin ordered commander of the 1st Ukrainian Front Marshal I. S. Konev to draw up a plan for an offensive towards Prague and submit it to GHQ for approval.

GHQ approved Marshal Konev's plan and early in May the general concept of the Prague Operation was determined. In addition to the 1st Ukrainian Front the operation was to be executed by the 2nd and 4th Ukrainian fronts which had taken up positions in areas west of Brno and Moravska Ostrava, ready to advance on Prague.

The operational and strategic situation was on the whole favourable for Soviet troops. The 1st Ukrainian Front, whose central armies had advanced from 30 to 50 kilometres north and northeast of Dresden, deeply bypassed the left flank of Army Group Centre and threatened it from the rear. They were within 130-150 kilometres of Prague. Marshal Malinovsky's 2nd Ukrainian Front fighting west and south of Brno had deeply outflanked the right wing of Army Group Centre and was 160-200 kilometres from the Czechoslovak capital. The 4th Ukrainian Front under General A. I. Yeremenko, wedged between the 1st and 2nd Ukrainian fronts, continued to push towards Olomouc and Prague in the face of stiff resistance by the 1st Panzer Army, its units being relatively far from Prague (250-300 kilometres).

The three Ukrainian fronts committed to the offensive 2,100,000 men, more than 30,000 guns and mortars, approximately 2,100 tanks and self-propelled guns and over 4,000 combat aircraft.

The German forces facing them north of the Danube had more than 900,000 men, with 9,700 guns and mortars, over 2,200 panzers and assault guns and 1,000 aircraft.

The concept of the Prague Operation was to strike two powerful blows at both flanks of Army Group Centre along directions converging on Prague. The objective was to encircle the main enemy forces east of Prague and liberate the Czechoslovak capital. The blows were to be dealt from an area northwest of Dresden by the troops of the 1st Ukrainian Front and from an area south of Brno by the 2nd Ukrainian Front. Simultaneously, the centre and the left wing of the 1st Ukrainian Front, the entire 4th Ukrainian Front and the armies on the right wing of the 2nd Ukrainian Front were to cut up the invested enemy group into parts, thus expediting its rout and compelling it to surrender.

In conformity with the general concept of the Prague Operation GHQ on May 1 and 2 set the fronts their respective tasks: at 01.30 hours on May 1, 1945, it directed the commander of the 1st Byelorussian Front to relieve the 1st Ukrainian Front in Berlin and south of it up to the line Luebben-Wittenberg not later than May 4, whereupon the commander of the 1st Ukrainian Front was to throw his right-wing forces into a swift offensive in the general direction of Prague. At 19.40 hours on May 2 GHQ ordered the commander of the 2nd Ukrainian Front to turn his forces westwards and strike in the general direction of Jihlava and Prague. The main strike groups of the two fronts were to go into action on May 7, while the 4th Ukrainian Front was to continue its drive in the Olomouc sector to meet the advancing right-wing forces of the 2nd Ukrainian Front.

The difficulty of preparing the Prague Operation consisted in that the 1st and 2nd Ukrainian Fronts, which were to deal the main blows, had to reshuffle drastically their divisions in a very short period of time, not more than three or four days. Things were hardest of all for the command and the HQ of the 1st Ukrainian Front: it was to transfer its two tank armies (3rd Guards and 4th Guards) from their positions at Berlin to an area northwest of Dresden, and to regroup four field armies, two tank armies, a mechanised and a cavalry corps, an assault artillery corps and many other reinforcing units. In order to reach the new positions the troops had to cover from 100 to 200 kilometres and take up assault positions for an offensive on Prague. The 2nd Ukrainian Front had to disengage the 6th Guards Tank Army and the 1st Guards Mechanised Cavalry Group and assemble them in new areas in preparation for an attack against Prague, incorporate the newly arrived 9th Guards Army and deploy it in the first line. The Front's other armies likewise had to cover considerable distances.

These difficulties notwithstanding, the troops of the 1st Ukrainian Front began to take up assault positions on May 5. The 2nd Ukrainian Front which was to take part in the Prague Operation regrouped shortly afterwards.

Having received a radio message that an uprising had

broken out on May 5 in Prague, the Soviet Command struck on May 6, a day earlier than planned, without waiting for the troops to complete regrouping.

TO THE ASSISTANCE
OF THE INSURGENTS IN PRAGUE

Informed by the German commandant of Prague, General Toussaint, that an uprising had broken out in the city, Doenitz's government in the morning of May 6 instructed the commander of Army Group Centre to withdraw his forces immediately to the west and surrender to the Americans. At the same time Schoerner ordered his troops to converge on Prague and crush the uprising. It was too late, however. The 1st Ukrainian Front's powerful attack took the enemy by surprise. The Soviet troops overwhelmed the resistance of the 4th Panzer Army northwest of Dresden and by nightfall on May 6 wedged into enemy positions to a depth of nearly 25 kilometres. Moreover, the Soviet offensive also frustrated the intentions of the commander of Army Group Centre to relieve the German garrison in Breslau (Wroclaw). At 18.00 hours on May 6 the garrison commander ordered his troops to lay down arms. After a three months' siege the 40,000-strong garrison surrendered to the 6th Army of the 1st Ukrainian Front.

Throughout May 6 the insurgents in Prague beat off the furious onslaught of the Germans who acted with especial brutality, especially in the workers' districts where SS units were thrown against the poorly-armed insurgents courageously defending the barricades. An important role in strengthening the morale of the insurgents was played by *Rude Pravo,* organ of the Central Committee of the Communist Party of Czechoslovakia, and *Prace,* organ of the trade unions.

Using armour, artillery and aircraft, the Germans overpowered the heroic insurgents, capturing a number of barricades and key objectives and breaking into the centre of the city. The enemy's superiority in strength was beginning to tell. The three panzer divisions which the German Command threw into action to crush the uprising reached the city's suburbs by nightfall on May 6 thus placing the insurgents in a grave situation.

Meantime, the 1st Ukrainian Front was hastening to the assistance of the insurgents. Having overrun the enemy positions on the west bank of the Elbe, the principal strike group reached the northern slopes of the main Rudohorie range by the evening of May 6. The following morning the 2nd Ukrainian Front and the other armies of the 1st Ukrainian Front joined in the operation. At the same time the 4th Ukrainian Front continued to push ahead in the Olomouc sector across difficult mountainous and wooded terrain. The Front Command ordered its mobile group and the mobile group of the 38th Army to set out in pursuit of the retreating enemy in order to reach Prague as quickly as possible.

Inspired by the struggle of the inhabitants of Prague the entire population of Bohemia and Moravia rose up against the nazis. The uprising in the towns and villages of Czechoslovakia fragmented the enemy's forces, depriving him of the chance of assembling them for a massive attack on Prague.

On the night of May 7 the Czech National Council, acting on the initiative of the Communists, called upon the people, and the working class in the first place, not to retreat, to continue the struggle and bring it to a victorious conclusion.

The Soviet troops made every effort to reach Prague with all possible speed, cut off the retreat routes of Army Group Centre to the west, prevent the Germans from smashing the uprising and destroying Prague.

On May 8, the 1st, 4th and 2nd Ukrainian fronts pressed ahead in the area between Dresden and the Danube. Simultaneously, the 3rd Ukrainian Front, operating south of the Danube, was pushing to the west. On the same day the 1st Ukrainian Front scored a major success: it surmounted the enemy's resistance along the Rudohorie line and captured Dresden, an important railway junction and powerful resistance centre in Saxony which covered the road to Prague from the north. Committing the 6th Guards Tank Army, the 2nd Ukrainian Front rapidly advanced towards Jihlava, driving on Prague from the south. The troops of the 4th Ukrainian Front liberated Olomouc in a bitter street-to-street engagement, opening the way for all its forces to attack Prague from the east.

On May 8 representatives of the German High Command signed the instruments of unconditional surrender in Karlshorst, a suburb of Berlin. The historic day of nazi Germany's complete and final defeat had arrived, and on the following morning German troops on the Eastern Front began to down arms and surrender to the Soviet forces. Army Group Centre, however, continued to fight; therefore the troops of the three Ukrainian fronts continued to pursue the German forces. The 1st Ukrainian Front advanced on Prague from the north, the 2nd Ukrainian Front from the south, and the 4th Ukrainian Front, which included the Czechoslovak 1st Corps, was bearing down on the city from the east.

The resistance of the insurgents weakened rapidly. Two thousand of them had been killed on the barricades. At this critical hour for the outcome of the uprising the tank armies of the 1st Ukrainian Front made an 80-kilometre lunge and early in the morning of May 9 entered the city, saving the Czechoslovak capital and its inhabitants from destruction.

At 04.00 hours the 63rd Guards and 62nd Guards tank brigades of the 10th Guards Tank Corps, and the 70th Guards Self-Propelled Artillery Brigade of the 4th Guards Tank Army broke into the city from the northwest. They were the first. Almost at the same time the 3rd Guards Tank Army (69th Mechanised Brigade, 16th Self-Propelled Artillery Brigade and the 50th Separate Motorcycle Regiment) entered Prague from the north. Within two or three hours their main forces had concentrated in the city. The main forces of the 4th Guards Tank Army had moved into Prague by midday. The advance units of the 13th and 3rd Guards armies entered Prague in the wake of the mobile units. By 10.00 hours the Soviet troops with the assistance of the population had cleared the entire city of the enemy.

On May 9 the mobile formations of the 2nd Ukrainian Front continued their rapid thrust on Prague from the southeast. The 6th Guards Tank Army which had crushed the enemy resistance in Jihlava was also pushing forward at a swift pace. Units of the 5th Guards Tank Corps entered the city's southeastern blocks. The armour units of the 7th Mechanised Corps and the 1st Guards Mechanised Cavalry Group also reached the city. In the evening the 4th Ukrainian Front's mobile group entered Prague, after covering 200 kilometres from an area northwest of Olomouc.

As a result of a swift manoeuvre executed by the troops of the 1st and 2nd Ukrainian fronts advancing towards each other, the main retreat routes of the German troops in Czechoslovakia were cut by nightfall on May 9. Disorganised, demoralised and deprived of control the main forces of Army Group Centre were taken into a giant ring, while the divisions of Army Group Austria, which managed to avoid encirclement, were being hammered on by the 2nd Ukrainian Front advancing to the west.

In the next few days the Soviet troops continued operations with the view to taking prisoner the invested enemy group and reaching the line where they were to link up with the US forces. On May 10 and 11 the bulk of the enemy troops was taken prisoner, the 1st and 2nd Ukrainian fronts linking up with the US 3rd Army along the line Chemnitz-Karlovy Vary-Plzen-Ceske Budejovice and further south.

The Ukrainian fronts fulfilled their assignments, achieving very impressive results. In the course of the Prague Operation the Soviet troops took about 860,000 prisoners.

4. RESULTS
OF THE SOVIET ARMY'S BATTLES
FOR CZECHOSLOVAKIA'S
LIBERATION

The chief political result of the Soviet Army's eight-month offensive in Czechoslovakia was her liberation from fascism which led to the appearance of a new people's democratic state—the Czechoslovak Republic. Thus, the victorious Soviet offensive overturned the plans of the emigre government in London to restore the bourgeois order in the country.

The national liberation movement, which unfolded in Czechoslovakia under the leadership of the Communist Party, merged with the offensive of the Soviet and Czechoslovak forces. Thanks to Soviet support and assistance the political line of the Communist Party of Czechoslovakia gained ascendancy in the national liberation movement. With the economic assistance of the Soviet people the Czechs and Slovaks were able to embark upon peaceful creative labour to rehabilitate and develop their economy and culture.

The liberation of Czechoslovakia also frustrated the last attempt of Germany's new government headed by Admiral Doenitz to turn the country into a sanctuary for a million-strong group of German forces where they would not have to surrender to the Soviet Army. By liberating Prague the Soviet Army ensured the victory of the Czech armed uprising, and also prevented a possible occupation of the country by American troops.

Strategically, the Soviet offensive in Czechoslovakia was a major achievement because it ended in a crushing defeat for the Wehrmacht: the Soviet troops destroyed, smashed and took prisoner 122 enemy divisions.[1] During the fighting in Czechoslovakia they took more than 1,200,000 prisoners, including those captured by the right-wing armies of the 2nd Ukrainian Front, seized 18,100 guns and mortars, about 3,200 panzers and nearly 1,900 combat aircraft, and destroyed a vast amount of equipment on the battlefield.

The operations in the Carpathians and at Prague helped the Soviet Army's main forces to smash the enemy at Budapest and Vienna and between Warsaw and Berlin.

The important political and strategic results achieved by the Soviet Army in the course of its offensive in Czechoslovakia and in other operations and battles of the Great Patriotic War were above all due to the enormous organisational activity of the Communist Party which inspired the Soviet people to fight and work heroically for the sake of complete and final victory over nazi Germany. They also offered fresh and striking proof of the high morale and fighting efficiency of the Soviet troops, their ardent patriotism and fidelity to their internationalist duty. Finally, they were a result of the truly titanic labour of the Soviet working people who kept their Armed Forces supplied with everything they needed to smash the enemy.

The Soviet people rendered enormous military and technical assistance to Czechoslovakia. During the war the USSR without compensation supplied the Czechoslovak troops with about 50,000 rifles and submachine guns, 3,954 machine guns, 1,374 guns and mortars, 1,283 anti-tank rifles, 151 air-

---

[1] Including the enemy divisions routed by the right-wing armies of the 2nd Ukrainian Front in battles at the southern approaches to Czechoslovakia during the fighting for Budapest.

craft, 1,262 motor vehicles, 142 tanks and self-propelled guns, and other weapons and equipment.

A large number of Soviet officers and men distinguished themselves in the battles in Czechoslovakia.

The Military Councils of the fronts and armies, political organs and Party and Komsomol organisations in divisions and regiments played a decisive role in explaining to the officers and men their military tasks and mobilising their efforts to fulfil them. On instructions from the Central Committee of the Communist Party and the Main Political Administration of the Soviet Army thousands of Communists of the three Ukrainian fronts carried on extensive political work in the troops.

Throughout the offensive of the Ukrainian fronts in Czechoslovakia, the ranks of the Communists and Komsomol members were augmented by the bravest and most efficient men. For example, 18,400 people were accepted to full or probationary Party membership in the 2nd Ukrainian Front from January to April 1945. In this period the number of Komsomol members among its troops increased by 14,400. In the course of the East Carpathian Operation 11,124 officers and men joined the Party and another 11,639 were accepted into the Komsomol in the 1st and 4th Ukrainian fronts.

The high combat skill and heroism displayed by the Soviet Armed Forces in Czechoslovakia received high praise from the Communist Party and the Soviet Government. For exemplary fulfilment of their assignments in the battles against the German invaders, for the liberation of Czechoslovak towns and for courage in action, more than 950 units of the 1st, 2nd and 4th Ukrainian fronts, including 260 units which had taken part in the Prague Operation, were awarded combat orders, and many officers and men were made Heroes of the Soviet Union. A second Gold Star of Hero of the Soviet Union was awarded to the commander of the 1st Ukrainian Front, Marshal I. S. Konev, and commanders of the Front's tank brigades D. A. Dragunsky, Z. K. Slyusarenko and M. G. Fomichev.

Military decorations were also conferred on Czechoslovak units which fought for the liberation of their homeland.

On 23 occasions Moscow saluted the Soviet, Czechoslovak, Polish and Rumanian troops for liberating Czechoslovak towns. Scores of units received titles in honour of the locality they had helped to liberate. In the course of the Soviet offensive in the Carpathians and on Prague the Supreme Commander-in-Chief conferred titles of honour, including Bratislava, Zvolen, Carpathian, Kosice, Presov and Prague, on 106 units of the three Ukrainian fronts concerned. The medal "For the Liberation of Prague" was awarded to 390,000 men including more than 40,000 Czechoslovak citizens.

In the battles for the liberation of Czechoslovakia the men of the Soviet Armed Forces displayed great physical and moral endurance, and many fell for the freedom and independence of the fraternal Czechoslovak people. More than 140,000 Soviet officers and men died in the 1944-1945 military operations in Czechoslovakia.[1] The Czechoslovak 1st Corps lost more than 4,000 men in the fighting against the common enemy.

Soviet-Czechoslovak comradeship-in-arms, which became the foundation of the inviolable friendship and fraternal co-operation of the Soviet Armed Forces and the Czechoslovak People's Army in the post-war period, was tempered in the fight against fascism, for Czechoslovakia's freedom.

The experience acquired in the joint operations on Czechoslovak territory in 1944-1945 became the corner-stone of post-war co-operation between the armed forces of the USSR, Czechoslovakia, Poland, Rumania and other socialist countries.

Immediately after the rout of the German invaders the liberated Czechoslovak people took to the road of democratic reforms and consolidation of the position of the working people, the working class in the first place, in the administration of the state.

People's Democratic Czechoslovakia began to rise as a single state of equal Slav peoples, the Czechs and the Slovaks.

The principal and guiding role in transforming society was played by the Communist Party of Czechoslovakia which wholly relied on the revolutionary activity of the working class, the peasantry and the working intelligentsia.

The crucial socio-economic reforms carried out in the country on the initiative of the Communist Party of Czechoslo-

---

[1] See *Krasnaya Zvezda*, March 26, 1971.

vakia in 1945, strengthened the people's democratic revolution and ensured its development into socialist revolution. The agrarian reform was launched in June, and in October the government decreed the nationalisation of key industries and large banks, and the initiation of a currency reform.

Following the victory of socialist revolution in 1948, the Czechoslovak people took political power into their hands and set up a dictatorship of the proletariat, inaugurating a new stage in developing people's democracy, socialist construction, with more revolutionary reforms it involved.

Socialist construction in Czechoslovakia unfolded in conditions of the strengthening economic and political co-operation with other countries of the socialist camp headed by the Soviet Union. The war-time comradeship-in-arms of the peoples of the USSR and Czechoslovakia developed into close co-operation and all-round fraternal assistance in post-war period. The Soviet Union furnished large-scale assistance in rehabilitating the Czechoslovak economy which had been seriously dislocated by the nazi occupation and the war.

As the years went by those counter-revolutionary elements that had survived the revolution and did not reconcile themselves to the fact that the country was successfully building socialism, worked on plans to pull the country out of the socialist camp and restore capitalism. In the mid-sixties they launched a vigorous ideological, economic and political struggle against the Communist Party of Czechoslovakia and at the same time prepared for an armed struggle. A grave threat loomed over the Czechoslovak Socialist Republic.

In fulfilment of their internationalist duty the Soviet Union, Bulgaria, Hungary, the German Democratic Republic and Poland, in August 1968 agreed to move their troops into Czechoslovakia in order to help the Czechoslovak people, to protect them against the threat of counter-revolution and the intrigues of reaction and imperialism.

The mighty forces standing guard over socialism, peace and the freedom of the peoples thwarted the designs of Czechoslovakia's enemies, and today no one and nothing can push her off the path of socialist construction. A guarantee of this is the existence of the community of socialist states, their ideological, economic, political and military links and mutual assistance.

Chapter X　　　END OF THE THIRD REICH.
　　　　　　　LIBERATION
　　　　　　　OF THE GERMAN PEOPLE
　　　　　　　FROM NAZISM

1. ON THE EVE
OF DECISIVE BATTLES

NAZI GERMANY'S AGONY

Having reached the Oder and Neisse along a wide front after smashing large German forces in East Prussia, Poland, East Pomerania and Silesia from January to March 1945, the Soviet Army was preparing for a battle for Berlin which was only 60 kilometres away. On the southern wing of the Soviet-German front the Soviet troops had wiped out enemy group at Budapest, liberated the whole of Hungary, a part of Czechoslovakia and the eastern regions of Austria, and were poised for an attack on Germany from the south as well as from the east.

On the Western Front the Anglo-American forces crossed the Rhine at the end of March and, encountering no organised resistance, drove towards Hamburg, Leipzig and Prague. By mid-April they gained the line Bremen-Wittenberge-Magdeburg-Dessau-Chemnitz-Strasbourg and were within 100-120 kilometres from Berlin.

Nazi Germany's days were numbered. Hitlerism was in death agony.

Germany's economic situation had deteriorated sharply. In March her steel output was a mere 15 per cent of the average monthly output in 1944; coal production dropped to 16 per cent and the output of coke to 38 per cent. Her general economic slump had a detrimental impact on war production which in March 1945 dropped 65 per cent as compared with July 1944, and she also lost her last sources of oil.

The military and political situation of nazi Germany, who had lost all her European allies in 1944, was characterised by her complete isolation on the international scene.

Inside the country the political situation had also worsened. The anti-fascists stepped up their struggle in the country, and the Communist Party of Germany headed by the prominent figures of the international Communist and working-class movement, Wilhelm Pieck and Walter Ulbricht, was in the forefront of the progressive forces of the German people. In a radio broadcast on January 25, 1945 Walter Ulbricht urged all anti-fascists to form armed detachments, unite with foreign workers and war prisoners and launch a popular struggle against nazism, for a new, democratic Germany.

On April 14, 1945 the Free Germany National Committee in an appeal to all the enemies of fascism declared: "End the nazis' mad war; the hour of liberation from nazi slavery has struck." A day later it issued a leaflet which said: "The land of socialism—the Soviet Union—and its victorious army, they are our true friends."

Nazi Germany, however, was still a powerful and dangerous enemy. When fighting for Berlin broke out she had 214 divisions on the Soviet-German front, including 34 panzer and 15 motorised, and 14 brigades and considerable stocks of weapons and ammunition.

In view of the military and political situation the nazi leaders intended to prolong the war and stir up contradictions within the anti-Hitler coalition. They were confident that the most unexpected changes could occur in a war of coalitions involving states with different social systems, which could alter the entire situation. Assessing the plans of the German Command at the final stage of the war the West German historian, Kurt von Tippelskirch, a former nazi general who took part in the fighting for Berlin, wrote that it had hopes of "holding out at least until inevitable ... conflicts break out among the Allies".[1] To this end the nazi leadership undertook a number of provocative actions.

In March 1945, for example, it entered into separate negotiations with the Anglo-US Command on the surrender of the German forces in Italy and it was only thanks to the Soviet Government's measures that the true nature of this venture was brought to light and the negotiations broke down. The nazi leadership made another attempt to enter

---

[1] Kurt von Tippelskirch, *Geschichte des zweiten Weltkriegs*, Bonn, 1956, p. 572.

into separate talks with Britain and the United States in the course of the Berlin Operation. They advanced the provocative slogan "Better surrender Berlin to the Anglo-Saxons than let the Russians enter it". In the hope of creating difficulties in the relations between the USA and Britain, on the one hand, and the Soviet Union, on the other, the German forces, at the beginning of April, in effect ceased all resistance on the Western front, and the German Command even shifted the 12th Army from the Western to the Eastern front when the Berlin Operation was already under way.

The Soviet Supreme Command considered that the best way to put an end to the machinations of the nazis was to destroy the Berlin group as swiftly as possible and capture Berlin.

The nazi leaders were fully aware that in order to draw out the war and provoke differences between the Allies they had to frustrate or, at least, hold up the Soviet offensive for as long as possible. This thought was set forth in a special appeal drawn up by the National Socialist (Nazi) Party on April 3 which stated that the outcome of the war was being decided in the East and not in the West, that the forthcoming major Soviet offensive was to be repulsed at whatever the cost and that by holding the Eastern front the German forces could achieve a turning point in the war.

The strategic plan of the nazi leaders was to hold their ground in the East at whatever the cost, check the Soviet offensive, conclude a separate deal with the USA and Britain and avoid unconditional surrender.

Despite heavy losses sustained in the winter of 1945, the German Command towards the middle of April augmented its forces on the Soviet-German front by 15 divisions.

The nazis attached great importance to the defences of Berlin. "The battle for Berlin," Hitler proclaimed, "is the battle for Germany."

The approaches to Berlin were defended by Army Group Wisla (corps-size Group Swinemünde, the 3rd Panzer and the 9th Field armies), the main forces of Army Group Centre (the 4th Panzer and the 17th Field armies) and the air defence forces of the Berlin area. In mid-April these forces had 85 divisions (about a million men), 10,400 guns and mortars, more than 1,500 panzers and assault guns and about 3,300 combat aircraft. The most powerful forces were concentrated in the Forst-Cottbus sector, and, especially, in the Kuestrin (Kostrzyn)-Berlin sector, where the Germans deployed a division per every three kilometres of the front, and had 60 guns and mortars, 17 panzers and assault guns per kilometre of the frontage.

The German Command began to build stable, deeply echeloned defences in February 1945, and when the Soviet troops launched the Berlin Operation, the Germans had already established powerful defences consisting of three lines extending to a depth of 20-40 kilometres along the Oder and the Neisse between the Baltic Sea and the foothills of the Sudeten. Together with the rear defence lines and the Berlin defensive area the total depth of the enemy defences was approximately 100 kilometres.

All towns and large villages were adapted for perimeter defence. A defence area was established around Berlin; it consisted of three circular belts and nine sectors in the city proper. Berlin's defences were organised for sustained resistance, which, as the order concerning the defence of Berlin pointed out, was to be waged with fanaticism and imagination, with resort to every trick, on land, in the air and under the ground.

There is every reason, therefore, to say that the American journalist Cornelius Ryan was making things up when he wrote that "Berlin's defences were an illusion" and that "Hitler and his military advisers" did not "act to fortify the city".[1]

Preparing for the battle for Berlin the nazi leaders strove not only to increase the number of troops there but also to raise their fighting spirit and strengthen their fanaticism. In an appeal to the soldiers of the Eastern front on April 19 Hitler said that he was sure that Berlin would remain a German city. At the same time he demanded that anyone who issued an order to retreat be shot on the spot, whatever his rank or post. "He who at this moment fails in his duty," he declared in the same appeal, "is a traitor to his people."

During the last months of the nazi regime a court martial of the 3rd Military District passed more than 15,000 death

---

[1] Cornelius Ryan, *The Last Battle*, London, 1966, p. 297.

Soviet troops firing a salute
to mark the restoration of
the border with Finland

Commander of the Karelian Front Marshal of the Soviet Union K. A. Meretskov (left) and Commander of the Northern Fleet Admiral A. G. Golovko (sitting). October, 1944

Soviet troops crossing the Norwegian border

Memorial to Soviet troops in
Oslo

Memorial to Soviet troops in
Budapest

Senior Sergeant V. Kosterev
and Junior Sergeant A. Pet-
ryaev hoisting a flag over
liberated Budapest

Soviet forces entering Vienna

Monument to Soviet troops
in the Austrian capital

Commander of the 1st Ukrainian Front Marshal of the Soviet Union I. S. Konev (second from left) and Commander of the 38th Army Colonel-General K. S. Moskalenko (first from left) at Dukla Pass

On the eve of the fighting for the Dukla Pass, 1944. Left to right: Commander of the 1st Guards Army Colonel-General A. A. Grechko, Commander of the 3rd Assault Artillery Division Major-General I. F. Sanko, Member of the Army Military Council Major-General I. V. Vasiliev, Deputy Commander of the 3rd Assault Artillery Division Colonel I. Y. Yevdokimov

Commander of the 4th
Ukrainian Front General of
the Army I. Y. Petrov in the
Carpathians

Soviet and Czechoslovak troops crossing into Czecho-slovakia via the Dukla Pass

Liberated Prague welcomes
the Soviet Army

Memorial to Soviet troops in
Bratislava
Byelorussian   Front.

Military Council of the 2nd Front Commander Marshal of the Soviet Union K. K. Rokossovsky (sitting, centre) and Chief of Staff Lieutenant-General A.N. Bogolyubov (standing). 1945

Commander of the Polish
2nd Army General K. Swierczewski discussing an operational plan with Soviet generals

Soviet sappers in Dresden
removing aerial bombs from
under a bridge across the
Elbe which the enemy intended to blow up

sentences. Moreover, there was a reshuffle among the top nazi officers. Himmler was removed from the post of commander of Army Group Wisla and replaced by Colonel-General Heinrici who was considered as one of the Wehrmacht's foremost experts in the organisation and conduct of defensive battles. At the end of March 1945 Chief of the General Staff of the Land Forces General Guderian was replaced by General Krebs. Prior to Germany's attack on the USSR he had been her military attache in Moscow and was regarded as a foremost authority on the Soviet Army.

Such were the German Command's strategic plans and most important measures to organise the defence of Berlin in the spring of 1945.

PREPARATIONS
FOR THE BERLIN OPERATION

The Soviet Command completed its work on a plan for the capture of Berlin at the end of March and beginning of April 1945.

On April 1 GHQ called a conference with the participation of the commanders of the 1st Byelorussian and the 1st Ukrainian fronts, Marshals G. K. Zhukov and I. S. Konev, and Chief of the General Staff General A. I. Antonov.

General S. M. Shtemenko who was also present wrote that after assessing the military and political situation in the theatre of war J. V. Stalin reached the conclusion that the Soviet troops "'...must take Berlin at the earliest possible date; the operation has to begin not later than April 16 and everything must be over within 12-15 days'. The front commanders agreed and assured GHQ that the troops would be ready on schedule".

The strategic concept of the operation was as follows: supported by long-range aviation, the 2nd and 1st Byelorussian and the 1st Ukrainian fronts were to rupture the enemy defences at a number of points in the area between Stettin (Szczecin) and Pencich, cut up his Berlin group into parts by swift thrusts of powerful groupings and then encircle and destroy it. Within 12 to 15 days of the operation, after capturing Berlin, the advancing forces were to gain the Elbe along a wide frontage, link up with the Anglo-US forces there, deprive Germany of the opportunity of continuing organised resistance, force her to capitulate and thus bring the war in Europe to an end.

Under the general plan of the operation the fronts were set the following tasks.

The 2nd Byelorussian Front was to force a crossing of the Oder, rout the Stettin group of enemy forces and, not later than on the 15th day of the operation, gain the Anklam-Demmin-Malchin-Varen-Pritzwalk-Wittenberge   line. It was to deliver the main attack by three field armies and three tank and one mechanised corps from an area north of Schwedt in the general direction of Strelitz. Conditions permitting, a part of the Front's forces was to exploit the success of the 1st Byelorussian Front by striking out in a southerly direction, compelling the enemy to roll up his defences along the Oder. A part of the Front's forces was to reliably cover the shore of the Baltic from the mouth of the Vistula to Berg Diwenow and from Berg Diwenow to Altdamm.

The task of the 1st Byelorussian Front was to smash the enemy east of Berlin and capture the capital of nazi Germany. Its main attack was to be launched from a bridgehead on the Oder west of Küstrin by four field and two tank armies, which were to reach the Elbe on the 12-15th day of the operation. In support of the main attack two blows were to be delivered, each by two armies, from the north and south. One blow was to be struck from an area northwest of Baerwalde in the general direction of Eberswalde and Sandau for the purpose of outflanking Berlin from the north; the second, from the bridgeheads on the Oder north and south of Frankfort-on-the-Oder in the general direction of Fuerstenwalde and Brandenburg in order to envelope Berlin from the south.

The 1st Ukrainian Front was to cross the Neisse, overpower the enemy forces in the Cottbus area and southeast of Berlin and within 10 to 12 days gain the Beelitz-Wittenberg line and further along the Elbe to Dresden. After the fall of Berlin the Front was to advance on Leipzig. The main blow to be delivered by five field and two tank armies was to be directed from Tribel in the general direction of Spremberg and Belzig. To support the operations of the main group from the south the Polish 2nd Army and part of the 52nd Army were to launch an auxiliary attack from the area of Kohlfurth in the general direction of Bautzen and Dresden. The Front's left-wing forces were to revert to rigid defence.

In view of the situation the preparations for the operation had to be completed within not more than 15 days despite the fact that the fronts had to carry out large-scale regroupings and build up considerable material reserves.

It was also necessary to hasten the beginning of the operation because reactionary circles in the Allied countries, British ruling circles in the first place, hoped to move their forces into Berlin ahead of the Soviet Army. Contrary to the decisions of the Crimea Conference, Winston Churchill insisted on moving the Anglo-American forces to the east of the Elbe. "I consider," he wrote to President Roosevelt on April 1, 1945, "that from a political standpoint we should march as far east into Germany as possible, and that should Berlin be in our grasp we should certainly take it."[1] His plans came to the knowledge of the Soviet Command.

Proceeding from the concept and purpose of the operation the Soviet Supreme Command concentrated enormous forces against Berlin: 19 field armies, four tank and four air armies, about 170 infantry and cavalry divisions, eight separate tank and mechanised corps, a total of 2,500,000 men, more than 41,000 guns and mortars, over 6,300 tanks and 7,500 aircraft. The Soviet forces had a 2.5-fold superiority in men, fourfold in artillery, 4.1-fold in tanks and self-propelled guns and 2.3-fold superiority in combat aircraft over the enemy.

In the first half of April the units were replenished with manpower, weapons and ammunition. Divisional HQ and the headquarters of larger formations were working on problems of co-ordinating the operations of the various arms of the service. Exercises were laid on to prepare the troops for crossing water obstacles, fighting in forests and cities and conducting night battles. Serious attention was focussed on training the troops for operations in Berlin, and a mock-up

---

[1] Winston S. Churchill, *The Second World War, Triumph and Tragedy*, New York, 1962, p. 399.

of the city was built for the purpose. To help spread battle experience the command issued special leaflets to men of all the arms.

The fronts' Party-political departments carried out a great deal of work in the preparatory period, concentrating in the first place on strengthening the Party and Komsomol organisations in the subunits. By the beginning of the operation they had from eight to 20 Communists each. This increase was achieved not only by transferring Communists from logistic establishments and headquarters to the troops in the field, but also as a result of the admission of new members. On the night preceding the offensive more than 2,000 officers and men of the 1st Byelorussian Front applied for Party membership. Preparations for the operation took place at the time when the Soviet Union was getting ready to mark the 75th anniversary of the birth of Vladimir Lenin and lectures and reports on his life and work were delivered in the units.

In an address to the troops on the eve of the offensive, the fronts' Military Councils outlined the Party's position on relations with the German people. It was pointed out that the Soviet soldier would never act like the nazi barbarians and never taint the dignity of a Soviet citizen; he would conduct himself on German territory in a way that the joyous tiding that the Red Army was a liberator army would spread even faster throughout the world.

The Polish 1st and 2nd armies also took part in the Berlin Operation. In the main the preparations for the offensive were completed by the middle of April.

2. THE ROUT
OF THE BERLIN GROUP.
NAZI GERMANY SURRENDERS

THE COLLAPSE
OF THE ODER-NEISSE DEFENCE SYSTEM.
THE ENCIRCLEMENT
OF THE ENEMY GROUP DEFENDING BERLIN

It was April 16, 1945. The troops and the headquarters of the 1st Byelorussian and the 1st Ukrainian fronts were checking the state of preparedness for the forthcoming operation. At 05.00 hours Moscow time, when the Oder was still shrouded in an early-morning mist, flashes lit up the sky over Berlin as the 1st Byelorussian Front began its artillery barrage. At 06.15 hours the artillery of the 1st Ukrainian Front opened up, shattering the air over the Neisse with the roar of thousands of guns, mortars, rocket launchers. At the same time the long-range aviation and the fronts' air squadrons struck a massive blow at the enemy's first and second lines, artillery positions and command posts. The last battle of the Great Patriotic War was on.

To take the enemy by surprise the infantry and armour of the 1st Byelorussian Front attacked before dawn. At 05.20 hours, as soon as the artillery and air bombardment was over, 140 searchlights directed their beams on the positions of the German 9th Army. The defenders were thrown into confusion by this new method of starting an offensive. The infantry and armour of the main group, consisting of the 47th, 3rd Striking, 5th Striking and the 8th Guards armies, under the cover of two rolling barrages, resolutely attacked the enemy positions. Between 06.15 and 06.30 hours the Polish 1st Army went over to the offensive north of Küstrin and the 69th and 33rd armies attacked from the area of Frankfurt to build up the strength of the main offensive. A bitter battle developed in the entire zone of the 1st Byelorussian Front.

By midday the main strike forces had advanced up to eight kilometres, reaching the second line of the enemy's defences along the Zelow Heights but failing to take it in their stride. In the afternoon the 1st Guards and 2nd Guards tank armies under generals M. Y. Katukov and S. I. Bogdanov were committed but still the assault forces could not capture the Zelow Heights on April 16.

The German Command realised that a Soviet penetration of the second line of defence would lead to dire consequences. To discuss the situation on the Eastern Front Hitler called a meeting of all the top-ranking nazis, including Borman, Goering, Doenitz, Keitel, Jodl and Krebs. It opened at 14.30 hours. In his situation report Krebs said that the German defences southwest of Küstrin had been pierced and that Heinrici intended to withdraw his troops from the area. Hitler, however, rejected this plan. The nazi leaders

dispatched the reserves of Army Group Wisla to reinforce
the troops manning the second line of defence and thus
retain their hold on the Zelow Heights. For its part, the Command of the 1st Byelorussian Front took steps to crush the
resistance of the enemy on this line as swiftly as possible.
Tanks and artillery were brought up for a powerful blow.

Fierce fighting for the Zelow Heights was resumed in the
morning. No less heavy fighting was under way north and
south of the Küstrin bridgehead. On that day, April 17, the
61st Army attacked the enemy on the right flank of the
Polish 1st Army. The offensive was now in progress along
the entire 170-kilometre-wide front.

The offensive of the Front's main strike group was preceded by a 30-minute artillery barrage against the enemy
strong-points which were also attacked by 800 bombers of
the 16th, 18th and 4th air armies under the command of
Colonel-General S. I. Rudenko, Chief Air Marshal A. Y. Go-
lovanov and Colonel-General K. A. Vershinin.

By nightfall on April 17, the Soviet troops had crushed
the fiercely resisting enemy, broke through the second line
of defence and captured the Zelow Heights: it had taken
them two days to advance a mere 11-13 kilometres. The
troops of the 1st Byelorussian Front had not gained sufficient space for executing a manoeuvre to split up and encircle
the Berlin group and had not yet overcome the enemy's desperate resistance. On the third day of the operation they had
to resume their efforts to break through the enemy's next
line.

The 3rd Guards and 5th Guards armies and the 13th Army
which made up the strike group of the 1st Ukrainian Front
attacked at 06.55 hours on April 16. They went into action
after a 40-minute artillery barrage under the cover of a
smoke screen laid by the 2nd Air Army along a 300-kilo-
metre front. The enemy was unable to observe the movements
of the Soviet troops or spot their crossing points on the
Neisse.

Under artillery cover the forward echelons crossed the
river, capturing bridgeheads on its left bank. The engineers
quickly put up bridges for the main forces. Resisting stubbornly, the 4th Panzer Army counter-attacked several times
in an effort to dislodge the advanced units from the bridge-

heads and re-establish defence along the Neisse. The Soviet forces repulsed the enemy and at 08.40 hours, after enough troops had crossed the river, they mounted a full-scale attack. At 14.00 hours the front commander committed General P. S. Rybalko's 3rd Guards Tank Army and General D. D. Lelyushenko's 4th Guards Tank Army in order to augment the penetrating power of the Front's strike group.

By the end of the day the group broke through the main line of defence on a 26-kilometre front and advanced 13 kilometres, wedging into the second line. The German Command threw in up to four reserve panzer divisions in an attempt to hold up the offensive of the 1st Ukrainian Front along this defensive line.

In the morning of April 17 Marshal Konev moved in his main armour forces. The enemy's resistance in the second line was crushed. By the end of the day the troops of the 1st Ukrainian Front had pushed ahead 18 kilometres in the crucial direction. Now, in order to gain the Spree and break through the entire depth of the German defences the Front's strike group had to advance another eight kilometres.

The Polish 2nd Army under General Swierczewski and General Koroteyev's 52nd Army which were moving towards Dresden pierced the enemy's defences and advanced up to 13 kilometres in two days of fighting (April 16 and 17).

The Germans made an all-out attempt to stop the Soviet advance on the Spree. The command of Army Group Centre used its reserves and the 4th Panzer Army, which had retreated under Soviet pressure, to defend this line. At the same time it was building up a powerful group near Görlitz which was to attack the 52nd and the Polish 2nd armies and reach Spremberg, which was in the rear of the 1st Ukrainian Front's strike group.

Keeping a careful watch over the fighting for Berlin, GHQ was concerned over the slow advance of the 1st Byelorussian Front that could upset its plan of encircling the Berlin group of enemy forces. This question was discussed by telephone by J. V. Stalin and the commander of the 1st Ukrainian Front I. S. Konev in the evening of April 17. The Supreme Commander-in-Chief ordered Marshal Konev to turn the

3rd Guards and 4th Guards tank armies to the northwest and attack Berlin from the south. These instructions were carried out immediately.

GHQ ordered the 2nd Byelorussian Front to go over to the offensive on April 20 and not later than April 22 strike a blow at Schönebeck, outflanking Berlin from the north.

By striking at Berlin from the southwest and north the 1st Ukrainian and the 2nd Byelorussian fronts could now encircle and destroy the enemy forces even if the 1st Byelorussian Front did not step up the pace of its offensive.

The 1st Byelorussian Front resumed the offensive in the morning of April 18 after a brief artillery bombardment and advanced from 4 to 8 kilometres. On the following day it covered another 9-12 kilometres, having broken through the third line on the Oder. Fighting was very heavy as the German Command continued to pour in fresh forces. From April 16 to 19 it threw in seven divisions, two brigades and up to 30 separate battalions, all from its reserve, in this sector of the front. The extreme intensity of the battles led Hitler into believing that Berlin would be able to hold out for another six or eight weeks.

The Soviet troops, however, broke down the enemy's stubborn resistance. By nightfall on April 21, the 1st Byelorussian Front had ploughed through the entire depth of his defence, right up to Berlin. The greatest gains were made in the zone of General F. I. Perkhorovich's 47th Army and the 3rd Striking Army commanded by Colonel-General V. I. Kuznetsov, whose advance units engaged the enemy on the city's northeastern outskirts.

The right-wing divisions of Colonel-General N. E. Berzarin's 5th Striking Army broke into the city's northeastern part and its main forces in co-operation with General V. I. Chuikov's 8th Guards Army and the 1st Guards Tank Army began to outflank Berlin from the east and southeast.

The advance brigades of the 2nd Guards Tank Army which was co-operating with the 47th Army and the 3rd Striking Army were moving westward, enveloping Berlin from the north.

Reliably backing the offensive of the main strike group the Front's right-wing armies (61st Army under General

P. A. Belov and the Polish 1st Army commanded by General S. Poplawski) by the evening of April 21 had advanced from 20 to 45 kilometres to the west.

The Front's left-wing armies (General V. Y. Kolpakchi's 69th Army and the 33rd Army under Colonel-General V. D. Tsvetayev) which supported the offensive of the main strike force on the left flank had advanced from 8 to 30 kilometres to the west.

As the 1st Byelorussian Front pushed on to Berlin from the east, the 1st Ukrainian Front, in fulfilment of GHQ orders, undertook a manoeuvre to attack Berlin from the south. Having discovered in the course of the offensive that the enemy's strongest positions in the third line of defence along the Oder were in the Cottbus and Spremberg areas, the front commander decided to pierce it and cross the river between these towns.

Building up their pressure, the 3rd Guards and 4th Guards tank armies and Colonel-General N. P. Pukhov's 13th Army in the morning of April 18 reached the Spree, forced it in their stride and captured bridgeheads north and south of Spremberg. As a result, the Soviet tank armies could now move towards Berlin. In just one day, April 19, they advanced from 40 to 50 kilometres and the 13th Army covered 20 kilometres. On April 20 the 3rd Guards Tank Army advanced another 40 kilometres. It captured Baruth, an important town on the road to Berlin, and by dusk reached Wuensdorf 10 kilometres south of Zossen.

The 1st Ukrainian Front's thrust into this area was so swift that High Command of the Wehrmacht and the General Staff of the Land Forces hastily moved from Zossen to Wannsee east of Potsdam, and some of the departments were airlifted to Southern Germany.

To step up the offensive on Berlin and complete the encirclement of the Frankfurt-Guben group in the forest southeast of Berlin, the commander of the 1st Ukrainian Front sent Lieutenant-General A. A. Luchinsky's second-line 28th Army into the battle. On April 21 the 3rd Guards and 4th Guards Tank armies attacked the enemy on the southern sector of the outer defence perimeter, pierced it on the following day and gained Berlin's southern outskirts. The enemy forces defending in Cottbus and north of it were

being outflanked by General V. N. Gordov's 3rd Guards
Army from the south.

The 13th Army and Colonel-General A. S. Zhadov's 5th
Guards Army pushed on westwards towards the Elbe.

In the Dresden sector, from April 19 to 25, the 52nd Army
and the Polish 2nd Army repulsed a powerful counter-attack
launched from Goerlitz.

On April 18 and 19 a part of the forces of the 2nd Byelorussian Front under Marshal K. K. Rokossovsky crossed the
Ost Oder, drove the enemy out of the flood plain between
the Ost Oder and West Oder. On April 20 the Front's main
forces assumed the offensive. Crossing the West Oder they
cracked the enemy defences on its left bank and pressed
westwards, overcoming fierce resistance.

Thus, in the course of six days the three fronts advancing on a 300-kilometre-wide sector tore asunder the enemy's
defences on the Oder and Neisse and inflicted a heavy
defeat on Army Groups Wisla and Centre, the 1st Byelorussian and the 1st Ukrainian fronts destroying more than 20
enemy divisions and paving the way for encircling the enemy
forces in Berlin.

On the night of April 22 GHQ ordered the 1st Byelorussian and the 1st Ukrainian fronts to complete the encirclement of the enemy Frankfurt-Guben group not later than
April 24, and at all costs prevent it from breaking through
to Berlin or to the west or south.

In the meantime, the nazi leaders were doing their utmost
to save Berlin from being taken into a ring. At 15.00 hours
on April 22 Hitler held his last extended military conference
in the Reich Chancellery. According to an entry in the OKW
journal and Jodl's testimony, Hitler decided to withdraw
all the troops fighting against the Anglo-Americans and
throw them into the battle for Berlin, personally supervis-
ing this operation through the OKW.

The 12th Army under General Wenck received orders to
withdraw from the Elbe and strike out towards the 9th Army
on the defensive southeast of Berlin and link up with it.
Keitel was put in command of this operation. Steiner's group
of forces was to advance on Berlin from the north, and
Admiral Doenitz was ordered to airlift sailors to reinforce
the Berlin garrison.

Nevertheless, the nazis failed to prevent the Soviet troops from closing the ring around Berlin. On April 24 the 8th Guards and the 1st Guards Tank armies of the 1st Byelorussian Front linked up with the 3rd Guards Tank and the 28th armies of the 1st Ukrainian Front southeast of Berlin, sealing off the enemy Frankfurt-Guben group. On April 25 the 4th Guards Tank Army of the 1st Ukrainian Front linked up with the 47th Army and the 2nd Guards Tank Army of the 1st Byelorussian Front west of Berlin near Potsdam, to have closed the ring around enemy troops in Berlin proper.

In this way the 1st Byelorussian and the 1st Ukrainian fronts, besides surrounding the enemy's main forces in the area of Berlin, also cut them into two isolated groups: one at Berlin and the other at Frankfurt and Guben.

Another momentous event took place on April 25. On that day the troops of the 5th Guards Army linked up with the advance units of the US 1st Army at Torgau on the Elbe. As a result, the German front was split: the German armies in Northern Germany were cut off from the armies in Southern Germany.

It took the Soviet troops only 10 days to break through the German defences on the Oder and Neisse, encircle the main forces of the Berlin group and create conditions to deal them a death blow.

During the breakthrough of the enemy defences and the encirclement of the Berlin group, internal resistance forces in Germany, braving brutal repressions, appealed to put an end to the senseless and bloody war. In some liberated German towns and villages people welcomed the Soviet troops as liberators. But the internal resistance forces were too weak.

END OF THE ENEMY'S
FRANKFURT-GUBEN GROUP

The Soviet Command forthwith launched an operation to wipe out the encircled groups of enemy forces. The group invested southeast of Berlin was to be cut up and destroyed piecemeal by converging blows delivered by the 1st Byelorussian and the 1st Ukrainian fronts. Anticipating that it might try to break out to the west, commander of the 1st Ukrainian Front Marshal I. S. Konev took steps to organise deeply echeloned defences along possible breakthrough routes. This was a crucial measure because the Frankfurt-Guben group, which was under the command of General Busse, the CO of the 9th Army, had 200,000 men, more than 2,000 guns and mortars and more than 300 panzers and assault guns, and was a formidable force.

This group was to be dealt with by the 3rd, 69th and 33rd armies of the 1st Byelorussian Front and the 28th Army and the 3rd Guards Army of the 1st Ukrainian Front backed by the main forces of the 2nd Air Army and part of the 16th Air Army. In armour and infantry the forces were equal, but the Soviet troops had a threefold superiority in artillery and mortars.

Launched in the morning of April 26 the operation was carried out in extremely difficult conditions. The Soviet troops advanced across heavily wooded terrain with numerous swamps and lakes in the face of powerful resistance from the enemy defending the passages between the lakes and forests.

In an effort to break out of the encirclement and link up with the German 12th Army at whatever the cost, the command of the invested group on the night of April 25 assembled a powerful force (three infantry, a panzer and a motorised division) and concentrated it on a narrow sector of the front, achieving superiority in infantry, artillery and armour. The enemy struck at 08.00 hours on April 26, tore up the Soviet lines and began to move to the west. The troops of the 1st Byelorussian Front managed to seal the breach and isolated this group from the rest of the surrounded forces. Towards the end of the day on April 26 a large part of it was wiped out.

In the following two days the enemy undertook several unsuccessful breakthrough attempts and on April 28 the commander of the German 9th Army reported to the headquarters of the Land Forces: "The breakthrough attempt has failed." On the night of April 28 the Germans made yet another attempt to force a breach, this time committing the greater part of their forces. They attacked at 01.00 hours on April 29. Bloody fighting raged for three days and nights, in the course of which the enemy managed to make some headway in the westerly direction but failed to break out of the encirclement.

As a result of the joint actions of the 1st Byelorussian and the 1st Ukrainian fronts the Frankfurt-Guben enemy group was cut up into small parts which lost contact with each other. The last of these parts was wiped out on May 1 at Belitz, where the German losses amounted to 5,000 killed and 13,000 taken prisoner. All told the Soviet troops killed more than 60,000 of the enemy, and captured 120,000 prisoners, more than 300 panzers and assault guns, 1,500 field guns and a large quantity of small arms, motor vehicles and various material.

By routing the Frankfurt-Guben group the Soviet troops killed the German Command's hopes of breaking the blockade of Berlin. The attempts of the German 12th Army to link up with the surrounded group were foiled by the staunch defence of General D. D. Lelyushenko's 4th Guards Tank Army and the 13th Army commanded by General N. P. Pukhov. Just as unsuccessful were the attempts of the enemy group at Goerlitz to strike in the rear of the 1st Ukrainian Front and impede its westward drive.

THE FALL OF BERLIN

The battle for Berlin was in its culminating stage. The city was completely surrounded by Soviet troops, the outer ring of encirclement being 30 to 50 kilometres away in the west. By April 26 the Soviet troops had occupied all the suburbs and were fighting for the central districts. The situation in Berlin was further aggravated by the fact that its population of two million had enough food to last it only two or three days.

The city's garrison numbered 200,000 men with 3,000 guns and mortars, 250 panzers and assault guns. The Soviet forces had twice as many men, 3.5 times as many guns and five times as many tanks and self-propelled guns.

Anxious to prevent unnecessary loss of life, destruction and the suffering of the Berlin population, the Military

Council of the 1st Byelorussian Front on April 23, 1945
offered the German Command and the command of the
Berlin garrison to cease their senseless resistance. This
humane proposal was turned down and the German Command desperately sought for ways to help the beleaguered
garrison from the outside. This is borne out by an entry in
the OKW journal dated April 25, 1945: "For the High
Command all tasks are now relegated to second place. The
main task is to help in lifting the blockade of the troops in
the capital." Accordingly, on the night of April 25 the troops
received the following directive: "All available troops shall
be thrown against the deadly enemy, Bolshevism. It must
be ignored that Anglo-American troops will be able to
capture considerable territory."

At the same time Hitler sent a telegramme to Doenitz in
which he wrote: "The struggle for Berlin is Germany's fatal
struggle. Compared to it all the other tasks and fronts are
of secondary importance. Therefore, I request you to support
this battle in every way, setting aside, if necessary, all the
other tasks of the Navy and surrendering to the enemy all
the strong-points under your command. Whenever possible,
it is necessary to airlift troops to the city and to bring them
in by sea and land to the fronts fighting at Berlin." Earlier,
the German Command failed in its attempt to use the 12th
and 9th armies and Steiner's group to help the troops defending Berlin.

On April 24, General Weidling, commander of the 56th
Panzer Corps entrusted with the defence of Berlin, received
Hitler's personal instructions to hold the city at all costs.
In their blind, frenzied desire to fight to the end the nazi
leaders were prepared to jeopardise the lives of its 2,000,000
inhabitants.

Since the city had been fortified for a drawn-out defence
and could be held with relatively small forces, the front
commanders decided to strike massive blows at narrow sectors, drive deep wedges into the enemy's defence, cut off
large sections of the city and then destroy the German forces
piecemeal. The Soviet Command decided that this task could
best be fulfilled by assault groups and detachments consisting of infantry and armour and supported by artillery and
engineers.

The storming of Berlin began with concentrated attacks by the bombers of the 16th, 2nd and 18th air armies, after which, on April 26, fierce fighting flared up along the entire perimeter of the city. As the Soviet offensive got under way the troops aimed their powerful blows at the centre of the city. The 1st Byelorussian Front (8th Guards Army, the 1st Guards Tank Army, the 5th Striking and 3rd Striking Armies, the 2nd Guards Tank Army and the 47th Army) deployed between Potsdam and Tempelhof attacked from the east, north and northwest, while the 1st Ukrainian Front (the 3rd Guards and 4th Guards Tank Armies and the 28th Army), which had outflanked Berlin from the south, lashed out towards the north.

The fighting was extremely furious from the outset. In organising the city's defence the German Command calculated that the German troops would bleed the Soviet troops white in hard-fought battles for each city block, each building and each floor, for each factory shop and thus stifle the assault. But nothing came of their intentions.

Realising that the Germans were primarily concerned with defending the streets and put up barricades and laid minefields, for this purpose, the Soviet troops began bypassing these obstacles. On April 26 and 27, as a result of skilful manoeuvres, they drove the Germans out of Tempelhof in the southern part of the city and Moabit in its northwestern part.

The surrounded enemy troops were squeezed into a narrow strip some 2-2.5 kilometres wide, extending 15 kilometres from east to west.

The nazis were thrown into utter confusion. Fully aware that the situation was hopeless Hitler on April 29 wrote his political testament. He expelled Goering and Himmler from the nazi party, removed them from all their posts and appointed Gross Admiral Doenitz as his successor in the capacity of state president and commander-in-chief of Germany's Armed Forces. In view of the sharply worsening situation in Berlin General Weidling submitted a plan for the German garrison to break out of the encirclement. Hitler, however, rejected it and ordered the troops to continue resistance.

Hitler learnt that Italian partisans had captured and executed Mussolini. Fearing that he might suffer the same fate, or be held to answer for his crimes, he committed suicide on April 30.

The battle for Berlin continued. The German resistance was especially stubborn in the city centre where fighting began on April 29. Being the site of government and administrative buildings, including the Reich Chancellery, with Hitler's underground headquarters, and also the Reichstag, a politically important target, this sector had been very carefully organised for defence. Each front, army, division and unit tried to be the first to break through to the Reichstag and raise the banner of victory over Berlin.

By nightfall on April 28 the 3rd Striking Army under General V. I. Kuznetsov was only 500 metres to the northwest of the Reichstag, with the Spree and Koenigsplatz in between.

In the night of April 28 the army began to prepare for the storming of the Reichstag, the final stage of the battle for Berlin. The building was a key strong-point in the city's central sector. All approaches to it were held under fire from small arms and numerous anti-aircraft guns emplaced in the neighbouring buildings and the adjoining square. The Reichstag itself was adapted to perimeter defence. All its windows and doorways were bricked up and embrasured. Its garrison consisted of diehard nazis, a thousand officers and soldiers from various units, mostly marine cadets from Rostock who had been parachuted into the city. It also included artillerymen, pilots and SS and Volkssturm detachments armed with a large number of machine guns, grenades and faustpatronen.

The 3rd Striking Army was all set for a heavy battle.

The task of capturing the Reichstag was assigned to Major-General S. N. Perevertkin's 79th Infantry Corps. By nightfall on April 29 it drove the Germans out of several nearby buildings and advanced to within 300-400 metres of the Reichstag. At night, the troops were bracing themselves for an assault.

At 13.00 hours on April 30 Soviet artillery began to pound the Reichstag. Thirty minutes later the Soviet troops went into attack only to be pinned to the ground by a squall of fire from automatic weapons, heavy artillery and anti-aircraft guns. As a result, they had to make fresh preparations for the assault.

The Banner of Victory over
the Reichstag

Junior Sergeant M. Kantaria
and Sergeant M. Yegorov
who raised the Banner of
Victory over the Reichstag

April 1945. Distribution of food to Berliners

Marshal of the Soviet Union
G. K. Zhukov signs the act
of nazi Germany's unconditional surrender

Soviet and American troops
on the Elbe River

Military Commandant of Berlin Hero of the Soviet Union Colonel-General N. E. Berzarin and Lieutenant-General F. Y. Bokov

Berlin. Memorial to Soviet
troops in Treptow Park

At the initiative of the command and the political division of the 79th Corps two groups of volunteers, each numbering 20 Communists and Komsomol members, were formed and placed under the command of two staff officers, Major M. M. Bondar and Captain V. N. Makov. Their task was to raise the banner of victory over the Reichstag. At 18.00 hours the Soviet troops with artillery support resumed the assault. It was spearheaded by battalions under Captains S. A. Neustroyev and V. I. Davydov and Senior Lieutenant K. Y. Samsonov. The Germans recoiled under their swift and furious onslaught. The Soviet troops broke into the building through the breaches in the walls, windows and doorways, and drove a part of the garrison into the cellars, forcing the remainder to take to the upper floors. Advancing with Captain S. A. Neustroyev's battalion the volunteer group under Captain V. N. Makov, including Senior Sergeants G. K. Zagitov and A. F. Lisimenko and Sergeant M. P. Minin, fought its way to the roof where they raised a red flag. On the night of April 30, on instructions from the commander of the 756th Infantry Regiment, Colonel F. M. Zinchenko, a group of soldiers commanded by Lieutenant A. P. Berest raised the banner of victory on the sculpture group crowning the pediment of the Reichstag. The banner which was attached by Sergeants M. A. Yegorov and M. V. Kantaria fluttered proudly over the vanquished Berlin.

After heavy and bloody battles the Reichstag garrison surrendered on May 2.

NAZI GERMANY SURRENDERS

As the fighting for the Reichstag was in progress other Soviet units continued the battle for the central part of Berlin. Breaking down the enemy's tenacious resistance, they split the surrounded German force into three small, isolated groups which lost all contact with the High Command and found themselves in an absolutely hopeless situation.

Goebbels and Borman who were in Berlin tried to open negotiations with the Soviet Command. On their instructions General Krebs, Chief of the General Staff of the Land

Forces, crossed the frontline at 03.50 hours on May 1 and was brought to the HQ of General V. I. Chuikov's 8th Guards Army. There he met deputy commander of the 1st Byelorussian Front General V. D. Sokolovsky who arrived shortly on Marshal G. K. Zhukov's orders. General Krebs produced a document signed by Goebbels and Borman which was officially informing the Soviet Command that Hitler had committed suicide, that a new government had been formed and that Krebs was authorised to enter into negotiations with the Soviet Command.

In an attempt to win time the nazi leaders proposed an end to the fighting in Berlin. The Soviet Command, however, declared that it could consent to a cease-fire only if the German forces unconditionally surrendered to all the Allies and warned that any further resistance on the part of the Berlin garrison would lead to needless bloodshed and loss of life among the city's population.

At 14.00 hours Krebs left to report the Soviet reply to Goebbels. At 18.00 hours Goebbels and Borman rejected the demand for unconditional surrender. This was yet another manifestation of the nazi leadership's foolhardiness and its complete disregard for the lives of millions of Germans who had entrusted their future to it.

The Soviet Command had no other alternative than resume attacks. At 19.15 hours on May 1, after a powerful 45-minute artillery softening-up the Soviet forces launched a general attack. Fighting lasted throughout the night. On the night of May 1 commander of the Berlin defence General Weidling, who was also commander of the 56th Panzer Corps, sent a truce envoy to inform the Soviet Command that his corps was ceasing resistance and surrendering. The command of the 1st Byelorussian Front demanded that the corps units down arms and surrender by 07.00 hours on May 2. At 06.00 hours General Weidling crossed the frontline and surrendered after ordering the Berlin garrison to capitulate. Shortly Fritsche, Goebbels's first deputy, issued a similar order on behalf of the government.

By 15.00 hours on May 2 the Berlin garrison ceased resistance and towards the end of the day the city was completely in Soviet hands.

German war prisoners led by the once arrogant and self-confident officers plodded desolately through the smoke-filled streets of vanquished Berlin. The *Drang nach Osten* did not end with a parade in Red Square as Goebbels and his propaganda machine had promised so often, but in the utter rout and inglorious surrender of the German forces in Berlin. The city lay in ruins, enveloped in flames and smoke. In 1933, Hitler promised the Germans that within ten years their capital would be unrecognisable. Well, he kept his promise.

Having smashed the Berlin group, the 1st Byelorussian Front took over the zone of the 1st Ukrainian Front, which was preparing to initiate the Prague Operation, and continued to pursue the 12th Army. By May 7 the Soviet troops had gained the Elbe along the entire length of the frontline where they linked up with the US forces. A large portion of the German 12th Army retreated to the river's west bank across pontoon bridges set up by the Americans, and surrendered to them.

Pushing swiftly to the west and northwest, the 2nd Byelorussian Front on May 3 reached the Baltic Sea coast and on May 4 gained the Wismar-Schwerin-the Elde line and linked up with the British troops. On May 5 the Front's forces occupied the islands of Wollin, Usedom and Ruegen and a few days later, together with the Baltic Fleet, liberated the Danish island of Bornholm, winning the gratitude of the people of Denmark.

In March 1946, when the Danish forces began to replace Major-General F. F. Korotkov's 132nd Infantry Corps stationed on the island, the Danish newspaper *Politiken* wrote: "The Russians will leave the best memories of themselves. Their discipline has been exemplary. They came as friends and brought liberation with them. We shall never forget this."

After three weeks of heavy fighting (from April 16 to May 7) the 1st and 2nd Byelorussian fronts and the 1st Ukrainian Front brought the Berlin Operation to a brilliant conclusion. They smashed the entire northern wing of the enemy's eastern front: 70 infantry, 12 panzer and 11 motorised divisions and a large number of combat groups, brigades, separate regiments and battalions, and captured about 480,000 prisoners and large quantities of equipment.

In the furious battles the three fronts lost more than 102,000 officers and men in killed. Their remains now rest in the common graves in Treptow Park and Pankow in Berlin. A magestic figure of a soldier-liberator bearing a saved child, and an allegorical figure of their Motherland, her head inclined in sorrow, have been erected in their memory.

The rout of the Berlin group of German forces and the occupation of Berlin presaged nazi Germany's utter defeat. The fall of Berlin completely paralysed her state and military machinery and deprived her of the opportunity to continue organised struggle.

The banner of victory raised by the courageous Soviet fighting men over the Reichstag signified the end of the grim and sanguinary struggle waged by the Soviet peoples and their Armed Forces under the guidance of the Communist Party in defence of their country and to liberate the enslaved peoples of Europe.

Soviet fighting men who took part in the Berlin Operation displayed high combat proficiency, courage and mass heroism. The title "Berlin" was attached to the names of 187 units which directly participated in the assault on the enemy capital. More than 600 officers and men were made Heroes of the Soviet Union, 13 others were awarded the second, and Marshal G. K. Zhukov and Major I. N. Kozhedub the third Gold Star of Hero of the Soviet Union. All the troops which had taken part in the storming of Berlin were awarded the medal "For the Capture of Berlin" struck especially to commemorate this victory.

Although the fall of Berlin sealed the fate of Hitler's Reich, Admiral Doenitz, who on May 1 assumed the post of Reich President, did his best to continue the war against the USSR at whatever the cost and establish contact with ruling circles in Britain and the United States. His political line was clearly set forth in his radio appeal to the German people on May 1 and his order to the Wehrmacht issued on the same day. In them he spoke about fighting on two fronts, but made it understood that military operations on the western front were of secondary importance and were to be terminated in the immediate future. In his address to the Army he said that he had assumed supreme command over all the units of the Wehrmacht, that he was resolved to continue the struggle against the Bolsheviks until the military units and hundreds of thousands of families in the east of Germany were saved from enslavement or destruction; referring to the British and Americans he said that he was forced to fight against them insofar as they hindered his struggle against the Bolsheviks.

On May 2, his government decided to "capitulate piecemeal", i.e., to surrender in the west and to continue operations against the Soviet Army. His representatives contacted British Commander Montgomery on the matter of ending hostilities in the whole of Northwestern Germany. At 08.00 hours on May 5 German armed forces in the Netherlands, Northwestern Germany, Schleswig-Holstein and Denmark downed arms and ceased operations against Montgomery's 21st Army Group. In this connection the HQ of the Wehrmacht Supreme Command wrote: "By downing arms in Northwestern Germany, Denmark and the Netherlands we are motivated by the fact that the struggle against the Western Powers has lost its meaning. In the East, however, the struggle continues. . . ."

The same day witnessed the capitulation of Army Group F under Colonel-General A. Loehr operating in Croatia and Southern Austria, and General F. Schulz's Army Group G fighting in Bavaria and Western Austria.

Army Group C under Colonel-General Vietinghoff in Northern Italy had surrendered several days earlier, on May 2.

In the hope of negotiating a separate capitulation of the entire southern group of German forces to the Americans, Doenitz sent his representative Friedeburg to Eisenhower. But the US Command turned down the proposal. Then Doenitz sent Jodl to Eisenhower in Rheims. The latter said that the surrender of the German troops was to be signed immediately on all the fronts and declared that if this demand was not fulfilled he would resume military operations in the north where they had been suspended with Montgomery's consent.

Jodl signed the preliminary protocol on the capitulation of all German forces on May 7 at Rheims. But this act was not final.

Recalling these historic events, Marshal Zhukov wrote that on May 7 he received a telephone call from Supreme

Commander-in-Chief J. V. Stalin who told him that Jodl had signed the act of unconditional surrender at Rheims and said that since it was the Soviet soldiers who had shouldered the main burden of the war and not the Allies, the surrender ought to be signed by the Supreme Commands of all the countries of the anti-Hitler Coalition, and not only by the Supreme Allied Command.

The Soviet Supreme Command proposed that the act signed in Rheims should be viewed as a preliminary protocol of surrender and to conclude the unconditional capitulation in the capital of the nazi state, Berlin. The Allied Supreme Command agreed.

On May 8 representatives of all the Allied Armies arrived in Berlin's suburb of Karlshorst. The Soviet Command was represented by Marshal G. K. Zhukov, the British by Chief Air Marshal A. W. Tedder, the US Armed Forces by Chief of the Strategic Air Force General C. Spaatz and the French Armed Forces by the Commander of the French Army General Delattre de Tassigny. At midnight on May 8 Field-Marshal Keitel, Admiral of the Fleet von Friedeburg and Colonel-General of the Luftwaffe Stumpf signed the act of Germany's unconditional capitulation. The "Thousand-year Reich" came to an ignominious end after existing for 12 years, four months and eight days bringing to a close one of the darkest pages in Germany's history. Hitler Germany was smashed militarily, politically, economically and morally.

The war in Europe was over. A new day, May 9, the day of victory, dawned, opening limitless prospects for peaceful democratic development before the peoples of Europe, including the German people, which had been liberated from the nazi yoke.

3. THE DEMOCRATIC DEVELOPMENT
OF THE GERMAN PEOPLE

LIBERATION OF THE GERMAN PEOPLE
FROM NAZISM. NEW TASKS

The German people were now confronted with the crucial problem of choosing the road of further development. The masses did not know which way to turn.

It was the Communist Party of Germany which had worked out its general line of struggle for the country's democratic revival, when she was still under nazi rule, and showed the German people the way out of the situation. An especially important role in this respect was played by Party Conferences in Brussels in 1935 and Berne in 1939, and the activity of the Free Germany National Committee which was established in 1943 and operated under the guidance of the Communist Party. In 1944, the Party's Central Committee drew up the Programme of Struggle to Achieve the End of the War, for Peace and the Establishment of a Free Germany and the Programme of Action of the Bloc of Fighting Democrats which laid down guidelines of the activity of the democratic forces at the final stage of the war and in the post-war period. In these documents the Communist Party set the following tasks to the German people: depose Hitler, smash the imperialist machinery of violence, punish the war criminals, pursue a peaceful foreign policy, recognise Germany's obligation to compensate for the losses she had inflicted on other countries in the war, develop a powerful people's democratic rule, place the economy at the service of the people, resolve the chaos and establish stable order, uproot imperialism, nazism and militarism, and re-educate the German people in the spirit of democracy.[1]

The Programme of Action of the Bloc of Fighting Democrats was destined to play an exceptionally important role in Germany's post-war development, for it indicated the way of building up a mass popular movement capable of eradicating nazism and creating a new, democratic Germany in the specific post-war conditions arising from the presence of the troops of the occupying powers and the probable alignment of class forces. The Programme envisaged joint efforts of the main classes and sections of the population in towns and villages—the workers and the peasants, the petty bourgeoisie and intellectuals.

In February 1945, as the end of the war was already in sight, the Political Bureau of the Central Committee of the Communist Party of Germany set up a commission under

---

[1] See *Geschichte der deutschen Arbeiterbewegung*, Vol. 5, Berlin, 1966, p. 420.

the chairmanship of Walter Ulbricht to work out directives for Germany's anti-fascist and democratic reorganisation and draft the main guidelines for the activity of the anti-fascists in the areas occupied by the Soviet Army.

In its activity the Communist Party of Germany proceeded from the joint decisions of the Allied Powers concerning Germany's post-war organisation adopted at the Crimea Conference.

During preparations for the Berlin Operation and particularly when it was in progress, the members of the Central Committee of the Communist Party of Germany and the Free Germany National Committee were vigorously laying the foundation for first practical measures ensuring anti-fascist, democratic reorganisation in the regions occupied by the Soviet Army. On April 30, 1945 a group of leading functionaries headed by Walter Ulbricht returned to Germany and set to work in Berlin.

After resolving matters of Germany's occupation by the Allies, the Soviet Military Administration in Germany (SMAG) assumed supreme authority in the Soviet Zone of Occupation. From the very first day, i.e., June 9, 1945, it acted as a class ally of the country's popular masses. It permitted the formation of democratic parties and organisations, the establishment of local self-government bodies and helped to bridle the forces of reaction. Order No. 2 of June 10, 1945 issued by chief of the Military Administration Marshal G. K. Zhukov stated:

"1. Permit the establishment and activity in the Soviet Zone of Occupation in Germany of all anti-fascist parties working for the complete eradication of nazism and the strengthening of democratic foundations and civil liberties in Germany and the promotion of corresponding initiative and activity of the broad masses of the people.

"2. Grant the working population in the Soviet Zone of Occupation in Germany the right to unite into free trade unions and organisations for the purpose of upholding the interests and rights of the working people. Grant the trade union organisations and associations the right to conclude collective agreements with employers, and also to set up insurance offices ... mutual aid, cultural, educational and other institutions and organisations. . . .

"5. In line with the above all nazi legislation will be abolished and also all nazi directives, orders, ordinances, instructions, etc., concerning the activity of anti-fascist political parties and free trade unions and directed against democratic freedoms, civil rights and interests of the German people."

At the same time the Western Occupation Authorities banned all political activity of the German population in their zones.

Relying on the support of the Soviet Military Command, the Political Bureau of the CPG Central Committee on June 11, 1945 issued an appeal to the working population in towns and villages. The appeal, which in effect was a concrete programme of action in conditions arising from the defeat of Hitlerism, pointed out that "Hitler's total war was the most unjust, the most barbarous and the most criminal war in the history of mankind", that "Hitler's greatest war crime ... was the treacherous, predatory attack on the Soviet Union which had never wanted a war with Germany and which, beginning with 1917, on more than one occasion had proved that it was a sincere friend of the German people".[1]

The appeal noted that Hitler was not the only one responsible for the crimes committed against humanity, that the blame for them also lay with all those Germans, men and women, who had submissively and indifferently allowed Hitler to seize power, wreck all democratic, and first and foremost workers', organisations and to clamp in dungeons, torture and execute the best sons of the German people. The responsibility lay with those Germans for whom Germany's greatness was in her armament and who had regarded militarism, military drill as the nation's only happiness and boon.

In the first place, stated the appeal, it was necessary to stamp out the last vestiges of Hitler's regime and his party; combat hunger, unemployment and homelessness; re-establish self-government bodies along democratic lines; protect the working people against the arbitrariness of the employers; confiscate the property of the nazi leaders and war cri-

[1] Walter Ulbricht, *Zur Geschichte der neuesten Zeit*, Vol. I, Berlin, 1955, pp. 370-72.

minals; abolish large landed estates and distribute land to land-hungry peasants and farm-hands; transfer all key utilities (transport, gas, water, power, etc.) to self-government bodies; recognise the undertaking to compensate for the damage caused by Germany to other countries.

Thus, the programme provided for extensive democratic reforms and the destruction of the foundations of German imperialism. The German Communist Party carried out these tasks by drawing all the democratic forces in the country into political activity. By the middle of July 1945, a united People's Front had been created in the country on the basis of the concerted actions of the four political parties which existed at the time: the Communist Party, the Social Democratic Party, the Christian Democratic Union and the Liberal Democratic Party. A united committee of 20 members (five from each party) was established to coordinate their activity.

A most important achievement in Germany's democratic development in the first post-war years was the smoothing over of the split in the German working-class movement through the establishment of unity of action of the Communist and the Social Democratic parties and the formation in April 1946 of a single Marxist-Leninist party of the working class—the Socialist Unity Party of Germany (SUPG).

Speaking at the unifying congress, Wilhelm Pieck noted: "The closing of the rift in the German working class and the merger of both parties into the Socialist Unity Party of Germany is an event of enormous historical importance for the German working-class movement and for the entire German people, too. We are putting an end to decades of discord between brothers in the socialist working-class movement and are re-establishing its unity. In this way we are creating a great force which will enable the working class to assume leadership of our people in the matter of re-establishing Germany, promoting genuine democracy, in establishing guarantees ensuring peace within the German people itself and also in laying the groundwork for building socialism."[1]

The Socialist Unity Party of Germany adopted the firm

---

[1] Walter Ulbricht, *op. cit.*, p. 313.

line of building socialism. But this proved to be possible only in the eastern part of Germany which the Soviet Armed Forces had entered. The two lines in Germany's development—one in the east, the other in the west—became manifest as early as the end of 1945.

In East Germany all denazification measures were carried out consistently and to the end, and the working people acquired broad democratic freedoms. The democratic reforms there led to the establishment on October 7, 1949 of the German Democratic Republic (GDR), the first peace-loving socialist state of workers and peasants in Germany's history. It was set up in reply to the division of Germany into two parts by the Western Occupation Authorities and the merger of the three Occupation Zones in the west (American, British and French) into the Federal Republic of Germany (FRG).

The Western Occupation Authorities did not uphold the democratic aspirations of the German people and went back on the agreed decisions reached at Crimea and Potsdam concerning Germany's post-war organisation. Pursuing their selfish, imperialist interests, they made sure that the omnipotence of the capitalist monopolies was preserved in West Germany. In contrast to the peace-loving socialist German Democratic Republic, the FRG is a capitalist state whose armed forces are an important part of the aggressive NATO bloc.

Of late, however, serious changes have taken place here. The FRG signed treaties with the USSR and the Polish People's Republic, which recognise the inviolability of the post-war frontiers; relations between the FRG and the GDR are being normalised on the basis of the recognition of their status as sovereign states; an agreement has been reached on West Berlin, and relations between the Federal Republic and Czechoslovakia and other socialist states are improving.

Such were the two lines which characterised the post-war development of East and West Germany.

SOVIET ASSISTANCE
TO THE GERMAN PEOPLE

The USSR did not seek a war with Germany and made every effort to avert it. In the war which was imposed by the nazi leaders the Soviet Union lost 20 million people and about 30 per cent of its national wealth. But the Soviet people, who were brought up in the spirit of proletarian internationalism, were never motivated by a desire to wreak vengeance on the German people.

The Soviet Union had no selfish interests towards Germany. The Soviet Armed Forces entered her territory for the sole purpose of fulfilling the agreed decisions of the Allied Powers, completing the rout of Hitlerism, helping the German people to cast off the nazi yoke, saving humanity from falling prey to nazism, making any further aggression by German imperialism impossible, granting democratic rights to the people and enabling it independently to solve all problems of democratising life and organising its state structure.

Internationalism manifested itself in all the actions of the Soviet Armed Forces, in the directives of the State Defence Committee of the USSR, GHQ, in the orders and appeals issued by the Military Councils of the fronts and armies and the concrete measures which were carried out in the course of the Berlin Operation and after Germany's defeat.

On January 19, at the time when the Soviet troops were fighting at the Vistula and Oder and driving towards Germany's borders, the People's Commissar of Defence of the USSR, J. V. Stalin, demanded that the German population should not be treated harshly.

The Soviet Army entered Germany as her liberator and not as conqueror. In this grim war the Soviet troops retained their noble spirit and humane qualities despite the fact that in almost every Soviet family someone had either been killed or crippled.

By unleashing the criminal war, the Hitlerite clique not only forced the German people to pay for it in blood but also placed it in extremely difficult material circumstances. The Soviet Government and the Command of the Soviet Armed Forces could not be indifferent to the suffering of the German people and did everything in their power to help them to return to normal life and to supply them with food in the first place, especially in Berlin, where the food shortage was most acute.

Speaking at a meeting on the occasion of the establishment of the Magistrate, General N. E. Berzarin, the first commandant of Berlin, said that when on April 25, 1945 his troops approached Berlin, J. V. Stalin's instructions to supply the Berliners with food had already been received.

It was extremely difficult to keep the almost three million Berliners supplied with food, since they required 24,000 tons of flour and 2,700 tons of grain and macaroni, not counting other products, a month.

To help solve this problem quickly and effectively, A. I. Mikoyan, member of the State Defence Committee and Vice-Chairman of the USSR Council of Ministers, and General A. V. Khrulev, Chief of Logistics of the Soviet Army, arrived in Berlin on May 9, 1945 on instructions of the State Defence Committee.

New daily rations were issued to the Berliners: workers performing hard manual work or those working in unhealthy conditions received 600 grammes of bread, 80 grammes of cereals and macaroni, 100 grammes of meat, 30 grammes of fats and 25 grammes of sugar; other workers received 500 grammes of bread, 60 grammes of cereals and macaroni, 65 grammes of meat, 15 grammes of fats and 20 grammes of sugar. The rest of the population received 300 grammes of bread, 30 grammes of cereals and macaroni, 20 grammes of meat, 7 grammes of fats and 15 grammes of sugar. Besides, each person was issued from 400 to 500 grammes of potatoes daily and 400 grammes of salt a month. Rationed coffee and tea were also issued. Scientists, engineers, doctors, people working in the fields of culture and art and also top officials of the city and district self-government bodies and the administrative personnel in industry and transport were entitled to the same rations as workers engaged in hard manual work or those working in unhealthy conditions. Other technical personnel, employers, teachers and clergymen received the same rations as those issued to the workers employed at ordinary enterprises. Special rations were distributed to people undergoing treatment in hospitals. A. I. Mikoyan ordered that 200 grammes of milk were to be issued daily to children under 13 years of age.

To supply the Berliners with food the 1st and 2nd Byelorussian and the 1st Ukrainian fronts set aside out of their own stocks 105,000 tons of grain, 18,000 tons of meat products, 4,500 tons of fats, 6,000 tons of sugar and 50,000 tons of potatoes (to be rationed over a period of five months) and 4,000 tons of salt and 350 tons of coffee (one-month rations).

The food supply problem was solved in an incredibly short period of time. Shops and stalls were opened at 08.00 hours on May 15, 1945 and began distributing food to the population, thus putting an end to all provocative rumours.

In keeping with a decision of the Military Council of the 1st Byelorussian Front 1,000 lorries, 100 motor cars and 1,000 tons of fuel and lubricants were handed over to Berlin self-government bodies. The logistical agencies of the Soviet occupation forces and Berlin's first commandant, General N. E. Berzarin, together with Walter Ulbricht's group and the local authorities, put in a vast amount of work to open theatres, cinemas, cafes, restore transport facilities, power supply and telephone service, put industrial enterprises into operation, bring in coal, improve the sanitary services and carried out other measures to normalise life in the city as quickly as possible.

It was indeed a titanic job. One of the leaders of the German Democratic Republic, Hermann Matern, said in those days that the population lacked a concrete idea of the tremendous efforts exerted by Soviet servicemen to help the Germans return to normal life, to overcome the aftermath of the catastrophe and to guide Germany on to a new road.

Only a socialist state could have pursued such an unselfish policy with regard to a conquered country. As regards the Anglo-American authorities, their attitude to the German people was totally different.

That many high-ranking British and American officials were not in the least inclined to help the German people was clearly indicated in President Truman's Directive to the Commander-in-Chief of the United States Forces of Occupation of May 10, 1945 which stated: "Germany will not be occupied for the purpose of liberation but as a defeated enemy nation."

In drafting its reparations plan, the Soviet delegation declared at the Crimea Conference on February 5, 1945, "the Soviet Government has always had in mind the creation of conditions ensuring the German people an average European level of life in the post-war period".

Taking into account the interests of the German people, the Soviet Union renounced a major part of the reparations to which it was entitled. Two hundred out of the 600 munitions factories subject to dismantling in the Soviet Zone of Occupation were left intact at the request of the Socialist Unity Party of Germany. At the beginning of 1947 a third of them were turned over to the Laender governments. In May 1950 another 23 factories were turned over to the German people; in May 1952—66, and in January 1954 the remaining 33.[1]

At the Potsdam Conference the Soviet side insisted on the immediate establishment of a central German government but the Western Powers prevented this from taking place. In this connection the Soviet Military Administration in October 1945 granted the newly formed provincial and Laender authorities the right to promulgate laws and ordinances. The Soviet Military Administration introduced the principle of equal pay for equal work, ensured full equality of women, took steps to protect juvenile labour and established an 8-hour working day.

Describing the Soviet Command's assistance to the German people, Walter Ulbricht said: ". . . at the time the German people could not firmly rise to its feet without outside help. The population of the German Democratic Republic will never forget the selfless peaceful work of the Soviet commandants and officers who had only recently fought at the fronts against the nazi forces; now with unprecedented energy they set about assisting the Germans, prompting them to work purposefully and selflessly. This fittingly crowned the liberation mission of the Soviet troops. . . .

"Millions of Germans are grateful to the Soviet Government and the Soviet Army for taking these broad measures once again which, this time after the termination of hostilities, saved millions of lives. Many Berliners recall with gratitude the Soviet soldiers who gave out bread and soup to the German population while fighting was still going on.

---

[1] See Stefan Doernberg, *Kurze Geschichte der DDR*, Berlin, 1964, pp. 44-46.

Foodstuffs provided by the Soviet Army helped the population of such large cities as Berlin and Dresden survive the
initial and the most difficult period."[1]

GDR—OUTPOST OF SOCIALISM

The formation of the German Democratic Republic, the
first socialist state of workers and peasants ever to arise on
German soil, became a turning point in the history of Germany and also in the history of Europe: the German
Democratic Republic is the first peaceful German state which,
for the first time in German history, does not threaten the
security of its neighbours, and is a reliable bulwark in the
common struggle of all the peace-loving peoples of the
world.

At the same time the birth of the German Democratic
Republic overturned the treacherous plans of the British and
American imperialists to inveigle the whole of Germany into
fresh aggressive actions against the forces of democracy and
socialism. These plans were expounded in a most straight-
forward manner by Henry Morgenthau, former Secretary of
the Treasury in the Roosevelt Administration, author of
plans of the division of Germany into a number of states.
". . . We need Germany," he wrote, "as a bulwark against
Russia and Communism."[2]

The German Democratic Republic has covered a glorious
road since its establishment. Guided by the Marxist-Leninist
Socialist Unity Party of Germany the working class and the
working peasantry carried out vitally important reforms
which led to the abolition of monopoly rule and the establishment of genuine people's rule.

"The victory of the Soviet Army and its Allies over Hitler's nazism," said Walter Ulbricht at a meeting in Berlin
on the occasion of the 20th anniversary of the GDR, "offered
us great opportunities to do away with the former cycle:
crisis-revival-war, and create guarantees ensuring that war
would never again start from German soil."[3]

---

[1] Walter Ulbricht, *op. cit.*, p. 63.
[2] Henry Morgenthau, Jr., *Germany Is Our Problem*, New York,
1945, p. 89.
[3] *Neues Deutschland*, October 7, 1969, p. 3.

Commander of the 2nd Far
Eastern Front General of the
Army M. A. Purkayev (cen-
tre) and Member of the
Front Military Council Lieu-
tenant-General D. S. Leonov

Military Council of the Pacific Fleet. Right to left: Member of the Military Council Lieutenant-General S. Y. Zakharov, Fleet Commander Admiral I. S. Yumashev and Chief of Staff Vice-Admiral A. S. Frolov

Pyongyang. A joyous wel-
come for the Soviet forces

Soviet forces in Dalny

Soviet representative General
K. N. Derevyanko signs the
act of Japan's unconditional
surrender

Memorial to Soviet troops in
Mukden

Victory salute in Moscow

June 24, 1945. Victory Parade in Moscow Red Square. Soviet soldiers casting Wehrmacht banners to the foot of the Lenin Mausoleum

As a result of the confiscation of the property of nazi and war criminals, which was carried out on the basis of a national plebiscite, more than 3,000 large enterprises had been turned over to the people by the end of 1947; 3,000,000 hectares of landed estates were parceled out to former farm-hands, land-hungry peasants and settlers. An estimated 520,000 former active nazis were removed from responsible posts in government and economic bodies and war criminals were tried and convicted.

By 1967, the GDR was already one of the world's ten most highly developed industrial countries for the volume of industrial production. It is the world's leading producer of lignite, the second largest producer (after the United States) of chemical products and ranks fifth in Europe for the output of electric power.

Socialist relations of production are dominant in the GDR: the socialist sector embraces 85.7 per cent of industrial and handicraft production, and 86 per cent of the effective area is cultivated by agricultural co-operatives.

All democratic parties and organisations: the Democratic Peasants' Party, the National Democratic Party, the Christian Democratic Union, the Liberal Democratic Party, the Confederation of Free German Trade Unions, the Union of Free German Youth and the Democratic Women's League of Germany are united around the Socialist Unity Party of Germany in the single National Front of Democratic Germany.

In its greetings to the Eighth Congress of the Socialist Unity Party of Germany, the Central Committee of the Communist Party of the Soviet Union wrote: "The profound social changes in the German Democratic Republic are of fundamental significance for the future of social progress, peace and security in Europe."

The German Democratic Republic consistently pursues a peaceful foreign policy. With other socialist states it firmly upholds the cause of peace. Its armed forces, as a part of the defensive Warsaw Treaty Organisation, are a bulwark of the common struggle of all the freedom-loving peoples of the world.

Hostility and distrust towards the Soviet Union which nazism had sown among the German people are now a

thing of the past. Today close bonds of fraternal friendship
bind the peoples of the Soviet Union and the German
Democratic Republic. Their relations are founded on proletarian internationalism, full equality and non-interference
in each other's internal affairs.

Chapter XI

LIBERATION
OF NORTHEAST CHINA
AND KOREA

1. THE MILITARY
AND POLITICAL SITUATION
IN THE FAR EAST
AND SOUTHEAST ASIA
IN THE SUMMER OF 1945

JAPAN'S AGGRESSION
AGAINST THE COUNTRIES OF EAST
AND SOUTHEAST ASIA
AND THE MILITARY OPERATIONS
OF THE ALLIES IN THE PACIFIC

As a result of tsarist Russia's defeat in the Russo-Japanese War of 1904-1905, Japan consolidated her positions in the Liaotung Peninsula, tore away the southern part of Sakhalin from Russia and imposed completely her rule over Korea.

Imperialist Japan's further aggressive designs were set forth in blunt terms in a memorandum drawn up by the head of the Japanese cabinet, General Tanaka, in 1927. "To conquer China," the memorandum stated, "we must first conquer Manchuria and Mongolia. To conquer the world, we must first conquer China. If we are able to conquer China, India and also the South Seas countries will fear us and capitulate before us. The world will then understand that East Asia is ours and will not dare to dispute our rights. . . . Having gained possession of all of China's resources, we shall proceed to the conquest of India and the South Seas countries, then to the conquest of Central Asia, and, lastly, Europe."

The memorandum stated that war between Japan and the Soviet Union was inevitable. "The programme of our national development," Tanaka emphasised, "will evidently make it necessary to cross swords with Russia." Developments showed that the Tanaka memorandum was a programme of Japan's subsequent policy and strategy.

In September 1931 the Japanese forces attacked China without formal declaration of war. By the end of the year they had fully occupied her northeastern provinces (Manchuria) and reached the borders of the Soviet Union and the Mongolian People's Republic. In March 1932 the puppet state of Manchoukuo was proclaimed on the occupied territory of China. On July 7, 1937 the Japanese provoked an incident and used it as a pretext to attack Yuanning in Central China, opening a new stage in the war against the Chinese people and creating a major seat of war in the Far East.

In the summer of 1938 the Japanese imperialists invaded the Soviet Union at Lake Khasan. But the defeat which was inflicted on them in the course of this provocation taught them nothing. Disregarding the warnings of the Soviet Government and the Protocol on Mutual Assistance signed on March 12, 1936 at Ulan Bator by the USSR and Mongolia, the Japanese militarists in May 1939 attacked the Mongolian People's Republic at the Khalkhin Gol.

Extending their Munich policy of non-interference to the Far East, the USA, Britain and France regarded imperialist Japan as a shock force in the struggle against the USSR in that part of the world.

On April 13, 1941 the USSR and Japan signed a five-year neutrality pact. Nevertheless imperialist Japan, which had joined the aggressive Rome-Berlin axis, had no intention to abide by the pact. Her stand became clear three days after nazi Germany's attack on the USSR, when in a conversation with the Soviet Ambassador Foreign Minister Matsuoka stressed that the Tripartite Pact was the foundation of Japan's foreign policy and if the present war and the neutrality pact came into conflict with this foundation and with the Tripartite Pact, the neutrality pact would be null and void.

The Japanese imperialists calculated that the USSR, relying on the neutrality pact, would shift a large portion of its troops stationed in the Far East to the Soviet-German front and also that nazi Germany would swiftly rout the Soviet Army. The Japanese General Staff planned to annex the Soviet Union's Far Eastern territories, and to divide the Soviet Union between nazi Germany and imperialist Japan along the Omsk meridian. Such, in particular, was the 1941 plan code-named Kan-Toku-En (Special Exercises of the Kwantung Army). In view of the expansionist intentions of the Japanese militarists, the Soviet Union was forced to maintain up to 40 divisions in the Far East while fighting a grim war against the nazi troops.

In the autumn of 1941, however, Japanese ruling circles

saw that nazi Germany's war against the USSR was acquiring a drawn-out character. Taking this into account, they
decided to "postpone" their attack on the USSR, but went
ahead with their aggressive plans against the USA and
Britain. On December 7, 1941 Japan opened hostilities
against the USA with the intention of seizing its colonies in
Southeast Asia and the Pacific basin.

In the first five months of the war the Japanese won a
series of easy victories: they captured Malaya, Singapore,
a part of New Guinea, Burma, the Philippines and Hong-
kong, occupied Guam, Wake, New Britain, Solomon and
other islands and from Burma invaded the Chinese province
of Yunnan. In this period Japan captured a vast territory of
4,242,000 sq. km., with a population of more than 200 million. Together with the occupied regions of China she controlled 9,801,000 sq. km., with approximately 400 million
inhabitants.

The war in the Pacific proved that Lenin was correct
when he wrote in 1920 that in that part of the world things
were heading towards an imminent clash between America
and Japan and that there were "quite definite indications
that the struggle is developing and making war between
America and Japan inevitable...".[1]

The Soviet Army's historic victories in 1942 and 1943
forced Japan to postpone and then give up her plans of
using a favourable situation on the Soviet-German front to
invade the USSR. And yet she continued to regard an attack
on the Soviet Union as one of the basic aims of her policy
and weakened neither her purposefulness nor her preparations for that offensive.

Soviet victories on the Soviet-German front created
favourable conditions for Allied operations in the Pacific and
also for the development of a people's war of liberation in
the Pacific countries enslaved by Japan.

In the spring of 1944, Japan's situation in the Pacific had
sharply deteriorated. Her troops were forced to withdraw
from Attu, Kiska, Solomon, Gilbert and Marshall islands,
a large part of New Guinea, New Britain and a number of
other strategically important territories.

---

[1] V. I. Lenin, *Collected Works*, Vol. 31, p. 46ʃ

Japan's strategic position became even more complicated in early 1945. Military operations had shifted from the central and southwestern parts of the Pacific to the South China Sea and the immediate approaches to Japan. Having re-captured the Philippines, the US forces severed Japan's sea communications with the South Seas. As a result, oil and oil products could only be brought to Japan via Indochina and China. A direct threat now hung over the Japanese forces in Indonesia, Indochina, on the islands of Hainan, Taiwan, Ryukyu and on China's east coast.

In March 1945, the US forces captured Iwo Jima. On April 1 they landed on the west coast of Okinawa and after three months of heavy fighting gained possession of the whole island. At the beginning of May 1945 the Allied troops liberated a large part of Burma, considerably weakening Japan's defences in other Southeast Asian countries.

And yet, in spite of their victories in the Pacific Ocean and Southeast Asia, the Allies did not inflict a decisive defeat on the Japanese invaders.

SOVIET ASSISTANCE
TO THE CHINESE PEOPLE
IN ITS WAR AGAINST JAPAN

When Japan attacked China in July 1937 Japan's rulers were sure that they would win the war quickly. But they were compelled to wage a drawn-out war against the Chinese people fighting for their national liberation; the war lasted almost eight years, passing through three successive stages: (1) strategic defence (July 1937-end of 1939); (2) strategic balance of forces (beginning of 1940-August 1945), and (3) counter-offensive undertaken by the Chinese people's armed forces following the entry of the Soviet troops in the war against the Kwantung Army. The Japanese ruling circles had no chance of defeating China in a drawn-out war which was bound to exhaust Japan's manpower, mineral, food and financial resources. The progressive forces in the world were united in their censure of the war which the Japanese imperialists waged in China and the Chinese people was offered their support, and above all the support of the Soviet Union.

In the mid-thirties the Soviet Government repeatedly strove to make China's ruling circles realise the need for joint efforts to avert war in the Far East. In April 1937 the Soviet Ambassador in China D. V. Bogomolov informed China that the USSR was prepared to sign a non-aggression pact and an agreement on mutual assistance with China and also offered her a loan of 50 million Chinese dollars for her defence needs. On July 5, 1937, the Soviet Government proposed that China, the USSR, the USA, Japan, Britain and France signed a regional pact of mutual assistance. But these proposals did not elicit a positive response from China's ruling circles.

Following Japan's attack on China and the spread of the national liberation war of the Chinese people against the Japanese invaders, the Communist Party of China (CPC) began to urge the Chiang Kai-shek Government to establish closer relations with the USSR. In its programme published on July 23, 1937, the CPC called for the immediate conclusion of a military and political alliance between China and the USSR. At the time the CPC leadership did not advance the thesis about "reliance on its own forces" and adhered to Comintern positions.

"The Land of Soviets," wrote the Communist *Ming Pao*, "had lived up to the expectations of the Communists and the Chinese people. It was the first to support China at the time of mortal danger. The Chiang Kai-shek Government was compelled to agree to negotiations that resulted in the conclusion on August 21, 1937 of a five-year treaty of non-aggression between the USSR and Chinese Republic which would be automatically extended for the ensuing two years." This Treaty was of major significance for the Chinese people, for it inaugurated "a new era in the relations between China and the USSR and in relations between other countries".[1] The Chinese people regarded the conclusion of the Treaty as a form of assisting China in her war against the Japanese invaders.

In September 1937 the Kuomintang, which pursued a policy of indecision and concessions to the aggressors and irreconcilability towards China's progressive forces, was

---

[1] *Ming Pao*, August 30, 1937.

compelled to enter into an agreement with the CPC on joint actions in the anti-Japanese war. Despite the fact that the Chiang Kai-shek Government opposed arming the people and organising a nation-wide rebuff to the Japanese invaders, the establishment of accord inside the country was a matter of enormous political importance.

The Western countries furnished Japan with economic and political support from the outset of her attack on Central and Northern China till the outbreak of the war in the Pacific Ocean.

Only one country, the Soviet Union, assisted China. Approximately a month after Japan's invasion of Inland China the Soviet Government offered China a loan. Subsequently it was agreed that the USSR would grant China a credit of US $ 500 million to be furnished over a period of several years.

China used the first loan to purchase arms and equipment for more than 20 divisions. Their delivery was started in October 1937 though the agreement on the first loan of $ 50 million was signed in March 1938. This was an unprecedented case in international practice. In July 1938 and June 1939, the USSR and China signed agreements on fresh loans of $ 50 and $ 150 million, respectively. At the request of the Chinese delegation, which arrived in Moscow in September 1937, the Soviet Government expedited the delivery of the first consignment of aircraft. The first 225 aircraft, including 62 medium-range bombers, 155 fighters and eight training aircraft, were to be delivered between September 25 and October 25, 1937. In the first stage of the anti-Japanese war China received 885 combat aircraft of various types from the Soviet Union.[1]

China also used her first loan and a part of the second one ($ 78,160,000) to purchase 82 tanks, 700 motor vehicles, 690 artillery pieces, 3,900 light and heavy machine guns, large quantities of shells, ammunition and aerial bombs, etc., all of which were delivered by the middle of February 1939. By September China had received a large consignment of weapons, including 250 artillery pieces, 4,400 machine guns, 500,000 shells and 150,000,000 rounds of small-arms ammu-

---

[1] *The Chinese Year Book, 1944-1945*, Shanghai, 1946, p. 315.

nition. The importance of these weapons could be judged
from the fact that in May 1939 China had 1,359 guns and
about 40,000 machine guns of various types. By 1940 the
Chinese Government had used up Soviet credits to the sum
of $ 173.2 million.

In rendering assistance to China the USSR proceeded from
the basis that in the final count it was not assisting the
Chinese Government but the Chinese people who were fighting for independence, since alongside the government troops
Soviet weapons were made available to the Communist-led
people's armies. This strengthened the position of the democratic forces, restrained Japanese aggression and created conditions for the development of a successful revolutionary struggle of the Chinese people against the Chiang Kai-shek clique.

But when a prolonged lull set in on the fronts of the
Kuomintang armies, and Chinese reactionaries switched their
efforts on breaking away from the United Anti-Japanese
National Front, the Soviet Union was forced to withdraw
its assistance to China and in 1940 suspended deliveries
under the third loan.

Soviet volunteer pilots and military advisers gave the
Chinese people substantial assistance. In the middle of
February 1939, there were 3,665 Soviet military experts in
China and in the summer of 1939 another 400 volunteer
pilots and aircraft mechanics arrived in the country.

Many of them, including 200 volunteer pilots, gave their
lives for the freedom and independence of the Chinese
people.

The group of Soviet military advisers in China included,
among others, V. I. Chuikov, P. S. Rybalko, P. F. Batitsky,
and A. I. Cherepanov. Many Soviet citizens, volunteer pilots
in the first place, who did much to enhance the country's
air defences were decorated by the Chinese Government.
For courage and exemplary fulfilment of their internationalist duty the Soviet Government awarded orders and medals
to several hundred volunteers, eleven of whom received the
title of Hero of the Soviet Union.

The Soviet Army's shattering rebuffs to the Japanese
forces at Lake Khasan in 1938 and at the Khalkhin Gol in
1939 gave the Chinese people fresh strength in its war against
Japan. They overturned the plans of the Japanese militar-

ists, inspired the Chinese people to fight even more resolutely and forced the Japanese forces to suspend their offensive
operations in Northern and Central China.

When nazi Germany attacked the Soviet Union the
people's liberation armies in China, the Kuomintang and
the Japanese forces in China fixed their attention on the
developments on the Soviet-German front fully aware that
the realisation of their plans depended entirely on the outcome of the titanic battles of the Soviet people. In these
circumstances the further presence of Soviet military advisers and volunteer pilots in China became meaningless.
Many Soviet citizens returned home, and in March 1942,
Soviet Military Attache, V. I. Chuikov, who had served as
adviser to the Supreme Commander-in-Chief of the Chinese
Army, was recalled.

The Chinese public opinion highly assessed Soviet aid
to China. A Chinese journal wrote: "There was a steady
stream of weapons, petrol and lorries from the northwest.
The sons of the Soviet Union modestly and unostentatiously
shed their blood ... in defence of China." Soviet aid to the
Chinese people received high praise even after the Chinese
Revolution in 1949. One of the books published in Russian
in Peking noted in this connection: "Since the beginning of
the war of resistance not a single government of any
imperialist power accorded us real assistance. Only the Soviet
Union rendered us large-scale assistance with its manpower,
material and financial resources."[1]

Yet, in spite of considerable assistance from the USSR,
the Kuomintang troops and the national liberation forces
beginning with 1940 undertook no active military operations
against the Japanese invaders.

Moreover, after nazi Germany's attack on the Soviet
Union, Mao Tse-tung who by then had strengthened his
position in the CPC, went back on the Party's internationalist duty to the world communist movement. In September
1941, at the most difficult moment of the Soviet Army's
struggle against the nazi invaders, he, in fact, turned down
the direct request of the Comintern and the CPSU for CPC
actions to avert a Japanese attack on the USSR.

---

[1] *On Chinese-Soviet Friendship*, Peking, 1950, p. 6.

In February 1942, instead of consolidating forces to rebuff the Japanese invaders, Mao Tse-tung launched what was called the "movement for putting the Party's style of work in order" ("cheng fen") which was essentially anti-Soviet and spearheaded against the Party's cadres adhering to Leninist positions and proletarian solidarity.

RESISTANCE
OF THE ENSLAVED PEOPLES
OF SOUTHEAST ASIA

The motive force of the Resistance Movement of the peoples in Japanese-occupied territories was the broad masses led by communist and other progressive parties, and the national bourgeoisie.

The national liberation movement in Southeast Asia attained its greatest scope in French Indochina, especially in Vietnam, in the Philippines and Burma.

At the head of the struggle of the Vietnamese people stood the Vietnam Independence League (Vietminh) which was established on the initiative and under the guidance of the Communist Party of Indochina. In December 1944 the first detachment of "propaganda by arms" under the command of Vo Nguyen Giap was formed on the basis of partisan groups in the mountains and forests of the Cao Bang Province. Simultaneously, another anti-imperialist military organisation, the Army of National Liberation, was formed. The creation of the people's armed forces played a very significant role in the national liberation struggle in Vietnam.

In the face of mounting resistance against the occupation regime, the Japanese Government was forced to resort to subterfuges, one of which was the proclamation on March 9, 1945 of Vietnam's "independence" under Emperor Bao Dai. The situation in the country was discussed at a plenary meeting of the Central Committee of the Communist Party of Indochina held from March 9 to 12 under the chairmanship of Ho Chi Minh. Representatives of the North Vietnam Patriotic Forces at a conference in April decided to merge the armed groups into a single Vietnam Liberation Army which launched military operations against the invaders. By June 1945, a large area embracing six provinces with a million inhabitants had been liberated. Following the unsuccessful Japanese punitive expedition against the Vietminh forces in May 1945, the 5,000-strong Liberation Army in co-operation with guerrilla detachments mounted a successful counter-offensive and by the end of July 1945, drove the Japanese out of a large part of North Vietnam. The flames of the anti-Japanese struggle also swept into Central and South Vietnam.

The Resistance forces were growing in the Philippines, too. In February 1942, thanks to the strenuous efforts of the Communists, a National Anti-Japanese United Front was formed which proclaimed a non-sparing war on the Japanese invaders, their puppets and traitors. On March 29 the Provisional National Council of the United Front convened a conference of freedom fighters at which it united all the operating detachments into the Hukbalahap.[1] Shortly after the conference this army came under the command of prominent members of the Communist Party Luis Tarus, Chairman of the Hukbalahap Military Committee, and Casto Alejandrino, his deputy, and in May 1942 Mateo del Castillo was elected its Political Commissar. It was then that the Hukbalahap, which was a disciplined people's army, mounted military operations in the provinces of Central Luzon.

When the US forces landed in the Philippines in October 1944, the Hukbalahap was in control of the situation on the country's main islands. In Luzon it had 20,000 armed fighters and another 50,000 were in the reserve; it was equipped with captured Japanese weapons and also managed to organise the production of its own rifles and shells. By then it had already fought 1,200 engagements, in which the Japanese invaders lost 25,000 officers and men in killed. In early 1945 the Hukbalahap numbered approximately 100,000 men.

The Soviet Army's historic victories over the German invaders in Europe did much to stimulate the anti-Japanese struggle in Burma. By August 1944, the Anti-Fascist People's Freedom League had been formed in the country. It included the Communist Party with its guerrilla detachments, the National Revolutionary Party of the Burmese bourgeoisie and other parties and public organisations. At the head of

---

[1] Short for Hukbong Bayan Laban sa Hapon, which in Tagalog means People's Anti-Japanese Army.

the League stood the Supreme Council representing the Communist and National Revolutionary parties and the Burma Defence Army. At the end of March 1945 the League emerged from the underground to head a national uprising in which an active role was played by guerrilla detachments and the Burmese National Army. Together with the British Army they drove the Japanese out of Burma. In May 1945 the armed forces of the Anti-Fascist People's Freedom League were the first to enter the country's capital, Rangoon.

The national liberation struggle against the Japanese invaders gained scope and scale also in Malaya and Indonesia. It had a diversity of forms and contributed to the rout of the Japanese forces and then to the establishment of national independence.

THE JAPANESE COMMAND PLANS
TO CONTINUE THE WAR
AGAINST THE ALLIED STATES

At no time during the Second World War did Japanese imperialism remove from its agenda the question of attacking the USSR. Between 1941 and 1945, the Japanese General Staff on three occasions revised its plans of war against the USSR, but their concept was invariably based on offensive operations. All of them assigned an important place to Northeast China and Korea, which were viewed as convenient springboards for aggression against the USSR, and in which the Japanese military had built up a powerful military-industrial base in the event of possible military operations.

In its preparations for war against the Soviet Union the Japanese Command attached considerable importance to building communications, air bases and airfields.

Whereas in 1931 Manchuria had 6,140 kilometres of railways and almost no motor roads, by 1945, the Japanese had built 13,700 kilometres of railways and 22,000 kilometres of motor roads. The railways could carry 90 troop trains, that is, to transport up to two Japanese divisions daily to the USSR border. In these years the Japanese also built 20 air bases, 133 airfields and 265 landing strips; altogether these 418 landing sites could handle more than

6,000 aircraft. Moreover, to accommodate the huge army which was to attack the Soviet Union, the Japanese built many cantonments that could house from 55 to 60 divisions, 150 hospitals with 75,000 beds and many supply bases and depots.

The Japanese Command decided to carry through a new plan of war. In the Pacific theatre of operations the Japanese troops reverted to defence in order to halt the advance of the US-British forces and prevent their landing in Japan, thus shortening the over-extended frontlines. The Japanese forces operating in Central China were to attack people's liberation armies and complete the long-continuing occupation of Central and South China. In Northeastern China and Korea the Japanese troops were to be on the defensive and be ready to launch offensive operations.

Under this plan the Japanese troops were to put up a stubborn resistance against the Soviet Army along a number of lines. Only in the face of overwhelming superiority of the Soviet troops were they to retreat to the Tumen-Changchun-Mukden-Chinchow line, where they were to take up stable defences, thwart the Soviet Army's advance in the southerly and southeasterly directions, retain their hold on Korea and the southeastern part of Manchuria as bridgeheads for active operations.

For this purpose Japan kept more than 5,365,000 men under arms, of whom 4,100,000 were in the ground and air forces, and 1,265,000 in the navy.[1] Of the total number of land troops 1,856,000 were stationed in Northeastern China and the occupied territories of Inland China, 490,000 were in the Southeast Asian countries, 338,000 in the Pacific islands and 1,416,000 in Japan proper. The main forces of the navy and the naval air arm were stationed at bases in Japan.

The backbone of the land forces deployed on the mainland were troops forming the Kwantung Army which consisted of the 1st and 3rd fronts (army groups), the 4th Separate Army, the 2nd Air Army and the Sungari Flotilla. After hostilities had broken out in Manchuria, the 17th Front

---

[1] See: *Japan's Economy in War and Reconstruction* by Jerome B. Cohen, New York, 1949, p. 288.

stationed in Korea and the 5th Air Army were incorporated in the Kwantung Army. All told, the Kwantung Army had 28 infantry divisions, eight infantry brigades, one special brigade (kamikaze)[1], one tank brigade and two air armies[2]— 1,040,000 officers and men, 1,155 tanks, 5,360 artillery pieces, 25 warships and 1,800 aircraft. Moreover, the commander-in-chief of the Kwantung Army was in command of the Manchoukuo Army, the troops of Inner Mongolia and the Suiyuan Army Group. Altogether these forces consisted of 13 infantry and cavalry divisions, 14 infantry and cavalry brigades and four separate cavalry regiments, a total of 280,000 men.

In the south of the Sakhalin Island and the Kurile Islands there were three Japanese infantry divisions, one infantry brigade, a separate infantry regiment and a separate tank regiment. All these forces were incorporated in the 5th Front which was subordinated directly to Imperial Headquarters and consisted of 100,000 officers and men, 60 tanks, 440 guns and mortars and seven aircraft.

So, in Manchuria and the adjoining areas the enemy concentrated four fronts and one separate army. Together with the Manchoukuo Army, the Inner Mongolia armed forces and the Suiyuan Army Group the Japanese had 1,420,000 effectives, 1,215 tanks, 6,700 guns and mortars, 25 warships and 1,907 aircraft. On top of that the Japanese Command concentrated its strategic reserves consisting of two field armies (from 6 to 8 divisions) at Peking which, if necessary, could be transferred to Northeast China.

Taking into account the specific features of the theatre of war and the great length of the border between Northeast China and the USSR and Mongolian People's Republic, the Japanese Command held the Kwantung Army's main forces

---

[1] Kamikaze, or suicide units, were formed for the purpose of killing enemy officers and destroying tanks, motor vehicles and other equipment. They attacked enemy officers from ambush and killed them with knives or daggers, and blew up tanks and other machines by throwing themselves under them with bundles of hand grenades, TNT and other explosives. Usually the kamikazes operated in small groups or singly.

[2] The 2nd Air Army was deployed in Manchuria and had up to 1,200 aircraft, the 5th Air Army which had approximately 600 aircraft was stationed in Korea.

in the Manchurian plain and deployed a third of its strength in the frontier zone calculating that the counter-attacks of its main forces would stop the Soviet Army and force it to revert to the defensive. After that the Japanese Command intended to launch a sweeping counter-offensive and invade the Soviet Far East. There was also a variant of the plan under which the Kwantung Army was to withdraw under the blows of the Soviet Army into Korea. There it was to set up a stable defence along the Tungminchang (Tumangan) and the Yalu Kiang (Amnokkan) rivers to avert the threat of an Anglo-US invasion of Japan, undertake an offensive against the Soviet Army and retrieve the lost territory.

The Japanese Command, however, considerably under-estimated the strength of the Soviet forces in the Far East. It hoped to inflict heavy losses on the Soviet troops on the Manchurian border and to smash by powerful counter-blows those divisions which managed to break through into Manchuria. A prominent Japanese general, commander of the 3rd Front Murakami, subsequently testified that "according to the plan worked out after May 1945, the advancing Red Army troops were to be engaged in a decisive battle along the Changchun-Zepingkai (Supingchieh)-Mukden line. ... Should the Soviet troops be defeated at Changchun and Mukden, the front's main forces were to pursue them along the railway (Chinese, Eastern Railway) to Karymskaya Station. ... The 1st Front was to push towards Khabarovsk, Nikolsk Ussuriisky (Voroshilov) and Vladivostok."

The military and political situation in the summer of 1945 was unfavourable for imperialist Japan, the organiser of a seat of war in the Far East. Her partners in the Tripartite Pact had already been routed, and the arduous and hopeless eight-year war in China, the four-year war in the Pacific and in Southeast Asia had gradually exhausted her economy. In view of the growing shortage of strategic raw materials she had to cut back ship-building and the production of armaments, military equipment and ammunition. Her great material losses in the war in China and the Pacific were not replenished.

Nevertheless, the Japanese imperialists would not concede defeat and conducted intensive military operations in the Pacific and in Southeast Asia. They still held strategically important regions in Northeast China and Korea where they concentrated a third of their ground forces and did not intend to weaken the million-strong group poised for action against the USSR and the Mongolian People's Republic.

2. THE USSR ENTERS THE WAR IN THE FAR EAST AGAINST IMPERIALIST JAPAN

THE SOVIET UNION FULFILS
ITS ALLIED COMMITMENTS

The United States and Britain, which kept postponing the opening of a second front in Europe during the years of the Soviet people's struggle against nazi Germany, tried hard to induce the Soviet Union to enter the war in the Far East at the earliest opportunity. Since the fragmentation of the forces of the anti-Hitler coalition could prolong the war against nazi Germany, the Soviet side at the Tehran Conference of the Heads of Allied Powers which took place at the end of 1943 agreed to enter the war against Japan only after nazi Germany's defeat.

The Crimea Conference (February 4 to 11, 1945) reviewed the military and political situation in Europe and Asia at the final stage of the war against nazi Germany, concerted plans for the final rout of the German and Japanese aggressors and formulated the fundamental principles of post-war peace and international security.

It also resolved the question of the Soviet Union's entry into the war in the Far East. The agreement which was signed on February 11, 1945 envisaged that the Soviet Union would join the war against Japan two or three months after Germany's capitulation, and on the following conditions:

"1. The *status quo* in Outer Mongolia (The Mongolian People's Republic) shall be preserved;

"2. The former rights of Russia violated by the treacherous attack of Japan in 1904 shall be restored, *viz.*:

"a) the southern part of Sakhalin as well as all the islands adjacent to it shall be returned to the Soviet Union;

"b) the commercial port of Dairen shall be internationalised, the pre-eminent interests of the Soviet Union in this port being safeguarded and the lease of Port Arthur as a naval base of the USSR restored;

"c) the Chinese-Eastern Railroad and the South-Manchurian Railroad which provides an outlet to Dairen shall be jointly operated. . . .

"3. The Kurile Islands shall be handed over to the Soviet Union."[1]

On April 5, 1945 the Soviet Government denounced the Neutrality Pact with Japan. In a statement giving the reasons for this move it said: ". . . the situation has been basically altered. . . and Japan, an ally of Germany, is aiding the latter in her war against the USSR. Furthermore, Japan is at war with the USA and Britain, which are the allies of the Soviet Union."

The Soviet Union's denunciation of the Neutrality Pact brought about the fall of the Japanese cabinet. But the new cabinet which was formed on April 7, 1945 by Admiral Suzuki also ignored the Soviet warning.

Japanese generals continued to adhere to this position and shrill about their confidence in Japan's ultimate victory even after nazi Germany's capitulation.

The Soviet Union's entry into the war to expedite the rout of Japan was further discussed at the Potsdam Conference of the three heads of government. Britain and the United States had no cause to doubt the position of the USSR, for the Soviet Government always considered itself by duty bound to fulfil its pledges to the Allies.

On July 26, 1945 a declaration was signed at Potsdam on behalf of the USA, Great Britain and China, calling upon Japan to surrender unconditionally. The Soviet delegation received a copy of the declaration only on the day it was signed. This fact mirrored the complexity of the relations between the USSR and its Allies. On the one hand, the United States would have liked the USSR to join the war against Japan, and, on the other, it did not want Soviet participation in resolving problems of Japan's post-war organisation. Striving to establish its own, undivided control over Japan's

---

[1] *The Tehran, Yalta and Potsdam Conferences*, p. 145.

post-war development the US Government resorted to atomic blackmail in the hope that the atom bomb would "make Russia more manageable".[1]

The United States decided to use the atom bomb, although it was obvious that the course of the Second World War and the Soviet Union's impending entry into the war in the Far East predetermined Japan's fate. President Truman gave the order to this effect prior to the signing of the Potsdam Declaration. On July 28 Japan rejected the Declaration and thus provided the necessary pretext for the US atom-bombing of Hiroshima and Nagasaki. Wholly unjustified from the military standpoint, this act was intended to further the selfish designs of the United States.

THE POLITICAL OBJECTIVES
OF SOVIET MILITARY ACTIONS
AGAINST JAPAN.
GHQ'S CONCEPT OF THE OPERATION

On August 8 the Soviet Government declared that as of August 9 it would consider itself in a state of war with Japan. A day later, on August 10, the Mongolian Government declared war on imperialist Japan and committed 80,000 troops for action.

The USSR and Mongolia entered the war against Japan motivated by the desire to eradicate the last seat of the Second World War as quickly as possible and with it the constant threat of an attack on them by the Japanese imperialists, by the desire to liberate, jointly with the Allies, the Japanese-occupied territories, spare the people further sacrifices and destruction which would be inevitable in a protracted war, and return to the Soviet Union Southern Sakhalin and the Kuriles which had been seized by Japan and hasten the establishment of universal peace.

Thrown into a state of confusion by the Soviet Union's declaration of war, Japanese ruling circles on August 9 and 10 in a feverish atmosphere discussed the question of accepting the terms of the Potsdam Declaration. The Japanese

---

[1] *Command Decisions,* Washington, 1960, p. 510.

25*

Army and the Navy, however, received orders to get ready for offensive operations.

The entire Soviet people enthusiastically approved the Soviet declaration of August 8, 1945.

By the end of June 1945 GHQ completed work on the plan of the operation in the Far East. The Soviet forces were to strike at the Kwantung Army with three converging blows aimed at the centre of Manchuria. The thrust from Trans-Baikal territory, from the Tamtsak salient in Mongolia, was to be delivered by the Trans-Baikal Front consisting of four field armies, a tank army and a Soviet-Mongolian cavalry and mechanised group; the 2nd Far Eastern Front (two field armies[1] and a separate infantry corps) was to advance from the area southwest of Khabarovsk; and the 1st Far Eastern Front (four field armies, a task force and a mechanised corps) was to strike out from Maritime Territory. The plan was to surround, dismember and wipe out the enemy.

The Trans-Baikal Front, which was assigned the decisive role in routing the enemy, spearheaded its thrust at Mukden (Shenyang), Changchun and Port Arthur, all key points in the Japanese defences whose fall spelled the end of hostilities. Striking out from Maritime Territory the 1st Far Eastern Front was to advance on Kirin along the shortest route to meet the Soviet troops driving from Trans-Baikal Territory. The offensive of the 2nd Far Eastern Front in the Amur area helped cleave and subsequently smash the Kwantung Army.

BUILD-UP FOR THE OPERATION

In keeping with a GHQ decision the Kwantung Army was to be smashed by the Trans-Baikal and the 1st and 2nd Far Eastern fronts operating in conjunction with the Pacific Fleet and the Amur Flotilla. High Command of the Soviet Forces in the Far East headed by Marshal A. M. Vasilevsky was in charge of the operation in which the troops of the Mongolian People's Revolutionary Army under Marshal

---

[1] The 16th Army was to defend the shore of the Tatar Strait. At the same time a part of its forces in conjunction with the sailors of the Pacific Fleet were to liberate the southern part of Sakhalin Island.

Choibalsan and Lieutenant-General Tsedenbal[1] also took part.

The three fronts consisted of 11 field armies, a tank army, three air armies and a task force, numbering 80 divisions (including six cavalry, two tank and two motorised infantry), four tank and mechanised corps, six infantry and 40 tank and mechanised brigades and the garrisons of fortified areas. All told, the Soviet side put up 1,578,000 men, more than 26,000 guns and mortars and nearly 3,500 combat aircraft. The Pacific Fleet had 427 warships and more than 1,500 aircraft. The Amur Flotilla numbered 83 warships. Three Air Defence armies were deployed to support the operations of the land forces.

The Soviet-Mongolian forces had a 1.1-fold superiority over the enemy in manpower, a four-fold superiority in guns, seven-fold superiority in tanks and self-propelled guns and a 2.5-fold superiority in aircraft.

3. LIBERATION
OF NORTHEAST CHINA

ROUT OF THE MAIN FORCES
OF THE KWANTUNG ARMY
IN NORTHEAST CHINA

The news about the Soviet Union's entry into the war against imperialist Japan was welcomed as a practical step to assist the peoples of Asia suffering under the yoke of the Japanese colonialists, and the first to hear it were the peoples of China.

In an address to the Chinese people just before the operation began, Commander-in-Chief of the Soviet Forces in the

---

[1] Being General Secretary of the Central Committee of the Mongolian People's Revolutionary Party, Yumzhagiin Tsedenbal was Head of the Political Department of the Mongolian People's Revolutionary Army. The Mongolian troops taking part in the operation were placed under the control of the Commander of the Trans-Baikal Front and were incorporated into the mixed cavalry and mechanised Soviet-Mongolian group commanded by Colonel-General I. A. Pliyev whose second-in-command in charge of the Mongolian troops was Deputy Commander-in-Chief of the Mongolian People's Revolutionary Army Lieutenant-General Z. Lkhagvasuren.

Far East Marshal A. M. Vasilevsky underlined: "The Red Army, the army of the great Soviet people, is coming to the assistance of its Chinese ally and the friendly Chinese people. Here, in the East, too, it is raising its standards as the army bringing liberation to the peoples of China, Manchuria and Korea from Japanese oppression and slavery."

On August 8, 1945 the Main Command of the People's Liberation Army of China sent a telegram to the Chairman of the USSR Council of Ministers, J. V. Stalin. "On behalf of the Chinese people," it said, "we warmly welcome the Soviet Government's declaration of war on Japan. The 100 million inhabitants and the armed forces in the liberated areas of China will in every possible way co-ordinate their efforts with those of the Red Army and the armies of other allied states in bringing about the rout of the hated invaders."

The three fronts went over to the offensive in the night of August 8. In the morning the Soviet Air Force delivered massive strikes at key railway junctions and military targets in Harbin, Changchun and Kirin. Having crossed the state border along a broad front, the Soviet troops smashed the Japanese security elements and entered Northeast China simultaneously from the west, north and east. The Pacific Fleet began to prepare landing operations and its aircraft and torpedo boats attacked ships and coastal defences in the ports of Yuki, Rashin and Seishin on Korea's northeast coast.

The population of Japanese-occupied Northeast China joyfully greeted the Soviet troops. In a cable to the Soviet Government the leaders of the Northeast China Committee of Salvation of the Motherland and the volunteer units in the liberated regions wrote: "We whole-heartedly approve of and thank the Soviet Army which had come to Tungpei[1] to liberate the people of Tungpei. The people of Tungpei will do everything they can to help the Soviet Army wipe out the Japanese aggressors and their henchmen in China."

The first day of the offensive brought the greatest success to the Trans-Baikal Front under Marshal R. Y. Malinovsky. Pushing forward in the overpowering heat of roadless semi-deserts, its units, co-operating with the troops of the Mongolian People's Revolutionary Army on their right flank,

---

[1] Tungpei—Chinese term for Northeast China.

crushed the enemy's resistance in all sectors. Having wiped
out the Japanese covering forces, the Front's strike group,
consisting of the 6th Guards Tank Army under General
A. G. Kravchenko, the 17th Army under Lieutenant-General
A. I. Danilov and the 39th Army under Colonel-General
I. I. Lyudnikov, surged forward.

By nightfall Soviet tanks advanced from 120 to 150 kilometres, and the forward units of the 17th and 39th armies
covered a distance of 60-70 kilometres. Japanese resistance
was the strongest at Tsitsihar which was of auxiliary importance. Relying on a line of strong-points following the Argun
river, the enemy tried to stem the offensive of General
A. A. Luchinsky's 36th Army. In stubborn fighting, however,
the Soviet forces swept through the Chalainor-Manchurian
fortified area, crossed the Argun and struck towards Hailar,
forging ahead 40 kilometres.

The 1st Far Eastern Front under Marshal K. A. Meretskov was pushing forward through the roadless taiga. On the
night of August 8 its advance units wedged between the
flanks of the fortified areas and smashed enemy strong-
points. In the morning of August 9 the Front's strike force
consisting of the 1st Army under Colonel-General A. P. Be-
loborodov and the 5th Army commanded by Colonel-General N. I. Krylov made a thrust towards Harbin. Upon piercing the zone of border fortifications, they advanced 20 kilometres. Lieutenant-General N. D. Zakhvatayev's right-wing
35th Army on the first day of the offensive crossed the Ussuri
and the Sungacha, negotiated a swampy region and advanced 12 kilometres. Colonel-General I. M. Chistyakov's
25th Army fighting on the left wing also advanced 12 kilometres.

General M. A. Purkayev's 2nd Far Eastern Front attacked
in the direction of Sungari and Jaoho. The 15th Army under
Lieutenant-General S. K. Mamonov, operating together with
the Amur Flotilla, forced the Amur north of Tungkiang.

Thus, on the first day Soviet and Mongolian forces attacked the Kwantung Army on land, sea and in the air along
the entire frontier with Northeast China and the east coast
of North Korea.

The successes of the Soviet Armed Forces in the Far East
created favourable conditions for the People's Liberation

Forces of China to go into action. On August 11, commander-in-chief Chu Teh ordered the 8th People's Liberation
Army to mount a counter-offensive.[1]

The Soviet offensive, however, was so swift that it was
all over with the Japanese forces before the 8th People's
Liberation Army had completed its preparations. Moreover,
it turned out that the operations of the Soviet fronts, the
Trans-Baikal in the first place, began just in time to extri-
cate the 8th People's Liberation Army in Manchuria from a
very precarious situation. A week prior to the Soviet Union's
entry into the war, considerable Japanese forces had surrounded the units of the 8th Army under General Chao
Wen-chin in the area of Pingchuan. They comprised a considerable portion of the troops in the liberated area which
were under the command of General Li Yun-chang and it
was only the swift thrust of the Soviet 17th Army that prevented the enemy from smashing the surrounded units of
the 8th People's Liberation Army of China.

"We are most grateful to the Red Army of the Soviet
Union," wrote General Chao Wen-chin to the 17th Army
Command. "We were in an exceptionally difficult position.
Having massed vastly superior forces, the enemy surrounded
us, severed all retreat routes and restricted our possibility to
manoeuvre. The Red Army saved us from destruction and
we are especially grateful to it."

Having broken down enemy resistance in all sectors the
Trans-Baikal Front by August 14 had crossed the Great
Khingan Mountains and the arid Chakar Desert. Advanc-
ing from 250 to 400 kilometres into Northeast China, it
reached the line Changhsing-Tolun-Tapanshang-Paicheng
(Taoan)-area west of Pokotu and struck at key military-in-
dustrial centres of Northeast China—Tsitsihar, Changchun,
Mukden, Jehol and Kalgan (Changkiakow). The Japanese
Command lost control over its troops, failing in all its at-
tempts to stem the Soviet drive.

Meanwhile the 1st Far Eastern Front had pierced the border
fortified positions in the coastal areas, advanced from 120
to 150 kilometres and was waging heavy battles for Mutankiang, a big town and communications hub where the Japa-

---

[1] See *Tsehfanjihpao*, August 12, 1945.

nese Command had assembled large forces in the hope of
preventing a Soviet breakthrough to Harbin and Kirin in
central Manchuria. Fighting for Mutankiang seemed to drag
out. In order to speed up the drive towards Changchun and
link up with the strike force of the Trans-Baikal Front, the
Commander of the 1st Far Eastern Front decided to outflank Mutankiang from the left. The fresh 10th Mechanised
Corps under Lieutenant-General I. D. Vasilyev developed a
sweeping offensive at Wangching and Kirin in the zone of
the 25th Army.

Closely co-operating with Rear-Admiral A. S. Antonov's
Amur Flotilla, the 2nd Far Eastern Front crossed the passes
of the Lesser Khingan and reached the town of Chiamussu. By
nightfall on August 14 the troops of the Front moved from
50 to 200 kilometres into Manchuria and reached the line
Heiho (Sahalian)-Sungiu-Hikang Paoching. The efforts of
the Japanese Command to stem the Soviet drive in the Sungari sector failed. On the same day the 16th Army under
Lieutenant-General L. G. Cheremisov and the Pacific Fleet
sailors began to liberate the age-old Russian land—the
southern part of Sakhalin Island.

The successful Soviet offensive and the threat of an Allied invasion of the Japanese islands placed Japan in an extremely difficult situation. On August 14 the Japanese Government informed the Governments of the USA, USSR,
Great Britain and China that the Emperor had accepted the
terms of the Potsdam Declaration. The Suzuki Cabinet resigned on the following day.

Still, the Japanese Supreme Command did not order a
cease-fire. In the evening of August 15 the troops of the
Kwantung Army received a cabled order from the General
Staff to burn immediately all banners, the Emperor's por-
traits and edicts and secret documents. In an attempt to win
time the Headquarters of the Kwantung Army which lost
control of its troops on August 14 broadcast an appeal to the
Soviet Command to end hostilities. But since the Kwantung
Army continued its desperate resistance, repeatedly counter-
attacked and did not lay down arms, GHQ ordered the Soviet forces to press on.

Between August 15 and 19 the Trans-Baikal Front captured the Changpei (northwest of Kalgan) fortified area on

its right flank, and the Hailar fortified area on its left flank, and advanced from 360 to 600 kilometres into Manchuria. At the end of the day on August 19 its right-wing troops approached the Changpei, Jehol and Chihfeng regions, the central units reached Mukden, Changchun and Kaitung, and the left-wing forces came up to Tsitsihar.

On August 15 and 16 the 1st Far Eastern Front pursued the offensive in all directions with the exception of Mutankiang where the 1st and 5th Armies were locked in exceptionally bitter battles with the Japanese 5th Army reinforced by the 122nd Infantry Division. Having thwarted the efforts of the Japanese Command to muster forces at Mutankiang for a counter-blow the Soviet troops crushed the resistance of the Japanese 5th Army which lost more than 40,000 men or. about two-thirds of its strength.

On August 16 the Soviet 1st and 5th armies broke through the strongly fortified line northeast of Mutankiang, forced the river of the same name, smashed the main forces of the Kwantung Army's 1st Front and captured Mutankiang. With the loss of this key stronghold, the remnants of the routed Japanese units began a disorderly retreat to the west and southwest under the incessant blows of the 1st Far Eastern Front. Setting out in pursuit, the Front's main forces swept towards Harbin and Kirin to link up with the troops of the Trans-Baikal Front and close the ring of encirclement around the Kwantung Army.

Between August 15 and 19 the 2nd Far Eastern Front inflicted a heavy defeat on the Japanese 4th Separate Army and a part of the 3rd Army. Having crossed mountainous and wooded country and swamps, the Soviet troops advanced 100-150 kilometres towards Tsitsihar and up to 300 kilometres in the Sungari sector and entered Kolochang, Lunminching, Shangchih and Poli regions.

On August 17, seeing the futility of further resistance and having lost control over his troops, commander-in-chief of the Kwantung Army General Yamada approached Marshal A. M. Vasilevsky with an offer to terminate hostilities. At the same time the Kwantung Army HQ radioed ceasefire orders to its troops. And yet Japanese forces continued to resist in many sectors.

On the same day Marshal Vasilevsky sent an ultimatum

to the Kwantung Army commander-in-chief demanding that
the Japanese troops cease all operations against the Soviet
troops along the entire front at noon on August 20, lay down
arms and surrender. As soon as the Japanese troops began
to down arms, he added, the Soviet forces would cease operations. On August 18 Japanese troops in some sectors began
to surrender, and the Soviet GHQ ordered to cease operations in these sectors.

On August 19 the Kwantung Army ceased resistance on
the greater part of Northeast China and North Korea and
began to surrender by the thousand. To disarm the Japanese
troops and take them prisoner as quickly as possible, to avert
possible destruction of industrial enterprises and the plunder
of material values, airborne troops were landed at a number
of towns, ports and naval bases in Northeast China, North
Korea, Southern Sakhalin and the Kurile Islands, and all
Soviet armies were ordered to form small and well-armed
mobile detachments.

On August 20 the three fronts linked up in the centre of
Manchuria and captured the large towns and administra-
tive and industrial centres of Harbin, Changchun, Kirin and
Mukden, where Soviet airborne task forces had been landed
on the eve of their arrival. At Harbin the Amur Flotilla
captured all the warships of the enemy's Sungari Flotilla.
The Pacific Fleet was landing troops in the Kurile Islands,
Southern Sakhalin and Korea. On August 23 units of the
Trans-Baikal Front captured Liaoyang and entered Port
Arthur (Lushun) and on August 24 captured Port Dalny
(Talien).

The disarmament and the reception of the bulk of the
war prisoners were completed by the end of August.
The million-strong Japanese Kwantung Army ceased to
exist.

The Soviet troops routed all the forces of the Kwantung
Army, the Manchoukuo Army, the Army of Inner Mongolia under Prince Teh Wang and the Suiyuan combat group,
about a half of the troops of the 17th and 5th fronts and the
Sungari River Flotilla—10 armies, combat groups and one
flotilla. The enemy's losses in manpower were 677,000, of
whom 84, 000 were killed. The Trans-Baikal and the 1st Far
Eastern fronts alone captured 3,700 guns, mortars and gre-

nade-launchers, 600 tanks, 861 aircraft, about 12,000 machine guns, more than 2,000 motor vehicles, approximately 13,000 horses, 679 depots and many other items of equipment.

SOVIET TROOPS
IN LIBERATED NORTHEAST CHINA

Northeast China was fully liberated by the end of August. At spontaneous meetings in the liberated towns and villages people turned out with Red and Chinese flags to express their gratitude to the Soviet Army.

Now that Northeast China was free, the Soviet Command had to solve a number of urgent problems. The very difficult task of normalising life in the liberated towns and villages, organising production, harvesting and supplying the population with food was entrusted to military commandants' offices set up in large inhabited localities and districts.

By September 10, 1945 the Command of the Trans-Baikal Front established 26 commandants' offices in Mukden, Changchun, Dairen (Dalny), Port Arthur, Dolonnor, Tsitsihar, Hailar and other important towns. Their efforts to bring life back to normal in towns were hampered by gangs of bandits. And since the local governors, city mayors and police chiefs who owed their posts to the Japanese did not combat their activity the matter was taken up by the Soviet commandants' offices. In Mukden, for example, the troops at the disposal of the local commandant's office in a fairly short space of time disarmed 9,000 bandits and smashed their Mukden centre.

The wide-ranging activity of the Soviet military commandants' offices helped normalise life in the liberated regions which were to be turned over to the Chinese authorities in keeping with the terms of the thirty-year treaty of friendship and alliance between the Soviet Union and China signed in Moscow on August 14, 1945.[1]

The Governments of the USSR and China expressed their

[1] The Moscow talks between the Soviet and Chinese Governments took place from June 30 to July 14 and were continued immediately upon the return of the Soviet delegation from Potsdam in order to work out a treaty whose purpose had been defined at Yalta: to assist China in her struggle for liberation from Japanese oppression. In addition to the treaty the two sides concluded a number of agreements.

determination to strengthen friendly relations, assist each
other in the struggle against aggression on the part of the
enemies of the United Nations, co-operate in the war against
Japan and in preserving universal peace and security in
the post-war period. A special agreement covered the relations between the Soviet commander-in-chief and the Chinese
administration following the entry of the Soviet forces into
Northeast China. Reaffirming China's sovereignty over this
part of the country and recognising the supreme authority of
the Soviet commander-in-chief in the zone of military operations, the treaty noted that "as soon as the returned territories cease to be zones of hostilities, the National Government of the Chinese Republic will assume authority over
civil affairs. . . ."

Practice showed, however, that the Kuomintang leadership had no intention of improving the situation in the liberated northeastern areas. On the contrary, Chiang Kai-
shek's emissaries touring the areas controlled by Soviet
troops deliberately created difficulties, organised campaigns
against the Soviet forces and activated armed detachments.

And yet, in spite of serious difficulties life in Northeast
China gradually returned to normal. The Soviet Command
took measures to reopen most of the Chinese primary and
secondary schools. Thanks to its assistance workers and employees at industrial enterprises in Mukden, Harbin, Changchun and many other towns received their long-overdue sa-
lary. It also managed to find the necessary money to pay
out unemployment grants to 70,000 people in Dairen. Stocks
of food were laid in towns through local chambers of
commerce. As a result, in September 1945, food and certain
necessaries were sold at fixed prices in some areas.

The majority of the population approved all the measures
which were carried out to democratise the administration.

The Command of the People's Liberation Forces took advantage of the favourable conditions arising from the rout
of the Kwantung Army and the presence of Soviet troops in
Northeast China. It received the opportunity to enlist volunteers throughout that part of China. The men who joined
the 8th People's Liberation Army were armed with captured weapons of which there was no shortage. Moreover, the

Command of the Chinese 8th Army used these favourable conditions to reorganise its forces. As far back as September 14, 1945, commander-in-chief of the 8th People's Liberation Army General Chu Teh asked the Command of the Trans-Baikal Front, whose units were stationed next to the military units of the Communist Party of China, to allow the 8th Army operating in the provinces of Jehol and Liaoning to remain in their areas. The Soviet Command began to withdraw its troops only after the 8th Army had completed the reorganisation of its units.

As a result of the reorganisation, the People's Liberation Forces increased numerically thanks to influx of volunteers from the provinces of Northeast China, and also qualitatively due to their conversion from the guerrilla-type organisation to that of a regular army and their equipment with captured weapons. By February 1, 1945, the armed forces of the Communist Party of China numbered 522,000 men, of whom 397,000 were stationed in North China.

The Soviet Command helped the leadership of the Communist Party to organise its work in Northeast China. In November 1945, for example, it returned Soviet units to Chihfeng to combat the subversive activities of bandit gangs.

During the presence of the Soviet Armed Forces in Northeast China a United Northeast Army was raised there. It included large guerrilla detachments operating in Manchuria and former POWs of the 8th and 4th armies who were working at mines and factories in Northeast China. Together with the 8th and the newly-raised 4th armies it was able not only to withstand the pressure of the Kuomintang forces but eventually to deliver a series of powerful blows which, in the end, resulted in the complete rout of the Kuomintang Army on mainland China. In these conditions the presence of the Soviet troops in Northeast China was no longer necessary, and at the end of April 1946 they pulled out of Manchuria.

The Chinese people gave a tremendous send-off for the Soviet Army. About 200,000 inhabitants of Harbin and adjoining villages took part in a meeting which ended in a march-past of the Soviet troops who made their way directly from Pachuchang Square to the railway station.

Thus, in April 1946 when the Soviet Army after fulfilling its mission of liberation withdrew from Manchuria, the People's Liberation troops constituted a formidable force. Fresh millions of working people of China joined the revolutionary struggle and favourable conditions had been created for continuing the fight against Kuomintang troops and consummating the Chinese Revolution. No small part in its victory was played by the Soviet Command's firm stand with regard to Port Arthur and Dalny.

THE BEGINNING
OF THE THIRD CIVIL WAR
AND THE VICTORY
OF THE 1949 CHINESE REVOLUTION

On August 25, 1945 the Central Committee of the Communist Party of China published a Declaration on the Current Situation in which it demanded recognition for the people's armed forces, designation of the areas of capitulation of the Japanese troops, recognition of all political parties and convocation of a conference for the purpose of forming a democratic coalition government of national unity.

The Brief Communique on the Talks Between Representatives of the Kuomintang and the Communist Party of China signed on October 10 recognised the need to democratise China and convene a political consultative conference. Putting forward these demands, the Central Committee of the Communist Party of China took into account the actual alignment of forces in China. During the offensive operations in Northern and Central China the People's Liberation Forces inflicted a series of defeats on the Japanese troops. In two months of fighting they killed, wounded or took prisoner more than 230,000 Japanese and puppet troops and liberated large areas with more than 18,717,000 inhabitants and 197 towns.

But the Kuomintang leadership from the outset ignored the will of the population in the liberated areas. As soon as the Kuomintang 5th Army entered Mukden its Command began to send troops to other towns of the province with orders forcibly to impose its own rule instead of the democratic bodies elected by the people during the Soviet Army's presence on Chinese territory. In a battle at Yingkow the People's Liberation Forces inflicted a serious defeat on the Kuomintang troops.

By June 1946, following the withdrawal of the Soviet troops from Northeast China, the Kuomintang forces, not without considerable assistance by the US troops, gained possession of central Manchuria, including the towns of Changchun, Kirin and Zepingkai. US warships landed more than 100,000 marines in Tientsin, Tsingtao and other North China ports and in Shanghai, and airborne troops were brought into Peking, Nanking and other important towns. US troops occupied a number of sections of North China railways to prevent them from coming under the control of the People's Liberation Forces. Under the protection of the US forces, the Kuomintang troops whom the Americans had armed and equipped took over Peking, Tientsin, Shanghai, Nanking and other key centres. Nevertheless, the United Northeast Army remained in firm control over the whole of Northern Manchuria with its centre, Harbin.

In July 1946, Chiang Kai-shek's armies launched a general offensive in North and Central China. By June 1947, thanks to enormous US military assistance they had occupied a number of cities in the liberated areas, including Kalgan and Yanan which for more than a decade were the seat of the leading bodies of the Communist Party and the People's Liberation Forces of China. Because of the intensification of military operations against democratic forces in China, negotiations between the Communist Party and the Kuomintang were broken off and the last representative of the Communist Party left Nanking in March 1947, after the Kuomintang offensive on Yanan.

By the middle of 1947, it became clear that in spite of certain successes scored by the Kuomintang troops, the campaign of the US-Kuomintang reaction against the liberated areas proved to be a failure. In the beginning of the second year of the war (July-September 1947), the People's Liberation Forces went over to the offensive and frustrated the Kuomintang's counter-revolutionary plans of spreading the war to the liberated areas and occupying them.

In the second year of the offensive the People's Liberation Forces gained considerable territory. In June 1948, the aggregate area of the liberated regions totalled 2,355,000 square kilometres, or 24.5 per cent of China's territory, with a population of 168 million (36 per cent of the country's total).

But the Kuomintang Army still controlled key strategic and communication centres in Southern and Central Manchuria (Mukden, Changchun), North China (Tientsin, Peking), the Central Plain (Kaifeng, Suchow) and Shantung Province (Tsinan, Chefoo). The presence of more than 2,000,000 Kuomintang troops in these areas prevented the liberated areas in Northeast, North and Central China from uniting into a continuous territory and constituted a threat of a fresh offensive.

The Kuomintang Command was most anxious to win a respite to regroup its battered troops and with the assistance of the United States raise new armies in the south of the country. But the Command of the People's Liberation Army of China[1], which by the autumn of 1948 had grown to three million effectives, did not give the Kuomintang troops the breathing spell which they needed so badly. In September and October it launched a general offensive for the purpose of routing the Kuomintang troops in Northeast China, liberating the Tientsin-Peking area, smashing Kuomintang armies in Central China and liberating the whole of Shantung Province. By mid-January 1949 the People's Liberation Army had freed the whole of Manchuria, North China and the Central China Plain from the rule of the Kuomintang reactionaries and their US patrons, thus achieving the aims of its autumn and winter offensive.

In subsequent battles it fully routed the Kuomintang forces and liberated almost the whole of the country.

The Soviet Army's assistance to the Chinese people in its anti-Japanese struggle, the rout of the Kwantung Army, the main force of the Japanese militarism on the mainland, and the liberation of Northeast China by the Soviet Armed Forces paved the way for the rout of the Kuomintang reactionary forces, the victory of the Chinese people's revolu-

---

[1] In March 1948 the People's Liberation Forces of China were renamed People's Liberation Army.

tion and the formation on October 1, 1949 of the People's
Republic of China.

4. LIBERATION OF KOREA

THE SOVIET ARMY COMES
TO THE AID OF THE KOREAN PEOPLE

For almost four decades the Korean people were under
the domination of Japanese imperialists. But they never
resigned themselves to the lot of slaves and waged an un-
remitting struggle for liberation. In the thirties the staunch
Korean patriots, under the guidance of the Communists, went
over to active forms of struggle; they unfolded a partisan
movement in Southeast Manchuria and the northern border
areas of Korea. The odds, however, were too heavy against
them, and the Korean people were unable to free themselves
from the Japanese invaders on their own.

In August 1945, having launched an offensive against the
Kwantung Army, the Soviet Armed Forces stretched a helping hand to the Korean people. Korea was liberated by the
25th Army of the 1st Far Eastern Front, Soviet marine units
and the Pacific Fleet warships.

At first the Front Command assigned a secondary role to
the 25th Army in the operation. Its task was to assume the
offensive on the left wing and support the main forces only
after the Japanese operational defence had been pierced.
After the entry of the main forces into the breach the 25th
Army was to push ahead in the general direction of Tungming, Lao Kay Chang and Tumen, force the defending
enemy to retreat to the south and on the 25th day of the
operation reach the line Wangching, Tumen, Hunchun. Acting in co-operation with the Pacific Fleet, a part of the army's
forces were to advance along Korea's eastern seaboard and
take part in naval landing operations in her northeastern
ports.

Military operations were to be started by composite detachments consisting of troops drawn from all the fortified
areas of the army and trained in surmounting enemy forti-

fications. The success of their offensive was to be exploited by the 386th and 393rd Infantry divisions.

Going into action at 01.00 hours on August 9, the composite detachments overwhelmed the unsuspecting garrisons of most of the enemy resistance centres who were asleep in their barracks and were unable to man the fortifications. When interrogated a high-ranking officer of the Japanese 3rd Army said that the "Soviet offensive was so unexpected that the Army HQ throughout the night of August 8 and up to 12.00 hours on August 9 did not know and was unable to find out what was taking place on the border and what was the situation of its units."

By 12.00 hours on August 9 all the detachments had captured the strong-points in the fortified areas, disrupted the enemy's tactical defences and created conditions for a successful offensive. The Commander of the 25th Army ordered the 39th Corps into action on the right flank and the 393rd and 386th Infantry divisions on the left.

On August 9 and 10 the army cut through the Japanese 3rd Army's tactical defence zone, captured the main strong-points of the Tungming and Tung Hsing Cheng fortified areas on the right flank, the Hunchun and Kaifeng on the left, gained the Tungming—Tung Min Tsi—Hunchun motor road and liberated the towns of Tungming, Tung Min Tsi and the regional centre of Nankado.

On the night of August 8, the Pacific Fleet's air arm and torpedo boats in co-operation with the land forces attacked Japanese coastal defence ships and key targets in the North Korean ports of Yuki (Unggi), Rashin (Najin) and Seishin (Chongjin). At the same time naval aircraft attacked the enemy's sea routes. Soviet planes and warships continued their strikes throughout the next few days. On August 9 and 10 Soviet bomber and attack aircraft flew 150 missions against Yuki and more than 400 against Rashin.

Very quickly the combined operations of the aircraft and the torpedo boats of the Pacific Fleet demoralised the enemy troops defending the seaboard and created conditions for landing naval task forces which were to seize North Korean ports. The task forces comprised several separate marine battalions, the 13th Marine Brigade and the 335th Infantry Division. The first group made up of scouts from the Fleet

HQ reconnaissance detachment commanded by Hero of the Soviet Union Senior Lieutenant V. N. Leonov landed at Yuki at nightfall on August 11.

On the same day the composite detachments and the 386th Infantry Division in action on the army's left flank reached the Korean border between Hoeryong and Keiko and a part of the army operating further to the right captured the towns of Lao Kay Chang and Hunchun.

To enable the 25th Army to exploit its success, the commander of the 1st Far Eastern Front reinforced it with the 17th and 88th Infantry corps and the 10th Mechanised Corps from the Front's reserves, and set it a new mission, *viz.*: its main forces were to pursue the offensive in the general direction of Kirin, cut the Japanese Army's routes leading from North Korean ports to Central and Eastern Manchuria, prevent the enemy group at Mutankiang from retreating to the south and the southwest and destroy it in co-operation with the 5th and the 1st armies. The army's left-flank divisions were to deal an auxiliary blow along the Korean coast and in conjunction with marines and the Pacific Fleet ships capture Yuki, Rashin, Seishin and Nanam, the main naval bases and ports in North Korea.

Yuki and Rashin fell on August 12. At the same time preparations were made for landing a task force and capturing the biggest port in North Korea, Seishin, whose proximity to the Soviet Union made it a particularly important objective. The Japanese had turned it into a stronghold with a 4,000-strong garrison. It was surrounded by two defence lines consisting of trenches, 180 bunkers and pillboxes with underground connecting passages. The strongest resistance points had been built on Komatsu Peninsula (Cape Komalsandan), dominating Seishin Bay from the north.

The Fleet's air squadrons and torpedo boats attacked the port prior to the landing operation, sinking several transports and wrecking depots, and the 140th Reconnaissance Detachment with a submachine-gun company conducted reconnaissance in strength. The landing party's main forces were to attack in three waves: the 355th Separate Marine Battalion was to spearhead the attack, to be followed by the 13th Marine Brigade and then the 335th Infantry Division. Sixty vessels were to transport and cover the task force.

Air support was furnished by three air divisions and one air regiment totalling 261 combat aircraft.

At daybreak on August 14 the 355th Separate Marine Battalion under Major M. P. Barabolko disembarked at the port of Seishin and began operations to extend the bridge-head. Counter-attacking incessantly, the Japanese tried to sweep the landing party back into the sea and by the end of the day considerably narrowed the Soviet bridgehead. Some of the Soviet subunits were pressed against the port's embankment and the piers and were fighting a mere 400 metres from the water's edge.

The 13th Marine Brigade under Major-General V. P. Tru-shin landed at dawn on August 15. Its assault battalions immediately engaged the enemy entrenched in port buildings. Supported by fire from naval guns, they soon cleared the port of the Japanese troops and together with the main forces of the landing party struck out towards the centre of the town. The enemy began to retreat to the outskirts and fortified hills where his main forces had assembled. Fighting was the heaviest for the Komatsu Peninsula and the hills northwest and west of Seishin.

At nightfall on August 16 the 393rd Infantry Division that was pushing on Seishin from the north attacked the Japanese forces fighting against the Soviet marines and thus determined the outcome of the battle. On August 17 the Soviet troops freed the town and port of Ranan (Nanam). On August 19 the 335th Infantry Division began landing in the port.

The Seishin landing was the biggest independent operation carried out by the Pacific Fleet in North Korea. By capturing the town and port of Seishin, the Soviet troops disrupted the Kwantung Army's supply routes with Japan via North Korea and considerably expedited the surrender of the Japanese forces and the end of the war in the Far East.

Soviet sailors, airmen and marines displayed courage and heroism in the course of landing operations in the North Korean ports, and many lost their lives in the battles for Chongjin (Seishin).

Having stepped up their drive towards Kirin, the 25th Army's main forces on August 16 captured Wangching and on the following day seized Tumen and Yangchi. In the fighting for Tumen special credit should be paid to the 40th Division's 231st Infantry Regiment. It was the first to reach the Tumen River, a major water obstacle blocking the advance of the Soviet troops. But thanks to deputy regimental commander for political affairs, Major Lyamin, who managed to organise an improvised crossing the Soviet troops reached Tumen on schedule. As a result of the 40th Division's swift thrust the numerically superior Japanese troops surrendered together with their headquarters.

Realising that the situation was hopeless, the Japanese 3rd Army began to surrender on August 18. In fulfilment of their internationalist duty the Soviet troops continued to liberate Korea. As a means of expediting the liberation of the whole of North Korea, the Soviet Command sent marine task forces to Idenchin (Etetin) on August 18 and Gensan (Wonsan) on August 21. For the same purpose the 384th Infantry Division of the 25th Army on August 24 sent airborne troops to Pyongyang (Heijo) and Kanko (Hamhung) which began to receive the surrender of large enemy garrisons. As it continued its southward drive, the 25th Army disarmed the Japanese troops, the police and gendarmerie and occupied the whole of North Korea. At the end of August the command and the headquarters of the 25th Army moved to Pyongyang.

In the course of the fighting which ended in the liberation of the Korean people the 25th Army lost 4,717 men, including 1,500 in killed. Soviet marine units, the air forces and Pacific Fleet ships also sustained considerable casualties.

The population of North Korea warmly welcomed the Soviet Army. At spontaneous demonstrations and meetings they expressed their gratitude to the Soviet socialist state and its army. The inhabitants of many towns and villages in liberated Korea helped to repair roads and bridges enabling the Soviet forces to push ahead at a rapid pace. The attitude of the Korean people to the Soviet Army was best expressed in an appeal to the people put out by the Committee of the Communist Party of the South Pyongan Province which said: "For years we had been fettered by the iron chain of Japanese imperialism and languished under its iron heel. But thanks to the heroic struggle of the great advanced power—the Soviet Union—the Korean people has at long last received freedom and sovereignty."

THE CREATION OF CONDITIONS
FOR DEMOCRATIC DEVELOPMENT
IN NORTH KOREA

The Soviet Government's policy towards liberated Korea was clearly defined in its first appeals to the Korean people.

In his order of October 10, 1945, the commander of the 25th Army announced: "The Red Army has entered North Korea to rout the invaders. It does not intend to introduce the Soviet order in Korea or gain territory. The private and public property of the North Korean citizens will be under the protection of the Soviet Military Authorities." The Soviet Command allowed formation and activity in North Korea of all anti-Japanese democratic parties working for the eradication of the vestiges of Japanese imperialism and strengthening the foundations of democracy and civil liberties.

The Soviet Command first and foremost concentrated on normalising life in towns and villages and establishing ties with the local population in the liberated regions of Korea. A very difficult task in a country which had lived through long years of Japanese imperialist rule and whose population had been indoctrinated in anti-Sovietism, it was entrusted to Soviet military commandants' offices (kommandaturas). By September 28 fifty-four kommandaturas were rendering every possible assistance to the North Korean population. For example, Lieutenant-Colonel Skopin, commandant of Tsinnampho, had 12 kilogrammes of foodstuffs (including 6 kilogrammes of rice and 6 kilogrammes of other cereals) issued to each inhabitant. Kommandatura officers held meetings with local committees, explained the Soviet Government's policy and delivered talks on the work of local industry, on the maintenance of order and discipline among the local population, on harvesting, on the protection of public enterprises, factories and mills, on the distribution of food to the population, and other topics.

The liberation of Korea paved the way for the development of the Korean Revolution and the establishment of an independent, genuinely democratic state. Political parties and public organisations sprang up everywhere. The Communist Party committees which were formed in the liberated provinces and large inhabited localities were most active. One of the first to be established was the Committee of the South Pyongan Province. Meeting in Seoul on August 20, representatives of the separate organisations of the Korean Communist Party passed a resolution on unification.

At the same time provisional local government bodies were being established. People's committees, organs of democratic rule, were set up in compliance with the will of the masses in North and South Korea. Their formation took place in the course of a sharp internal struggle between individual groups orientated on various political forces, with the result that contrary to the interests of the country's democratisation many of them were cluttered up with pro-Japanese elements. The development of the Korean Revolution, after Korea had been freed from the Japanese colonisers, took place in the difficult conditions of the country being artifically divided into two zones, a circumstance that made an imprint on its progress in the two parts of the country.

The US imperialists whose troops were stationed in the southern part of the country did not want to promote her democratic development and took steps to keep it divided.

In North Korea, where Soviet troops were stationed, the masses within a short period of time carried through deep-going revolutionary reforms. These reforms were initiated and guided by the Korean Communist Party. In October 1945 the Communist Party of North Korea set up an Organisational Committee which concentrated on democratising local government bodies and normalising life in the northern part of the country.

On October 14, 1945 a hundred thousand people took part in a rally in Pyongyang to mark the country's liberation and the beginning of the construction of a new, democratic Korea in her northern regions. The ten-day preparatory period which preceded the rally was highlighted by city-wide meetings of the population, dissemination in the Korean language of the order issued by the Commander of the 25th Army on the occasion of Korea's liberation and a large number of talks delivered to various sections of the population concerning the liberation mission of the Soviet Army. Addressing the rally Korea's national hero, Kim Il Sung, organiser of the Korean people's partisan struggle, said: "In the darkest years of Japanese domination we turned our eyes with hope to the land of socialism, and our hope has come true. In August 1945, the mighty Soviet Army routed the Japanese Kwantung Army and liberated Korea. For centuries to come we shall be grateful to the Soviet Union, our liberator."

At a conference in February 1946, representatives of provincial, city and district people's committees, political parties and public organisations of the northern part of the country elected a Provisional People's Committee of North Korea. The period of the Committee's activity (1946) has gone down in the history of the Korean people as a year of great democratic reforms in all spheres of political, economic and cultural activity in North Korea.

The Soviet Military Administration and the troops of the 25th Army won the gratitude of the Korean people for their very effective assistance to the Provisional People's Committee in carrying through democratic reforms, bringing life back to normal in North Korea and, first and foremost, in its efforts to restore the ruined economy. "It was the first time in the history of mankind," wrote the Chairman of the Korea-USSR Cultural Relations Society, author Lee Ghi En, "that soldiers were building houses and factories, mines and blast furnaces, that they were creating and not wrecking."[1]

Only an army brought up in the spirit of the great ideas of proletarian internationalism could act in such a way.

At a conference in July 1946, democratic parties and public organisations formed a United Democratic National Front (UDNF) which developed into a mass organisation of more than five million people. The Communist Party of North Korea, which now has 134,000 members compared with 6,000 in December 1945, became its leading and guiding force.

---

[1] *New Korea* No. 1, Pyongyang, April 1950, p. 47.

The struggle for democratic reforms strengthened the unity of the working class and enhanced the authority of the Communist Party. As a result, the Communist and the New People's parties of North Korea merged in August 1946 to form the Workers' Party of North Korea. A few years later, in July 1949, the Workers' Party of North Korea merged with the Workers' Party of South Korea to form the Korean Workers' Party, the vanguard of the country's working class and the peasants.

In November 1946, elections were held to North Korean provincial, city and district people's committees, and in December to rural and village people's committees. In February 1947 the Congress of the Chairmen of People's Committees elected the highest legislative organ—the People's Assembly of North Korea which at its first session formed the People's Committee of North Korea headed by Kim Il Sung.

Having solved the central question of the revolution, the question of power, the North Korean labouring masses under the leadership of the working class and its vanguard—the Korean Workers' Party—set out on the path of fundamental revolutionary changes in the socio-economic sphere. In this vital task they relied on the economic base which the Soviet Military Administration had under its control. The command of the 25th Army not only preserved North Korea's national wealth and turned it over to the people's government, but selflessly helped the Korean people to restore the industrial enterprises which had been wrecked by the Japanese, and build new ones. Paying tribute to the Soviet troops the Chairman of the Council of Ministers of the Korean People's Democratic Republic, Kim Il Sung, wrote: "The great Soviet Army stationed in the northern part of the country extended a hand of selfless assistance to the Korean people in their effort to restore factories, railways and mines. In all parts of our republic officers and men of the Soviet Army worked enthusiastically side by side with our workers and specialists and left us the valuable fruit of their dedicated labour."[1]

---

[1] Kim Il Sung, *"On the First Anniversary of the Agreement on Economic and Cultural Co-operation between the Soviet Union and the KPDR", Minjen Chosun,* March 17, 1950.

Striving to end the division of the country, the Korean Workers' Party carried out a number of measures designed to bring about the formation of a united democratic state. These measures included general elections to the country's highest legislative body. Held on August 25, 1948 at the initiative of the Korean Workers' Party they drew large numbers of people in both North and South Korea to the polls and resulted in the formation of the Supreme People's Assembly made up of representatives of South and North Korea. At its first sitting on September 9 the Assembly adopted the Constitution and proclaimed the establishment of the Korean People's Democratic Republic. The rise of a people's democratic state on Korean territory was one of the most auspicious results of the liberation mission of the Soviet Armed Forces in the Far East.

"The direct liberation of Korea from the yoke of Japanese imperialism by the Soviet Army," wrote Kim Il Sung, "led to the establishment of the Korean People's Democratic Republic and the victorious development of the national liberation movement.

"If the Soviet Army did not liberate Korea we could not have established our Korean People's Democratic Republic and our national liberation movement could not have made such victorious headway. The victory of the Soviet Union in the Second World War, therefore, opened a new chapter in the history of the Korean people. . . ."[1]

The first session of the Supreme People's Assembly of the Korean People's Democratic Republic appealed to the Soviet and US governments simultaneously to withdraw their troops from Korea. Meeting this request, the Soviet Government announced the decision of the Presidium of the USSR Supreme Soviet to pull all Soviet troops out of North Korea not later than January 1, 1949.

The Soviet troops, whose evacuation was completed on December 25, 1948, were given a warm and friendly send-off. In a letter to the Soviet Government the people of Korea wrote: "More than once in the course of her age-old history Korea had been invaded by foreign troops. Their swords

---

[1] Kim Il Sung, *Selected Works*, Vol. 3, Pyongyang, 1953, pp. 349-50 (in Korean).

struck down patriots and killed the civilian population; they burnt down towns and villages, turning them into heaps of ashes. Only the Soviet troops came to us as liberators and not as conquerors. Emancipated from oppression our land breathed freely. We saw the radiant sky, our land began to blossom. Songs of freedom, joy and happiness are being sung."[1]

In memory of the Soviet soldiers who fell in the battles for the liberation of Korea, the citizens of free Korea erected memorials and monuments in many cities. In Chongjin stands a monument to the Soviet marines who were killed in the fighting for the city. The citizens of Wonsan erected an obelisk near the port with the following inscription on its pedestal: "Here lie the men of the Navy of the Soviet Union who died heroically for the freedom and independence of the Korean people from Japanese oppression." In Pyongyang people come to pay their respects to the Soviet soldiers buried in the cemetery in the eastern part of the city, and on mount Moranbon a majestic granite Liberation Monument carries the inscription: "Eternal glory to the heroic Army of the Union of Soviet Socialist Republics which liberated the Korean people from Japanese bondage and ensured Korea's freedom and independence. August 15, 1945."

While far-flung democratic reforms were being introduced in North Korea, in the southern part of the country measures were being taken to form a puppet government subservient to Washington in violation of the decisions of the Moscow Conference of the Foreign Ministers of the USSR, USA and Great Britain (December 1945). In 1948 the notorious UN Trusteeship Commission, which the United States managed to establish thanks to the majority vote it controlled in the UN, launched its anti-popular activity in South Korea. Resorting to blackmail and other spurious methods it framed elections on May 10, 1948 whose results enabled the US imperialism to establish a puppet state—the Republic of Korea.

The US Government turned down the Soviet proposal for the simultaneous withdrawal of Soviet and US forces from

---

[1] *Izvestia*, February 16, 1949.

Korea and ignored the request of the Government of the
Korean People's Democratic Republic to pull out its troops.
Commander of the US Occupation Forces in South Korea,
General Hodge, told newsmen that American forces would
not be evacuated in the immediate future.

The imperialist policy of the United States in the occupied southern part of the country led to the split of Korea
into two parts. North Korea began building socialist society,
while South Korea became a state fully dependent both economically and politically on the United States of America.

5. THE SIGNIFICANCE
OF THE VICTORY
OF THE SOVIET ARMED
FORCES IN THE FAR EAST

The Soviet Armed Forces in the Far East routed the Japanese Kwantung Army and liberated Northeast China and
Korea, the main objectives of their operations in the Far
East, in the course of a single 24-day campaign. And although it was carried out with truly lightning speed, its
scope, dynamism and its end results make it one of the most
important campaigns of the Second World War. The Soviet Armed Forces conducted their military operations on a
frontage of more than 5,000 kilometres and an area of
1,500,000 square kilometres with a population of more than
70 million. The Soviet Army's mighty blows forced the
Kwantung Army to surrender and predetermined Japan's
complete defeat.

The act of Japan's unconditional surrender was signed
on September 2, 1945 on board the US battleship *Missouri*
anchored in Tokyo Bay. It wrote *finis* to the Second World
War which lasted six years and ended in the complete rout
of nazi Germany and imperialist Japan.

By smashing the Kwantung Army and forcing Japan to
surrender, the Soviet Union saved hundreds of thousands of
Allied soldiers from inevitable death and millions of Japanese from terrible privations and suffering; it also prevented
the further annihilation by the Japanese invaders of the
peoples in the occupied countries whose losses were already
enormous.

The Soviet Union's entry into war and its decisive role in speeding up victory over Japanese imperialism plus the enhanced prestige of the USSR in the world arena wrought a fundamental change in the situation in East and Southeast Asia. The victory of the Soviet Armed Forces in the Far East created exceptionally favourable conditions for the swift development of the national liberation movement of the peoples in that part of the world, and particularly of the peoples of China, Korea, Vietnam and Indonesia. The peoples of China, North Korea and the Democratic Republic of Vietnam chose the road of socialist construction.

The lightning, shattering blows struck by the Soviet Armed Forces at the Japanese troops in Northeast China spurred into action the Vietnamese patriots headed by the Communist Party of Indochina. On August 13, when panic had already spread among the invaders in Indochina, the Communist Party of Indochina convened a conference which agreed to begin a general armed uprising and emphasised the need to fight against the restoration of French colonial rule. This was the voice of the United National Front of Vietnam (Vietminh) which had five million people ready to go into battle under its standards.

The decision of the Central Committee of the Communist Party of Indochina and the National Committee of Vietminh was enthusiastically endorsed by the All-Vietnam National Congress which met on August 16. The Congress set up the Vietnamese National Liberation Committee headed by Ho Chi Minh which assumed the functions of a Provisional Government, and approved the Vietminh programme.

This decision was a reflection of the armed uprising in Ha Tinh Province which broke out on August 11 and in Quang Ngai Province which began on August 13. A demonstration of 100,000 people which was held in Hanoi on August 19 led to the establishment of people's rule in the city. In Saigon people's rule was established on August 25.

The August Revolution was a genuinely popular, anti-imperialist revolution of the Vietnamese people who had been fighting for many years for national liberation. An important role in the revolution was played by people's armed forces which in August 1945 totalled 5,000 men. On Sep-

tember 2, 1945, at a mass rally in Hanoi, Ho Chi Minh read
out the Declaration of Independence and proclaimed the
formation of the Democratic Republic of Vietnam. The
Vietnamese people entered the era of liberation from co-
lonialism, the era of a new, free and independent Vietnam.

Emphasising the significance of the Soviet people's victories in the Second World War, President Ho Chi Minh
wrote in 1945 that under the guidance of the Communist
Party of the Soviet Union the Soviet Army smashed fascism
and thus created exceptionally favourable conditions for the
development of world revolution. As a result of its victory
in the Far East in 1945 the Soviet Union in fact liberated the
peoples oppressed by Japan.

In August 1945 the news that the Soviet Armed Forces
had defeated the Kwantung Army's picked divisions precipi-
tated the Indonesian Revolution which ended 350 years of
Dutch domination. The Indonesian Republic was proclaimed
on August 17.

The long and bitter struggle of the Filipino people for
their country's independence ended in victory on July 4,
1946.

In Burma, in spite of the collapse of the united anti-imperialist front (October 1946), the struggle of the broad masses acquired such proportions that the British colonialists
were unable to paralyse it.

After the expulsion of the Japanese invaders from Malaya
in 1945, democratically elected people's committees were set
up in the country under the guidance of the Communists. In
September, however, a large British force landed in Malaya
and reimposed British colonial rule under which the country
remained for many years.

The people of Cambodia and Laos began a courageous
fight against the French colonialists.

Compelled to recognise the independence of the majority
of Southeast Asian countries won by their peoples in revolutionary wars, the colonialists at the same time took steps
to preserve their domination in that part of the world. In
conditions of a general upsurge of the world democratic and
liberation movement the national liberation struggle of the
Southeast Asian peoples attained its greatest scope.

The defeat of the Japanese Kwantung Army and Japan's surrender, therefore, had a beneficial impact on world historical development. The last seat of the Second World War, which had been fanned by Japanese militarism, was extinguished. The road for democratic development was now open to the countries of East and Southeast Asia.

Chapter XII   THE HISTORIC
                  SIGNIFICANCE
                  OF THE LIBERATION
                  MISSION OF THE SOVIET
                  ARMED FORCES

1. SOCIALISM—
AN INTERNATIONAL SYSTEM

RESULTS
OF THE LIBERATION MISSION
OF THE SOVIET ARMED FORCES

The Second World War, which had involved the heaviest fighting on the Soviet-German front, ended in the utter defeat of Germany and imperialist Japan. It was a great victory for the freedom-loving peoples of the world.

The main result of the war was the radical shift of the balance of forces on the world scene in favour of socialism.

The contribution made by the Soviet Union in the war proved beyond any doubt that there are no forces in the world capable of destroying socialism and bringing people devoted to the ideas of Marxism-Leninism, dedicated to the socialist homeland and rallied around the Leninist party to their knees. The results of the war are a stern warning to the imperialist aggressors and a severe and unforgettable lesson of history.

The Soviet people and its Armed Forces led and guided by the Communist Party played the decisive role in defeating fascism. By their devoted courage and heroism they not only upheld the freedom and independence of their country but also saved mankind from fascist slavery, a difficult and honourable duty to the peoples of the whole world.

The Armed Forces of the United States, Britain and other countries who had been flung by the force of circumstances into the ranks of the anti-Hitler coalition, also dealt telling blows at the enemy. The allied forces of Poland, Czechoslovakia, Yugoslavia and Albania, and in the final phase of the war the troops of Bulgaria, Rumania and Hungary bravely fought side by side with the Soviet troops. The People's Liberation Army of China and the Mongolian People's Army made their contribution to the struggle against the Japanese invaders.

The fighters of the Resistance Movement which had been inspired and organised by communist and workers' parties also helped to weaken the war efforts of nazi Germany and imperialist Japan. The most effective force of the anti-fascist liberation struggle was the working class which rallied together patriots from all classes and social strata.

In a number of European and Asian countries the expulsion of the invaders and the expansion of the democratic movement engendered an intensive development of a revolutionary situation. But the possibility of its erupting into revolution depended on specific internal and international conditions. With the help of their armed forces the US and Britain tried to impede the democratic movement and even went so far as wage an open war against the people, as was the case in Greece, for instance. The Anglo-US imperialists openly backed reactionary regimes in other countries, too.

The victory over fascism had a profound impact on the course of historical development and meant a major turning point in the life of many peoples and states. The statement adopted at the Meeting of Communist and Workers' Parties in Moscow on June 17, 1969 characterised the victory over German nazism and Japanese militarism, as a prerequisite for accelerating historical progress, for the advance and triumph of socialism throughout the world. The collapse of the fascist bloc undermined the positions of world imperialism, violating for a long period the historically-formed balance of forces in the capitalist world. This in turn further intensified uneven development of modern capitalism. The positions of some countries on the world scene were gravely undermined (Germany, Japan, Italy), or seriously impaired (Britain, France), while the United States rose to the leading position in the capitalist world.

Having affected almost 80 per cent of the world population, the Second World War aggravated the general crisis of capitalism and ushered in its second stage. One of its manifestations was the intensification of the crisis of the imperialist colonial system and the resulting considerable shrinkage of the sphere of imperialist expansion.

The defeat of fascism stimulated the growth of democratic forces, especially of the working class whose influence strengthened in all countries. This in turn accelerated the development of social processes in the capitalist world.

The Soviet Union's victories in the war wrought a great change in the peoples' world outlook; they tremendously augmented the prestige of the Soviet Union, the Soviet socialist system, the Communist Party of the Soviet Union and the entire world communist movement. Back in 1919 Lenin said with reference to the war which the young Soviet republic was waging at the time: "The workers and peasants are ... drawn to our side despite the infinite gravity of our war."[1] These words can be applied to the Soviet Union's effort in the Second World War, too.

These victories demonstrated the advantages of the Soviet socialist system over capitalism, the superiority of Soviet military thought, organisation and skill over the military thought, organisation, strategy and tactics of the capitalist armies, the advantage of the Soviet Army as a liberation army fighting for a just cause, for the interests of the working people.

The war exposed the futility of imperialism's efforts to smash socialism by force of arms and thus solve the main contradiction of our epoch, the contradiction between capitalism and socialism, in its favour.

The heroic war effort of the Soviet people and its Armed Forces was decisive not only in defeating the aggressive forces of imperialism; it also influenced post-war developments, promoted the strengthening of socialism and peace forces in all spheres and weakened capitalism. A very important role in making the world what it is today is played by the steadily and rapidly enhancing might of the Soviet Union and other socialist states, their peaceful foreign policy and the Peace Programme advanced by the 24th Congress of the CPSU.

The active, forward-looking foreign policy of the CPSU, emphasised the April 1973 Plenary Meeting of the CPSU Central Committee, rests on the great strength and prestige of the Soviet State and support of the entire nation; it promotes positive changes in the world situation. The position and the unity of the fraternal socialist countries have strengthened considerably, the influence of their concerted policy on international developments has increased, peaceful co-

---

[1] V. I. Lenin, *Collected Works*, Vol. 30, p. 224.

existence as a standard of relations between states with different social systems has gained broad recognition and a change is taking place from cold war to a detente. The imperialist aggression in Vietnam has come to an end.

In the course of the war the Soviet troops destroyed or took prisoner 607 enemy divisions. Not less than half this number, including 93 divisions which downed arms following Germany's unconditional surrender, were wiped out or taken prisoner while the Soviet Army fought on foreign territory. The Soviet troops also routed or took prisoner 49 divisions and 27 brigades of imperialist Japan's land forces and large air and naval forces.

Thanks to their high level of political consciousness, combat efficiency, heroism and courage, the Soviet Armed Forces fulfilled with honour their noble mission of liberating the peoples of Central and Southeast Europe and Asia. For more than a year the Soviet troops fought in foreign countries. Entering countries which had fought against the USSR, they had no thought of revenge. They came as liberators and lived up to their great mission carrying their banners unblemished through the countries of Europe and Asia. Above all this was due to the ideological work carried on by the CPSU prior and during the war to educate the Soviet people and the members of the Armed Forces in the spirit of internationalist solidarity with the working people of all countries.

When Germany capitulated the Soviet troops were in Central Europe, hundreds of kilometres away from the USSR. On September 2, 1945 Soviet forces in the Far East were in Northeast China, and those that had entered Korea stopped at the 38th parallel in keeping with an agreement between the USSR and the USA. It was envisaged that the division of Korea into zones of responsibility of Soviet and US forces was a temporary measure designed to enforce the capitulation of the Japanese troops in the country.

The Soviet Armed Forces liberated, either fully or partially, the territories of ten European countries with a total area of a million square kilometres and 113 million inhabitants. They also partially liberated the territories of two Asian countries having an area of more than 1,500,000 square kilometres and a population of approximately 70 million. Thousands of inhabited localities, including 507 towns, were freed. The heroic struggle of the Soviet Army played a decisive role in the expulsion of the fascist invaders from all European countries.

It required enormous efforts on the part of the Soviet Armed Forces to fulfil their great mission of liberation. Eleven Soviet fronts, two air defence fronts, four fleets, 50 field armies, six tank armies, 13 air armies, three air defence armies and three flotillas took part in the fighting on the territory of foreign countries. From July 1944 to the end of the war approximately 7,000,000 Soviet troops participated in the liberation of European countries, and more than 1,500,000 Soviet troops, half of them transferred from the Soviet-German front upon the conclusion of the war in Europe, participated in the liberation of Northeast China and North Korea in August and September 1945.

More than a million Soviet officers and men were killed in action in foreign countries and over 2,000,000 were wounded or listed as missing. The Soviet troops also lost thousands of tanks, aircraft, guns and mortars and large quantities of other weapons and equipment there; they fired thousands of tons of ammunition.

VICTORY
OF THE PEOPLE'S DEMOCRATIC
REVOLUTIONS

Liberation day, which many countries of Central and Southeast Europe and Asia observe as a national holiday, was not only a day on which they regained their lost freedom but one which also opened before them the historical road towards social progress, towards socialism.

This fact is mentioned in the CPSU Central Committee's Theses *On the Centenary of the Birth of V. I. Lenin*: "The rout of the shock forces of world imperialism—German fascism and Japanese militarism—the fulfilment by the Soviet Army of its liberation mission, contributed decisively to the success of the people's democratic revolutions in a number of countries of Europe and Asia."[1]

---

[1] *On the Centenary of the Birth of V. I. Lenin*, Moscow, 1970, p. 24.

During the war and nazi occupation, the bourgeoisie and landlords in these countries discredited themselves by treacherous collaboration. This considerably weakened their positions after liberation and eventually they ended up as political bankrupts. At the same time there was a growth in the cohesion and political awareness of the working class and its leading force—the communist and workers' parties. Nevertheless, in the majority of the countries of Central and Southeast Europe petty-bourgeois parties managed to retain some influence.

It was this alignment of forces that determined the rate of development, the nature and the motive forces of the revolution which was consummated in Albania, Bulgaria, Czechoslovakia, Hungary, Poland, Rumania and Yugoslavia at the final stage of the Second World War and in the initial post-war period. The anti-fascist democratic revolution which began to unfold in East Germany after the rout of nazism resulted in the formation in 1949 of the German Democratic Republic, the first peaceful socialist state ever to emerge in Germany. Anti-feudal, anti-imperialist revolutions were victorious in Vietnam and North Korea. A few years after the end of the Second World War a people's revolution triumphed in China.

Revolutions in the countries liberated by the Soviet troops sprang from the anti-fascist Resistance Movement in the course of which the general democratic national liberation struggle conducted by the people against the foreign invaders fused with the class struggle of the working people headed by the proletariat against the wealthy national bourgeoisie which had sold itself to the fascist invaders.

The groundwork, therefore, for the victory of the people's democratic revolutions had been prepared by the entire course of historical development in these countries. Above all, it was a result of the development of internal objective factors and the presence of propitious external conditions which evolved from the Soviet Union's decisive role in smashing nazi Germany and her satellites. People's Democracy—a new form of social political organisation—whose class content was the revolutionary democratic dictatorship of the proletariat and the peasantry headed by the working class, was born.

In the course of the people's democratic revolutions, which in the majority of countries had been consummated by 1947 or 1948, the Communists initiated and carried through revolutionary reforms in the economic and political spheres and also restored and extended the democratic rights and freedoms of the working masses. At the same time certain problems of a socialist nature were also solved. The leader and the principal motive force of the revolution was the working class which acted in alliance with the peasantry, the petty-bourgeois elements in town and country and the progressive intelligentsia.

During the acute and resolute struggle waged by the working class under the guidance of Marxist-Leninist parties and with the active support of all working people in all spheres of social activity—economic, political and ideological—the people's democratic revolutions began to overgrow into socialist revolutions. In its class content this amounted to the establishment of the people's democratic form of the dictatorship of the proletariat.

All this fully confirmed Lenin's idea about the transformation of the "dictatorship of the proletariat from a national dictatorship (i.e., existing in a single country and incapable of determining world politics) into an international one (i.e., a dictatorship of the proletariat involving at least several advanced countries, and capable of exercising a decisive influence upon world politics as a whole)".[1]

The post-war period witnessed the formation of the world socialist system embracing Albania, Bulgaria, Czechoslovakia, Hungary, the German Democratic Republic, the Democratic Republic of Vietnam, the Chinese People's Republic, the Korean People's Democratic Republic, the Mongolian People's Republic, Poland, Rumania, the USSR and Yugoslavia, and later Cuba.

At the present time the majority of the socialist countries of Central and Southeast Europe are entering a new period in their development, they are completing socialist construction and are preparing to launch the building of communist society. Only in China and Albania whose leaders are pursuing a policy of anti-Sovietism and petty-bourgeois adven-

---

[1] V. I. Lenin, *Collected Works*, Vol. 31, p. 148.

turism, there exists the danger that the people's socialist gains may be forfeited.

The rise and consolidation of the world socialist system have made it possible to expose the real substance of the capitalist system and weaken it to a greater extent. Imperialism has for ever lost its monopoly in solving world affairs which it possessed up to October 1917, and is no longer the dominating force on the world arena.

The world socialist system has become the leading anti-imperialist revolutionary force of the contemporary epoch; imperialism's inability to suppress the liberation movement of the peoples of the world is above all due to the growing might and cohesion of the community of socialist countries.

The International Meeting of Communist and Workers' Parties held in Moscow in 1969 characterised the role of the world socialist system in the following terms: "Relying on its steadily growing economic and defence potential, the world socialist system fetters imperialism, reduces its possibilities of exporting counter-revolution, and in fulfilment of its internationalist duty, furnishes increasing aid to the peoples fighting for freedom and independence, and promotes peace and international security."[1]

Working people in Poland, Czechoslovakia, Bulgaria, Korea and other European and Asian countries rightfully regard their liberation by the Soviet Army as a decisive factor of the birth and development of their people's democratic system, for it was the Soviet Army that performed for them "the heaviest part of the job, that of routing the invaders", as Klement Gottwald put it.

From the day they began to build a new life, the countries of Central and Southeast Europe and Asia relied on the Soviet Union, a strong political bulwark without which their working people would have never been able to retain power in the face of the pressure exerted by the capitalist states.

The presence of the Soviet troops in some of the people's democracies in the first post-war years prevented imperialism from exporting counter-revolution, fettered their internal reactionary forces and ensured freedom of action for the

---

[1] *International Meeting of Communist and Workers' Parties, Moscow, 1969*, Prague, 1969, p. 23.

forces of progress, democracy and socialism. Georgi Dimitrov said it not for the presence of Soviet troops on Bulgarian soil "Bulgaria would have been occupied by hostile foreign troops with all the ensuing consequences fatal for her present and future. . . . This being the case the Bulgarian people looked upon the Soviet troops which had to remain in our country under the armistice agreement not as occupants but as dear guests and benefactors. When the Soviet troops left our country, the people saw them off with a feeling of profound affection and gratitude".[1]

It must be said, however, that the liberation of a number of European and Asian countries by the Soviet Armed Forces and the presence of Soviet troops on their territory for a period of time merely created favourable opportunities for democratic development, whereas the transformation of these opportunities into reality depended chiefly on the internal revolutionary forces.

"Socialist revolution is not an item of import and cannot be imposed from without," stated the representatives of Communist and Workers' Parties at their meeting in Moscow in November 1960. "It is a result of the internal development of the country concerned, of the utmost sharpening of social contradictions in it. *The Communist Parties, which guide themselves by the Marxist-Leninist doctrine, have always been against the export of revolution. At the same time they fight resolutely against imperialist export of counter-revolution.*"[2]

In order to discredit the Soviet Union, bourgeois ideologists deliberately put a false colouring on the liberation mission of the Soviet Armed Forces in the Second World War and assert that the Soviet Union's policy in the liberated European and Asian countries was centred on implanting the "Soviet regime" there. For example, in his dismay over the victory of the Soviet Army at Stalingrad J. Edgar Hoover wrote: "Stalingrad not only marked the turning point in

---

[1] Georgi Dimitrov, *Selected Works*, Vol. 2, Moscow, 1957, p. 500 (in Russian).
[2] *The Struggle for Peace, Democracy and Socialism*, Moscow, 1960, p. 73.

Soviet fortunes in World War II, it also marked the beginning of the Communist offensive in which seven European nations lost their freedom. . . ."[1] Here is what F. Wagner, a bourgeois historian from West Germany, writes: "Of all the countries 'liberated' by the Soviet Army, it was only in Yugoslavia and Albania that the Communist Parties themselves established their domination. In all other countries Soviet bodies had to work to 'liberate' the former from capitalism."[2]

Writing about the governments in countries which are building socialism, US foreign policy historian, former US diplomat in the USSR, George F. Kennan claimed that basically these governments were not genuinely national in character. "In the view of the West," he wrote, ". . .these regimes were imposed by the skillful manipulations of highly disciplined Communist minorities, trained and inspired by Moscow, and supported by the presence or close proximity of units of the Soviet Armed Forces."[3]

In other words, Hoover, Wagner, Kennan and other falsifiers of history allege that revolution was brought to European and Asian countries "on the bayonets" of the Soviet Army. But facts disprove these slanderous fabrications. Why were there no revolutions in Austria, Iran and other countries where the Soviet troops remained for a considerable period of time? Simply because there were no internal prerequisites for revolution in them. Another important reason was that the troops of the Western imperialist powers which were stationed in parts of the territory of some countries (Germany, Austria, Korea and Norway) not only impeded all democratic reforms; they actively supported reactionary monopoly forces. Obviously, the fact that the Soviet Army had participated in their liberation had left its imprint: the political activity of the masses intensified, the communist parties and other democratic forces strengthened their positions and the prestige of the Soviet Union rose. The working people could see and feel that the Soviet troops were their friends and comrades.

---

[1] J. Edgar Hoover, *A Study of Communism*, New York, 1962, p. 130.

[2] F. Wagner, *Die Teilung Europas*, Stuttgart, 1959, p. 111.

[3] *Foreign Affairs*, January, 1960, p. 179.

There are other facts which Mr. Kennan cannot fail to know. Soviet troops had never been in the Democratic Republic of Vietnam, Albania or Cuba, and their presence in China and Yugoslavia was confined to a limited area. Nevertheless, there were internal forces in these countries which proved capable of taking advantage of the favourable international situation and carrying through a revolutionary upheaval.

The results of the Second World War most emphatically prove that the Soviet Union invariably upheld the principle of national sovereignty. It is common knowledge that the USSR helped many states in Europe and Asia not only to restore their national independence but also to strengthen their genuine sovereignty.

Having liberated the peoples of the countries of Central and Southeast Europe, the Armed Forces of the Soviet Union vividly demonstrated the inviolable connection between patriotism and internationalism. They reasserted the indubitable truth that these countries won national independence thanks to the decisive role played by such an international force of socialism as the Soviet Union. At the same time developments in these countries confirmed the Marxist premise that national liberation was inconceivable and impossible without a class struggle.

THE USSR DEFENDS
THE NATIONAL INDEPENDENCE
OF THE LIBERATED COUNTRIES
AND RENDERS THEM
ALL-ROUND ASSISTANCE

With the Second World War over, the Soviet Union considered that its internationalist duty was to continue its all-round assistance to countries liberated by the Soviet Army.

Proletarian internationalism formed the basis of the Soviet Union's relations both with countries that had been occupied by nazi Germany, and with the former members of the fascist bloc. Having fought against the fascist regime and not against the peoples of these countries, the USSR continued its internationalist policy after their liberation, directing it in the new conditions at the national revival of

Bulgaria, Hungary, Rumania and East Germany. It prevented the revival of the forces of militarism and reaction in these countries enabling their peoples to advance along the peaceful road of social progress and consolidate their independence.

The USSR furnished extensive, all-round assistance to the fraternal countries immediately after the war although the Soviet people had their hands full, healing the wounds which the nazi invaders had inflicted on their country.

The friendly policy which the USSR pursued in its relations with the People's Democracies became especially manifest during the preparations for and the conclusion of peace treaties with Bulgaria, Hungary and Rumania at the end of 1946 and beginning of 1947. At the time Western imperialist circles did everything in their power to impose unfair conditions for a post-war peace settlement on these countries so as to be in a position to meddle in their internal affairs. With this aim in view, as John C. Campbell, secretary of the US delegation to the Paris Peace Conference, admitted, they tried to obtain "a foot in the door of eastern Europe, politically and economically".[1]

Thanks to the efforts of the Soviet delegation the peace treaties that were signed at the Paris Peace Conference in the main ensured the interests of both the victor powers and the peoples of Bulgaria, Hungary, Rumania and other defeated states. The Soviet Union's participation in working out post-war organisation predetermined the democratic nature of the peace terms with the defeated states and safeguarded their national independence.

The USSR continued to render economic, political, moral and, when necessary, military assistance to the People's Democracies, in the ensuing period.

Defence, including the use of armed forces, of the gains of socialism, which is an important factor of the contemporary revolutionary process, constitutes an organic element of the internationalist policy of the Soviet Union and other socialist countries. Proletarian internationalism and complete equality characterise the treaties of friendship, mutual as-

---

[1] John C. Campbell, *The United States in World Affairs 1945-1947*, New York and London, 1947, p. 55.

sistance and post-war co-operation which the Soviet Union concluded with Czechoslovakia and Poland during the war, and its treaties with Rumania, Hungary and Bulgaria signed early in 1948. These treaties contain the mutual commitments jointly to take all possible measures to avert any threat of a repetition of aggression on the part of Germany or any other state which would have directly united with Germany or in any other form.

The treaties of friendship, mutual assistance and post-war co-operation concluded among the people's democracies were likewise an expression of new, internationalist relations.

In 1949 the Soviet Union began rendering all-round military assistance to the People's Republic of China. It was the first to recognise people's China and on February 14, 1950 the two countries signed a treaty of friendship, alliance and mutual assistance. From 1950 to 1953 the Soviet Union, China and other socialist states assisted the people of the Korean People's Democratic Republic in its patriotic war of liberation against the US aggressors.

The Communist Party of the Soviet Union, the Soviet people in general, have done everything possible to support the peoples of all the socialist countries. With the formation of the world socialist system, the internationalist tasks of the Soviet Armed Forces have grown immeasurably. Stationed on the territories of other countries in the post-war years, the Soviet troops continued to fulfil their internationalist mission in new conditions and with different means. They helped the people to overcome the aftermath of fascist dictatorship and abolish the threat of occupation, to rehabilitate the economy, and promote cultural activities and education. In the liberated countries they saved many priceless architectural monuments and works of art.

During and after the war Soviet military authorities took care of liberated inmates and prisoners-of-war whom the nazis had horded into camps from all parts of Europe. They received material support and medical treatment and arrangements were made for their return home.

In the initial post-war period Soviet sailors helped Rumanian, Bulgarian and Yugoslavian sailors to remove mines from the Danube between its mouth and Vienna, and also from other water bodies adjoining these states. The sailors of the Baltic Fleet took part in demining operations in the Gdansk, Pomorie and Lübeck harbours, the Pacific Fleet sailors removed mines from Korea's coastal waters, and the Northern Fleet sailors helped clear mines from the waters washing the coast of Northern Norway.

Besides the economic tasks which the young people's democracies had to tackle immediately upon liberation, they were also confronted with the serious problem of defending themselves. The communist and workers' parties followed Lenin's advice that if the proletariat wants "to hold power, it must ... prove its ability to do so by its military organisation".[1] The struggle against the intrigues of imperialism, the defence of their homeland, became the most important functions of the young socialist states.

Drawing upon the enormous experience of the CPSU and taking the specific national features of their countries into account, the Communist and Workers' parties were behind the establishment of new, genuinely people's armies. Their backbone consisted of units which had been raised on Soviet territory during the war, and fought together with the Soviet Army, and also of the commanders and men of the guerrilla detachments who courageously battled the enemy during the occupation.

When the people's democracies set out re-organising their armed forces in the first post-war years, the Soviet Union sent its military experts and weapons and took part in the establishment of their defence industries. The development of the Soviet Armed Forces always stood as a good example to be followed by the armies of the people's democracies.

A very important contribution to the strengthening of friendship between the USSR and the peoples of Bulgaria, Hungary, Germany, Rumania and Korea was made by Soviet representatives on Allied control commissions and other military administrative bodies that were set up in these countries in the final period of the war and functioned in the first post-war years.

Soviet military authorities played a special part in normalising life in Germany where there were no central ad-

---

[1] V. I. Lenin, *Collected Works*, Vol. 29, p. 153.

ministrative bodies for some time after the war, and where at first Soviet military agencies assumed all the functions of administration and supply. At the same time they actively participated in the establishment of local self-government, rehabilitation of wrecked factories, mines and railways, revival of cultural activity, education and science. The Soviet people shared their abundant economic and political experience with German anti-fascists.

In the light of these and many other facts the efforts of bourgeois falsifiers to undermine the respect of the liberated peoples for the Soviet troops are clumsy and ridiculous. The West German historian Jürgen Thorwald, author of several books on the Soviet Army's operations in foreign countries, alleges that Soviet soldiers maltreated the populations of the liberated countries, destroyed their material and cultural values and plundered their national wealth. The conduct of the Soviet troops in foreign countries is presented in a similar way by Guderian and other nazi officers, and in the memoirs of some American generals.

Facts, however, refute all these fabrications. People are able to distinguish lie from truth, and bourgeois slanderers, no matter how hard they try, will never be able to defame the liberation mission of the Soviet Armed Forces.

Evaluating the role played by the Soviet military authorities in rehabilitating the East German economy, Walter Ulbricht wrote: "Were it not for the dedicated and unselfish activity of the working people and the regular assistance and instructions of Soviet officers and men, the German anti-fascists would have never been able at the time to cope with the enormous tasks of rehabilitating the economy.... Thanks to the assistance of Soviet officers, German democrats were able to utilise in full the wisdom of the Soviet people, a people which in the course of most bitter battles surmounted enormous difficulties, built a new life and acquired enormous experience in all matters of running the state and carrying out giant plans and also in fighting its enemies. Brought up by the Communist Party of the Soviet Union, the Soviet people in army uniform worked selflessly for the sake of peace and friendship of peoples."[1]

---

[1] Walter Ulbricht, op. cit., Vol. I, pp. 90-91.

Never before in the history of wars had an army behaved so nobly on the territory of foreign countries. Such behaviour was characteristic only of the armed forces of a socialist state.

Their high mission fulfilled, the Soviet troops began to pull out of the countries they liberated shortly after the termination of hostilities. The local population gave them a warm send-off. The bulk of the Soviet forces in Yugoslavia withdrew immediately after the Belgrade Operation.

In keeping with the GHQ directive of June 27, 1945, Soviet troops began to withdraw from Czechoslovakia in the autumn of the same year.

In September 1945 Soviet forces pulled out of Northern Norway. On the Danish island of Bornholm the Soviet troops stayed for 11 months: most of the units of the Soviet infantry corps stationed on Bornholm left the island in October 1945. Early in 1946 the Soviet Government decided to evacuate all its forces from Danish territory ahead of schedule and the last naval vessel with Soviet troops on board left the island on April 15.

The presence of the Soviet troops in other countries was in conformity with corresponding multilateral international treaties or bilateral agreements. For instance, under the February 10, 1947 peace treaties signed with Bulgaria, Hungary and Rumania, which entered into force on September 15, 1947, the Soviet Union undertook within 90 days of the conclusion of the treaties to pull its troops out of these countries. At the same time the Soviet Union acquired the right to station its troops in Hungary and Rumania to protect and maintain communications with the Soviet occupying forces in Germany and Austria.

Under its peace treaty with Finland the Soviet Union obtained a 50-year lease of the Porkkala-Udd area where it intended to build a naval base. In 1955, however, it gave up its leasehold interests and in early 1956 withdrew its troops from the area.

The Soviet Union has always upheld the national interests of the Korean people. The US delegation at the Crimea Conference declared that Korea would be ready for independence not earlier than within 20 or 30 years. At the end of the war the US State Department insisted that American forces should occupy the whole of Korea. But when the swift offensive of the Soviet troops opened the way for liberating Korea without US participation, President Truman advanced the idea of dividing Korea along the 38th parallel to enforce the capitulation of the Japanese troops by the Soviet and American commands north and south of this line respectively. In fact, however, the Korean people was liberated by the Soviet Armed Forces alone—US forces landed in South Korea on September 8, that is, after Japan's capitulation. In September 1948, the Supreme People's Assembly of the Korean People's Democratic Republic requested the Soviet and American Governments immediately and simultaneously to withdraw their forces. The Soviet Union evacuated all its armed forces from Korea by the end of 1948, but the United States forces continued their occupation of South Korea.

The Soviet Government no less scrupulously honoured China's sovereignty. In the course of Soviet-Chinese talks in Moscow in August 1945, the head of the Chinese delegation was told that the Soviet Armed Forces would pull out of China's northeast provinces within three months after the end of the war. Shortly after Japan's surrender, the Soviet Government informed the Chiang Kai-shek Government that it intended to withdraw the Soviet troops from Manchuria within the shortest time possible.

Soviet forces were evacuated in March and April 1946. The Kuomintang Government repeatedly sought the Soviet Union's agreement to permit Chiang Kai-shek forces to enter the Liatung Peninsula from where they could attack the People's Liberation Army of China from the rear. The Soviet Government was, however, strongly opposed to Dalny and Port Arthur being used for military purposes for that would have been in violation of the agreement of August 14, 1945.

In the third civil war which the Chiang Kai-shek forces unleashed, the Kuomintang sustained a shattering defeat and on October 1, 1949 the Chinese people proclaimed the establishment of the People's Republic of China. In February 1950 the USSR and the PRC signed an agreement on the Chinese Changchung Railway, Port Arthur and Dalny, under which the Soviet Government agreed to pull its troops out of the jointly used naval base of Port Arthur by the end of 1952. But the beginning of the foreign intervention in Korea and the US occupation of Taiwan and also the conclusion of a separate peace between the Western Powers and Japan made it necessary to postpone the withdrawal of the Soviet forces from Port Arthur. In the course of the Soviet-Chinese talks in October 1954 it was agreed that Soviet troops would be withdrawn from Port Arthur by May 31, 1955, and this was done.

On May 15, 1955 a State Treaty on the restoration of an independent and democratic Austria was signed in Vienna. Under its terms the occupation troops were withdrawn from Austria after it had come into force.

At present Soviet troops are stationed in the GDR, Poland, Hungary and Czechoslovakia in keeping with the Warsaw Treaty and bilateral agreements. Their legal status is stipulated in the agreements between the Soviet Union and the German Democratic Republic of March 12, 1957, between the Soviet Union and the Hungarian People's Republic of May 27, 1957, between the Soviet Union and the Polish People's Republic of December 17, 1957 and between the Soviet Union and the Czechoslovak Socialist Republic of October 16, 1968.

Together with the troops of the fraternal armies the Soviet forces are discharging a responsible and honourable service, standing guard over the socialist community.

PEOPLE'S GRATITUDE

The peoples of the whole world are grateful to the Soviet Armed Forces who had honourably fulfilled their internationalist duty in the Second World War. Their deep gratitude is recorded in official documents, it has been voiced by prominent politicians and statesmen and ordinary citizens, it has found expression in works of art, books and songs and has been embodied in numerous memorials and monuments. Most important, however, is that the image of the Soviet soldier-liberator, a symbol of heroism and humanism, has been indelibly imprinted in the hearts of the peoples he liberated.

The high moral qualities of the Soviet troops engendered in the peoples of foreign countries sincere respect and affection for the whole Soviet people and its socialist ideals and admiration for its successes in building a new life and educating a new man.

The decisive role which the Soviet Union and its Armed Forces played in liberating the countries of Central and Southeast Europe and Asia was reflected in the first constitutions of these countries, a new phenomenon in constitutional law. For instance, the Constitution of the Polish People's Republic said that "the historic victory of the Union of Soviet Socialist Republics over nazism liberated Polish lands, gave the Polish people the opportunity to win power and created conditions for Poland's national revival within her new and just frontiers". "The Rumanian People's Republic," stated the Constitution of that country, "appeared as a result of the historic victory of the Soviet Union over German nazism and the liberation of Rumania by the gallant Soviet Army...."

This thought permeates numerous letters by the citizens of the countries liberated by the Soviet forces. In February 1949, shortly after the Soviet troops completed their withdrawal from North Korea, the Korean people sent a letter with about 17 million signatures to J. V. Stalin. "The Korean people," it said, "will never forget the heroic deeds of the Soviet soldiers and shall pass them from generation to generation as wondrous tales that will eternally evoke in the people warm affection for and gratitude to the Red Army."

"The day of Rumania's national liberation by the Soviet Army," reads a letter from a meeting which was held in Bucharest on the occasion of the 7th anniversary of Rumania's liberation by the Soviet Army, "became the decisive turning point in our country's history. Our people are eternally grateful to the soldiers of the land where socialism was born who shed their blood for the freedom and happiness of our people and the whole of humanity."

In their greetings the participants in the meeting on the occassion of the 5th anniversary of Czechoslovakia's liberation declared: "The heroic Soviet Army which defeated nazism returned the peoples of Europe, including us—Czechs and Slovaks—to life. Without the Soviet Union not only would there have been no free Czechoslovak Republic but, in general, there would have been no life for our people."

Dwelling on the Soviet-Czechoslovak agreement regulating the activity of the Soviet troops and military authorities on the liberated territory of Czechoslovakia, Klement Gottwald wrote: "Only few cases are known to history when a great and powerful ally entering a country to liberate her from the foreign domination had so generously transferred the administration of the country into the hands of her people. Nothing illustrates more vividly the genuinely liberatory mission of the Red Army than this fact."

"On the limitless expanses of the Russian land, in the Ukraine and all parts of the Soviet Union," said Janos Kadar at a meeting in Budapest marking the 15th anniversary of Hungary's liberation, "live people who had shed their blood on Hungarian soil. They fought for the freedom of our people. Our people think of them with profound appreciation and express their heartfelt gratitude."

During the war a large group of Tehranians in a letter attached to a gift parcel to the Soviet soldiers thanked the Red Army "which crossed into Iran, frustrated the nazi plans aimed against the USSR and liberated us Iranians from the horrors of war which the nazis were preparing on the territory of Iran".

German anti-fascists are profoundly grateful to the Soviet Army for liberation from fascism and its enormous assistance in the building of a new, democratic Germany. The working people of Germany expressed these sentiments with especial poignancy during the celebrations of the fourth anniversary of the rout of nazism when a monument was unveiled in Treptow Park in Berlin, the last resting place of the Soviet soldiers who had fallen in the battle for the city.

Nations have expressed their gratitude to the Soviet Army in many other ways. For instance some European and Asian countries observe their national holidays on days directly connected with the liberation mission of the Soviet Armed Forces. Poland marks her national revival on July 22, the day when the Soviet Army and the Polish 1st Army began the liberation of the country in 1944. August 23 is a national holiday in Rumania. On that day in 1944, during the victorious offensive of the Soviet Army, an anti-fascist people's uprising broke out in the country. Bulgaria's day of national liberation is observed on September 9 and is also connected with the Soviet Army's march of liberation into the country in 1944 and the uprising in Sofia. The Hungarian people observe their national holiday on April 4. On that day in 1945 the Soviet forces drove the last nazi invader out of the country. May 8, the day when the Wehrmacht surrendered unconditionally in 1945 is a national holiday in the German Democratic Republic. The peoples of the Czechoslovak Socialist Republic observe Liberation Day on May 9; on that day in 1945 the liberation of the Czechoslovak people was completed.

Grateful citizens in the liberated countries have erected monuments in honour of Soviet soldiers. An old Czech speaking at a meeting in Topola declared: "Monuments to fallen heroes are beacons for the living, reminding them of the magnanimity of the Russian soldiers."

The noble exploit of the Soviet troops in the last war has inspired many European and Asian authors to write fine books about the unforgettable days of joint struggle against nazism and the great liberation mission of the Soviet Armed Forces.

Thousands of Soviet officers and men were awarded orders and medals by foreign governments for courage and heroism in the fighting for their countries' freedom. On its part the Soviet Union, in recognition of the exploits of its foreign comrades-in-arms who had fought against the German invaders, awarded orders and medals to thousands of foreign citizens of whom 22 were made Heroes of the Soviet Union.

Many members of the Soviet Armed Forces, from marshals to privates, were made honorary citizens of foreign towns. Squares, streets, industrial enterprises, schools and cultural institutions have been named after Soviet officers and men.

To this day thousands of foreigners correspond with Soviet servicemen who took part in liberating their towns or villages and who continued to render them all-round fraternal assistance, when the fighting was over.

2. A GREAT MILITANT ALLIANCE

THE WARSAW TREATY—A NEW PHASE
IN THE MILITARY UNITY
OF THE SOCIALIST COUNTRIES

Marxism-Leninism makes the point that the essence of proletarian internationalism lies not only in mutual political,
economic and moral support of the working people of different countries, but also in direct military assistance to one
another in case of need. This premise is the theoretical foundation of the military co-operation of the socialist countries.

"We say: unity of the military forces is imperative; any
deviation from this unity is impermissible", Lenin underlined.[1] This thought is mentioned in the CPSU Central Committee's theses, *50th Anniversary of the Great October Socialist Revolution*, which state that the idea of proletarian
internationalism has found a new, vivid embodiment in diverse forms of co-operation, including co-operation in defence matters between socialist countries. Since military
unity mirrors the essence of the new system in the countries
of the socialist community, the military alliance of socialist
countries is an objective necessity of their social development and rests on their political, economic and ideological
unity. It is also important that the military unity of the fraternal peoples has deep-rooted traditions going back to the
civil war in Russia, the fight against fascism in Spain and
particularly to the years of the Second World War.

The interconnection of the international and the national
in the military unity of socialist countries, and especially in
the activity of the Warsaw Treaty Organisation, consists not
only in the compounding of their common efforts which aug-
ments their might, but also in that by ensuring the defence
of their country's socialist gains they simultaneously bolster
the defence of the socialist community, i.e., they fulfil their
internationalist duty to the entire community.

The need for the military unity of socialist countries arises
from the existence of two opposing socio-economic formations—socialist and capitalist—and imperialism's aggressive

---

[1] V. I. Lenin, *Collected Works*, Vol. 30, p. 326.

policy. In our day and age the need for such unity is even more imperative because, despite its major historical setbacks, international imperialism is still a powerful and dangerous enemy capable of plunging mankind into the carnage of another war.

"Certainly, the aggressive forces of imperialism will not lay down their arms for a long time yet; there are still adventurers who for the sake of their selfish interests are capable of kindling a new military conflagration," said Leonid Brezhnev.[1]

The organisational forms of military co-operation of the socialist countries, which are contingent on a set of international and domestic factors, are just as important as its common principles. In the initial post-war years, for instance, their military co-operation was expressed in bilateral treaties. Later, in view of the continuing arms race, NATO's increasing military preparations and the revival of militarism and revanchism in West Germany, they agreed on the need to form a collective military alliance to ensure their security.

At a meeting in Warsaw in May 1955 eight European socialist countries signed a Treaty of Friendship, Co-operation and Mutual Assistance. The socialist countries of Asia welcomed the treaty and said that they were prepared to co-operate with its signatories. The Warsaw Treaty is basically unlike the aggressive imperialist agreements and blocks. It is a treaty of self-defence, friendship and international unity —the shield and sword of the socialist countries. Developments on the international scene showed that the establishment of the Warsaw Treaty Organisation was a timely and necessary step. The military alliance of the socialist states and their armies not only guarantees the inviolability of the borders of the socialist community; it is also an important restraining factor capable of bringing war-mongers to their senses.

Thanks to the Warsaw Treaty Organisation the world socialist system has become a mighty bulwark of the sovereignty and independence of all countries threatened by imperialist aggression.

---

[1] *Pravda*, July 12, 1973.

Meeting in Prague in January 1956, the Political Consultative Committee approved the statute of the Joint Command and accepted the proposal of the GDR delegation that its country's armed contingents be included into the Joint Armed Forces. This step was taken in response to the formation of a revanchist West German Bundeswehr whose leaders and inspirers openly advocated an attack on the German Democratic Republic.

The conclusion of the Warsaw Treaty with its underlying principle of "one for all, all for one" signified the appearance of an international defensive organisation alongside the existing forms of co-operation between socialist countries. Such co-operation opened still greater opportunities for the Warsaw Treaty countries to draw upon the vast combat experience of the Soviet Armed Forces and equip their armies with modern weaponry.

The Soviet Government made it clear more than once that the Soviet Union would defend the borders of the fraternal countries just as resolutely as its own.

After the conclusion of the Warsaw Treaty important changes took place in the world raising the people's hopes for a durable peace. Working for a detente, the Soviet Union and other socialist countries reduced their armed forces.

The Western Powers, however, did not reciprocate this serious move. They did not terminate the arms race and the accelerated formation of the Bundeswehr in West Germany, and began openly to interfere in the internal affairs of the socialist countries. For example, they vigorously backed the organisers of the counter-revolutionary mutiny in Hungary in October 1956. Fulfilling its internationalist duty, the Soviet Government, at the request of the Hungarian Government, promptly came to the assistance of the fraternal country in her hour of need. Uniting their efforts, the Hungarian working people and the Soviet troops crushed the counter-revolution and saved the socialist gains of the Hungarian people who also received substantial material and moral support from other socialist countries.

Even though the imperialists did not stop their subversive activity against the socialist countries after the failure of the counter-revolutionary venture in Hungary, the countries of the socialist community took steps to weaken international tension and resolutely worked to strengthen world peace.

The meeting of the Political Consultative Committee of the Warsaw Treaty Countries which took place in Moscow in May 1958 was an important step in this direction. The government leaders of the socialist countries attending the meeting decided to make yet another reduction of their armed forces in 1959. The Moscow meeting also approved the Soviet proposal backed by Rumania to pull out Soviet troops stationed in Rumania in keeping with the provisions of the Warsaw Treaty and to reduce the Soviet forces in Hungary.

In the following years the socialist countries displayed complete agreement on key foreign policy problems.

Carrying out the recommendation of the Warsaw Treaty countries the German Democratic Republic, for example, in August 1961 introduced a range of drastic measures to cut short the intrigues of West German revanchists.

In 1962, when the threat of US military intervention loomed over revolutionary Cuba, the Soviet Union and other socialist countries cooled the zeal of the aggressor by demonstrating their determination to give military support to the Cuban people. Committed to the principles of proletarian internationalism, socialist countries rendered enormous assistance to the Vietnamese people in its long years of dramatic struggle against imperialist aggression, and are rendering extensive all-round assistance to the Arab peoples and all peoples fighting for freedom and national independence.

Placing their biggest stakes on nationalistic elements, bourgeois ideologists are striving to undermine the unity of the peoples of the socialist countries. Marxists-Leninists have at all time come out against nationalistic distortions, against attempts to "drag" socialism into "national confines". The long years of existence of the world socialist system prove conclusively that the national interests of each socialist country are most effectively taken care of when the struggle for them merges organically with the struggle for the common interests of the entire socialist community.

To counter the insidious efforts of aggressive imperialism to weaken the socialist community and break it up from within, and the anti-Soviet campaign conducted in recent years by the Chinese leaders, socialist states and all peace-loving forces have to display even greater unity of action than ever before. At its Plenary Meeting in April 1973 the Central Committee of the CPSU underlined the need for constant vigilance and preparedness to rebuff any intrigues of aggressive, reactionary imperialist circles.

THE FURTHER STRENGTHENING OF THE MILITARY UNITY OF THE SOCIALIST COUNTRIES AT THE PRESENT STAGE

The Marxist-Leninist Parties of the Warsaw Treaty countries are continuously strengthening their military unity which took shape during the war and in the post-war years, and at present embraces a wide range of questions. The revolutionary changes that have taken place in the Soviet Armed Forces have had a beneficial impact on the armies of the socialist countries and enabled them to increase their might and improve their combat efficiency.

In the course of joint exercises Soviet troops generously share the valuable experience acquired by the Soviet Armed Forces in the course of the Second World War and in the post-war years with the personnel of the Armed Forces of other socialist states.

In recent years the Parties and Governments of socialist states have taken a wide range of steps aimed at further strengthening and perfecting the Warsaw Treaty. Of especial importance in this connection are the decisions taken by the Political Consultative Committee of the Warsaw Treaty states at a meeting in Budapest on March 17, 1969. This meeting approved the statute of the Committee of Defence Ministers of the Warsaw Treaty states, a new statute on the United Armed Forces and the Joint Command and other documents further improving the structure of the defensive Warsaw Treaty Organisation and its administrative bodies.

An important factor determining the expansion of military co-operation of the Warsaw Treaty states is the increasing unity of views on the fundamental questions of military theory and the practical development and combat training of their armed forces. Today the Armed Forces of the socialist states are developing in accordance with a single socialist military doctrine whose political conclusions are universally recognised in the socialist community. These conclusions promote the aims of defending the socialist gains and serve as guidelines for the development of their armed forces. The military theory, the combat experience and training of the armies of the socialist countries enrich the storehouse of advanced military science.

Reciprocal visits by military delegations, friendship festivals of socialist countries, sports contests and cultural activities also stimulate further the expansion and development of their military co-operation. Very important are regular consultations arranged for military experts of the fraternal countries organised under the auspices of the Joint Armed Forces HQ, the USSR Defence Ministry, the General Staff and the Main Political Administration of the Soviet Armed Forces. The fraternal armies also regularly share their experience of political work among the troops which they conduct mainly for the purpose of educating the men in the spirit of internationalism and comradeship-in-arms.

As in the past the Soviet Union is rendering the fraternal armies great assistance in the training of officers.

The CPSU and the Soviet Government have always shown unflagging interest in the further consolidation of the military co-operation of the socialist states. Speaking at a Kremlin reception in honour of military college graduates on July 8, 1968, General Secretary of the CPSU Central Committee Leonid Brezhnev noted: "With the threat of war still unaverted the fraternity of our peoples in work, in the building of a new society is naturally supplemented by comradeship-in-arms. The Warsaw Treaty countries have acquired extensive experience in various fields of military co-operation. Relying on this experience we shall continue to strengthen our collective defence."[1]

Soviet officers and men stationed in foreign countries have played their part in cementing the unity of the fraternal armies. The whole world knows that Soviet servicemen at a risk to their lives saved people and property when

---

[1] *Krasnaya Zvezda*, July 9, 1968.

natural disasters struck in the German Democratic Republic, Hungary, Poland, Czechoslovakia, the Mongolian People's Republic and Yugoslavia, removed mines from a vast area in Algeria and took part in various emergency jobs.

The Communist and Workers' parties and governments of socialist countries have expressed high appreciation for the noble deeds of the Soviet servicemen. In 1967, for example, the Government of the German Democratic Republic awarded medals and decorations to nearly 1,600 servicemen of the Group of Soviet Forces in Germany. All told, over 10,000 Soviet officers and men have been decorated with orders and medals of the socialist countries.

In August 1968 the armed forces of five socialist states, motivated by their sense of internationalism, entered Czechoslovakia. It was stated in the document adopted at the December 1970 Plenary Meeting of the Central Committee of the Communist Party of Czechoslovakia that "the entry of the allied troops of five socialist countries into Czechoslovakia was an act of international solidarity, meeting both the common interests of the Czechoslovak working people, and the interests of the international working class, the socialist community and the class interests of the international communist movement. This internationalist act saved the lives of thousands of men, ensured internal and external conditions for peaceful and tranquil labour, strengthened the Western borders of the socialist camp, and blasted the hopes of the imperialist circles for a revision of the results of the Second World War".

Cemented with the blood spilt in the joint struggle against common enemies, the comradeship-in-arms of the socialist countries is a dependable guarantee of the inviolability of the frontiers and revolutionary gains of the socialist peoples.

"As a result of collective measures," states the Resolution of the 24th Congress of the Communist Party of the Soviet Union on the Report of the Central Committee of the CPSU, "the military organisation of the Warsaw Treaty countries has been strengthened. The armed forces of the allied powers are in a high state of readiness and are a reliable guarantee of the paceful labour endeavour of the fraternal peoples."[1]

---

[1] *24th Congress of the CPSU*, Moscow, 1971, p. 212.

* * *

The year 1945 has gone down in the history of mankind as a year of the great victory of the freedom-loving peoples over the dark forces of fascism. A decisive contribution to this victory was made by the Soviet people and its Armed Forces. Not a single army of the capitalist states had to shoulder such incredible hardships and score such brilliant victories in battles which lasted 1,418 days and nights as those that fell to the lot of the Soviet Army. The Soviet soldier faithfully discharged his patriotic duty. With might and main he defended the great gains of the socialist revolution, the state and national independence of his land and saved the Soviet people from enslavement and extermination by nazism.

In the past war the Soviet Armed Forces performed their mission of liberation with honour. They helped many nations throw off the fascist yoke and saved mankind from nazi bondage.

Their great international exploit in the Second World War will never fade from the memory of the peoples.

Very important changes have taken place in the world since the end of the war. "Today," said Leonid Brezhnev in the Kremlin of July 11, 1973, "we are witnessing, and not only witnessing but actively participating in a momentous change in the entire post-war history: the transition from a period of hostile confrontation in international affairs, when the storm-laden tension could have erupted in a vortex of war, to a period of a more stable peaceful coexistence, reasonable and peaceable co-operation between socialist and capitalist states based on mutual benefit and equal security."[1]

Alongside all this, as the leaders of the Communist and Workers' Parties pointed out at a friendly meeting in the Crimea on July 30 and 31, 1973, "there are still forces which, acting in the spirit of the 'cold war', are opposing detente and advocating intensification of military preparations and the swelling of military budgets". Therefore, the participants in the meeting pointed out, it was necessary to display unflagging vigilance with regard to the policy of these forces

---

[1] *Pravda*, July 12, 1973.

and counteract their efforts to mislead world public opinion, sow discord and enmity between peoples and take advantage of detente to undermine the positions of socialism.[1]

Today, as in the years of the Second World War, the Soviet Armed Forces are dependably guarding the peaceful labour of the Soviet people, the socialist gains in the Soviet Union and all socialist countries, the interests of the working people of the whole world. Together with the fraternal armies of other socialist countries they represent an invincible force capable of smashing any aggressor. Their might is the decisive factor of a strong and lasting peace on our planet.

---

[1] *Pravda,* August 1, 1973.

REQUEST TO READERS

Progress Publishers would be glad to have your opinion of this book, its translation and design and any suggestions you may have for future publications.

Please send your comments to 21, Zubovsky Boulevard, Moscow, USSR.

Художественный редактор *В. Камкина*
Технический редактор *Л. Полякова*

Подписано к печати 3/IV-1975 г.
Формат 84×108/₃₂. Бум. л. 7.
Печ. л. 23,52+2,94 п. л. вклеек. Уч.-изд. л. 27,80.
Изд. № 17730. Заказ 1719. Цена 3 р. 41 к.

Издательство «Прогресс»
Государственного Комитета
Совета Министров СССР по делам издательств,
полиграфии и книжной торговли.
Москва Г-21, Зубовский бульвар, 21.

Ордена Трудового Красного Знамени
Московская типография № 7 «Искра революции»
«Союзполиграфпрома» при Государственном
Комитете Совета Министров СССР по делам
издательств, полиграфии и книжной торговли.
Москва Г-19, пер. Аксакова, 13.